# YOUR NEW HOUSE

The alert consumer's guide to
buying and building a quality home.

ALAN & DENISE FIELDS

## Copyright Page and Zesty Lo-Cal Recipes

Framing of Spelling Errors by Alan Fields
Nailing of Punctuation Mistakes by Denise Fields
Cover, interior design and guitars by Epic Design

Congas, cuica, stand-up bass and tambourine by Denise Fields
Flugelhorn, bassoon, steel guitar and drums by Alan Fields
Backing vocals on "Real Estate Agents" by Jewel
Keyboard solo on "The Builder" by Randy Newman
Additional guitar and harmony vocals on "The Paper Trail" by John Hiatt

More special thanks to our panel of expert editors, whose insight and comments were invaluable: Michael Malinowski, Keith Gumbiner, Anita Holec, Jim Parker, Kathy Fragnoli, T.C., and, of course, Patti Fields.

Denise Fields appears courtesy of Helen and Max Coopwood.
Alan Fields appears courtesy of Patti and Howard Fields.

**This book was written to the music of the Barenaked Ladies, which probably explains a lot.**

Distributed to the book trade by Publisher's Group West, Berkeley, CA 1-800-788-3123. Printed in the USA.

*Updates to this book are posted at www.YourNewHouseBook.com*

To order this book, call 1-800-888-0385 or order online at www.windsor-peak.com. Or send $15.95 plus $3 shipping to Windsor Peak Press, 436 Pine Street, Suite 9000, Boulder, Colorado 80302. *Quantity discounts are available.* Questions or comments?Contact the authors at (303) 442-8792. Or fax them a note at (303) 442-3744. Or e-mail the authors at questions@yournew-housebook.com. Or write to them at the above address.

Library of Congress Cataloging-in-Publication Data
Fields, Alan 1965–
Fields, Denise 1964–
   Your New House: The Alert Consumer's Guide to Buying and Building a Quality Home (2nd edition)/Alan and Denise Fields
   Includes index.
   1. Homes—United States—Construction. 2. Consumer education—United States. 3. Shopping—United States.
93-93751 LIC
ISBN 1-889392-11-1

*Version 4.0*

# Table of Contents

**Introduction**

## Chapter 6
## House by Design

## Chapter 7
## Bring on the Builder

## Chapter 8
## The Paper Trail: Protecting Your Rights
## with a Good Contract

*Part II*
*Go! Building the Home and*

## Chapter 9
## Key Inspection Points, Part 1: The Skeleton House

*The Dog and Pick-up Truck Builder, as rendered by Jon Caldara*

# Icons

 Biggest Myths

 Eco-Friendly Alternative

 Email from the Real World?

 Getting Started: How Far in Advance?

 Key Inspection Points

 Money Bombs: Scams to Avoid

 New Homebuyers in Cyberspace: What's on the Web?

 Questions to Ask

 Reality Check

 Sources

 Step-by-Step Strategies

What Will It Cost You?

# PART 1 POWER
## HOME BUYING

### GETTING READY, GETTING SET!

# Reality Check:
# Bob Vila is NOT
# Building Your Home

**C H A P T E R 1**

Let's say right here and now that building or buying a new house is an insane experience. In fact, a recent survey of "people who should be slapped silly" ranked "folks building a house" third... right before "bungee-cord jumpers" and just after "people who get on the freeway doing 25 mph."

And trust us, we know what we're talking out. We built a home . . . and lived to talk about it.

Actually, to be more accurate, we didn't build anything. A builder and a crew of misfits, ex-felons and drunkards labored on alternate Tuesdays to build our house. We just stood by in horror with our mouths and our checkbook wide open. In the end, we signed a piece of paper saying that we would pay for this thing for the next thirty years.

So, you are contemplating the same journey? To see if you are ready to buy a new home, please take the following test:

1. Take this book in your right hand.
2. Position the spine of the book so it faces you.
3. Whack your self in the head three times.

Welcome to the New Home Buying Journey, where smacking yourself on the forehead with a real estate book seems like the most logical thing you'll do for the next six to twelve months.

For some reason, the process of buying a new home is a 9.9 on the 10-point difficulty scale in the category of "Things You Can Buy as a Consumer." It's as if a team of government scientists had carefully engineered the process of buying a new home to maximize confusion and frustration . . . while simultaneously removing your life savings from your bank account.

So, that makes our mission clear: to try to make some SENSE out of this mess for you, the new homebuyer. And, while we're at it, let's save you from some nasty scams and rip-offs that have ensnared other new homebuyers.

In the end, we hope you get the new home you've hoped and

dreamed for—and paid for with some hard-earned bucks. But before you start fantasizing about gourmet kitchens and three-car garages, fasten your seat belts and set the phasers to "stun." It may get ugly.

## So, Who Are You Guys, Anyway?

You might be wondering why we're writing this book. We aren't builders, developers or real estate agents. We think the toaster is a

# Yes. You Should.

**S**o, a new home is a perfect solution for everyone, right? Not exactly. We found plenty of pitfalls that can trip up the new homebuyer. Let's look at the 5 REASONS WHY YOU SHOULD BUY A NEW HOME . . . AND WHY YOU SHOULDN'T.

### 5 Reasons to buy a new home.

**1** **Everything is, well, NEW.** All the home's systems (heat, A/C, appliances) are fresh out of the box. With older homes, you are basically buying someone else's problems—and that often means constantly fixing items that are just waiting to break after you move in.

**2** **Floor plans that fit today's lifestyles.** Most new homes feature open floorplans with spacious kitchens and master bedrooms/baths. Contrast that to older homes, many of which were designed in the "cave man" period of architecture: dark, tiny spaces, chopped up into useless floor plans. Sure you can remodel an older home into one that reflects today's lifestyles—but with the big expense of a major re-do, what's the point?

**3** **Nice community amenities.** Many new home communities feature parks, walking trails, and other amenities. New homes often mean newer schools as well.

**4** **Wired for the 'net.** Even low-end production houses offer wiring packages that enable you to have high-speed Internet access, networked computers and satellite TV. Many are also pre-wired for security systems.

**5** **No need for extensive updating.** New homes are finished with items that reflect today's fashions. With an older home that needs "updating," you could be hit for thousands of dollars for new carpet, paint, tile, etc. And did we mention the avocado green sinks in the master bath?

complex power tool. We couldn't tell a router from a band saw if it snuck up and bit us on the fanny.

Nope, we're just average, ordinary homebuyers—like you. When we decided to buy (and build) a new house, we immediately trotted down to the bookstore to find wise advice on the topic. Blame it on an occupational hazard—as writers, we always think the answer is in a book.

We made a beeline to the "House & Home" section and searched for wisdom from the all-knowing and all-seeing God of Home Improvement.

# NO. You Shouldn't.

## 5 Reasons to NOT buy a new home.

**1** **You're going to pay a premium for all that new stuff.** The figures don't lie: new homebuyers get to pay EXTRA for all those new gadgets. The latest figures: an average new home sells for $226,680. Contrast that with an "old" home, which is a paltry $146,600. (Source: National Association of Home Builders and National Association of Realtors, 2002 surveys). See charts later in this chapter for a breakdown of average costs for a new home.

**2** **I have a life, thank you.** Have some spare time on your hands to decide on tile colors . . . light switch styles . . . doorknob finishes? Buying a new home requires a tremendous commitment of time to do everything from interviewing builders to selecting finishes.

**3** **You need a home RIGHT NOW.** A trip to Mars is quicker than buying the average new home, which can take four to six months to construct. And that doesn't include time for shopping, planning, design and more. Even if you happen upon a production or spec home nearing completion, it can take weeks or months to customize the finishes to your liking.

**4** **You want to live close to the city.** Speaking of Mars, most new homes are built on the edge of town—and that can mean a lengthy commute to jobs, shopping and more. And it's hard to tell if the builder's promises of "future" parks, schools and amenities are just sales hype. If you buy a resale home in an existing neighborhood, at least you are getting a known quantity.

**5** **Over-crowded schools.** Yes, schools near new home communities are often new. But they can also be vastly overcrowded. That's because school districts seem to be forever playing catch up in building new facilities in high-growth (read: new home) areas.

Yes, we're talking Bob Vila.

Surely, Bob would dispense reassuring words of wisdom that would guide us on this new home journey. Surely, Bob would tell us everything we needed to know.

After sifting through piles of books on fixing toilets and how to make a million dollars in real estate, we found what we thought was the answer: a Bob book entitled *Bob Vila's Guide to Buying Your Dream House.*

Since we're cheap, we first read some sample passages in the bookstore before deciding to buy the book. Smugly, we poured over the book, secure in the knowledge that we had found the ANSWER TO OUR PRAYERS.

Suddenly, our excitement turned to gloom as we read Bob's advice on new homes, in a chapter titled "To Build or Not To Build." After going on at some length about why building a house is so difficult, Bob writes:

*Building a new home can also be a brilliant solution. You may have a special shot at a choice piece of land. You may be living in a region where builders are desperate for work. You may be in a position in which financial factors are not constraining. If so, good luck and God's speed.*

That's it. No chapters of endless advice. No words of wisdom. Just "Good luck and God's speed." Thanks, Bob.

Bob then goes on for the remaining 280 pages to talk incessantly about how wonderful *old* homes are. Bob apparently has not seen old homes in our area. We have, and it isn't pretty—lovely 1970's-era homes with obsolete floorplans, "deferred" maintenance, and an extensive need for "updating" when it comes to every decorative item of the home.

Despite Bob's comments and our better judgement, we weighed all the reasons pro and con and decided to build anyway . . . and write this book. We should point out this book is much more than our personal experiences in building a home. First, we interviewed homebuyers, agents, builders and consumer advocates across the country. We also attended homebuilder conventions to scope out the latest products, trends and tips. Along the way, we discovered the *Four Truths About Buying a New Home No One Tells You.* Let's break it down:

# Four Truths About Buying a New Home No One Tells You.

**1** **Bob Vila is not building your home.** You've seen those TV shows like "This Old House," where Bob, Norm or Steve and a crew of careful craftsmen lovingly restore a home. The workers ruminate endlessly about the correct way to install this door or that siding. Many homebuyers think they are getting this level of care when they build or buy a new home. And why not? It's not like builders are giving them away.

Sorry, folks, this type of skilled building is seen only on television. Real life means building crews who are more like Larry, Curly, and Moe—bumbling idiots who couldn't tell their butt from a two-by-four. The only thing these guys ruminate on endlessly is which bar they'll hit at quitting time.

One homebuyer we interviewed said she was shocked at the level of workmanship on her $300,000 semi-custom home. Sloppy carpentry, lousy cabinet installation, incompetent roofers—the buyer was amazed at what a "new" home actually means in today's marketplace.

This is the ultimate reality check on building a new home: Bob Vila is not your builder. As a result, you need to protect yourself. That's the goal of this book: we'll tell you exactly how you can do this and get the best deal for the dollar.

**2** **You get to pay for all those wonderful advancements of science.** Building a home at the dawn of the 21st Century is a quick lesson in environmental "correctness." Water-saving toilets, extra insulation, super-efficient furnaces are now required by law in many communities—and who do you think pays for all this? You, in the form of higher home prices. Sure, some of this stuff may pay dividends down the line (in lower utility bills), but you still have to pay for all these expensive toys today.

Stringent environmental laws translate into tougher building standards and limited supply of certain materials. And when the supply goes down, it's you that's left holding the bag. When you decide to build a new home, you enter the mysterious world of Lumber Shortages, Drywall Rationing and other strange market conditions caused by hurricanes that strike Indonesia.

The result: a home built today may be more "politically correct" than one built in 1969—but you get to pay for the privilege.

For all the gory details, check out the charts later in this chapter that list the "average" costs of building a new home today.

**3** **It always takes more time, money and patience than the original estimate.** So, your builder says he can build you a $315,000 home in just four months? Six months later, you're pulling your hair out because that home is now $360,000 and isn't even finished yet.

The percentage of homes finished on time and on budget must be small enough to fit on the head of a pin. Nearly every homebuyer we've interviewed across the country recounts a similar story—it cost more and took longer than they anticipated. Recognizing this at the outset is the best course. In the following chapters, we'll give you specific suggestions for minimizing the pain.

**4** **"New construction" does not mean "soundly constructed."** High price does not mean high quality. In the bizarre world of new homes, "new" doesn't have the same meaning as other "new" products, like a new car. A new home means only that no one has lived there yet—and that's a plus and a minus.

"New" does not mean the house was soundly constructed. A quickly slapped-up tract house with the cheapest of cheap materials may be "new," but it could cause years of headaches.

And just because you're spending a lot of money does not mean you're getting commensurate quality. A $300,000 house may be loaded with cheap windows, a lousy paint job and poor roofing—if you don't pay attention, you might get a house that's really worth much less than you're paying . . . especially if you're stuck with repair bills and costly maintenance.

Some builders seem keenly aware that most of their customers have no clue when it comes to differentiating quality from shoddy construction. Ray Redden, president of Redden Properties, an Atlanta, Georgia builder said in a recent issue of *Builder* magazine, "Most home buyer's perception of quality starts (and finishes) with how much molding there is in the house." And sadly, there is a ring of truth to that insulting statement. The best solution to protect yourself from shoddy construction is to arm yourself with knowledge. While you can't become an genius in construction overnight, you can surround yourself with experts who won't be fooled by a shoddy house that's disguised with pretty molding. More on this strategy later.

# Who Should NOT Buy or Build a New Home

Even if you can cope with those four truths about building a new home, there are several types of buyers who should NEVER buy a new home. Yes, you read that right—there are some folks who should be banned from even walking into a model home, for their own safety (and sanity). Sure, real estate agents like to pitch new homes to any-one with a pulse—but some of these folks could sell ice to Eskimos. What you won't read in those slick new home magazines are the types of buyers who should NOT buy new homes. If you're in one of these groups, we advise you to think twice:

◆ **New-to-towners.** Just moved to a new area? Think you already know where the good neighborhoods and schools are? Think again. It takes more than a few weeks or months in a new town to really get the lay of the land. Asking a real estate agent for advice is dangerous. Most work for the seller (or builder, in this case)—hence, they'll prom-ise you it's a great neighborhood just to get that commission. Never mind the toxic waste dump down the street or the lousy schools that score on the bottom of standardized tests . . . you probably won't notice them until after you've closed on the home.

Another subtle reason that "new-to-towners" should not build: most are unfamiliar with local construction methods and practices. If you move from a dry climate to a wet one, you might not realize that builders are supposed to do special types of waterproofing or pest-control techniques. Case in point: termites. In Montana, they aren't much of a problem. In Florida, builders must take special care to build a home to avoid termite infestations. Assuming builders use the same or similar practices as those in your previous hometown is a major mistake.

The best solution would be to rent a home for a year or so—that way you really know which locations are best and what places are the dregs. By taking your time, you can talk with previous homebuyers, builders, architects and others about local construction and what you really should get in your new home. If renting is not an option, consider buying an existing home that's been thoroughly checked out by a private inspector.

◆ **Long-distance buyers.** So, you're being transferred to a new location? It seems like the perfect time to buy a new home. Perhaps there's a partially built home in the "right neighborhood" that will be finished when you move to town. Sounds great, huh?

Ah, there's nothing that makes shoddy builders happier than snaring a long-distance buyer. If you're hundreds (or thousands) of miles away, there's nothing to keep them from taking you for a ride. Doing sloppy work, switching to cheap materials, "forgetting" to add expensive features—when the buyer's away, the scum will play. Any unsupervised builder could be a one-way ticket to housing hell.

Retirees often fall into this trap. Building a dream vacation or retirement home may be a life-long goal—but doing it long distance is too great a risk. "Back home" most of the builders are reputable, you say. Don't assume that's the case in your retirement destination. Areas with the most defective housing (North Carolina and Florida, for example) also just happen to be hot retirement markets. Coincidence? Don't bet on it.

◆ **Couples with shaky marriages.** Building or buying a new home exacts a huge emotional toll. From the anxiety of committing yourself to that scary mortgage to the stress of making a trillion decisions, this is not for the faint of heart. Adding the stress of building a home to career and family responsibilities is a precarious undertaking.

Some couples try to fix a failing marriage by building a home—big mistake. They might think that since such a massive project requires a "team effort," it will bring them back together. The reality is that the stress usually does these marriages in. While we are not psychologists, it's our opinion that anyone with marriage difficulties should think twice about such a huge undertaking.

Does this mean that every couple who fights over the right color for the faucets will end up in divorce? Of course not. Thousands of couples successfully navigate the emotional land mines of the new home process every year. But don't say we didn't warn you. Fasten your seat belts—this will be a bumpy ride.

◆ **Cash-strapped buyers.** If you've scraped and saved for years to come up with that 20% down payment, you may think you have enough money to build a new home. But remember one truism of new home buying: it always costs more than you originally thought.

A million things can push up the final price. Cost overruns caused by weather delays are common. "Hidden expenses" such as the low-ball allowance game (which we'll describe later) can zap you for hundreds if not thousands of dollars. Throughout this book you'll notice "money bombs"— watch out for these pitfalls, which can unexpectedly cost you big money.

And don't forget about "extras" that aren't included in most new homes—two prime examples are window coverings and landscaping. Did we mention that curtains and shades for all those pretty new windows can run $1000 or more? And have you priced the cost of sod lately? Many buyers forget to factor these items into the cost of a new home.

As a result, we strongly recommend that you have a cash buffer of at least 5% of the home's price. Ten percent is even safer. That means if you're building or buying a $300,000 home, you should have another $15,000 to $30,000 stashed away to deal with emergencies. (An alternative would be to increase your mortgage by that amount—assuming you are willing and able to handle the bigger mortgage payments.)

If you don't have this cash buffer, consider alternatives: scale back the house's amenities to provide a buffer zone. Instead of that $300,000 home, perhaps you should aim for $280,000 or $270,000. Or

## SHOULD THIS BOOK BE RATED NC-17?

In reviewing this book, the *San Francisco Chronicle* wrote: "A terrific consumer guide that can scare you half to death but save you big bucks and years of grief."

Now, we aren't reprinting this review here to toot our own horn. Instead, we'd like to discuss the "scare" factor in any consumer guide. Yes, we realize there are some guides out there that bash an industry just to boost book sales. But that's not our objective. We seek to educate new home buyers by documenting what can go wrong (and right) when buying a new home. We'd be the first to acknowledge there are caring, competent builders out there and many new home buyers are satisfied with their purchases.

Yet, the fact is after researching the new home market for 10 years and interviewing hundreds of new home buyers, it CAN be a scary world out there. New home rip-offs, scams and shams can and do hurt thousands of consumers each year. While the exact number isn't known, we do know from our email volume alone, this is a big problem that isn't going away.

But, as writers, how can we present this material without thoroughly scaring every reader into thinking every builder is a scam artist and every new home purchase is a Steven King novel in the making?

The answer: we have no idea. The mere cataloging of all the things that can go wrong might look daunting. Yet, our philosophy is "forewarned is forearmed." We hope none of the scams and rip-offs chronicled in the next several chapters happens to you. But the best way to make sure you are protected is to first, learn about what CAN happen. And then take concrete steps to safeguard you, your life savings and your new home.

We also realize that some folks will read this book and decide NOT to build a home. And that's fine. If you realize you don't have the time, inclination or effort it takes to make your new home purchase as safe as possible, then don't do it. If you go forward, however, we urge caution and careful preparation.

delay your purchase until you can save the extra money or earn the extra income to cover higher payments.

Even if you have enough cash in the bank and a great marriage and have lived in an area for more than a year, you may have a simple question on your mind: what's this going to cost me? Fair enough. In the next section, let's break down the cost of an average new home.

## Whrt doés rn rverrge new home cost?

"Sticker shock" is a good way to describe most folks' reaction to new home prices today. A hot housing market in recent years has driven new home prices into the stratosphere in many cities, despite the ups and downs of the national economy.

It's easy to accuse builders of price gouging, especially in hot markets. Yet, it's important to realize much of the "cost" of a new home has little to do with bricks, lumber and kitchen tile. There are many hidden costs in buying a new home, not the least of which are all the layers of "government approvals" and other red tape that can add thousands to the average house. Here is a break down of the typical cost of a new home, based on a survey of 42 metro areas in 1998 by the National Association of Home Builders; we updated it with 2002 figures from our own research.

*Chart A: The average lot for a new house costs $53,516. Here's a breakdown:*

| Lot Cost | $ Amount | % of Total |
|---|---|---|
| Raw lot cost | $30,082 | 56.2% |
| Development costs | | |
|     Cost of processing approvals | 1,799 | 3.4 |
|     Site preparation | 4,075 | 7.6 |
|     Site improvement | | |
|         Paving | 4,859 | 9.1 |
|         Water & sewer | 4,593 | 8.6 |
|         Erosion & sediment | 1,076 | 2.0 |
|     Impact analysis | 748 | 1.4 |
|     Water/electric hookup | 1,260 | 2.4 |
|     Land dedication or fee in lieu | 168 | 0.3 |
|     Bonding/escrow fee | 349 | 0.7 |
|     Financing cost | 2,129 | 4.0 |
|     Tree preservation & planting | 762 | 1.4 |
|     Wetland preservation | 235 | 0.4 |
|     Value of unbuilt land as green space/parks | 536 | 1.0 |
|     Other costs | 845 | 1.5 |
| Total development costs | $23,434 | 43.8% |
| Total Finished Lot (raw+development) | $53,516 | 100.0% |

*And that's just the land. On the next page, we'll go over actual construction costs.*

*Chart B: The average new home racks up $124,276 of construction costs.*

| Construction Cost Breakdown | $ Amount | % of Total |
|---|---|---|
| Building permit fees | $1,108 | 0.9% |
| Impact fees | 1,182 | 1.0 |
| Water & sewer inspection | 1,207 | 1.0 |
| Excavation, foundation, backfill | 11,952 | 9.6 |
| Steel | 1,406 | 1.1 |
| Framing, trusses & sheathing | 25,052 | 20.2 |
| Windows | 4,769 | 3.8 |
| Exterior doors | 1,415 | 1.1 |
| Interior doors & hardware | 2,322 | 1.9 |
| Stairs | 558 | 0.4 |
| Roof shingles | 3,226 | 2.6 |
| Siding | 5,350 | 4.3 |
| Gutters & downspouts | 785 | 0.6 |
| Plumbing | 7,318 | 5.9 |
| Electrical wiring | 4,669 | 3.8 |
| Lighting fixtures | 1,292 | 1.0 |
| HVAC | 5,110 | 4.1 |
| Insulation | 1,793 | 1.4 |
| Drywall | 6,807 | 5.5 |
| Painting | 4,734 | 3.8 |
| Cabinets, countertops | 6,167 | 5.0 |
| Appliances | 1,675 | 1.3 |
| Tiles & carpet | 5,971 | 4.8 |
| Trim material | 3,861 | 3.1 |
| Landscaping & sodding | 2,250 | 1.8 |
| Wood deck or patio | 821 | 0.7 |
| Asphalt driveway | 1,873 | 1.5 |
| Other | 9,603 | 7.7 |
| **Total construction costs** | **$124,276** | **100.0%** |

*Chart C: Putting it all together: The TOTAL average cost of a new home.*

| Sale Price Breakdown | $ Amount | % of Total |
|---|---|---|
| Finished lot cost (see Chart A) | $53,516 | 23.6% |
| Total construction cost (see Chart B) | 124,276 | 54.8 |
| Financing cost (builder's costs) | 4,266 | 1.9 |
| Overhead & general expenses | 12,955 | 5.7 |
| Marketing cost (including buyer financing) | 3,180 | 1.4 |
| Sales commission (agents/sales reps) | 7,650 | 3.4 |
| Profit | 20,837 | 9.2 |
| **Total sales price** | **$226,680** | **100.0%** |

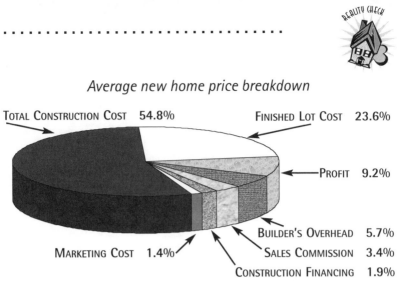

*Average new home price breakdown*

Total Construction Cost   54.8%

Finished Lot Cost   23.6%

Profit   9.2%

Builder's Overhead   5.7%

Sales Commission   3.4%

Construction Financing   1.9%

Marketing Cost   1.4%

*Source: National Association of Home Builders survey of builders in 42 metro areas.*

# The Fine Print on these Costs

Now, you'll note the bottom line is $226,680, the average cost of a new home in the U.S. But that's not the FINAL cost to you, the home buyer. Nope, you'll have to factor in the following:

**1** **Mortgage costs.** Origination and other mortgage costs (prepaid taxes and insurance, for example) will add thousands to your final bill. For example, let's say you make a 20% down payment on that new home ($45,366). That leaves a mortgage of $181,344. If a mortgage lender charges you a "one point origination fee," that equals $1813—money that's above and beyond the purchase price. (More on mortgages in Chapter 2).

**2** **Closing costs**. Mortgage fees are just the beginning—at the closing of your home, you'll also be asked to "pre-pay" a certain amount of property taxes and hazard insurance. Then be prepared to cough up more money for title insurance, "underwriting fees," and other closing costs—bottom line: add another $1000 to $3000 to your bill for this "average house."

**3** **Landscaping.** Oh, did we forget to mention that new home does NOT have any grass, trees or shrubs? Most builders charge extra for these niceties, that is if they offer them at all. With some builders, you're on your own. Budget another $2000 to $8000 for this.

**4** **Window coverings.** All those shades, curtains and blinds you see in the model home are extra as well. Sure, you can shop around for deals on window coverings, but still expect to shell out $1000 to $3000.

**5** **Miscellaneous.** You don't plan to use that ratty old couch in your brand new home, do you? All those new spaces may need new furniture, which ain't cheap. You may need to budget money for new furnishings, as well as other décor items and "extra upgrades" for the new home you can't live without.

Now, take a calculator and add it up. Here's a worksheet:

| | |
|---|---|
| Target Home Price | _____ |
| Mortgage Costs | _____ |
| Closing Costs | _____ |
| Landscaping | _____ |
| Window Coverings | _____ |
| Misc. | _____ |
| **Your Actual FINAL costs:** | _____ |

It's easy to see how that "average" $226,680 home price really translates into $235,000, $245,000 or more when all is said and done.

# Behind the Numbers: Nasty Surprises That Inflate Home Prices

Take another look at those charts detailing what an average new home costs. Home builders say 10% of the price is due to "unnecessary regulation." A quick glance at Chart A reveals some "development costs" that could be easily attributed to excessive red-tape: cost of processing approvals ($1799), impact analysis ($748), impact fees ($1182) and more. Basically, these are paperwork items counties and cities require builders to complete and pay for before they can get permits to build.

Yet, some of those government requirements (such as parks, green space, and wetland preservation) are exactly the items that show up on buyer surveys as key amenities. Hence, the market might force builders to build these amenities even if the government didn't.

Inspection and permit fees are another item that might look excessive at the outset—but does any consumer want to buy a home that hasn't been inspected to make sure it meets minimal building and safety codes? Having a city or county building inspector visit your home multiple times costs money, plain and simple. Sure those bureaucracies could be run more efficiently in many cases, but the alternative (letting builders police themselves) is a prescription for disaster in our opinion.

More interesting in these figures are some big ticket items most buyers have no idea they are paying for. Take the "sales commission" line in Chart C. Amazing that the average new home price includes a whopping $7650 in commissions for real estate agents. Notice the agent is paid more money than the entire cost of plumbing in your new home ($7318). As we discuss in Chapter 5, we think this expense is quite unnecessary—and we'll give you tips on how to get that $7650 put in your new home, instead of in an agent's pocket.

What about all the profit the builder makes? That $20,837 figure on a $226,680 may only account for 9.2% of the home price but remember that is AFTER the builder has accounted for "overhead and general expense" (pickup trucks, donuts, etc). Most businesses are lucky to eke out a 5% profit on sales; grocery stores are happy with a 1% profit. So, we don't cry for builders when they claim their profits are too small.

Of course, builder profit margins vary from contractor to contractor. In chapter 2, we'll list the profit margins of several large builders.

# The Goal: Take Control of Your New Home Purchase

Whether you plan to build the "average" new home or a high-end "dream home," buying or building this monster will be the most expensive thing you've ever purchased. And if you look at a new home like any other consumer purchase, it might surprise you how little research and preparation goes into the buying process.

When buying a car, most folks will do extensive research before any purchase, checking out crash tests, pouring over reliability reports, taking test drives and more. Heck, some people will consult three consumer magazines for rankings before they buy a $50 toaster.

Yet, what happens when folks buy a $225,000 home? Most just walk into a builder's model and fall in love with a kitchen tile treatment. That's it. Many buyers are seduced into spending hundreds of thousands of dollars by fancy decorating or other items in a model new home—even though their new home may not even contain any of the items from the model!

Few buyers ever delve into a builder's background or track record. The same folks who would never buy a car without seeing a window sticker of standard equipment and options will never get that level of detail on their new home. And, worst of all, many new home buyers reveal sensitive and confidential information about themselves to a real estate agent, never asking WHO that agent works for.

It's as though folks put on their "home buyer's caps" and turn off their brains.

In writing this book, we hope to do something radical to the new home buying process: get consumers to TAKE CONTROL. And our approach isn't an unproven, experimental method—the goal of this book is to teach you simple yet effective ways of buying a new home that makes sure you get the quality you've paid for. And to avoid rip-offs and scams that bilk some out of their life savings.

The key to this book is our strategy of buying a new home: the Paper/Scissors/Rock Method. We'll explain this theory briefly in this chapter and then expand on each concept as we go forward into later chapters.

We should point out, however, this book is not a "do-it-yourself" guide where you pound the nails. Instead of "how-to," this is a "how-NOT-to" book. We hope to show you how not to get ripped off, spend too much money or get an inferior home. The only way to accomplish this is to hire a team of professionals, who are screened for their reliability and monitored for quality during the job. Through savvy consumer maneuvering, you can get a quality new home at a price you can live with.

We think of this book as a two-way street—we encourage you to write, email or call us with your experiences. If you discover a problem we haven't discussed or a great tip that you think would help other home buyers, please contact us. You can call us at the number listed on the "How to Reach Us" page at the back of the book. Our address, fax number and e-mail address are on the same page, so feel free to drop us a note.

# THE KEY INGREDIENTS OF A QUALITY NEW HOME

Think of the paper, scissors and rock as the key ingredients in the recipe of your new home. Here is a brief description of each component:

## The Paper

The basis of a quality home starts before one brick is laid: the "paper" that makes up your agreement with the builder. As you'll note in chapters 6 and 8, this is much more than a boilerplate contract. The paper must protect you as a consumer. To do this, you need:

◆ Detailed plans for the house and foundation drawn by a qualified professional. The safest course is an experienced, residential architect and structural engineer. A soils test should be done to ensure that the proper type of foundation is designed.

◆ A thorough contract that specifies all the "standards and materials" to be used—down to the brand of siding, shingles, faucets and more. Installation of the materials should be clearly spelled out.

◆ A clear warranty that doesn't limit your consumer rights. Some builders try to sneak in clauses that restrict "implied warranties" or methods of compensation if things go wrong.

## The Scissors

You'll need a tool to "poke" the builder to make sure he or she lives up to the paper. The scissors are actually a team of watchdogs who work for you, not the builder:

◆ An experienced structural engineer to inspect the foundation and other critical construction points.

◆ A retired contractor/private inspector/engineer as a home inspector who can flag other problems. In chapters 9 and 10, you'll learn about the key inspection points.

◆ An architect to make sure the builder follows the design and uses the materials as specified on the blueprints.

◆ A real estate attorney to make sure the contract gives you maximum legal protection in line with your state's laws.

Note that the "scissors team" does not include municipal housing inspectors. Nor does it include the real estate agent—most agents work for the builder and know zip about new construction. We'll discuss the issue of agents later in Chapter 5.

## The Rock

The "rock" in the new home building process is gold—the money (your money) that builds the house. Always keep in mind the Golden Rule of House Building: *He who holds the gold makes the rules.* If you control the money, you stand a better chance of getting a quality home. Here's how you do it:

◆ Finance the construction by taking out the construction loan in your name. Someone must finance the construction process—we argue it should be the homeowner, not the builder or developer. In Chapter 2, we'll tell you how to do this.

◆ Control the bills: any money disbursed from the construction loan should be paid only after the work is completed to your satisfaction. You sign off on all the checks and see all the bills for the home.

◆ The money goes directly to the subcontractors or suppliers.

◆ The builder gets the profit only after the home is completed to your satisfaction. This is done at the closing. While draws are allowed to reimburse direct expenses (permits, approval fees, etc.), the big profit check isn't written until the end. By holding the gold until the end, you give the builder a powerful incentive to do it right.

*Reality check:* this part of our strategy is perhaps the hardest to control. Large production builders and even smaller custom home builders will INSIST that they (not you) control the construction financing. Others insist on large deposits or payments as the construction progresses. In areas where new homes are in hot demand, builders may have a "take it or leave it" attitude when it comes to this and many other parts of the transaction. The goal here is to build in as MANY of the above protections as you can. We'll show you how in the coming chapters.

Finally, be aware that even if you have complete control over the "rock," there are downsides and costs to this as well. You may have to purchase the land or building site outright—this early down payment may be many months before your new home is finished. Also, the paperwork can be a hassle.

# Jargon Check

Before we continue headlong into this process, let's pause for a second to make sure we're all on the same page. Real estate folks love jargon—they've never met an acronym they didn't like. Here are a few terms you'll encounter and our interpretation of their meanings.

## The Three Flavors of New Houses

**1** **Tract or production homes.** A production house is mass-produced by a builder or developer in a tract-style development. Drive into a subdivision in Anytown, USA, and you'll notice cookie-cutter homes that are cloned from one or two basic styles. With many production builders, the emphasis is on PRODUCTION—that is quantity, not quality. They want to slap up as many houses as possible. As a result, you must choose from one of a small number of predetermined styles. In the past, you couldn't change anything about a production home, except for the color of the carpet or paint. Sure, builders offered "upgrades" such as nicer carpeting or better appliances, but the basic house (the rooms, windows, etc.) stayed the same.

The good news is that many large production builders are offering today's buyers more customization. The Vintage Hills community in Reno, Nevada offers seven base plans and a whopping 267 variations to choose from. A computer that tracks the costs from these additions helps keep the home purchase from becoming an accounting nightmare.

In Voorhees, New Jersey, The Orleans Co. enables buyers at the Lakes at Alluvium community to go hog wild customizing plans, according to a recent *Builder Magazine* article. One buyer enhanced their new home's view of the lake with a picture window added above a direct-vent gas fireplace. The plan originally called for a wood-burning fireplace, which would have precluded the window. The buyer also dropped the cathedral ceiling in the living room to make room for an extra bedroom upstairs.

Before you get too excited, we should note that most customization is occurring with upper-end homes, such as Chicago-based Sundance Homes, which offers customization in a community that starts in the $300,000 price range. However, building industry consultants predict that customizing will spread to even lower-price communities in the coming years.

Whatever the level of customization the builder offers, the advantage to production homes is still their price. All those "economies of scale" and "builder's special" materials drive the prices of production homes below those of fancy custom homes.

**2** **Semi-custom homes.** These homes exist in a gray area between production and true custom homes. While the builder once again provides a series of floor plans and styles, the buyer can "customize" the home by changing several interior aspects. Want the master bedroom closet to be larger or the dining room to be smaller? Most semi-custom builders can adjust the walls to fit your needs. (The only things that can't be moved are "load-bearing" walls, which are walls that hold the weight of the home. Any move of a load-bearing wall would require the home to be re-engineered.)

Semi-custom builders are often smaller companies than production builders. By doing a few homes at a time, they can offer more personalized service and customization for their customers. According to a recent industry survey, 23% of new homes were built by semi-custom builders (that compares to 70% for tract home builders who offered standard designs and designs with option packages).

One caveat: we've discovered several builders that have deceptively marketed their homes as "semi-custom." A builder that offers to "customize" the home by changing the color of the kitchen tile or exterior paint is not a true semi-custom builder. Many production builders like to pretend that they are doing semi-custom homes to dupe buyers into thinking they're more than just a tract home builder. Actual semi-custom builders can change (for a price) almost any element of the home.

**3** **Custom homes.** Only 8% of all homes built in this country are custom-built for buyers. The home is designed from scratch to meet the buyer's needs and wants, often by a professional architect who is working for the buyer (not the builder). Typically, the lot or building site is owned by the home buyer—this can be a roadblock if land is scarce or expensive. Also, the land may need to be purchased outright; coming up with this cash early in the process can be a challenge as well.

Production and semi-custom builders would like you to think that all custom homes cost $500,000 or more. The truth is custom homes are more affordable than you think. You can build a custom house in the price range of many production and semi-custom homes, if (and that's a big if) you can find a piece of land to build it on. How? First, you don't have to pay the 6% to 7% real estate agent commission that's built into the production-home price. This savings usually covers part of the cost of hiring an architect or design professional. Most importantly, you control the quality of the materials that go into your home.

Why do custom homes always seem to cost so much money? It has more to do with custom-home *buyers* than the homes themselves. Many "custom" buyers are interested in high-end features such as huge gourmet kitchens, whirlpool baths, fancy cabinets and so on. Load up any home with these expensive features and the price will soar.

Many custom builders we've interviewed are willing to build in the "affordable" price ranges—they just don't advertise it. Granted, the lower price home will be smaller and will have fewer features than the more expensive homes, but the house will be built to your exact needs.

And that's the best advantage to building a custom home: You get a house that fits you, not some pre-fab "Average Family." If you need a home office with a fax line, you get it. If you want a kitchen with an island rangetop, it's yours. In a sense, a custom home is a finely tailored suit or dress that exactly fits you.

## Where the buyer fits in: spec or pre-sold?

Whatever the home type (production, semi-custom or custom), new homes also fall into two general categories—spec or pre-sold.

◆ **Spec homes.** These homes are built on "speculation"; that is, the builder is taking a risk by starting construction without a buyer. Hopefully, one will come along at some point and buy the home. If the buyer shows up at the midpoint of construction, some minor alterations (colors, finishes) may be done to the home. However, the basic floor plan is usually literally set in concrete. In hot markets, some production and semi-custom builders may gamble on building a few spec houses, since the likelihood of finding a buyer is good.

As you'll read later, the advantage to buying a spec house is that it may be ready quickly. You don't have to wait until something is built from scratch. Unfortunately, when you buy a spec home, you're also vulnerable to many scams. Since you weren't there at the beginning, several critical construction stages may have come and gone without your supervision. The pouring of the foundation and/or footings is a good example. It's hard to tell whether the footings were done correctly when they're now buried under four feet of dirt. If you buy a spec home with a defective foundation, you may only find out later when the home shifts.

◆ **Presold homes.** As the name implies, the home is "presold" to a buyer before construction begins. All types of builders (production, semi-custom and custom) will gladly sell you a home before one shovel of dirt is moved. Of course, just because the home is presold does not mean the builder gets all (or any) of his profit before the home is completed. It's just a commitment by you to buy the home—if it's built in accordance with your contract, design plans and specifications.

The biggest advantage of going "pre-sold" is that you monitor the construction from day one. Your team of watchdogs (architect, inspector, etc.) can catch any problem before it's set in stone. On the other hand, this takes time—you may have to wait three to six months (or even a year) until the home is completed.

## GETTING ORGANIZED

There are only one to two trillion details involved with building or buying a new home. As a result, it pays to try to organize this mess.

We recommend a three-ring binder with pockets. Put a spiral notebook in the binder—use it to jot down details during meetings, trips to plumbing supply centers, etc. Another useful organizing tool is an filing cabinet—you'll use this to hold brochures and other material you'll gather during this process. Files can be labeled with categories such as contracts, kitchen cabinets, lighting, plumbing fixtures, design ideas, etc.

# Why You Should NOT Build a House Yourself

*"If you completely absorb the information we provide here, you should be able to build your own house."*
—From a "do-it-yourself" book on home building published in 1990.

Visit any bookstore and you'll discover dozens of "do-it-yourself" house building books. These books passionately try to convince you that building a house yourself will be the most rewarding, least expensive method of getting a new home. Pound the nails yourself and you could save that fat 15% profit the builder is charging!

The mantra of "do it yourself" building is fed by all those Home Depots out there and stoked by TV shows that promise instant construction knowledge.

However, there are many aspects of doing-it-yourself that get scant attention from do-it-yourself books, home centers and TV shows. Slick salespeople and TV hosts don't always reveal potential problems for the do-it-yourselfer.

For example, you can't build a house without a building permit, obtained from a local building department. Many building departments will only issue permits to licensed contractors. Do-it-yourselfers don't count.

Lenders also are often unwilling to lend money to an unlicensed contractor. One aspiring do-it-yourselfer wrote to syndicated columnist Robert Bruss about this problem. "I can't find a bank which will make a construction loan to a do-it-yourself contractor such as myself," the home buyer said, adding that the bank gave as its reason that "virtually their only foreclosures on construction loans have involved do-it-yourselfers." And, can you blame the lenders? Would you lend $200,000 or $300,000 to someone who's never built a home before?

Along with the technical and financial difficulties of building your own home, there is another big roadblock: time. Do you know how much time it takes to build a home? To get bids from sub-contractors? To schedule workers and deliveries of materials? Building a home is a full-time job and the average house can take anywhere from three to six months (or even a year) to construct. If you have another full-time job and expect to work on the home on the weekends, your home building project could last a year or more.

Among the biggest risks of doing it yourself is Murphy's Law of Home Building: whatever can go wrong, will go wrong. You're on the hook if a problem with the home's construction occurs. By contrast, if you hire a professional builder to construct your house and an unforeseen problem occurs, it is the builder's responsibility to solve the problem. With few exceptions (soil problems, to name one), the cost should be absorbed by the builder. Any increase in materials costs also will be paid by the builder (if they are working on a fixed-price basis). And builder's get contractor's discounts that the do-it-yourselfer may not be able to qualify for.

Finally, the best sub-contractors like to work for professional builders, not do-it-yourselfers. The prospect for repeat work motivates the subs to do the best job possible. When you're building a home by yourself, the electrician, plumber and roofer all know they will probably never see you again.

As book authors we may be blasphemers to say this, but we believe no book can teach you how to be an expert plumber or electrician. It takes years of experience to be a good builder—you can't just substitute a 250 page book or a two-hour video tape for this level of expertise. While building a home may not look that complicated, you also have to navigate a minefield of regulations, building code requirements and other laws. The bottom line: leave the work to the professionals.

Also, consider videotaping and/or photographing the progress of your house. Not only does this make a great keepsake, but also if anything goes wrong, you will have some evidence of the building process. Another good idea: buy a fax machine. Faxing documents, approvals and change orders will save an incredible amount of time and could speed the process of your new home's construction.

Finally, a word to the wise: get wired. If you are not on the Internet or email, do it now. You'll use the 'net to research builders, building products and others. Email will be an easy way to communicate with contractors, suppliers and more. (Okay, not everyone has email yet, but more folks are going online each day).

## How to Use This Book: Meet the Money Bombs

In order to make the material in this book easier to use, we have divided up the chapters into sections like "Questions to Ask" and "Step-By-Step Strategies." We use icons to make these sections easier to identify.

One icon you may want to pay special attention to: money bombs (noted with the above icon). These are special scams and rip-offs that can trip up new home buyers. A money bomb might be anything from cheap materials "hidden" behind the walls of your new home to defective installation of products such as skylights, mechanical systems, etc.

We call these pitfalls "money bombs" because these ticking time bombs tend to explode and cost you money—sometimes lots of money. The "bomb" may go off just a few weeks after you move in or it could take years. A leaking skylight will be apparent after the first hard rain; however, a lousy paint job may not be apparent for a year or more— that's when you notice the paint is fading and needs to be re-done at a huge expense.

A reality check: yes, homebuilders are in this business to make a profit. Like any good capitalist, that means selling you a home at the highest price, while holding his costs as low as possible. Slashing the costs on a new home by substituting cheap materials or cutting corners on labor might be good for a builder's bottom line—but where does it leave you?

The answer: as a home buyer, you should at least be aware of the "trade-offs" a builder makes to make a profit. Some cost-cuts may be unnoticeable; others can cause you big problems down the line. The purpose of the "money bombs" is to point out the construction "trade-offs" that save the builder money, but can end up costing you in the future.

As a buyer, sometimes you have a choice to "upgrade" your new home to eliminate a builder shortcut—for example, paying extra for a quality window brand as an upgrade instead of accepting the builder's generic-brand choice. Other times you have no choice but to walk out of the builder's office and go elsewhere.

How widespread is defective construction? According to the Better Business Bureau, complaints about home construction are the second-largest consumer problem reported to local BBBs (the only area that causes more trouble is used cars). And the during the building boom of the 1990's, complaints to the BBB about shoddy builders doubled nationwide. Determining the exact extent of defective construction is difficult since many defects don't show up for months or years.

So, how many new homes are riddled with defects? It's hard to say—there are no reliable statistics or studies on the problem. When we interview inspectors who look at new homes, they claim many (perhaps two out of every three) new homes have "serious problems." In our office, we've amassed large files of "new home nightmares" that have appeared in local newspapers, on radio and on TV.

In their defense, builders say only a "small percentage" (they say 1% or 2%) of new home buyers are dissatisfied with their homes. Hey, with a million new homes built each year in the U.S., there are bound to be to a few lemons, right?

Yet, we think "customer satisfaction" surveys mask the extent of the problem, which in some high-growth areas like Texas and California can be epidemic. Why? If you buy a new home that's a lemon, you're not likely to complain. Since your life's biggest invest-ment is locked into the property, there is a BIG incentive to quietly patch up the home and try to pass it along to the next sucker. Yes, it is illegal to sell a defective home without disclosing the problems, but it happens with great frequency—it's the dirty little secret of the real estate business.

Perhaps a better measure of how many defective homes are out there in North America is what we call the Hurricane Test. Yep, there's nothing better to test the structural integrity of a home than 100 or 200 mph winds. Take the experience of Hurricane Andrew, which cut a swath of destruction in South Florida in 1992. The roofs of 100,000+ homes were blown away, along with much of the rest of the houses as well. According to an investigation by structural engineers, much of the damage was due to defective construction: seriously flawed roofs and homes were no match for strong winds.

Yet, here's the kicker: according to analysis by the *Miami Herald*, the homes most damaged by the hurricane where built recently in the 1980's and later. By contrast, subdivisions right across the street that were of older vintage often suffered LESS damage. The reason is clear: homes built in the last 10 to 20 years were riddled with defects that directly contributed to their destruction in Hurricane Andrew.

The bottom line: recognize the shortcomings of the new home market today and take steps to protect yourself. In the next several chapters, we'll try to educate you what to watch out for.

# What's New In This Edition

What's the biggest change in the new home market in recent years? In one word, it would be the Internet—the explosion of web resources you can use to plan your new home is amazing. You can apply for a mortgage online, research various builders and even check out detailed info on building products.

In the last edition of this book, we added more web sites and 'net resources . . . and this edition continues that trend. In each chapter, you'll see a section called "New Home Buyers in Cyberspace: What's on the Web?," which reviews the hottest web sites for new home buyers. We've also added web site contacts for most of the sources cited in this book.

We've also added coverage of the latest controversies on defective building products like synthetic stucco (called EIFS systems) and the growing problem of mold in new homes. We'll discuss the latest experimental building products, including what's working and what's not.

Finally, we've updated the book with the latest trends in new home design and added more bargain sources for lighting, flooring and other finishing items.

If that weren't enough, you'll also discover a handy phone/web directory in the back of the book. With one glance, you can see the phone numbers and web site addresses for all the companies and contacts we reference in the book.

# How Much New Home Can You Really Afford?

H ere's a quick quiz: what's the most expensive purchase you'll ever make?

If you answered "a new home," you're close but no cigar. Nope, the biggest purchase is your home's *mortgage*. When you factor in all the interest payments, you'll pay SEVERAL TIMES your home's purchase price for a mortgage.

For example, let's say you buy a $250,000 home and put 20% down. That leaves a mortgage of $200,000. At 8% interest, you'll pay over $528,309 in interest and principal over the next 30 years!

With such big bucks at stake, you can see why the mortgage business is full of lenders who'd love to have you pay *them* those big bucks in interest. So, you would think the actual process of GETTING a mortgage would be easy, right? Ha!

For some unknown reason, lenders make applying for a mortgage slightly less exciting than a root canal. From mountains of paperwork to confusing loan programs with acronyms like ARM's and FHA's, it's easy to get lost in the mortgage jungle.

So, let's cut to the chase and try to make sense out of the mortgage process. Along the way, we'll discuss the hot trend for home mortgages: getting a mortgage online. We'll review the best web sites for loans, rates, and research.

## The Ultimate Reality Check: 3 Mistakes to Avoid

This chapter is at the front of this book for one reason: you can't buy a new home unless you know the answer to the Money Question: How much can you spend on a new home? By getting this answer now, you can avoid these three mistakes:

◆ **Falling in love with something way outside your price range.**
It's fun to look at fancy houses with marble floors and giant master bedrooms. The problem is that marble is intoxicating—you can forget what planet you (and your bank account) are on.

◆ **Wasting time on false starts.** Not knowing exactly what you can afford will not only cost you time, but also it could very well cost you money. If you plan to build a $370,000 custom home and hire a design professional, you'd expect him or her to design a home for that amount of money. But what if you discover you can only spend $345,000? Forget that fancy kitchen, that extra bathroom, the three-car garage—all of these changes may cost you extra money to have the plans altered.

◆ **Getting in over your head.** Sure, you might be able to afford that big mortgage—but do you really want to make those payments for the next, say, 30 years? When you sit down with a lender (whether person or online), you'll get detailed info about your payments: principal, interest, taxes and insurance. The bottom line hit to your wallet may be surprising. Just because a lender will let you borrow the equivalent of Bolivia's national debt does not mean you WANT to borrow that much money. Other needs, like saving for retirement and college funds, may reduce the amount of money you want to pay monthly for your mortgage.

# The Goal of This Chapter

Through all the rigorous credit checks and paperwork hassles of getting a mortgage, it's important to keep your eye on the prize: the goal of this chapter is to get a "pre-approval letter" from the lender. This letter essentially says they've checked you out and are willing to loan you up to X amount of dollars on a new home. A pre-approval letter is a powerful bargaining chip with builders—it shows you're serious and ready to rumble.

We learned the lesson about the value of a pre-approval letter the hard way. On the first house we built, the mortgage lender told us our financing was secure, yet delayed getting us the formal letter for several days. During that time, the builder refused to start the project. As a result, our home's construction fell a week behind schedule. While that wasn't earth-shattering, it combined with other delays to raise the stress level up another notch.

Note: there is a big difference between getting "pre-qualified" for a loan and "pre-approved." Many lenders and web sites (reviewed later in this chapter) will do a free "pre-qualification" for you—this involves calculating your buying power. Basically, you tell the lender your income, debts and other financial info and the lender tells you ROUGHLY how much of a loan you can get.

Pre-approval is more rigorous—the lender is now actually committing to loan you money for that new house (provided it appraises for the sales price and other conditions). As you can imagine, this commitment requires you to prove your income/assets. You may also have to pay for a credit report and any application fees ($100 or more)—and those expenses may not be refundable in case you change your mind.

In the next section, we'll go over some more mortgage jargon that you may encounter in your home search.

# Stuff to Know

Yep, mortgages are a world unto their own, with a special lexicon of words only a banker would love. Because of limited space, we'll only discuss a few of the most common terms here.

◆ **Points.** A point is a prepaid interest charge. One point is equal to 1% of the loan. If your loan is $200,000 and the lender is charging one point as an "origination fee" (a common fee lenders charge buyers to process their loan), you pay $200. So, in essence, you are only receiving $198,000 in loan proceeds—but you must pay back $200,000 PLUS interest. Great deal, right? Perhaps the best thing you can say about points is that they are tax deductible (as of this writing).

Obviously, it pays to shop for the lender with the lowest points, as well as the lowest application/processing fees. In down markets, some builders may offer to pay points as an incentive—shop around to see whether this is truly a good deal or merely a gimmick.

◆ **Escrow.** In this chapter, we recommend putting any deposits for a new home in escrow. But what is that? Escrowed funds are held by a third-party (usually a real estate agent or title company) until certain conditions are met. An escrowed deposit is only released to a builder once the home is completed (after closing).

◆ **Private mortgage insurance (PMI).** PMI is required by lenders on homes that have low down payments. If your loan is more than 80% of the sales price, the lender may require you to pay monthly premiums on a PMI policy. We'll discuss PMI in depth later in this chapter.

◆ **Locks.** Mortgage rates fluctuate daily. Some lenders offer you the ability to "lock" in a rate before closing. When interest rates are expected to rise, buyers like to lock in a low rate. Locks vary from 7 to 30 days. We've even heard of 60-, 90- and 150-day locks. (Any lock for more than 30 or 45 days will probably require some kind of fee, either in points or a higher interest rate.) A 30-day lock means you must close on the home within 30 days to get that rate. If the home isn't ready, the lock expires and you may have to re-lock. The rates for longer locks tend to be higher, since the lender is assuming the risk that rates may rise in the future.

◆ **Two-step mortgages.** Mortgage rates used to come in only two flavors: fixed or adjustable. Yet, in the last 10 years, a new mortgage has emerged: the two-step. It's sort of like the Neapolitan flavor of mortgages—a two-step is fixed for a period of time (one, three, five, or seven years) then is adjustable after that. For example: a "5/25" is fixed for five years at one rate and then adjusts to the market rate for the last 25. The advantage of these loans: that first rate (for five or seven years) is typically lower than the market. That might be a great deal if you plan to only live in the house for a few years. If you decide to stay, of course, you can always refinance your mortgage to lock in a fixed rate.

If all this stuff is making your head spin or you are a first-time buyer, you might consider some additional help. Later in this chapter, we'll review several mortgage web sites that have excellent tutorials for beginners—and it's all free.

# The Two Paths to A New Home

Getting a mortgage for a new home can be more complicated than a loan for a resale home. That's because you may choose to be involved with the financing of the construction of your home, for reasons described below. Lenders split such transactions into two separate loans: a construction loan and a permanent mortgage.

Here's an overview of the two paths to buying a new home:

◆ **Straight purchase.** You give the builder a small deposit and the balance of the money at closing. The builder finances the actual construction. This is most common with production houses, where the builder/developer owns the land and you have very little ability to "customize" the house beyond the color of the carpet, paint and a few other cosmetic details.

Now this method sounds quite simple, but there can be hidden pitfalls. Essentially, YOU'VE agreed to buy this home but the BUILDER is managing the money that's being used to construct the home. What if the builder mismanages the money? Say, the builder pockets the loan money and "forgets" to pay the subcontractors and suppliers on your home? That's what happened to dozens of homebuyers in Texas in recent years. They found numerous "liens" slapped on their homes by unpaid subs. Later in this chapter, we'll discuss some ways to protect yourself if you do a "straight purchase"

◆ **Consumer-active construction financing.** If you are building a semi-custom or custom home, you may have the opportunity to be involved in the financing of your new home. While this may sound like big hassle, there is an upside: by taking out a construction loan in your name, *you* are in control. You control how the money is spent on your house. You see all the bills and can confirm that your house contains those items before cutting a check to a supplier or sub. The builder is kept on a short leash.

As you can imagine, some builders will not want to give you this kind of control over your new home project. Like everything else, this is a negotiation—if the housing market is hot, builders may have a take it or leave it attitude on this issue. The sad reality is that few new home buyers (perhaps less than 15%) take control of the construction loan for their project.

Lenders will give you two options when it comes to construction loans: a "straight" construction loan or a combination loan called a "construction to perm" loan. The advantage of the latter loan is reduced closing costs. Why? If you build a new home with a straight construction loan followed by a permanent mortgage, you will have TWO closings (one for each loan). That means two origination fees, two credit report fees and more. By consolidating both loans into a construction to perm loan, you do one closing. Details on each program vary from lender to lender, but it is generally more economical to go with the construction to perm loan.

To understand why consumer-active construction financing is so important, let's take a look at the Golden Rule of New Home Buying or Building.

## The Golden Rule of New Home Buying or Building

*"He who holds the gold makes the rules."* Sounds a little harsh, doesn't it? But that's the reality of real estate today—by simply taking control of the "gold," you dramatically stack the odds in favor of getting a quality house. Lose control and the chances of getting a "lemon" are higher.

What is the "gold"? Quite simply, it's the money used to build your new house. That money pays for the bricks, windows, shingles, paint, light switches and everything else in and on the house. And, oh yes, part of the money goes to the builder as profit for his time and effort.

Where does the gold come from? You, of course. Whether you pay for the house from your own pocket or get a loan from a bank, you're the person on the hook. Ultimately, you'll be paying monthly installments on this house for 30 years. This year consumers will shell out $150 BILLION to buy new houses—and that doesn't include the interest to be paid over the next 30 years.

That's a lot of money. But would it shock you to learn that most consumers voluntarily give up control on the majority of all new homes bought today? Builders and developers control the "gold" in a whopping 85% of all new houses sold.

How do builders control what is really your money? By getting the construction loan in their name, they finance (and control) the building of your home. The builder controls your money, doling it out to subcontractors and suppliers as they perform the work on your house. At the end of the construction, your "permanent mortgage" pays off the builder's construction loan—anything left over is their profit.

Savvy builders realize that controlling your money gives them a free hand in building your house—and maximizing their profit. By controlling the "gold," they can manage the project as they see fit. That might work out fine in the end for most home buyers, but there is a great potential for abuse. Less-than-ethical contractors use the control over a home's construction financing to hide all sorts of "improprieties." They can substitute cheaper materials since you never see the bills. Maybe you'll notice the cheaper brand of windows or less expensive siding—and maybe you won't.

Perhaps most dangerous is the builder's ability to pull his profit out of your house even before one shovel of dirt is moved. That's right, the builder can "draw" large chunks of profit from the construction loan long before you move in. Despite federal banking regulations that prevent such practices, we've seen many cases of builders who have done just that. Scam artists can siphon huge sums of money from construction loans and leave you with a half-finished house—and guess who's on the hook to pay back this money? Hint: It's not the builder.

The best strategy is for you to hold the gold. You can do this by insisting that the construction loan is in your name and that no money is disbursed on your new home without your signature. Construction loans are typically set up like your average checking account. Each check must be signed by both you *and* the banker. The builder can't spend any of your money without your approval.

What about the builder's profit? We believe the builder should not receive one dime of profit until the house is completely finished to your total satisfaction. The money (your money) is the builder's biggest incentive to make sure the house is right.

Of course, holding the profit until the end doesn't mean you're holding all the money back. It is fair for the builder to expect you to pay all the other expenses associated with building your house. Building materials and supplies are one major category, as is subcontractors' labor. As you'll note later, we recommend paying the subcontractors and other suppliers directly, as opposed to giving the money to the builder and hoping he pays these folks.

Reimbursing the builder for his actual out-of-pocket expenses during construction is also kosher. For example, the builder may have to pay $1000 for a building permit or other governmental approvals for your house—you should reimburse the builder for this.

A gray area to be negotiated are items such as "overhead": This could include the builder's office expenses, salaries for a foreman or superintendent, etc. But how much of the builder's office rent, telephone expenses, and other "soft expenses" are due to your house? How about the other house(s) the builder is doing at the same time? While the lumber delivered to your house is truly your expense, "overhead" expenses are harder to classify.

The best rule of thumb is to pay any expenses the builder incurs that are directly related to your house. Any indirect expense (office rent, phone, advertising, donuts) will not be paid out of your construction loan—but instead from the lump-sum profit payment made at the end of your house's construction.

# Step-by-Step Strategies.

**Step 1: Determine your needs.** The first step in any mortgage process is to assess your needs: is a permanent mortgage all you need, or are you interested in construction financing as well? How much mortgage can you qualify for? In the next section, we'll provide you with web sites that have online mortgage calculators to help with this info.

**Step 2: Shopping.** Whether you get a mortgage online or from a lender in your home town, you'll need to compare the rates and various "programs"—fixed rate, adjustable rate, etc. More on these later in the chapter. Narrow your search to three to five lenders that are final contenders.

**Step 3: Interviews.** Meet with at least three lenders (or call online lenders to set up telephone consultations). Be thorough in your evaluation—ask all the questions mentioned later in this chapter and raise other issues you have questions about.

**Step 4: Apply for a loan.** This phase includes the application itself. Yes, you can do some of this online, but even web-based mortgage companies will ask for documentation of income and assets. For construction financing, you may have to ask your architect/designer or builder to complete a cost estimate on the project.

**Step 5: Pre-approval.** After all the paperwork is submitted, get a commitment from the lender on the approval date. You may have to hassle them to make sure they hit this deadline—call once a week to see how things are going. A good lender will keep you informed on the process. Once you get pre-approval, the lender's job isn't over, however. They will continue to process your loan (and perhaps need additional documents) to get to final approval. Note: there is a some good news on this front—computerized processing of loan applications has cut the time needed for approval in recent years.

**Step 6: The construction closing.** If applying for construction financing, there will be a "closing" for this loan. Basically, you sign a lot of paperwork and the account is established.

**Step 7: Draws (construction loans only).** During the construction process, you may meet with the lender once a month or so to complete the "draws." These are payments to the builder, subcontractors and suppliers to reimburse them for work done on your home.

**Step 8: Permanent closing.** Finally, the home is finished and the closing of the permanent loan is held. We strongly urge you to have an attorney review the closing documents. Another wise tip: have your accountant review the closing statement, which calculates pro-rated taxes and other items that come out of your money. Most accountants will do this for a small fee (less than $100).

# How much profit is fair?

If your contractor or architect prepares a cost estimate for your project, you may see a strange figure at the bottom line of this piece of paper: the builder's "profit."

At this point, let us digress into a brief discussion about builder's profit—and how much is "right" or "wrong." That's a question we get asked frequently by new home buyers. How much profit is fair for the builder?

Of course, there is no one right answer. First, you must understand there are several types of "profit." Gross profit is roughly defined as the sales price of the home less the builder's "hard costs" (lumber, bricks, carpet, etc). Note this does not include the builder's overhead, management time, and other "soft costs" (office expenses, Krispy Kreme runs and so on). Builders who have sharp accounting skills can allocate those costs to come up with a "net profit."

When you see a profit figure for a contractor on a new home, it is usually gross profit. If you look at average gross profit margins (profit as a percentage of the home's sale price), they are all over the board—some builders eke out a 5% gross profit on a home. Other contractors in a hot market can make 20% to 30% or more. While those profit figures might look huge to consumers, remember they are gross (not net) profits. Builders can make a nice-looking gross profit on a new home but still lose money because their net profit is weighed down by excessive overhead.

## PROFIT MARGINS OF THE LARGEST PUBLIC HOME BUILDERS

| BUILDER | 2001 GROSS MARGIN* |
|---|---|
| D. R. HORTON | 21.6% |
| NVR | 21.4% |
| K B HOME | 20.4% |
| RYLAND GROUP | 19.7% |
| BEAZER HOMES | 18.7% |
| TOLL BROTHERS | 15.2% |
| LENNAR/US HOME | 12.4% |
| CENTEX | 11.9% |
| PULTE | 9.8% |
| MDC HOLDINGS | 7.5% |

*Gross margin is the percentage of revenue left after paying all direct production expenses. 2001 figures.

Large builders report their profit margins to Wall Street. On the previous page is a chart of the "gross margins" (the percentage of revenue left after paying all direct production expenses) for several big public builders.

You'll notice that builders who specialize in entry-level production houses have lower profit margins than those like K B Home and Toll Brothers, who target the luxury market. Hence, Centex may walk away with only $22,000 on a $200,000 sale, while Toll Brothers may pocket a fat $61,000 profit on a $400,000 home. But, don't cry for Centex—the company's huge volume makes up for slim profit margins. In 2001, Centex sold $6.7 billion in homes, compared to Toll Brothers $2.2 billion.

We should note that profit margins not only depend on the niche the builder targets, but also the economy in general. In good times, you might see hefty 15% to 25% gross profit margins. When the economy tanks, some builders are lucky to make a profit at all and others are satisfied with one in the single digits.

Are fat builder profits to blame for today's sky-rocketing new home prices? Well, they may play a part. But, the biggest difference is the price of land. In 1950, land accounted for only 11% of the average new home's cost. It's twice that today, in percentage terms.

## Getting Started: How Far in Advance?

How much time should you budget for the mortgage process? We'd suggest at least 60 days for the shopping, application and approval process.

Yes, you will see newspaper ads that claim lenders can approve you in just "10 days or LESS!" But that doesn't include the time it takes to do the application and compile all the documents a lender needs. The speed in which you submit needed documentation greatly affects how long the mortgage process takes.

Are online mortgage sources quicker than banks? Not necessarily. E-loan, the biggest online mortgage lender, says it takes about three weeks from the time you submit the *complete* application until approval. That's about the same as most bricks-and-mortar lenders. Add in several more weeks for shopping and you're up to 60 days.

The bottom line: don't wait until the last moment to start mortgage shopping. The more time you leave to compare rates and programs, the better.

## Sources for Mortgage/Construction Loans

◆ **The Builder.** Large production builders often have their mortgage subsidiaries. Even mid-size might have mortgage arm or at least a relationship with a mortgage broker (see below for more on brokers). The smallest builders usually have a local relationship with a bank or mortgage broker. Whatever the builder size, you'll likely get pitched to get a loan from the builder's lender. We'll discuss three cautions to this route in the following box.

◆ **The 'Net.** The web is the hottest source for mortgages today. We'll review the best sites later in this chapter. A word of caution: most online mortgage sites are run by mortgage brokers (described below). Later,

# The Builder-Lender: Fox in Sheep's Clothing?

Like all big builders, Pulte has their own mortgage subsidiary that it encourages buyers to use. But how effective is that pitch? Buried deep inside Pulte's financial reports, we found the surprising answer: 56% of all Pulte buyers also get their financing from Pulte.

That success can be attributed to do words: special deals. Many big builders have learned the same tricks as car dealers—financial incentives (rebates, low-interest loans) are a powerful sales tool. Many home buyers sign up for a builder's mortgage because the builder is offering a "special sale" with $2000 towards closing costs. Or a adjustable mortgage with a super-low starter rate.

But what are the pitfalls when the builder is also the lender? Here are three cautions:

**1** **Watch the rates.** Sure, a builder's sales rep says they have the best rates in town. But do they really? Conduct a reality check by checking rates from at least three other sources (more on how later in this chapter). One buyer in Vermont told us her builder promised a great deal on a mortgage, plus a $1000 toward closing costs. After checking, however, the buyer realized the builder was charging a quarter-point higher interest rate than other lenders—hence, you'd pay for the $1000 closing cost "gift" with high mortgage payments.

**2** **Under pressure.** When you consider your mortgage options, expect a good amount of pressure to go with the builder's lender. Some unscrupulous sales reps sometimes imply you don't have a choice—you MUST go with their lender to buy the home. That isn't true, of course. You can choose whatever mortgage source you want.

**3** **Illegal questions.** What's your religion? Do you have kids? Are you married? Those questions are all illegal for any builder to ask. But don't be surprised if an over-eager builder sales agent goes over the line in trying to "pre-qualify" you for a mortgage. We've heard reports that builders have asked questions about a buyer's religion or marital status, despite clear federal laws prohibiting such practices.

we'll discuss some of the pitfalls of using such broker sites, including some precautions you should take in shopping for a mortgage online.

◆ **Banks, savings and loans, credit unions.** The amount of home mortgages these companies do can vary, but they are good sources to check.

◆ **Mortgage lenders.** These companies make loans directly to consumers; since they specialize in mortgages, their rates and program options may be more attractive than banks. In additional to conventional mortgages, these lenders also originate the majority of VA and FHA loans. For the uninitiated, VA and FHA loans are government-backed mortgages that offer special benefits to qualified home buyers. The Department of Veteran Affairs, for example, guarantees VA loans to veterans of the U.S. Armed Forces to help them buy homes with no down payment. In contrast to VA loans, anyone can qualify for government-backed FHA loans, but pre-set spending limits and hefty upfront costs have dimmed the attractiveness of these mortgages. On the upside, FHA loans do have low down payments, about 5% of the home's price.

◆ **Brokers**. Brokers don't actually make loans, but act as middlemen introducing buyers to lenders. Like any middleman, there is a cost for their service. On the plus side, a broker can shop among several lenders for the best deals. That might be good if you have a "challenging" mortgage need (unusual property, employment situation, etc). BUT . . . you pay for this service. Some brokers charge fees and points that would be higher than if you went directly to a mortgage lender or bank. Later in this chapter, we'll discuss precautions in dealing with online mortgage sources—most of these tips apply to brokers as well.

◆ **Government agencies.** Did you realize that state and local housing agencies occasionally make below-market-rate mortgages available to first-time buyers and others who meet low or moderate income requirements? Most loans are administered by financial institutions. Check the "Blue Pages" of your phone book for a local/state housing agency for more information.

## Sources to Find the Best Rates

What's the current interest rate on a fixed-rated mortgage? In the past, homebuyers didn't have many sources to get that question answered. Sure, you could ask a real estate agent, who might have been sent a "rate quote" sheet from local lenders. But that sheet was always a few days old, so you never know what the "current rates" actually were unless you picked up the phone and called several lenders.

Even more unreliable were the real estate sections of your local newspaper—sure they might have charts of mortgage rates and even ads from local lenders. But here's a dirty little secret of the mortgage business: those rates are almost always bogus. Lenders advertise artificially low rates to "tease" home buyers to call them. By the time you phone in the next Monday to get a current quote, the actual rates are always higher because Alan Greenspan sneezed twice today.

Fortunately, the 'net has changed all this. Today, you can get a "real-time quote" from an unbiased source like HSH (reviewed later in this chapter). All in all, the 'net has forced lenders to be more honest, since their own web sites typically list "today's rates"—hence, there's no more falling back on the old excuse that the "advertised rate in the newspaper was too low because the market suddenly changed today."

In the next section, we'll review the best sites to check current rates.

## New Home-Buyers in Cyberspace: What's on the Web?

The internet is a treasure trove of information on mortgages. Even if you don't want to get a mortgage online, you can research various rates, learn about different loan programs and get answers to general questions. If you are a first-time buyer, there are several sites with great mortgage tutorials. What makes the web so handy is the interactive nature of these sites: most have various calculators and tools that let you determine monthly payments given different loan amounts and interest rates. You can also determine your buying power based on your financials (and a lender's requirements) and get pre-qualified. Some sites will even recommend a loan program for you, based on your requirements.

And best of all: it's all free. All the web sites reviewed in this section give away all this info at no charge.

As with everything on the web, the explosion of e-commerce is amazing. In 1996, only 60 lenders offered online mortgages. By 2000, that number ballooned to 3000 lenders! While we can't review all of those sources, here's a round-up of the best 'net sites for mortgages:

### Eloan
**Web site:** www.eloan.com, see Fig. 1 on the next page.
**What it is:** The biggest online mortgage broker.
**What's cool.** It's the mother of all mortgage sites, with in-depth advice and research tools. The easy-to-navigate site includes sections on "Home Finance 101" and "What to Expect." Eloan's loan calculators (to see what how much loan you can quality for, payment amounts and more) are easy and quick to use. Once you apply for a loan, you can track the progress of your application with their "E-track" feature. You can also have the site send you an email when rates drop to a certain level. Eloan claims you can save 80% off standard lender loan fees.
**Needs work.** Eloan claims it offers lower fees than traditional lenders, but that doesn't mean your quote is free of "junk" charges. We priced a loan that had just a half-point origination fee—but Eloan estimated a charge of $250 for "processing" and $425 for "underwriting." As with any lender, compare ALL the fees and charges to make sure it's a deal.

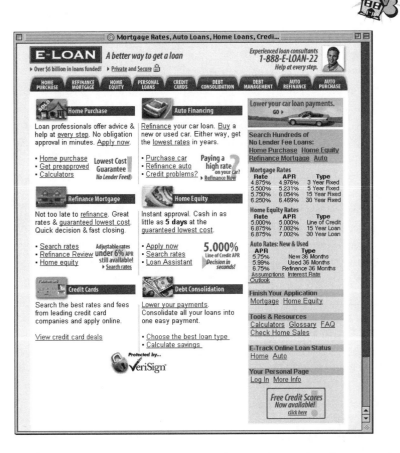

**Figure 1:** Eloan's tracking features (to watch your loan's progress) are among the best on the 'net.

## HSH

**Web site:** www.hsh.com

**What it is:** The world's largest publisher of mortgage and consumer loan information.

**What's cool.** They don't make loans, accept ads, take commissions or sell your name. HSH is like the *Consumer Reports* of mortgage info—they report on current rates and provide general advice. How does HSH come up with its info? It regularly surveys 2500 lenders nationwide and updates the rates daily. In addition to the web site, HSH also sells the "Homebuyer's Mortgage Kit" ($20, plus $3 shipping) which includes a 56-page guide to mortgage shopping and a list of lenders and rates in your area. You'll learn how to trim up-front fees, get worksheets on loan types and more.

**Needs work.** Well, it isn't very pretty to look at—the site's navigation could be easier. HSH's "average mortgage rates" combines both regular and "jumbo" (loans over $300,000) rates, which can make interpreting their data somewhat tricky. It might make more sense to split those two categories into separate figures. Because of the site's cluttered appearance, you have to stumble around to find useful reports (like their Weekly Market Trends forecast).

## Microsoft's Home Advisor

**Web site:** homeadvisor.msn.com

**What it is:** Microsoft's real estate site.

**What's cool.** As you'd expect, Microsoft delivers a slick site with lots of useful info—we liked features like the "roadmap" for learning about the mortgage process, calculators entitled "How Much Can You Afford?" and more. The "Shop for Rates" section is excellent—you use drop-down menus to pick your state, loan type (fixed vs. adjustable) and the loan amount then click the "update" button. Voila! Instant rate quotes for the loan amount you need. We also loved the "Rate Tracker" service, which sends you a daily email update on rates. Microsoft's 10-step process for loan application is streamlined and easy to understand

**Needs work.** Microsoft only has a limited number of lenders available to make loans on its site. And it is not licensed to make loans in all states as of this writing. While we liked the extensive research section, reports like "Know What to Negotiate" were too brief to be very helpful.

### Other sites to consider:

◆ **Bankrate.com** offers daily mortgage rate info, including in-depth analysis of rate trends. We liked the easy-to-use site with message boards, calculators and other research tools.

◆ **Countrywide.com** is the best example of the "bricks and clicks" mortgage companies, combing a web site with online quotes and a nationwide network of offices with real human beings to answer questions.

◆ **Getsmart.com** bills itself as the "online marketplace" for consumer and business borrowing. The web site has linked with iQualify.com which lets homebuyers receive an automated loan underwriting analysis and approval in minutes. Getsmart is a subsidiary of Providian Financial Corp.

◆ **iOwn.com** is a San Francisco-based mortgage broker (now owned by CitiGroup) with an innovative web site. Their "RateShopper" tool lets buyers compare loan programs and the estimated lifetime costs of each offering—we loved the interactive payment graphs. "LoanStatus" enables you to track the real-time progress of your loan online. iOwn.com has 23 lender-partners and charges a half-point fee to process a loan.

◆ **IndyMac.com.** This Pasadena, Calif. Based site scored at the top of a recent survey of online mortgage sites, thanks to their excellent customer service. The site pledges to beat any other loan offer by $300 and offers live online chats with its customer service agents.

◆ **LendingTree.com** is one those "blind dates" mortgage sites—you fill out a form with your personal data and they try to find a loan for

# Shopping Savvy for Online Mortgages

Shopping for a mortgage on the web is all the rage, but there are still are some precautions you should take. Here's an overview:

◆ **Online mortgage sites come in three flavors:** direct lenders (those sites that make loans directly to consumers), mortgage brokers (who, like all brokers, don't make loans but hook you up with a lender) and referral services (who merely refer you to lenders). The key: know who are dealing with. You can typically discover a site's background by clicking on an "About Us" button. Some sites are "blind dates"—you fill in your info first and then they try to find a lender for you.

◆ **Beware extra fees.** Shopping online is supposed to save you money, right? Well, some sites are merely mortgage brokers who make their money from "yield-spread premiums." These brokers convince buyers to take a mortgage that's higher than the going market rate—and then the broker pockets a hefty commission from the lender for this. As always, compare ALL of the loan's costs (fees, rate, points) to make sure you are getting a good deal.

◆ **Look for the APR.** The "Annual Percentage Rate" of a loan is more than just the interest rate—the APR factors in ALL of a loan's fees and charges to arrive at the "true cost" of borrowing. Yes, all lenders are suppose to disclose this to you. Do all mortgage web sites employ this much candor? No. Make sure you see the APR before committing to the mortgage.

◆ **Get the lock in writing.** Print any and all rate quotes you get. In case of a computer crash (yours or theirs), you may need this documentation to prove you locked your loan rate.

◆ **Ask about privacy policies.** Before you enter your annual income and other sensitive financial info into a site, be sure to check the site's privacy policy. Some unscrupulous sites have been known to slice and dice your financial stats, selling them to telemarketers. The bottom line: if the site doesn't guarantee your privacy, then don't do business with them.

◆ **Confirm track records.** Unfortunately, the youthfulness of the web does have a downside—even the most experienced online mortgage players have been in business for just a few years. Call the BBB and other consumer protection groups like your state attorney general's office to make sure the lender has a clean record. Another tip: confirm the lender has a valid license to make loans in your state (some sites actually list their license numbers online).

you. Unfortunately, there are no rates posted online; you have to wait (two business days) to see what deal you can get (the site promises offers from at least four lenders). The web site has beefed up its customer service in the past year, sending out emails to answer frequently asked questions and other enhancements.

◆ **Mortgagebot.com** is a online lender with an excellent site—the company offers loan decisions within three business offers and quick closings. Their rates are very attractive.

◆ **Mortgagelocator.com.** This site bills itself as the "National Directory of Online Virtual Lenders." You can search by state for lenders, surf a mortgage message board or take part in a real-time chat to get your questions answered. This site doesn't do any loans itself; instead you are referred to other lenders in your area.

◆ **Quickenmortgage.com.** You've got to fill out an extensive loan application before you get to see the names of lenders, but this site does have some useful features. The advice sections are solid and include general articles on home-buying from real estate authors.

◆ **Realestate.com.** This site offers help in finding local mortgage professionals or you can shop the rates of national lenders. Their interactive calculators include helpful graphs and tables to explore mortgage options.

# Questions to Ask

We've divided this section into two parts: the first concerns construction loans and the second focuses on "permanent" mortgages.

## Construction Loans

**1** **What are your procedures for construction loans?** This gives you an idea of what requirements must be met and the steps to get there.

**2** **Can you give me a written estimate of all fees?** These would include origination fees, application fees, credit-check charges, closing fees and so on.

**3** **Do you need a permanent mortgage commitment letter?** This is a critical area—most lenders will require that you have a permanent mortgage commitment before they're willing to approve a construction loan. Some lenders will limit the construction loan to the size of the permanent mortgage.

**4** **Do you offer construction to permanent loans?** Are there any savings in fees if I give you all my business? Some lenders offer "savings" if you get both loans from them. For example, the construction loan lender may require a credit report. If you go to another bank for your permanent mortgage, you may have to pay for this twice.

**5** **Will I have to deposit money into the construction account?** You may have to cough up some money at the outset. If the construction is estimated at $300,000, but the permanent mortgage will only be $265,000, the lender may require you to deposit another $35,000 into the construction account. If you own the lot, you may be able to pledge it as collateral—this could lower the initial deposit.

**6** **What's the procedure for payment of "draws"?** Is my signature required on every check? It better be—the worst case is when the builder has the power to draw money out of this account without your permission. Some banks pay draws based on bona fide bills that are presented to the home buyer. Another method is described in the next question.

**7** **If you authorize draws based on a loan officer's inspection of the house, what experience and training does this employee have?** Some banks pay the builder based on the percentage of completion for certain elements. For example, if 50% of the roof is com-

## Email from the Real World

**A Michigan reader wonders what happened with the savings from their "one-time closing" loan:**

*"We have a construction-to-permanent loan on our new home that offered a 'one-time closing.' Now as the home is finished, we've been notified by the lender that there will be an additional $2500 in closing costs, like underwriting fees, title insurance and a $350 application fee. If we closed last year, I'm wondering why we're being charged closing costs again? Does this sound proper to you?"*

No, it does not. Perhaps the lender "forgot" the terms of the earlier deal, but most construction-to-permanent loans offer the savings of a "one-time" closing—you only pay closing costs (like application fees, title insurance) ONCE. You may still have to pay some pre-paid escrows (for interest, taxes, insurance, etc.) at the final closing of your home, but that shouldn't include any of the loan fees. One smart protection: make sure you get any promises like this in writing. That way if there is a change in loan officers, you're covered. In the above case, the home buyer had to get his attorney involved before the bank relented on the double-charging of fees.

pleted, the builder (or subcontractor) gets 50% of the estimated roof cost. Is that smart? We don't think so—we think the builder should finish the roof to your (or your inspector's) complete satisfaction before getting any money. Later in the "money-bomb" section of this chapter, we'll describe a real-life story of how this method scammed a homeowner out of thousands of dollars.

If the lender insists on this draw method, demand "veto" power over draws for work that is not totally completed. Check the experience level of the lending officer who is signing off on these inspections.

**8** **What protection do you offer from liens?** Smart construction lenders should have a special lien waiver that they stamp on the back of every draw check. When a subcontractor or material supplier endorses and deposits the check, he agrees that the bill has been paid in full and that a lien won't be filed against the property. (Technically, a lien—or more properly a mechanic's lien—is a claim placed against your house by unpaid workers or material suppliers.) Another strategy to protect you from liens: have the subs and builder sign lien wavers, which are separate documents that waive their rights to file any liens against your home.

Here's an ages-old real estate scam: builders who take money from homeowners and then "forget" to pay their subcontractors. The subs then file liens against the house, forcing the homeowner to pay twice for his or her house, in essence,. A good tip to avoid this: some title insurance companies offer "extended coverage" policies that give protection against mechanic liens. The cost is usually a $200 to $600, depending on the home's cost—ask the builder whether they are willing to pay for this. Even if you don't control the construction loan, mechanic lien insurance is a wise investment.

The bottom line: a good construction lender should have a strategy to protect you from mechanic liens.

**9** **What tests for the lot are required?** Examples could be a soils test to determine what type of foundation is necessary. Other possible tests/reports may include a survey of the lot and/or appraisal of the plans. If a septic system is required, a "percolation" test may be called for by the lender before the construction loan is approved. We'll go into more detail on these tests later.

## The "Permanent" Mortgage

**1** **Please provide me with a written estimate of all fees and charges.** These could include application fees, credit reports, origination fees, appraisals, and all closing and recording fees. Mortgage insurance premiums also may be required for homes with down payments that are less than 20% of the sales price.

**2** **What is the annual percentage rate (APR) for your current loans?** Truth-in-lending laws require all lenders to disclose this to you—the APR is the real rate you pay after you factor in all those special charges and fees. Generally speaking, every "point" you pay adds 1/8% to the loan rate. Hence, an 8% mortgage with two points is equivalent to an 8.25% APR.

**3** **How long will it take for approval?** In the old days, loan approval could drag on for 30 to 60 days. Yet, recent improvements in mortgage processing (including computerized underwriting) has cut that time to just days or at most a couple of weeks. The exception: a refinancing boom. If there is a sudden drop in rates, a surge of applications to refinance or purchase homes can delay approval up to a month.

**4** **What proof of income is required?** Many lenders require a copy of your tax return or pay stub to verify your income. If you're self-employed, that may be just the beginning. You may have to provide profit and loss statements (along with a balance sheet) as well.

**5** **What "lock-in" options are available?** Are there any lock fees? Most lenders will let you lock-in rates 30, 45 or 60 days in advance of closing. That way you can guarantee yourself a certain interest rate (if you think rates will rise). Some lenders have "lock fees" or may require you to pay a deposit. Longer locks are available, but at a price. In our area, lenders offer 90 day locks if you're willing to pay a one-half percent higher rate.

**6** **Do you offer "no-doc" loans?** No-doc means "no documentation"—these are loans that require no documentation of income, employment and so on. As you might have guessed, such loans are available to buyers who make hefty down payments (over 25% to 30%, for example) and have an impeccable credit history. Tight federal lending requirements have restricted many "no-doc" loans—now lenders are offering "low-doc" loans as an alternative. A low-documentation loan is one with expedited approval, providing you put down 30% or more of the purchase price.

**7** **Given the house we're considering, what loan product is best suited for us?** The lender should give you a range of options.

**8** **Can I pay my own property taxes and insurance?** Some lenders require that they collect property taxes and insurance for you, since you're so darned irresponsible that you may forget to pay them. These "impounds" (great word, huh?) are zapped into your payment every month; the lender then takes this money and pays the insurance company and county tax department once a year. The big rip-off is that most lenders don't pay any interest on these monies—so they get to keep your funds for a year interest-free. Our advice: see whether you can pay the taxes and insurance yourself.

# CREDIT SCORES: WHAT'S YOUR FICO?

Back in the ancient days of mortgage processing (say, 1999), loan approval meant waiting days if not weeks for something called "underwriting." This is a mysterious dark art was practiced by guys named "Herbert" in non-descript office buildings in suburban Cleveland—Herbert would pour over your credit files, income verification and other files to determine whether you should be approved or denied for that nice mortgage loan.

Yet, like everything these days, Herbert and other human underwriters have been replaced with a computer. The new computerized credit evaluation systems are known as "credit scoring." Here, a computer crunches your credit history and spits out something called a credit score; the most common type is a FICO, named after Alan Greenspan's dog. (Just kidding. FICO actually stands for Fair Isaac Company, which was one of the first inventors of the credit scoring methods used today).

FICO scores are on a 300-900 point scale: 720 or above is considered great, 680 to 720 is good, above 620 is acceptable. What if your score is below 620? Any FICO between 580 to 620 is a problem, but might be acceptable to government-backed programs like FHA. If your score is under 580, it isn't likely you'll be approved—or you might have to accept a loan with a super-high interest rate.

What determines your FICO? It's a complex mix of your payment history, income level, open credit card accounts, balances and more. Payment history is a biggie—make your payments on time and you get more FICO points.

Since 2000, most lenders now approve their loans electronically (Freddie Mac and Fannie Mae's web sites let them do this quickly). These computerized approvals are heavily weighted toward credit scores.

What's the advantage for home buyers? First, this approval can now be done in just days instead of weeks or even months under the hold system. Second, there's less need for documentation today—you are less likely to be asked for a pay stub or bank statement. Finally, there's a lot less of the last minute hitches, thanks to a balky underwriter who needs just one more piece of financial info.

Of course, there is a dark side to FICO: namely, if you have a low score, it can be very hard to raise. It can take a year or more to try to "repair" a low score; lenders that might "worked something out" now feel bound to the God of FICO.

So, what's your FICO? You can get it from web sites like MyFico.com (which offers a report with your FICO score and credit reports for $12.95) or ask your lender. As we were going to press, a new bill was proposed in Congress (the Consumer Credit Score Disclosure Act of 2001) that would mandate full disclosure of FICO scores when you apply for a mortgage.

If you'd like to get your credit report, consider sites like MyInstantCreditReport.com, which for $29.95 will produce an online credit report culled from the three major credit reporting agencies. Best of all, it takes 60 seconds to get the info.

Should you share your FICO or credit report with your builder? No, all a builder needs to know is that you are approved or not approved for a loan . . . NOT whether you have a 750 score or one that is merely 620. We're always weary of giving a builder too much info and a high credit score might a contractor less willing to negotiate with you over price or upgrades (why should we give you a better deal, Mr. Smith? You're loaded!). Conversely, if a builder knows you have a relatively low FICO score (but loan approval), they might be less willing to do a deal with you, especially if they have another buyer interested in the house with a higher FICO.

## Email from the Real World

**A homebuyer from San Antonio felt rushed into paying a deposit on a new home:**

*"We fell in love with a model home at one builder's development. The builder's salesperson asked us for $1000 plus one-half the cost of the upgrades in order to start construction. What concerns me is that we don't even have a loan yet! Friends at work have said that they didn't have to put anything down until closing, even with new construction. Others have said not to do anything until I have a confirmation letter from a mortgage company stating that the loan is approved."*

Yes, some builders are rather anxious about getting their hands on your money. But we would NEVER recommend putting down a deposit on a new home UNLESS you were pre-approved (or at least, pre-qualified) by a bona-fide lender. In the worse case, you could place the deposit and then find you can't buy the home—and lose the deposit. Less-than-honest contractors may be trying to squeeze money out of you, even though there's a chance you won't be able to buy the home (which is no loss to them, since they'll sell it to someone else).

How much down payment is "standard"? It depends on the market. If builders are begging for business, they may do no-deposit deals. Others may require significant deposits. Ask your buyer's agent for intelligence on the market in your area. As always, any deposit should be placed in ESCROW and not dispersed to the builder before closing.

# Biggest Myths about the Mortgage Process

**Myth #1** *"I'm convinced all mortgage lenders exist solely to rip-off consumers with ridiculous fees and outrageous requirements."*

In defense of mortgage lenders, many of the hoops lenders make consumers jump through are not only for their protection but also for yours. If you take on a mortgage that is beyond your ability to pay back, who wins? Nobody—you might lose your house to foreclosure, and the last thing the lender wants is to own your house or evict you and try to sell it to someone else.

Most of the lender's requirements are mandated by state and federal guidelines—the lender is simply following the law. If there is any point on which to criticize lenders, it would have to be on the very poor job they've done to educate consumers about this process. Many of the fees lenders charge are passed through to third parties. Take a home's appraisal, for example: banks require an appraisal to make sure the house is worth enough to justify the mortgage. A $200 to $400 fee is collected from the consumer and sent directly to the appraiser. The lender doesn't take a cut. But all consumers see is this money coming out of their pocket and going to the lender at (if only temporarily). A good lender should tell you exactly where every penny is going.

**Myth #2** *"I assume that the private mortgage insurance premium insures me against defaulting on my mortgage. If I can't make the payments, doesn't this insurance protect me?"*

Sorry, that's not how it works. Private mortgage insurance (PMI, explained earlier in this chapter) protects the *lender*, not you, in the case of a default. That's right, you must pay the lender's insurance bill. And unfortunately, it's not an insignificant sum. PMI effectively adds 1/8% to 1/4% to your mortgage's interest rate—which means hundreds of dollars a year (and thousands over the life of the loan). If you fail to pay the mortgage, PMI bails out the lender. You get soaked.

The reality is that you would have to pay this insurance bill anyway. If it were not paid directly, the lender would probably raise the interest rate on your loan by the same amount as the PMI. The insult is that PMI is zapped into your mortgage every month, a constant reminder that you're picking up the lender's bill. The "in-your-face" aspect of this charge is probably most offensive to consumers.

Blame lenders again for failing to educate consumers on PMI—many consumers are left with the false impression that PMI protects them. Perhaps lenders are embarrassed to tell the truth. The only way to avoid PMI is to put down more than a 20% down payment—not an easy task for today's hard-pressed home buyer. Another strategy is to shop around—lenders have different loan "products" that have varying amounts of PMI. Finding a mortgage with a smaller PMI is an important shopping criterion.

One money-saving tip: ask the lender whether you can stop paying the PMI after you've accumulated a certain amount of equity in your home (typically more than 20% of the home's value). This can happen rather quickly if home values are rising. It's smart to ask about the procedures (and requirements) to cancel PMI in the future.

# The Lock Game
## The Pressure to Get the Best Rate Can Create Move-In Headaches

One of the toughest challenges for home buyers is the question: to lock or not to lock?

Most lenders offer 30- to 60-day locks to insure that you get an interest rate you can live with. If rates go up in that time frame, you get the lower rate—as long as you close within the lock period.

And there's the rub. We've met many home buyers who locked too early and subsequently tried to rush closing because interest rates climbed. However, if the house isn't ready, the lender may very well refuse to close—forcing you to re-lock at the new, higher rate.

Some lenders could care less, letting you move into a partially finished house. The problem is the builder will receive most if not all his money at closing. Hence, his incentive to finish the house to your satisfaction might be diminished. Sadly, some builders will only perform when a giant carrot (your money) is dangled in front of them.

Therefore, the worst-case scenario is locking too soon and then interest rates rise significantly in that 30- or 60-day period. The pressure to close early and move in could be excruciating. Of course, less scrupulous builders realize this and might try to slip inferior work by you.

The best advice is to build in a buffer zone. If the builder says the house will be done August 1, you might want to lock July 1 with a 60-day lock. That way you have until September 1 to close on the house. Then, if the builder comes to you in late July and says that delays will push back closing, you won't have to panic. Gauging how accurate the builder's closing date estimate is can be tricky—ask your private inspector (or architect, if you have one) about how the house is progressing.

As for figuring out which direction interest rates are heading, good luck. No one really knows. Check out the *Wall Street Journal* or HSH.com for predictions from the "experts" on the direction of future mortgage rates. And then flip a coin.

# Money Bombs
## Construction Loans

**Money Bomb #1: Builders who hold the money cards.**
*"My friend had a nightmare experience with the builder. By controlling the construction loan, the builder took large draws to pay his own profit long before the house was completed. He drained all the money out of the construction loan and then skipped town—leaving an unfinished house and a devastated family."*

Fraud with new home construction isn't something you'll see discussed in glossy real estate magazines, but it does happen. And, sadly, very few builders are ever caught and convicted of absconding with construction loan proceeds. So, even though the chances of this happening to you are small, you should take precautions. The obvious protection: control the money. Get the construction loan in your name, not the builder's. If you can't control the construction financing, make sure your deposit is kept in escrow until closing. Before closing on the home, confirm all the sub-contractors and suppliers have been paid and have them sign lien wavers. Purchase lien waver insurance from your title company in order to get an extra layer of protection.

**Money Bomb #2: Inexperienced inspectors and fraudulent draws.**
*"Our so-called reputable builder took us for a ride. The foundation was faulty, the roof installed wrong, the framing a total disaster. Now we have a half-built house and $125,000 in damages. To make matters worse, our construction loan lender approved $10,000 in draws to the builder on work that was not completed and materials that weren't even delivered to our house."*

That's a true story from an unlucky home buyer in Spartanburg, South Carolina. We analyzed this case and found two key problems with the construction financing (not to mention the incompetent builder). First, the bank gave money to the builder based on a "percent-completion" basis. Instead of the sub-contractor bills being paid directly to the subs after the work was finished, the *builder* received money based on "estimates" of work completed.

The only problem was that the loan officer was inexperienced (to put it charitably). He had no training in construction. Zip. Consequently, when the builder claimed the roof was 50% completed or certain materials were delivered, the loan officer took the builder's word for it. Now the consumer owes $52,000 to the bank for a seriously defective, half-built house—and the kicker is $10,000 of that money was given to the builder for work that wasn't even done. The bottom line: you're on the hook. Search for a lender that will protect your rights (the percent-completion method has major rip-off potential) and a loan officer with construction knowledge and experience.

### Money Bomb #3: The "double invoice" and billing errors from hell.
*"We caught a $7000 error on our house—the window company billed us for our windows twice!"*

Mistakes do happen. Occasionally, an invoice for work done on your house will be incorrect. For our house, we caught one bill for lumber delivered to another house down the street. Obviously, checking the bills for accuracy is critical. If you're building a custom or semi-custom house, an architect may offer this service. If you're doing this yourself, check with the builder to confirm bills. A little "slip" could cost you thousands.

### Money Bomb #4: "Quit claim" deeds.
*"We couldn't get a construction loan to build a home on a lot we own. The builder suggested we 'quit claim' the lot to him and he would get the loan. Is this kosher?"*

Watch out—a quit claim deed gives the builder the title to your lot during construction ... a potentially dangerous situation. Depending on the contract, if you fire the builder, he may still own the lot. If you can't get financing, this may be a last resort. Be careful and seek the advice of a real estate attorney on the best way to protect your rights.

## Permanent Mortgages.

### Money Bomb #1: Surprise fees and 11th-hour disqualification.
*"My wife and I qualified for an 80% loan (20% down payment). At the last moment, the lender changed his mind and only offered us a commitment for a 75% loan. The sudden change forced us to put up another $7500 in down payment. Ouch!"*

Loan requirements do change from time to time—and they always seem to get tougher. The best tip is to get a pre-approval letter from a lender as quickly as possible. Note that this is not a lock on mortgage rates, but is just a general commitment to loan you a certain amount of money at or below a certain interest rate. Another major rip-off is unscrupulous mortgage brokers who surprise you with last-minute fees. The fact is that federal law requires mortgage lenders to provide you with a good faith estimate of fees and charges within three working days after the mortgage application is submitted. Hence, any last-minute charges could be illegal. Consult with your attorney and consider giving the lender an ultimatum—fly straight or you lose my business. Be prepared to switch lenders—even if this means delaying the home closing.

## Money Bomb #2: Monster adjustable loans.

*"We call our adjustable rate mortgage (ARM) a bungee-cord loan. At any moment, the rate seems to spring from one point to another. The result is we get hit with higher payments."*

Adjustable rate loans are just that—adjustable. Some ARMs are tied to extremely volatile indices such as Treasury Bills; as a result, the interest rate on your loan can change sharply month to month. The bottom line: your home mortgage is pegged to your biggest life investment. An ARM holds tremendous risk—go into this with your eyes open.

## Money Bomb #3: Oops! Duplicate charges, errors and fictitious fees. *"Before closing on our new home, we had the settlement sheet from the lender checked over by our accountant and attorney. Amazingly, they found four errors—including a duplicate charge for loan processing that would have cost us $500!"*

Most home buyers don't pay much attention to the closing statement. They assume that since the lender has those impressive calculators with buttons for cosines and derivatives, the numbers must be right. Right?

Guess again. Consumer advocates and attorneys point out that it's not uncommon for settlement sheets to have "mistakes." Some are unintentional typos, but others make you wonder. And, as you might

## Email from the Real World

**A homebuyer from Nevada was stung by a "discount" appraisal.**

*"We applied for a loan through a bank to purchase a lot; the loan officer sent an appraiser to take a look at it. The bank responded that the appraiser gave then a "range-value" (the lot was worth $100,000 to $120,000) and they wanted us to cough up the difference between the low end of that range and our purchase price. Our real estate heard that said HOLD IT! Turns out the bank just paid the appraiser for an "opinion of appraisal" instead of a full-blown appraisal. This saved the bank a few hundred dollars, as the opinion is much less than the full appraisal. Also frustrating: the appraiser was from out of town and was unfamiliar with the area."*

Appraisals are just like any other product: you can go cheap or expensive. Banks that try to save pennies can hurt you if their bargain appraiser low balls the value of your lot. And make sure the appraiser is NOT from out of town. The more familiar the appraiser is with your area, the better.

expect, errors usually favor the lender.

Some common goofs: simple errors in the loan information. Double check the rates and points to make sure you get what you were promised. According to a recent article in the *Wall Street Journal* on mortgage loan mistakes, "one District of Columbia man recently was charged for flood insurance even though he lived on the fifth floor of a building on top of a hill."

Duplicate charges (such as being charged both an origination fee and a processing charge) are another rip-off, as are inflated or fictitious fees. Miami attorney Charles Baird says one dubious fee is the escrow waiver fee, "which charges you for the privilege of paying your own insurance," he told the *Journal*. Other scams: document transportation fees and inflated recording fees. "For instance, in one case that San Francisco attorney Thomas Jenkins investigated, a lender charged a client a $135 recording fee—even though the actual filing fee in California is less than $25," the *Journal* reported.

## Money Bomb #4: Real estate broker "referral fees".

*"A real estate agent strongly recommended we use a certain mortgage lender. One advantage he cited was a faster application process—the agent is hooked up via a computer. As he started typing in our application, he mentioned that he was collecting a $300 'referral fee' that would be charged to us! We were shocked!"*

We find these "relationships" between real estate agents and lenders to be a major rip-off. Many agents try to charm home buyers into getting a mortgage this way, claiming this "one-stop shopping" deal will save time and hassle. The reality is that their computer is hooked up to only ONE lender. That one lender can lock out competitors that are offering lower rates or costs—as a result you could end up losing thousands of dollars for this "time-saving convenience."

How many consumers are duped like this? A recent survey by the U.S. Dept. of Housing and Urban Development found that a whopping 40% of all home buyers choose a lender based on a recommendation from a real estate agent. Many mortgage lenders are aggressively trying to recruit real estate agents to set up computerized "mortgage centers." Even more scary is the fact that a new federal ruling has taken the caps off such referral fees—now agents can rake in any amount of money they please to "refer" you to a lender via a computer hookup.

And sometimes the "referral fees" are not disclosed to the consumer. Illegal kickbacks from mortgage brokers to their "friendly" real estate agents are widespread in areas such as California, the Southwest, the Midwest and the Philadelphia/Washington, D.C. corridor. A recent federal probe called the problem "epidemic." The result (whether the referral fee is above or below the table) is higher mortgage costs passed on to consumers. The best advice: shop around. The rate surveys mentioned earlier in this chapter are a good place to start. And be suspicious of that smiling agent who strongly suggests you use his "favorite" mortgage lender.

# Closing Costs: The Good-Faith Estimate.

One of the better euphemisms in real estate is the "good-faith" estimate of closing costs. The federal government requires all lenders to provide such an estimate within three days of submitting the application. One wonders, if the feds didn't force lenders to give a "good faith" estimate, what type of estimate would it be?

Anyway, it's important to understand just what closing costs are, since they can zap you for thousands of dollars. These costs are divided into two categories: closing fees and prepaid charges/escrows. Here's a brief explanation of these costs.

**Closing fees** *may include such items as:*

◆ **The loan origination fee.** This ranges from nothing to 1% of the loan amount. Basically it's the lender's fee to "process" your loan.
◆ **Discount points.** As explained earlier, this is prepaid interest.
◆ *Appraisal fee ($200 to $500; the national average is $305).* Just to make sure the property is worth what the builder/seller says it is.
◆ **Credit report** *(about $40).* To check your credit history.
◆ **A final inspection fee** *(about $100).* To make sure the home is still standing.
◆ **Settlement fee** *(less than $100).* A junk fee to close the loan.
◆ **Document preparation fee** *(another $200).* See "settlement fee" above.
◆ **Tax certificate (about $10).** When purchasing land, this certificate verifies that the real estate taxes on the property have been paid. You may also pay a flood certification fee (about $20) to insure the property isn't in a flood plain.
◆ **Recording fees (usually less than $50).** To record the deed at the county courthouse.
◆ **State documentary fee.** Essentially, a tax on property transfer—usually about 10¢ per $1000 of the sales price.
◆ **Survey/improvement location certificate.** This certifies that your home was built on your lot. About $200 to $400.
◆ **Underwriting fee.** More profit for the lender. Roughly $100.
◆ **FHA Mortgage Insurance/VA Funding Fee.** For FHA loans, buyers may be required to pay a premium for mortgage insurance. The funding fee for VA loans is just money for the government.
◆ **Danish charge.** Just kidding! In most states, buyers don't have to pay for any pastries served at closing.

**Prepaid and escrow charges** are advance payments the bank would like you to pay up front, thank you. For example, the lender may require 30 days' interest in advance, the first year's homeowner's insurance and private mortgage insurance (PMI) up front. Finally, the lender may ask you to cough up six months of property taxes at the time of closing.

**Tip:** Ask the lender whether you can pay your own taxes and insurance, thus avoiding all this up-front cash at closing. Some lenders may offer to waive the escrows for a fee, ranging from $100 to one-quarter of a point of the mortgage amount. Other lenders have no fee to waive the escrows.

## Actual closing costs for a $120,000 mortgage

LOAN FEES:

| | |
|---|---|
| LOAN ORIGINATION FEE | $1040.00 |
| APPRAISAL FEE | 250.00 |
| CREDIT REPORT | 55.00 |
| FINAL INSPECTION FEE | 100.00 |
| SETTLEMENT FEE | 85.00 |
| TITLE INSURANCE | 200.00 |
| DOCUMENT PREPARATION FEE | 100.00 |
| RECORDING FEES | 35.00 |
| IMPROVEMENT LOCATION CERT./SURVEY | 85.00 |
| UNDERWRITING FEE | 100.00 |
| REALTY TAX SERVICE FEE | 66.50 |
| **TOTAL CLOSING COSTS** | **$2116.50** |

ESTIMATED PREPAID/ESCROWS:

| | |
|---|---|
| PREPAID INTEREST (30 DAYS) | $812.06 |
| 1ST YEAR'S HOMEOWNER'S INSURANCE | 490.00 |
| TAXES (6 MONTHS) | 600.00 |
| **TOTAL PREPAIDS** | **$1902.06** |

**GRAND TOTAL CASH NEEDED AT CLOSING  $4018.00**

That's right, if you were buying this home, you'd need to cough up $4018 in *addition* to the down payment. It's important to factor in these costs when doing your budget.

We should also note that if you are purchasing the land separately and then financing the building of the home with a construction loan, you will actually endure *three closings:* one for the land, another for the construction loan and a final one when the home is completed. In this case, be sure to ask for a good-faith estimate of costs for all three closings. A buyer's broker (we'll introduce you to these guys later) or title company will be able to help you on the closing costs for the land, while the construction lender should provide figures for the building loan. Finally, the permanent mortgage lender will give you costs for the final closing. (You can eliminate one of these closings with a construction to perm loan as described earlier).

# The Building Team

There are no solo performances when you build a home—it's strictly a team effort. From the workers who pound the nails to the bankers who lend the money to buy the nails, you are joined on the house-building journey by all sorts of folks.

But exactly who should be on your team? Who's the opposition? Who are the referees? Getting a quality home begins with assembling a quality building team. Here are the key players.

## The Designer: The Rodney Dangerfield of Home Building

Architects often get a bad rap in this country. Fewer than 10% of new houses are designed by an architect who's working directly for the consumer. Why? Perhaps it's the pervasive myths about architects that some buyers still hold today. Talk to folks out in the real world and you often hear the following myths:

### Biggest Myths about Designers/Architects

**Myth #1** *"Architects are too expensive—only rich people building huge houses can afford them."*

Builders like to repeat this myth as a way to scare buyers. The truth is that architects, on average, charge between 6% to 10% of the construction cost to design a typical home. Sure, famous architects' fees in large cities can be 15% to 20% or more. But the reality is that an architect's fee for a $200,000 home is likely to be about $14,000. Other architects charge an hourly fee that may be an even better deal.

That may sound like a lot of money, but consider what you get in return: professionally drawn plans, complete specifications/materials lists, and (with some architects) bidding and negotiation services. Many architects also serve as watchdogs to monitor the construction.

**Myth #2** *"Architects are just wild-eyed dreamers who design pretty but EXPENSIVE houses."*

In fact, architects who specialize in residential design are most interested in building an attractive, yet *affordable* home. The scary truth is a good architect will probably *save* you money. Instead of getting an overpriced, poorly built production home, you're more likely to get a custom home with quality construction.

By bidding out the project to several builders, you can get the best value for your dollar. Most important, an experienced residential architect is an expert at materials costs and efficient design.

Some of this misperception is fed by the large number of architects who specialize in commercial projects (schools, shopping centers, etc.). Occasionally, these guys will design a house—usually with less than desirable results. Their lack of residential experience shows.

**Myth #3** *"Architects only draw a set of plans. I can hire a designer or buy a plan from a book for less money."*

Architects CAN simply draw a set of plans for you, but typically their involvement extends much further. As you'll see later in this chapter, they become the consumer's advocate during construction as well, overseeing the work of the builder and making sure the plans are followed.

A design from a plan book (available through bookstores) is less expensive—about $500 to $900 for a set of blueprints. However, you get (or don't get) what you pay for. The quality of these plans varies dramatically—some are more detailed than others. Furthermore, you have to fit a generic design to your needs and building site, which might require paying a contractor to re-draft the blueprints (at an additional fee, of course).

Some home buyers also try to save money by hiring a designer or drafting services firm. As you'll see in Chapter 6, there are several problems with this route as well. While the level of detail is better from drafting services than plan-book blueprints, they still can't match a careful architect. They don't provide the construction supervision or the engineering expertise either.

**Myth #4** *"My builder told me he can approximate most of what an architect can do. So, what do I need an architect for?"*

Some contractors will try to sell you on the convenience of "one-stop shopping"—they can not only build a house, but design it as well. Such "design-build" firms are popular in many large cities and you might encounter one in your home search.

But just how good is the builder at design? While there are always exceptions, most good builders make lousy designers. Why? An architect or design professional sees a house as a series of spaces; a builder sees a house as a pile of bricks and wood, a puzzle to be assembled as cheaply as possible. While builders have some understanding of how to arrange a floor plan, a design professional takes the long view. How does it fit your lifestyle? Does it have room to grow?

Architects try to design a house in which people can function—if you frequently entertain guests, a spacious kitchen area is a must. If you spend time in the bathroom relaxing, a bath that is roomy, sunny, and luxurious is more appropriate than a small closet a builder might design.

We can always tell a home designed by a builder versus a professional architect. The builder-designed house is often generic and boring, with features thrown in as an afterthought. You can almost walk through these homes blind-folded—just about every cliché in home design is used and abused.

So, what can a good architect do for you? Think of the architect as an advocate on *your* side (and payroll) who will help navigate the choppy waters of zoning restrictions, building codes, profit-hungry builders and a myriad of design options and cost trade-offs. Not only will they design the house of your dreams, but they also will help make sure that dream doesn't turn into a nightmare, by supervising the actual construction.

## Sources for an Architect

**1** **American Institute of Architects (AIA), 202-626-7351; web: www.aiaonline.com.** The national headquarters can refer you to local AIA chapters—most will be able to provide a list of local residential architects in your area. Also, the AIA has pamphlets, booklets and a video that may be helpful in choosing an architect. For more information call 1-800-365-ARCH or go online to www.aiaonline.com.

**2** **Word of mouth.** Next time you see a house you like, ask the homeowner for the name of his or her designer. If they used a design professional, find out whether he or she was easy to work with.

**3** **Parade of Homes.** These annual events for charity are a great way to see the work of local architects. Most of these high-priced mansions are designed by residential architects, not by builders. And don't be dismayed by the Parade of Homes palaces—most Parade architects also will design houses in a more realistic price range. (We should note that while we think Parade of Homes shows are a great place to get ideas or meet architects, we're less thrilled about finding builders and contractors at such events. We'll explain more about that later in Chapter 7.)

**4** **Architectural schools.** Local colleges or universities that have architectural schools are a possible source of referrals. They might recommend an alumnus practicing nearby.

## The Two Types of Architects

Mention the word *architect*, and the first name that pops into your mind is probably Frank Lloyd Wright, the designer of the Guggenheim Museum in New York (with its distinctive, curving staircase). Frank did design other things besides museums, including quite a few homes and even furniture. His "Prairie style" made many of his homes design classics.

Yet, Wright didn't design those houses to meet any home buyer's tastes—the designs were purely Wright's whimsy. In this sense, Wright is the ultimate *"signature architect."*

While it's nice to admire the work of a signature architect, most consumers have more practical concerns when it comes to home design. Frankly, you need an architect interested in designing a home to fit your lifestyle—a *"customer-driven architect."*

Fortunately, most residential architects fall into the customer-driven mold. They look at you, your family, and your lifestyle before they begin designing a house. They ask all the right questions and develop a design *with your input.* In our opinion, this is the most sane and rational way to go.

Of course, that doesn't mean you won't run into a few signature architects out there. Such designers specialize in a certain style of home—if you don't like that design, it makes no sense spending your time visiting with them.

## Architecture by the Numbers

There are 17,000 architectural firms in the U.S. Only 10% of all the money architects make is derived from residential construction—the rest comes from commercial projects such as office buildings or schools. You can see why young architectural students are encouraged to go into commercial rather than residential work.

About one-third of all architects are "sole practitioners." These folks are more likely to specialize in residential construction than are large firms with lots of employees. It's not that big firms don't design new houses, it's just that they tend to focus on bigger projects for bigger bucks—like shopping centers. You should compare and contrast the service you get from one-person operations with that from larger firms to see who's right for you.

The use of architects by home buyers to design new homes also varies by region. Architects seem less popular in the Upper Midwest and the Great Plains states. Another area that sees a lower use of architects for new homes is Texas and the surrounding states of Oklahoma, Arkansas and Louisiana.

Meanwhile, in the Pacific Northwest and California, architects are more in vogue for new homes. Another area where architects are hot is the Mid-Atlantic states of New York, New Jersey and Pennsylvania.

In the process of researching this book, we interviewed several home buyers who found it more challenging to find an architect in rural areas. This doesn't mean you can't find a good residential architect in a small town in Kansas—it just means you might have to look harder or see whether you can find one in a nearby town or city.

# Getting Started: How Far in Advance?

Leave plenty of time for interviews, visits to the architect's past projects, proposals and reference checks. This takes about 30 to 60 days. Considering that the design process itself can take one to three months (or longer) and construction another four to six months, it makes sense to start looking for an architect about 12 to 18 months in advance of when you want to move into your new home. These are conservative estimates. Your new home may take much longer depending on how hot the market is in your area.

# What Will It Cost You?

The three ways architects bill for their time are:

**1 Percentage of construction costs.** If a full-service architect charges an 8% fee and your home budget is $325,000, the charges would total $26,000. Many architects use this method, but critics point out a few problems. If you're billed as a percentage of cost, what incentive does the architect have to keep costs down? Consider this method carefully before going with it. If this is the only option, ask the architect to put a cap on the cost of the house—if the architect is a pro, he or she will know costs and be able to design within your budget. Of course, fees vary depending on the service. Expect to pay 3% to 5% for barebones design only. You may pay as much as 15% for full service (negotiation with contractors, construction supervision, etc.) in major cities, although the average in the U.S. is about 6% to 10%.

**2 Dollars per square foot. Here you pay the architect a certain fee per square foot.** A 2000-square-foot home at $3 per square foot would run $6,000. The logic here: the more square feet, the more work for an architect to design. By not scaling the fee to construction cost, an architect has more incentive to keep costs down, so the theory goes. As one architect explained to us, "Why should I get more money if you put in a fancy Kohler toilet versus an inexpensive one? It takes the same amount of time to draw the toilet on the plan anyway."

Overall, expect to pay from $3 to $12 per square foot—that's for everything from design to actual construction management. The best architects will break down per square foot fees depending on the phase. For example, one architect we visited told us his fee for design development was $500 plus 80¢ per square foot (for a one-story house). Construction documents were priced at $1000, plus $1 per square foot.

**3** **Hourly fee.** A flat, hourly fee is the third alternative. Putting a cap on the total hours that can be billed makes sense. Some like this method since it completely divorces your home's size or cost from the architect's compensation. Few architects offer this, but it may be worth seeing whether you can negotiate such a deal.

◆ **Other costs.** In addition to the basic costs, architects may charge for additional services. These may include fees for an assistant project supervisor, revisions (drawings or specs), work caused by change orders, and evaluation of substitutions made by the contractor. Other optional services also may include providing financial feasibility studies, planning surveys, or site evaluations.

Some architects combine different payment options. For example, one architect we spoke with charges an hourly fee for a design schematic and a lump sum for design development, construction documents, and bids/negotiations. Administration or supervision of the construction is an hourly fee. This architect's hourly fee varies depending on whether she does the work or has one of her assistants do it ($95 per hour for architect, $35-$45 for staff).

The AIA contract breaks down payment into five phases: schematic design phase, design development, construction documents, bidding or negotiation, and construction phase (more on these phases later in this chapter). One sample breakdown could be the following:

| | |
|---|---|
| Schematic Design Phase | 10% |
| Design Development | 15% |
| Construction Documents Phase | 60% |
| Bidding or Negotiating Phase | 5% |
| Construction Administration Phase | 10% |
| **Total Basic Compensation** | **100%** |

For example, if the total architect's fee is $20,000 on a $300,000 house, then a payment of $2000 would be made at the end of the schematic design phase and so on.

We should note that other residential architects charge fees during the preliminary work (such as 25% for the schematic design phase, 10% for the refined schematic design phase, 35% for the preliminary construction documents, and, finally, 30% for the final construction documents). Then, bidding/negotiation and construction administration are done on an hourly fee basis.

Because of the complexity of compensation schedules, you should get a written and detailed fee schedule at the outset.

## Reality Check

Certainly, architects aren't a necessity for every project and many people on tight budgets will be tempted to forgo an architect in order to add a few more amenities. However, there are several fundamental elements you must consider—curb appeal, a sound foundation, and a properly designed roof. While it may be tempting to cut corners on these items to add a whirlpool tub or upgraded carpeting, think twice. If the house looks like an ugly, cookie-cutter tract home, your home's value is diminished—no matter how nice the carpeting.

When would you not use an architect? One possible scenario: building a very simple house on a flat lot. If you use a builder's design,

## Going Naked: Make Sure You're Covered

One of the key questions you should ask an architect is whether he or she has professional liability insurance to cover "errors and omissions." This insurance, called E & O, is an important protection for home buyers.

Why? Well, nobody's perfect. Architects can and do make mistakes. Since the builder will NOT take any responsibility for defects in design, such a defect rests on the architect to remedy.

For example, let's take your new home's foundation. Your architect makes a major mistake—under-sizing the foundation footers that support the house. No one catches the mistake, including the builder and the county building inspector. You move in and soon find that your foundation settles to Australia. Walls crack, floors bow, and tile pops off bathroom walls. The damage could be catastrophic—the cost to jack up the house and re-pour the footers to correct size is estimated at $40,000. The resulting damage to the home's interior is another $30,000. Who's going to pay this bill?

That's why many architects carry E & O insurance. Theoretically, you put in a claim to their insurance company and they pay to fix the problem. Now, if you've ever dealt with any insurance company, you probably realize that reality may not be as simple as this. Insurance companies have experts on staff to make sure they swiftly collect premiums and, just as swiftly, deny claims. However, if you can document that the problem is the result of the architect's error or omission, you stand a much better chance of recovering if the architect has E & O insurance.

In a perfect world, all architects would carry such insurance. The reality is that half of all architectural firms in the U.S. do not have professional liability insurance, according to a recent survey by the American Institute of Architects. In industry jargon, such architects are "going bare," an apt description.

Even more frightening: three out of every four sole practitioners are going bare. That's right, the architects that are most likely to design new homes are also the most likely to be without professional liability coverage.

make sure he or she has consulted with an engineer to determine that the foundation is well designed. Several inspections by a private inspector to supervise the construction would be quite prudent.

Another possible case where you may forgo a design professional is a "kit home." For example, several companies sell kits for "do-it-your-selfers" to put up a log cabin house. The pieces are clearly marked and the instructions are usually detailed enough not to need an architect (again, consult with an engineer about the foundation).

As you might expect, the larger the firm, the more likely they'll have E & O insurance. For architectural firms with two to four employees, the percentage without insurance drops to 56%. Only 11% of companies with 10 to 19 employees go bare. We suppose if there is any argument to go with a larger architectural firm, it may be the fact that more carry this important insurance.

One major reason architects don't have E & O is the cost—the average firm pays in excess of $20,000 to $30,000 per year for this valuable insurance. However, this figure varies widely depending on the size of the company. Sole practitioners and small firms pay considerably less. Considering the peace of mind to you, the consumer, that seems reasonable.

In addition, architects can also purchase errors and omissions insurance for a specific project or additional insurance for a particularly large or expensive home design. If the architect you're considering cannot afford "full-time" coverage, this might be a good compromise.

As a side note, some builders also carry E & O insurance. One builder in California told us that his insurance company threatened to cancel him unless he removed the word "designer" from his business card. Why? The builder wasn't really a qualified designer: he had no experience or credentials. Hence, insurance companies also tend to police the industry by refusing to insure so-called professionals who don't really have the relevant skills or credentials.

With all this discussion of mistakes, you may wonder "how often do architects goof?" Well, that same survey by the AIA revealed that only 13% of all architectural firms reported a claim on their E & O insurance in a recent year. That means 87% of all firms had no claims. Even more encouraging: 94% of sole practitioners who carried insurance had no claims.

Of course, this is little comfort if you fall into that other 6% and have a serious mistake made on your house. For you, the error rate is 100%. Hence, it's best to play it safe and find an architect or designer that carries this insurance . . . just in case.

# Step-by-Step Strategies: Finding a Good Architect.

**Step 1: Initial meeting.** Discuss the general parameters of your project. Bring magazine pictures with you as well as some ideas of your likes and dislikes. Discuss your lifestyle as candidly as possible with the architect so he or she can get a feel for your needs. Also at this meeting, look through the architect's portfolio of past houses to get an idea of his or her capabilities and style. As important as any other aspect of the architect is your personal chemistry—make sure you like him or her.

**Step 2: Visit actual houses and job sites.** Get a list of residential projects the architect has done and visit them (the architect may need to set these visits up for you). If he or she has any jobs in progress, this is the time to take a look at them as well.

**Step 3: Get a proposal with fee estimates.** At this point, narrow down your choices. Now's the time to talk turkey. What would a project like the one you envision cost? If the architect uses a combined payment fee like we discussed above, be sure to get the details of each phase. This will alleviate any future confusion.

**Step 4: Ask for references.** If you're worried the architect will just give you the best three projects he's ever done, ask for the *last* three projects he's completed. When you call the references, ask "yes or no" questions such as:

◆ Did the architect listen carefully to your needs and wants?
◆ Did the project cost more than originally estimated?
◆ Did the architect meet his own deadlines for the design phase?
◆ Did the architect accurately estimate costs of materials?
◆ Was the architect an effective advocate for you during the bid/negotiation phase with the builder?
◆ Did the architect adequately monitor the construction?
◆ Did the architect get along with the builder?

Also in this step ask for and call financial references such as banks. Later in Chapter 6, "Designing the House," we cover more steps in the design development process.

## Questions to Ask an Architect

(The source for this section is the American Institute of Architects' "Questions to Ask Your Architect" handout.)

**1** **Who will design my project?** With whom will I be dealing directly? These are important questions because many architects have a staff or assistants who actually do some of the drafting. If an assistant will be drafting and designing your home, the cost should be less than if the architect does it. A clear understanding of who your liaison will be is important. And it's a good gauge of how committed the architect is to your project—if you're farmed out to an inexperienced assistant, other projects may have higher priority.

**2** **Given your current workload, can you meet our time-frame and deadlines?** How much time should we schedule for the design process? In the real world, most buyers have deadlines. A candid and frank discussion of the architect's schedule is crucial.

**3** **How are the fees established?** What will be the fee for my house? Are you willing to accept an hourly fee with an overall spending cap? No matter what method the architect uses to determine compensation, you need a bottom-line estimate for comparison.

**4** **What is the payment schedule?** There are all kinds of possibilities, so make sure you have all the details. Confirm with your lender regarding the possibility of financing the architect's fee—the lender may have certain requirements for this.

**5** **What are the steps you'll follow in the design process for my house? How will you organize it?** A systematic and organized approach to this process is a mark of a professional. (Chapter 6 discusses the design process in more detail.)

**6** **What is your experience and track record with cost estimating?** If the architect has a contractor's license or has spent time in the building field, he or she may have a better idea of costs. Keeping your new home within your budget will be directly related to the architect's knowledge of current construction costs.

**7** **If the scope of the project changes (such as reducing the square footage or increasing the size of a deck), will there be additional fees?** Get an idea up front what additional costs you may incur.

**8** **Do you offer any construction supervision services? What is the scope of such services?** If you don't offer this service, can you recommend a construction manager or private inspector? Monitoring might include only three inspections (foundation, framing and finishing), but most likely will involve many more visits to the site. (In chapters 9 and 10, we provide you with a detailed breakdown of possible inspection points.)

**9** **Describe to me your philosophy of house design.** An experienced pro should have a well-thought-out answer. Look at pictures of past and current projects. Any professional should have such a portfolio available for you to view.

**10** **Can I see examples of the architectural plans?** You should see plans that include several elevations, a detailed framing plan, foundation plan, specifications and more. The level of detail often separates less skilled designers from experienced architects.

**11** **Do you see any potential conflicts of interest on this project? Do you have a relationship with the builder?** Some architects may design production lines for area builders. Such a previous or current relationship represents an obvious conflict of interest—how can the architect be your advocate while at the same time receive money from the builder for another project?

A related question: does the architect sit on the board of an architectural control committee in your subdivision? This can be a plus or minus, depending on the level of political infighting in the homeowners' association.

**12** **What type of insurance do you have?** Does this cover errors and omissions? Can you provide me proof of insurance? An extremely important question—see the previous box for more information on this topic. Proof of insurance could be a copy of the first page of the policy or a letter from the insurance carrier indicating the person is insured.

**13** **Who owns the blueprints?** Many home buyers mistakenly think that the blueprints (and the rights to their home design) belong to them after the house is built. Actually, most architects' contracts specify that the architect retains ownership of the design and may re-use it in the future. This is an especially important issue with high-priced homes, where the uniqueness of design may be part of the home's value. If you want to make sure your home's design is not replicated across town, you'll want to come to an agreement on the ownership of the design.

**14** **Are you willing to negotiate parts of your standard contract?** Many architects use the standard American Institute of Architects (AIA) contract. Critics point out the contract has several shortcomings, which we'll discuss later in Chapter 8, "The Paper Trail." You may want to ask the architect whether he or she is willing to modify their standard contract to address these issues.

## THE PRIVATE INSPECTOR/CONSTRUCTION MANAGER

What is a private inspector? Construction manager? They are important watchdogs who make sure the construction is going according to plan. If you don't hire an architect or are using an architect only to design your house but not to oversee the construction, we recommend hiring a private inspector or a construction manager. For large or expensive houses (over $300,000), it may pay to have both an architect and a construction manager/private inspector to oversee construction.

Who can be a private house inspector? Unfortunately, just about anyone who prints up a business card. Only a handful of states regulate this growing business, so home inspection is a wide-open field for abuse.

The best inspectors are retired contractors or licensed engineers with residential construction experience. Such individuals would be most likely to spot problems with new construction. Many home inspectors specialize in evaluating older or re-sale homes; their cursory, "cosmetic" inspections would not be appropriate for a new home construction project.

There are several key stages in the construction when you should have a private inspector look at your new home. We discuss these in detail in chapters 8 and 9. Here is a brief outline:

## Key Inspection Points

**Foundation**: Layout and footings inspection. This can be divided into two parts: when the hole is dug (to check for proper depth of footings) and after the foundation walls are up.

**Framing:** Rough-in of plumbing, electrical, and mechanical systems. The framing inspection should also gauge the correct use and installation of the home's support structure.

**Finishing:** The details that make a house a home, such as drywall, trim, flooring, cabinets, etc.

**Closing:** Prior to closing, a final "punch-list" is created of any items the builder needs to repair or install.

What if you need more supervision than a home inspector? The answer may be a construction manager. This person is typically a contractor or retired contractor with years of building experience. The construction manager usually supervises day-to-day operations at the building site, overseeing the construction in your interests. While construction managers are most often seen on expensive homes (over $300,000 or $400,000) when an architect isn't involved in administering construction, this may be an option to consider for your house.

Now, at this point, you may be wondering—why do I need a private inspector or construction manager? Isn't the builder supposed to supervise the construction? Yes, in theory, the builder is supposed to diligently supervise your home's construction. No shortcuts are ever taken and the correct materials are always installed in a professional manner. The reality for some homebuyers is, sadly, quite different. Supervision is spotty or non-existent. Unsupervised subcontractors are an invitation to disaster. Furthermore, some unscrupulous builders try to pull a fast one on homebuyers, knowingly passing off substandard work or substituting inferior materials. That's why you need a private inspector or construction manager working for you—you're basically evening the odds.

Are all builders incompetent and out to rip you off? Of course not. But ask yourself—could you tell whether a main beam was installed incorrectly? How about the plumbing? Roof trusses? Even some competent builders get stretched too thin and fail to supervise their homes properly. Unless you're intimately familiar with good construction practices (and even some builders are clueless on this one), you should have someone on your team whose sole job is to protect *your* interests, not the builder's. Builders may want you to "trust" them; your motto should be "TRUST BUT VERIFY."

## Getting Started: How Far in Advance?

Hire a private inspector or construction manager after you choose an architect but *before* you hire the general contractor. This timing is optimal because the inspector may be able to offer his or her opinion on the building practices of the builders you're considering. If the inspector isn't familiar with a builder's work, consider visiting some of the builder's jobs in progress with the inspector to evaluate the quality.

## What Will It Cost You?

Charges for a private inspector could range from $25 to $125 per hour. Assuming the average home requires about eight hours of inspection, the total tab could run $200 to $800. For extensive inspections or in large metro areas, the total bill may be closer to $1000 or $2000.

Construction managers can cost between 3% and 5% of the total construction cost. Hourly fees are also sometimes charged at a rate of $50 to $100 per hour. For an average $300,000 home you could expect to pay $9000 to $15,000.

## Sources for Finding a Private Inspector.

**1** **Two national associations can refer you to local inspectors.** The National Association of Home Inspectors (800-448-3942 or 612-928-4641; web: www. nahi.org) has more than 1000 members. You can get names over the phone or online.

The American Society of Home Inspectors (ASHI) (800-743-2744;

web: www.ashi.com) has 5500 members. ASHI requires inspectors to perform 250 inspections before joining the group. The association has an automated system where you can get a list of local members faxed to you (or you can get this list online).

Even though most associations require members to subscribe to a code of ethics, you're still on your own to check references carefully.

**2** **State associations.** Many states, including Florida, California and Texas, have state real estate inspection associations. In your local library, you may want to check out the Gale Directory of Associations to see if your state has an association of home inspectors.

**3** **Architects.** These folks frequently work with inspectors and engineers. In fact, when an architect doesn't have structural engineering training, he or she often subcontracts out the foundation plans to a qualified structural engineer. The engineer may offer on-site inspection as part of his or her service.

**4** **Homeowners associations.** Grass-roots consumer groups can help you find a good home inspector. In Texas, contact Homeowners Organization for Mediation and Education (HOME) at (817) 861-7000 or (877) 802-8937 (web: www.flash.net/~carlton2/home.htm). Another group in Texas is Homeowners for Better Building (www.hobb.org). Home buyers in Kansas City can turn to Homeowners Against Deficient Dwellings (HADD) at (816) 781-1590, web: www.hadd.com.

**5** **Real estate attorneys.** Lawyers might know inspectors and engineers who have been used as experts in lawsuits involving faulty construction in your area.

**6** **Yellow Pages.** A last resort. Look under the categories Engineers-Foundation, Engineers-Structural, Engineers-Geotechnical/Soils, Building Inspection Service, Inspection, or Construction Management.

## New Home-Buyers in Cyberspace: What's on the Web?

### American Society of Home Inspectors
**Web:** www.ashi.com, see Fig. 1 on the next page.
**What it is.** Inspector referrals and other good info.
**What's cool.** ASHI's web site lets you pop in your zip code to find a list of home inspectors within 25 miles (or you can expand the search up to 250 miles). The resulting list even includes email addresses for inspectors (when available) so you can make quick contact. The site also has other useful features, including a "Consumer Alerts" section with articles on current inspection topics. We also liked the "Technical Information" area (in the Home Inspectors section) with useful links to sites with building code info and other construction topics.

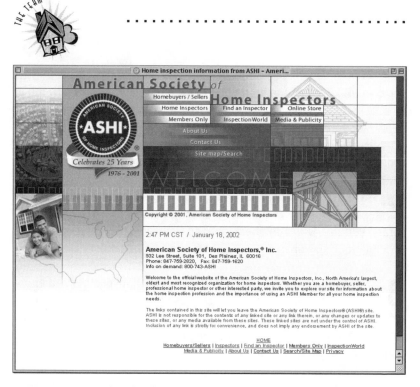

**Figure 1:** ASHI's (www.ashi.com) easy to use web site let's you zero in on local private inspectors.

**Needs work.** The site's FAQ for homebuyers is too simplistic and borders on propaganda. While it is nice to learn how ASHI certifies inspectors, more info on inspections for new construction would have been helpful. A picture gallery of contractor goofs would be a nice addition to the site.

**Another site of merit:**
◆ **Improvenet.com** lets you search for architects, designers or contractors for your project. Best of all, the site pre-screens these professionals to make sure they are legit. Another neat feature: you can run a credit/legal check on a contractor for $29.

# Why Municipal Building Inspectors Can't Be Trusted

One of the biggest myths that new home buyers fall victim to is the belief that city or county building inspectors will protect them from getting ripped off by unscrupulous builders. "Home building is one of the most regulated businesses in America," builders are fond of saying. "Municipal inspections protect the consumer from defective construction."

Wrong. In researching this book, we found a clear pattern of evidence that indicates just the opposite—homebuyers *cannot* count on city or county building inspections to save them from rip-offs.

To understand why, you must first realize what those municipal inspectors are actually enforcing—the building code. What is a building code? The code is a series of rules typically enacted at the state level to ensure construction meets a *minimum* level of safety standards. Note the key word in that sentence is MINIMUM. Counties and cities occasionally stiffen the code to adapt to local conditions—such as coastal areas that must brace for hurricanes.

What are inspectors NOT enforcing? Your contract. These inspectors are not there to make sure the work is done in a professional manner. For example, vinyl flooring can pass inspection for code violations even if it is poorly installed without a sub-floor, leaving "lumps" in the floor. Government building inspectors are not there to certify that there are zero defects or that the work was done in accordance with your agreement. All they're looking for are those bare minimum standards outlined in the building code.

Sadly, you can't always count on building inspectors to even do that job. We found five reasons that government building inspectors are a miserable failure at protecting consumers:

◆ CORRUPTION. In 1995, an Illinois building inspector was indicted on bribery charges after an investigation of "shoddy or nonexistent building inspections of new homes in unincorporated Will County," according to the *Chicago Tribune*. An investigation of the building department's files revealed that as many as 50% of new homes built during 1993-4 had no inspections at all. Many of those homes received occupancy permits despite "glaring" code violations.

A May 2001 article by the Boston Globe ("Luxury by Design, Quality by Chance") described a lawsuit by New Jersey homeowners who documented how corruption by local building inspectors led to a subdivision riddled with defective homes. "So far, revelations emerging from at least 15 lawsuits filed against the developer by the homeowners include sworn accusations of free liquor and other gratuities distributed to local building inspectors by the developer, and dozens of instances in which the firm started construction without permits and required inspections."

In the mid 1990's, a Cincinnati TV station videotaped building inspectors "playing golf, going shopping or conducting personal business when they were supposed to be working. The station said employees falsified time sheets, inspection logs and mileage records," according to the *Cincinnati Post*. Later the same station aired reports that showed "a county building inspector admitting homeowners were often allowed to move into new houses that had not been given a final building inspection. The report also showed a building contractor, who refused to be identified, saying that 'inspectors often tagged houses as inspected when they never examined them.' " These home buyers were victims of what the industry calls "drive-by inspections."

Think those are isolated cases? Think again. In Frederick, Maryland, building inspectors were found to be moonlighting as subcontractors for the very same builders they were inspecting. In an editorial in the *Frederick Post*, the paper noted wryly, "Can we assume that someone goes out to inspect a construction site, for example, says it's wonderful and then we discover the same person is also working on that site? It would be like the inspector is inspecting his own work. Bet it passes inspection."

In New York City, 14 employees of the city Buildings Department were indicted on charges of "squeezing $150,000 in bribes from builders and owners over a five-year period," according to the *New York Daily News*. The corruption was described as "systematic, widespread, high-dollar and driven by supervisors." In Philadelphia, corruption in the building department has a long, colorful history that goes back to 1951—the year the Department of Licenses and Inspections was created. The *Philadelphia Inquirer* quoted the mayor of Philadelphia as saying that "ever since I've been with the government—from day one—I've heard about the passing of $10 bills and $20 bills to inspectors to speed up a building permit or overlook an inspection of some kind."

Among the more recent cases, an enterprising building department official in Cooper City, Florida was indicted for bribery, extortion and conspiracy in 1999. The FBI caught this guy shaking down Florida builders for $5000 to speed plans through the permit process and another $10,000 to "help" contractors pass inspections.

You can spot a telltale sign of possible corruption by examining building permits that are posted outside homes under construction. The permit lists each inspection, date and any corrections needed. "Be very suspicious if the card has only approvals and no citations for needed corrections," said Dr. Don Jacob, a consumer turned activist in New York who was saddled with $30,000 in repairs from a defective new home. "Some inspectors sign off cards for their contractor friends and never look at the construction. They may only drive by the construction site. In one city, builders were bringing cards to inspectors in a local donut shop and getting them signed off. Inspectors were never going to the construction sites."

◆ INCOMPETENCE. Even if municipal building inspectors aren't corrupt, they may very well be incompetent. You'd think that cities and counties would hire inspectors with engineering or construction backgrounds. The reality is quite different—requirements vary widely from area to area. While many building departments may require a college degree, it could be in basketweaving or some other relevant field.

The training and certification inspectors receive also varies from the barely adequate to the incredibly abysmal. Some departments hand out inspecting positions to political cronies of the mayor or city council. You can see a prescription for disaster coming: instead of well-trained inspectors with engineering and construction experience or schooling, the inspector in charge of making sure your new home is free from dangerous code violations may be a bureaucrat's crony with as much construction knowledge as . . well, you can fill in the blank.

Some states and counties are better than others. But the best building codes in the country are worthless if the people left to enforce them are idiots. The scary thing is there's no way to tell whether the

## Email from the Real World

Not all states have incompetent inspectors. A reader in Southern California emailed us information on that state's municipal building inspectors, which she claimed are among the toughest in the country:

*"Because of our stringent earthquake codes, state and county governments (under duress from insurance companies) take home inspections very seriously. Since the 1931 quake in LA, these governments have made damn sure that their own inspectors know what they are doing. They go to school, take brush-up classes and are closely supervised. Inspectors are respected by architects and strike terror in the hearts of builders. Californians who are building do pay for this service, of course. We are looking at something on the order of $6000 in assorted fees charged by the county for a typical house."*

area where you're building has competent or incompetent inspectors. Unless you're convinced otherwise, assume the worst and take the precautions outlined in this book to heart.

◆ TIME PRESSURES. Let's assume the municipal building inspector for your house is neither corrupt nor incompetent. Unfortunately, you're not home free. There's yet another roadblock that prevents new homes from being properly inspected: time.

Many building inspectors are overworked at best, forced to do a staggering number of inspections in an eight-hour day. This problem is especially acute in areas that have housing booms.

In Atlanta, Georgia, more than 120,000 new homes were built in a recent five year period. In an article on shoddy builders across the country, the *Los Angeles Times* reported that "Cobb County, Georgia's 10 inspectors 'take about 15 minutes per house call,' said Bob Harrison, manager of inspectors. That's an improvement over the nine minutes harried housing inspectors took three years ago but falls way short of the 40 minutes it should take to inspect the framing of a home," he said.

It should scare you to no end to know that the inspector who really needs 40 minutes to thoroughly evaluate the framing of your house—the critical structural element that literally holds up your walls and roof—is giving it only 15 quick minutes.

Even if the area where you're building isn't booming, the inspection department can be woefully understaffed. Governments put a higher priority on visible services such as police and fire protection. Home building inspection is left on the back burner.

Housing markets can shift quickly from "cool" to "hot," with the boom resulting in increased new house construction. Suddenly, three inspectors who could have handled the load in normal times are swamped with four times the number of inspections to do in the same period of time. An overworked inspector who is doing rushed inspections is just as dangerous as an incompetent or corrupt inspector.

◆ **LAWS WITH NO TEETH.** Some communities have housing laws with holes big enough to drive a cement truck through.

North Carolina again comes to mind. While the state requires contractors to be licensed to build a new house, the penalty for not doing so is a whopping fine of $50. That's it, $50. We're sure unlicensed contractors who are building $250,000 homes are quaking in their boots when faced with this type of punishment.

Incredibly, in some areas of the country, there is no systematic check to determine whether contractors are licensed or not. Therefore, unlicensed contractors can "pull a permit" to build a house and dupe consumers into thinking they're legitimate.

Even more amazing: loopholes in laws also let contractors build houses *without permits*. A few states allow unlicensed contractors to build houses without a permit if the house is for their personal use. Some builders use this loophole to claim they're building a house for themselves, only to quickly turn around and sell it.

Of course, some communities have tougher codes. Lake Forest, Illinois, requires 17 to 20 inspections to enforce a detailed code that calls for quiet plumbing and jiggle-free floors. Of course, you pay for all those municipal inspections through expensive permit fees that can top $5000 per house. The reality is that Lake Forest is the exception—many areas have toothless laws that are enforced by bungling inspectors.

◆ **POLITICAL INFLUENCE.** Builders and developers are big-time contributors to political campaigns. Their big money contributions can buy them a sympathetic ear at city hall and a powerful lobby at state legislatures. How does that affect so-called impartial building inspectors?

Who do you think pays the salaries of building inspectors? Yes, it's the city or county. While inspectors may be certified and trained by the state, their paychecks are in the hands of local politicians.

Hence, we've seen cases of blatant political bullying, in which builders and developers ask their friends in government to "ease up" on enforcement of the building code. "Hey, we're choking under all this government regulation," the builders cry, "why are you trying to crush the creators of the American Dream?"

In the Southeast, we found at least one case of a building inspector who was fired after he refused to "ease up" on contractors who were blatantly violating the state's building code. He found another government job, but was ordered by superiors (county bureaucrats) not to speak to reporters about the situation. As you can see, it's hard to get rock-solid proof on this phenomenon but many inspectors admit off the record that it's a common occurrence.

We also interviewed a former building inspector for Shreveport, Louisiana who was fired after 11 years on the job. Her offense? She busted a builder who was doing high-end homes for not filing correct plans with the building department. The builder complained to the mayor and guess who won? The building inspector also blew the whistle on so-called "drive-by" inspections, where inspectors sign off on work without ever seeing it.

**The bottom line.** You as a consumer must take responsibility for making sure you're getting a quality home. Relying on inspectors employed by government building departments is dangerous at best. If the inspectors aren't corrupt or incompetent, they're often overworked. Even if the inspectors are fine, the consumer protection laws for new homes can be riddled with loopholes or watered down by political influence.

The best path is to use your own "scissors" to poke the builder into building a quality new home. Those scissors are private professional inspectors with experience at evaluating new construction.

## What's the most common mistake inspectors uncover?

Yes, not all municipal housing inspectors are corrupt idiots who do drive-by inspections. Some actually do their job and do it well.

In a recent article on inspectors in *Builder* magazine, good inspectors discussed the most common problems they find with new homes. And what do they say is the number-one reason builders fail inspections? "Failure to follow the approved set of plans," said the article.

We found that point to be quite telling. Builders go through an extensive plan review process at most building departments, which checks the plans for all kinds of technical items like proper-size joists and beams and load-transfer points. Translation: items that make sure your home doesn't fall down.

Yet, out in the real world, builders often "forget" to make sure their workers and subcontractors actually follow the approved plan. Sure, sometimes it might be an honest mistake. Other times it's intentional—a builder who's cutting corners to save money or rushing to finish a project that's running late.

Another common problem: builders who are ignorant when it comes to the building code, those set of laws that make sure a house is safe and sound. "I bet less than 50 percent of builders have ever looked at a code book," said a municipal housing inspector in Lane County, Oregon. "I used to be a contractor and didn't study the code until I took the test for this job."

What's this mean for you, the smart home buyer? Even if you get a nice set of blueprints complete with detailed specifications, you still have to make sure the builder is actually following those plans. And don't assume your builder is an expert in the building code. Trust but verify.

## Questions to Ask Private Inspectors

**1** **What is your experience in evaluating residential construction?** How long have you worked in this area?

**2** **What credentials do you have?** Do you have a contractor's license, an architect's license, or an engineering degree? Since most states don't regulate private inspectors, this is critical—avoid anyone whose education or experience is limited. As a side note, you may want to ask if they belong to a national association of home inspectors.

**3** **Have you worked for this builder in the past?** Conflicts of interest may arise if the builder has ever employed the inspector or construction manager in the past. As with architects, any inspector or manager who has been paid a salary by the builder may be less willing to work on your behalf.

**4** **What are some common problems with new construction in my area?** Experienced answers might cite low-quality lumber grades, foundation problems, etc. The answer to this question should be in plain English and clearly understandable—jargon is a no-no.

**5** **Can I see a copy of one of your reports?** When studying the report, note whether the inspector simply has addressed cosmetic problems (paint nicks, unfinished trim work) or has made a more detailed examination. Some inspectors use a checklist, while others prefer narrative reports—we like the latter for new construction. If a checklist is used, notice how detailed it is regarding common problem areas such as foundations.

**6** **Is there a guarantee of prompt service?** If something is wrong, you need to have a written report to back up your claims in a timely fashion. While the builder probably will fix a problem without written evidence of a goof, it's nice to establish a paper trail in case a major problem develops down the road.

**7** **Do you take photos?** Most inspectors don't, but you might as well ask. A picture of defective construction is strong proof to present to the offending builder/subcontractor.

**8** **Do you fix any defects?** If the answer is yes, it's a big red flag—an ethical inspector should never profit from defects he uncovers.

# Money Bombs with Inspectors

### Money Bomb #1: Greenhorn inspectors.

*"My friend just bought a home and hired an inspector who did a lousy job. The inspector was new to the business and only did a brief, cosmetic inspection that missed several problems."*

These are the inspectors who just got into the business by printing up business cards. Usually, they have no experience and little knowledge of common problems such as soil conditions. Be sure to ask for references and check them out. Ask the inspector about his or her education or certification.

### Money Bomb #2: "Captive" inspectors.

*"I hear there is a private inspector in town who's the darling of local real estate agents. He apparently passes every property he inspects as a favor to his 'agent' friends, who in turn give him a steady stream of referrals."*

Real estate agents often are the "gate-keepers" of potential clients for inspectors. Many inspectors receive as much as 80% of their business from real estate agents. What does this mean for you?

Nearly all real estate agents are working for the seller, not the buyer. If an inspector turns up problems that are detrimental to selling a house, the real estate agent may be inclined to stop recommending that inspector—no agent wants to recommend a "deal killer" inspector since agents only get paid when a deal closes. The inspector knows who butters his bread and may give passing grades to projects in order to get repeat business.

Therefore, whatever you do, don't hire an inspector recommended by a real estate agent working for the seller/builder. This is why real estate agents weren't listed above under Sources. Use one of the other sources and check references carefully. (The exception: recommendations from a buyer's broker are more credible. More on buyer's brokers in Chapter 5.)

Be aware that many private inspectors get "bad" reputations among real estate agents because they become too good—that is, too good at ferreting out defects and problems with new homes. If a real estate agent fears a particular inspector, that's exactly the person who should be inspecting your home.

Some agents have taken the words "conflict of interest" to a new level when it comes to inspectors. A recent article (March 2001) in the Jupiter (FL) Courier newspaper reported on a case in point: a large Florida real estate company, Arvida, charged home inspection companies "$4000 to receive 12 months of publicity on Arvida's web site and in printed materials distributed at 105 Florida offices," the article stated. "In addition, Arvida is paid a $20 referral fee each time the inspection company does an inspection for an Arvida agent." Another article in the Palm Beach Post pointed out that if home inspectors paid the

$4000, they'd be one of just three vendors recommended to buyers.

Inspectors called that $20 fee a kickback (Arvida called it a "marketing fee") and the Florida Association of Building Inspectors warned members the deal was unethical.

### Money Bomb #3: Construction manager conflicts of interest.
*"We were about to hire this construction manager until we learned he was a former employee of the builder. Isn't that a clear conflict of interest?"*

Two situations might occur if you use a construction manager who knows your builder too well.

**1** **They're too friendly with one another.** This might occur if the manager used to work for the builder or if they just happen to be friends. The whole reason for hiring a construction manager is to keep a tight rein over the builder. If they're buddies, the manager may be unlikely to enforce your wishes.

**2** **If the construction manager and the builder are stiff competitors and don't like each other.** This situation could lead to many more hassles than you bargained for. After all, the manager is not supposed to be an ogre in this process, just an advocate for your interests. Excessive conflict on the job site is never helpful.

The solution to both these problems: hire a construction manager who doesn't work in the same area as the builder. For example, choose a manager who works in a nearby county or subdivision, but doesn't know your builder or the neighborhood intimately.

### Money Bomb #4: Builder's excuses that block your inspector.
*"My builder told us we could not have a private inspector look at the house under construction. He cited some wild excuse, saying his insurance company prohibited this for liability reasons."*

What a joke. Some builders will do anything to keep consumers from looking "under the hood" of their homes. Sure, some builders will allow an inspector to see a home after it is finished—and well after any potential problems are covered over with dirt, concrete or drywall. Builders may invent all kinds of excuses about this—a favorite is to say that their insurance company forbids anyone (you or the inspector) from coming onto the property during construction. This is a great bluff.

Challenge the builder to present a written copy of the policy with that provision. Even if such a provision exists, ask the builder if you can call the insurance company to confirm this prohibition against inspectors. Ask the insurance company for a waiver for your inspector. If the builder refuses to cooperate, consider another builder.

# Real Estate Attorneys

How does a real estate attorney protect your rights as a consumer? It's up to the attorney to review all the contracts you will be asked to sign as a part of your new house. Specifically, he or she should pay special attention to your rights including warranty coverage (warranties will be explained more fully in Chapter 8).

Builders stack the odds in their favor by having packs of lawyers on a leash. Seminars sponsored by local builder associations give builders insights on how to avoid "liability problems" (translation: legal problems from constructing defective houses).

Since most contracts used in new home purchases are written by the builder or his attorney, you can be darn sure every word is crafted to favor the builder. Other, less sophisticated builders pursue an opposite course: their contract may be so ambiguous or poorly written that you're in danger of falling into the "verbal promise trap." Such builders make wonderful verbal promises to you, but later no one can remember who agreed to what.

## Sources to Find a Real Estate Attorney

◆ **Local lawyer referral services:** Practically every city has some sort of free lawyer referral service. Some radio or TV stations also offer "Ask a Lawyer" nights for local consumers who have legal questions. Contact your local bar association for information.

◆ **Other professionals:** Architects and accountants also may come in contact with good real estate attorneys. The key to a good real estate lawyer is finding one with new construction experience.

## What Will It Cost You?

Lawyers ain't cheap. Face it—the cost of a lawyer to merely review your contracts can be as little as $75 per hour in small towns or up to as much as $200+ in larger cities. It shouldn't take much more than an hour or two to review any contracts.

If you want the lawyer to be present at closing, as well as to review the closing documents, you'll have to pay for another hour or two. The total tab could be anywhere from $200 to $500. Consider placing a cap on the lawyer's "billable hours"—get it in writing that the lawyer won't exceed the cap without your written permission.

## Money Bombs with Real Estate Attorneys

**Money Bomb #1: Lack of construction experience.**
*"My brother is an attorney who said he could help us with the construction of our new home. However, he seemed to be clueless when it came to the legalities of new construction."*

Many real estate lawyers are well versed in dealing with closing documents and contracts on "used" homes, but may not be as experienced with new construction. Because of the complexities of construction law, hiring a specialist is prudent.

**Money Bomb #2: Curse of a one-lawyer town: conflicts of interest with builders**
*"When we hired a local real estate attorney to help us with our new construction contract, we didn't know he was friends with our builder. Later, when we had problems with the builder, the lawyer was unwilling to help us out. Now we have to find a new lawyer to represent us."*

In small to medium-size towns the reality is there often aren't that many attorneys who specialize in real estate or new construction. Hence, the attorney you choose to represent you also may have represented the builder at one time. Home buyers are at a disadvantage since the builder can bring the attorney more repeat business than a one-time transaction.

In the book *And They Built a Crooked House*, author Ruth Martin describes her family's traumatic experience building a home in Cleveland. A conflict of interest with their attorney cropped up as a major problem. Although the attorney revealed at the beginning that he had worked with the builder, he downplayed any conflict. Then when a serious dispute occurred, the attorney backed out of representing the buyer—claiming that his relationship with the builder was too valuable. The resulting chaos was a contributing factor to the new home disaster. (If you interested in hearing the whole story, check out the bibliography later in this book for more info on the Martins' book).

## New Homebuyers in Cyberspace: What's on the Web?

Yes, you can get legal advice from the law firm of Net, Web And Cyber—and unlike most lawyers, this advice is free and available 24 hours a day. In this section, we'll give you an overview of the best web sites for legal advice. Of course, these sites are no substitute for a real estate attorney—you should always have a live, actual lawyer review your construction contract, handle the closing papers and help with troubleshooting. Yet, these web sites are great for quick answers for many real estate law questions.

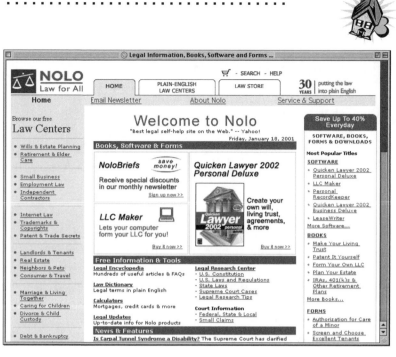

**Figure 2:** Nolo.com is a great site for quick answers to real estate law questions.

◆ **Nolo.com.** Here's one of our favorite law sites. Nolo.com (see Figure 2 on the next page) is the online outpost of the self-help legal publisher Nolo Press. On this site, you'll be able to surf their large catalog of do-it-yourself law books and software, sift through a legal dictionary and more. Best feature: "Ask Auntie Nolo," a section with plain-English answers to legal problems. Also cool: Nolo has a huge cache of legal documents and forms you can download (for a small fee) and customize on your home computer.

◆ **FreeAdvice.com.** This site has a decent real estate section with general advice on buying/selling, mortgages and zoning issues. The online legal library is quite impressive, as is this site's offer of a "free consultation" to determine your rights if you run into legal problems with your contractor.

◆ **Findlaw.com.** It's a bit cumbersome to look at, but this massive legal site has numerous links for new home buyers to explore. The chat rooms and message boards will let you vent over legal troubles and perhaps get an answer from a visiting attorney.

◆ **Law.com.** Another big legal site, Law.com has a useful self-help legal guide with a long list of topics (including several under Real Estate). Enter your city/state and you can view specific links that are helpful.

# Other Possible Team Members

Think about one or more of these professionals to add to your dream building team.

◆ **Design specialists.** An interior designer may be helpful, especially for the selection of finishes. Some interior designers have formal schooling in architectural design. A lighting designer is another specialist that might help your project, as might a landscape architect.

◆ **Buyer's broker.** A buyer's broker is a special type of real estate agent who works for you, the buyer. (More on this later in Chapter 5.) We recommend using a buyer's broker to purchase the lot or building site (if you are building a custom home) or to negotiate on a tract, semi-custom or new spec home in an existing development. That way you guarantee the agent is representing *you* in all negotiations. Many consumers aren't aware that traditional real estate agents are working for the seller (or builder)—not the buyer.

◆ **Insurance company.** A "hazard" insurance policy that guards against fire and other perils will need to be in place at the time of closing. You may want to ask your insurer whether they have any construction-related policies to protect in case of a fire during construction (if you own the lot).

# Who Is NOT on Your Team?

◆ **Real Estate Agents (for the house).** If they aren't a buyer's agent, they aren't working for you. That's about 99% of all agents out there. Whose team are they on? Frankly, their own—most agents are fixated on that commission. Technically, they are legally and ethically bound to get the highest price and best terms for the builder.

◆ **The lender.** While lenders are technically working with you, they are most worried about their money. Most could care less whether you get a quality house. While some lenders may be able to help if a dispute occurs between you and the builder, most simply shrug their shoulders. Making sure they get your payments on time is their major concern.

◆ **Mother Nature.** Weather forecasters on TV can't seem to guarantee the weather in the next hour, so don't expect to have smooth sailing with Mother Nature throughout the construction. Not only can bad weather delay construction, but it may delay pre-construction activities (such as a soil test) as well. If the builder tells you it will take four months to build your house, add another month to the estimate. This way, if it pours rain or dumps snow, you won't be disappointed when the house isn't finished on time. And if the weather is perfect (along with everything else), you'll be pleasantly surprised when your house is finished early.

◆ **Homeowners associations.** In "covenant controlled" communities (condos and townhomes and, increasingly, with single-family homes), homeowners associations (HOA's) often control the *design* of houses that can be built in the subdivision. In fact, many associations set up separate architectural control or review boards to comment on and approve building plans—we'll discuss HOA's in-depth in the next chapter.

Check with the association for the community you want to live in *before* you decide to buy a lot and build. Get a copy of the covenants and speak to homeowners in the area to discover any potential problems. Also, let your architect know what the "standards" are in the community so you don't waste money and time altering a rejected design.

◆ **Labor shortages.** In "hot" building regions, the supply of construction labor may be very tight. The lack of subcontractor availability can double the amount of time it takes to complete a house. What took four to six months in a normal market may now take seven to nine.

In one community we studied, framers were especially hard to come by. Some houses stood idle for a month or longer after the foundation was poured. Some markets can turn from "cold" to "hot" seemingly overnight. If you plan to build in such a market, be prepared. Recognize that labor shortages could add weeks or months to the builder's optimistic timeframe.

◆ **Labor strikes.** Although they may not be as common as labor shortages, labor strikes do occur. For example, a drywallers strike in California in the early 1990's significantly slowed new construction.

◆ **The scam artists.** When you build a house, you deal with dozens of people and companies. Some are more ethical than others. Scam artists might be subcontractors who intentionally do inferior work. In other cases, a smiling salesperson may sell products that don't live up to the manufacturers' claims. Choosing a builder who is reputable helps raise the odds of getting good subs—but there are no guarantees. Having an inspector on your side is the only sure way to guarantee that inferior work is corrected.

If your builder or architect suggests trying a product you aren't familiar with, do some research before agreeing to use it. For example, thousands of houses were built in the 1980s using an experimental plastic pipe system, instead of copper, for plumbing. The folks who bought those houses have since incurred expensive repairs to fix damage from leaky pipes. In fact, the manufacturer has begun paying claims to settle class-action lawsuits brought by angry homeowners. A little advance research might have helped these consumers avoid such serious problems.

◆ **Delays.** The biggest enemy of any buyer is the seemingly inevitable delays. The wrong materials arrive at your home site. Subcontractors don't show up when scheduled. Or at all. And so on.

Here's an example of what delays can do: a builder had scheduled the carpet installation for a Tuesday. Instead of showing up at 8:00 a.m., the carpet installer saunters in at 5:30 p.m. This throws off the entire schedule—delaying the final inspection, cleaning and closing of the house.

The builder's biggest headache (and the reason you don't want to build a house yourself) is the scheduling of the subs. Like an expensive and time-consuming game of dominoes, one delay can cause another, which leads to a cost-overrun. The result is a vicious circle that raises the frustration level beyond description.

Like most home buyers, we had dozens of delays on our home—some major and others minor. For example, a wrong kitchen cabinet was delivered (the manufacturer's mistake), delaying the installation of countertops by a week. However, the house ran only two weeks late in the end—being the cynics we are, we planned for a delayed closing anyway.

What about the builder? Whose team is he or she on? Gee, it would be nice if every builder were on your side. The reality is the builder is also trying to make a profit at the same time he's trying to make you happy. Unfortunately, some (critics would say many) builders let their thirst for profits win out over your interests. To boost sagging financial fortunes, some builders and developers get desperate, taking home buyers down with them. You should probably pretend that you and your builder are on the same team, but, at the same time, take steps to protect yourself.

# If Dirt Were Dollars: Finding the Right Location for Your Home

**S**o, where exactly are you going to put this new house? Finding just the right location for your new home is going to involve a good amount of searching, compromise and trade-offs. Also, you must become your own detective to uncover the past history of the lot—discovering that the "dream location" for your new home was once a toxic waste dump after you buy it could ruin your whole day.

Basically, there are four types of potential sites for a new home:

**1** **"No Competition" Lots.** These are sites in existing developments that are owned by one builder. You want the lot? Then you must also hire that builder. Many production-style developments are run this way. Hence, the quality of such homes can range from "passable" to "your worst nightmare." Even more expensive lots in "exclusive" communities are sometimes sold this way. We've heard horror stories from consumers who fell in love with a lot—only to discover later that the builder/developer was an expert at building defective homes. On the plus side, if the lot is owned by a reputable builder, then you are good to go. This is also a time-saver, as your search for the house and lot are combined. One side note: occasionally, some of the "no-competition" lots will let you choose your own architect or designer. At least this gives you a little more protection.

**2** **"Managed Competition" Lots.** Many communities of production or semi-custom homes allow you to choose from a list of "approved builders." Often, you can pick your own designer or architect and bid out your plan to these builders. Of course, the only problem may be that none of the approved builders has the skill or experience to do your home. Developers of these communities claim they have screened "approved" builders, but that assertion is dubious at best.

Here's a strategy around the restrictions: ask the homeowners association or developer whether you can get an exception to the rule. Approved builder lists are often done to keep "tract" style builders from building in exclusive communities. The reality is you may be granted an exception if you can prove that your home design (by a professional designer or architect, of course) and builder are up to the so-called standards of the community. It may be well worth the effort.

**3** "Free Market" Lots. These building sites are not "attached" to any builder. You buy the land and then use any builder you desire. Obviously, the flexibility of this arrangement is its chief advantage. Of course, most areas don't have many "free market lots." You may have a long search—and end up choosing a location farther from town. Some of these sites have services such as natural gas and city sewers—others are more "rustic," requiring septic systems and the like. Don't let the "undeveloped" nature of such lots scare you off, however.

**4** Partially-Built Spec Homes. In some cases, you may find a partially built home that is still on the market. (In jargon, this home is a "spec" since it was built on speculation, instead of presold to a buyer.) The advantage, of course, is that the builder has already picked a spot, obtained financing and started construction. On the downside, that "spot" may not be the best for you. Furthermore, there is significant risk in buying a partially built home—for example, you can't check the foundation since it already has been poured and the footings are buried. Insisting on a complete set of plans and specifications as well as independent inspections by a private inspector will help, but it's still a gamble. Nonetheless, you will still use the same "location analysis" techniques to determine whether it's the right place for you.

## Step-By-Step Strategies to Scoping out a Location: Phase I.

**Step 1: Narrow your search to a general area and determine it's zip code.** Go to your local library and find the *Sourcebook of Zip Code Demographics* (published by CACI Marketing Systems; www.demographics.caci.com*).* This book is a wealth of information with answers to such questions as: What percentage of families in that area have young children? Which area has the highest per capita income? Every county in the country is covered in detail.

**Step 2: Surf the web for neighborhood info.** A good place to start is USA City Link (www.usacitylink.com), which has links to all sorts of civic sites. Another source: see if your real estate agent has access to a CD-ROM called "Know Thy Neighborhood" (published by eNeighborhoods, www.eneighborhoods.com). This software gives you up-to-date info on neighborhood demographics, school data, housing values, crime rates, climate reports and more.

**Step 3: Identify two to three possible neighborhoods that have new home building sites available.** You can determine this by simply driving around, checking the local paper, or asking a buyer's broker for hints.

**Step 4: Score each neighborhood on a 1 to 10 scale** for the following quality-of-life measures: school district, commute time, access to highways/shopping, and other things important to you.

**Step 5: Check the availability of various services.** How close is the nearest grocery store? Other shopping? Where's the nearest recreation center? How far away are the elementary, middle and senior high schools?

**Step 6: Evaluate the neighbors.** Are the lawns well taken care of? What types of cars are in the driveways? For kids, do the "Big Wheel" test—see whether any toys are left outside (the tell-tale sign of children). Get out and walk around. If you're looking on a weekend or in the early evening, chances are you can visit with potential neighbors.

**Step 7: Give a prospective lot a "once over."** Visit it during different times of day, including rush hour—how's the traffic flow? Are you on a sleepy cul-de-sac or a busy thoroughfare? How's the traffic noise? If you're near an elementary school, how loud is it during recess?

**Step 8: Locate a buyer's broker** (see Chapter 5 for tips). Direct the broker to look for available lots in your target neighborhoods.

**Step 9: Check zoning for nearby empty land** with your city/county planning department. That lovely meadow just down the street may be slated for a giant, smelly factory. Or a high-rise condo building.

**Step 10: Who can build on the lot?** Any builder? Just three? One? Can you have your own architect? This might decision might be controlled by a developer, who has limited the number of contractors to a pre-screened list. Or you might have to seek approval from a homeowner's association regarding your contractor or architect. See Chapter 7 for tips on evaluating production builders.

**Step 12: If it looks like a go, do some sleuthing on the "history" of the lot.** See the box later in this chapter called "Environmental Detectives" for more information.

# Step-by-Step Strategies to Scoping Out a Location: Phase II

**Step 1: Bring the architect and/or builder out to the lot for a "look-see."** Have them walk around the lot before you buy it. The goal is to identify any possible concerns—is that wet spot a drainage problem? Is the lot's slope going to add significantly to the cost?

The architect or builder may do this for free or they may charge you a nominal hourly fee. Whether the lot looks challenging or simple to build on, it may be well worth the effort to have an "expert" give an opinion before you buy.

**Step 2: Confirm the site's available "services" (or lack thereof).** This includes access to a municipal water and/or sewer system, natural gas lines, electrical service, cable and phone lines. Does the area have high-speed Internet access? Much of this information is in the Multiple Listing Service listing for the property. However, don't take a real estate agent's word on the availability of services—call the utility company and confirm electrical or natural gas service at that address. You can also ask your local planning or building department for details on available services.

The lack of services could mean significant extra cost. No cable TV may mean installing a satellite system. If the area is undeveloped, you may have to pay a significant fee to the utility company to bring in service. If you have a home office, make sure the phone company will let you install multiple lines to your home (for a fax, modem, etc.).

**Step 3: The next step is to do the "tests."** If you're buying a "free-market" lot, these tests will be your responsibility. If the builder already owns the site, make the purchase of the home contingent on seeing the written results. Depending on the area you are building in, you may want to do all or none of these tests—ask your inspector or architect regarding the norms in your area. Here's a rundown of the possible tests:

◆ **A Soils Test:** This is done by an engineer or geologist who drills several small holes 12 to 15 feet deep in the lot. Core samples are taken to determine the "sub-soil conditions"—basically what's underneath the top soil. Is there clay? A layer of rock-hard limestone? The results will influence the type of foundation (including the need for and size of footings) and the excavation costs. This test costs $250 to $350. Add in engineering for the foundation and the total cost can soar to $1000 to $2000. Skipping this step (to cut corners, time) is a potentially dangerous decision. See the Money Bomb section later in this chapter for more details. *(Note: In some areas, soils tests are replaced by an "open hole inspection": after the foundation is dug, a soils engineer comes out to look at the hole. He or she checks the rock and makes sure the planned foundation is adequate.)*

◆ **A pesticide test.** Is your lot in a subdivision that used to be a farm? Fruit orchard? Some other agricultural use? If so, you should insist on having the lot tested for pesticide residue. We'll discuss this issue more in depth later in this chapter.

## Email from the Real World: Get a Map!

**A reader in Michigan set in this story about how a soils test saved her $30,000**

*"Last July we found property that we liked on a canal in Michigan. We put a deposit of $4000 on the lot. Then we found your book. We had never heard of soils tests, but thankfully we followed your advice and had the land tested. The testing cost $1500 but showed the lot had been filled in and would require an extra $30,000 to build an engineered foundation with pilings! If we hadn't read your book, we'd be out $120,000 for a lot that required an extra $30,000 in special foundation work!"*

What more can we say? Buying a lot without a soils test is penny-wise and pound foolish.

◆ **Percolation Test:** Also know as a "perc test," this is done for lots that don't have access to a municipal sewer system and, hence, require a septic system. A perc test is done by digging a hole, pouring in a certain amount of water and timing its disappearance. This is done to determine how quickly water will drain from the future septic field. The depth of the hole for the perc test varies, depending on local code. In northern climates, a perc test may only be possible when the ground isn't frozen. If the test has already been done, get a copy. In cases where deep perc holes are required, this test also may determine the soil condition. Cost: $200 to $700.

**Step 4: Check zoning for certain prohibitions.** For example, some communities that are still stuck in the Dark Ages prohibit home offices. Height restrictions and other regulations could nix your plans for a grandiose home. Your local county or city building or planning department should have a complete list of zoning requirements.

**Step 5: Determine the association/government fees for building on the lot.** Certain community associations may ask you to put down a "deposit" to guarantee you will obey their covenants, conditions and restrictions. If you play by the rules, you get your money back. Associations sometimes also charge a "submittal" fee to review your plan to make sure their architectural rules are met. Municipal building departments may have certain "fees" to have your plans reviewed and make sure they're in compliance with building codes. These fees may be in addition to the cost of getting a building permit. Knowing all these costs up front is obviously important in evaluating one site over another.

# Environmental Detectives: Sleuthing the Sludge

**I**t's every home buyer's biggest nightmare—you move into your dream house and suddenly discover an odor in the backyard. You go to investigate and find a green ooze seeping up from the ground.

Alarmed, you call the health department and learn your home sweet home was a toxic waste dump in a previous life. Or a landfill. Or perhaps it's all those gasoline tanks down the road—have they spilled any gas that could seep into your yard?

Think this only happens in Love Canal? Think again. Dozens of homeowners in Fairfax, Virginia recently discovered the worst when they found a toxic brew of petroleum by-products leaking into their basements. The culprit? A nearby collection of gas tanks that had a history of leaks. Many of the homeowners faced bankruptcy when they couldn't sell their homes because of the problem.

While this sounds discouraging, it's not impossible to find out the past environmental history of your home site—and the surrounding area. We found a web site called Smart Home Buy (www.smarthome-buy.com). Enter a property address and you can find out environmental info, crime stats and natural hazard potential (such as earthquakes and floods). Cost: $4.95 per report (or $14.95 for 10 reports).

These reports tell you everything nearby that could be a possible hazard, from a little dry cleaner store to a nuclear power plant. If a truck carrying hazardous chemicals spilled in an accident on a nearby highway, you'll know it.

If the Fairfax homeowners had spent the time to investigate their neighborhood before they bought their homes, they would have discovered the subdivision was right next to a gasoline storage facility that had a long history of leaks—saving themselves untold amounts of grief and money.

**Step 6: Consider a survey to determine just what you're buying.**
Do you know how big your lot is? What about the lot's "topography"? Just because there is a "pin" or "marker" indicating each corner, how do you know that it is correctly placed? They may have been put there by a previous lot owner who was merely guessing at the site's dimensions. More blatant fraud occurs when the pins are placed in knowingly wrong locations or are moved, creating the appearance of a bigger lot. The fact is, unless you have a formal survey done, you may not know exactly what's on your lot and what's on your neighbor's. Some lenders require a survey, which costs $150 to $500, before you can get a construction loan. The cost can be affected by several factors such as trees (heavily treed lots cost more) and access (easy access = lower price). Another way to save on a survey: ask the surveyor if the lot can be measured every five feet (instead of the standard two feet). One caveat to surveys is a "what came first, the chicken or the egg" type dilemma. In order to do a good topographic survey of a lot, you may need to clear some trees. That obviously is a problem if you don't own the lot

Some potential problems can look rather harmless—a nearby gas station or dry cleaner store is required to be registered with the EPA since they use or store hazardous chemicals. If they've had a spill or any other problem in the past, you have a chance to learn about it if it was reported to the EPA. And that's the biggest potential shortcoming of these reports—it can't pick up problems that have not been reported to the government. Hence, if your neighbor installed a diesel gas tank underground and didn't report it to the state or federal environmental officials (as required by law), this report would miss it. While it obviously isn't foolproof, it's better than nothing.

Let's say you get a report on your potential new home site and some problems are turned up. (Vista Info told us some "dirty" sites can have reports exceeding 25 pages.) What should you do next? To determine whether you have a serious situation or not, you probably need to hire an environmental engineer to do a site evaluation. In addition to looking in the phone book, you can also get a referral by contacting the Environmental Assessment Association at (320) 763-4320; www.iami.org/eaa.cfm

How bad is the problem? According to a recent *Money* magazine article, "some 40 million Americans live within four miles of one of the 1235 sites that have made the U.S. Environmental Protection Agency's Superfund National Priority List—sort of the most wanted list of hazardous waste—and about 50 to 100 new sites turn up each year."

We strongly recommend you check out your home site before purchasing. Discovering your home is built on a hazardous waste site after you move in is not worth the risk.

yet (but want a survey to verify dimensions). You may have to make your bid contingent on a survey, which will let you remove X trees.

**Step 7: Adjust your bid to the lot conditions.** Now you're ready to offer some money to the lot owner. Your bid should be based on what you're buying. That perfect lot may have a rock-hard layer of bedrock under the surface, forcing an extra $5000 in excavation costs. If you know all the facts before you negotiate, you can make a more intelligent bid.

## What Will It Cost You?

The "general rule of thumb" is that the lot should cost 25% to 35% of the total price (lot plus house). The reasoning is simple—you don't want to put a giant, expensive house on a cheap lot with awful views or a tiny backyard. Similarly, a cheap house on an expensive piece of land doesn't work either.

Obviously, rules are made to be broken—if you find the perfect location, go for it. In some areas, land is so expensive that you may have a hard time hitting the 35% mark—lenders may be willing to make an exception. In California, the land may account for 45% to 50% of the total price.

When you acquire land, the costs include:

◆ **The actual land price.**

◆ **Tests.** Most of the costs are the buyer's responsibility. The seller may already have completed a survey or percolation test in some cases.

◆ **Tap fees.** These costs are to "tap" into the local utility lines (electrical, natural gas, sewer, water and so on). Some lots have the tap fees paid already.

◆ **Consultant fees.** You may want to pay for an hour of your architect's or builder's time to visit the potential site to give you their opinion about it's suitability.

To pay for all this, you have several options:

◆ **Cash.** The old standby.

◆ **Bank loan.** Occasionally, you may find a lender to loan you about 50% to 75% of the lot's value.

◆ **"Seller carrybacks."** In some areas, the seller may take back a note on the property. You make a down payment and make monthly payments to the seller. You can use a short-term carryback (one to three years) to finance the land while you go through the process of preparing to build on the lot.

# Siting the House

Finding the right location is just the beginning. Now you must decide where on the lot your home should sit. "Siting" the house should not be a quick, haphazard decision. Here are some thoughts on this process:

◆ WHAT VIEWS DO YOU WANT TO SEE? Anything you want to avoid? Positioning the house on the lot to take advantage of any view is a delicate task.

◆ CHECK ZONING AND ANY COVENANTS. Certain rules may dictate how far back your home can be from the front, back and side property lines. These may be county or city zoning "set-backs" or community covenants. Height restrictions and other regulations are also an issue in some areas.

◆ CONSIDER HIRING A LANDSCAPE ARCHITECT FOR PARTICULARLY CHALLENGING LOTS. If you have a flat lot with few trees, siting the house may not be difficult. However, if the lot slopes or has lots of little hills and valleys, you may want to call in a pro. If you have an architect, he or she should be able to recommend a landscape architect to help you site the house. The landscape architect will maximize the view from the street and the position of the house relative to potential landscaping.

◆ **CURB APPEAL IS THE GOAL.** The key to having a quality house with strong resell appeal is to understand how the house will look from the street. This first impression is crucial if you plan to sell the home later. A facade that's dominated by a giant, ugly garage may detract from the home's value, despite how beautiful the inside is.

◆ **SOLAR "VIEWS."** In cold climates, southern exposure helps warm the home through "passive solar energy." Some folks like morning sun to shine into the kitchen or breakfast nook. In areas where the summer heat is intense, a room with a large expanse of windows that faces west could be difficult to cool. Many homes in the South that have no southern or western exposure are considered more desirable. The same logic applies to driveways—in cold climates, driveways that face the north or are shaded by trees and get little sun are a negative (the snow doesn't melt as quickly).

The determination of the best solar siting of your home is tricky. If you visit the lot in June, the sun will be high in the sky—much different than in the dead of winter. In cold climates, if you can view the lot in the winter, you may have a different perspective on where to place the home and driveway. The point is to think through these issues carefully.

◆ **DRIVEWAY.** In snowy climates, a driveway should be level and a straight shot to the garage. Ask anyone who's tried to negotiate a driveway with a sharp turn that's covered with ten inches of snow and you'll understand why—slow down to take the turn and you're toast. Similarly, a driveway with a "negative slope," where the driveway slopes down from the street to the garage is a major no-no ... you can easily slide down an icy surface into your living room. A driveway that snakes its way through lots of trees might be nice to look at, but impossible to plow.

In climates with heavy rain, you want rainwater to drain naturally off the driveway into the street—not pool near your garage. "Negative slope" driveways may require an expensive drainage system to keep water away from the house.

## How Big Is The Average New Home Lot?

Lot sizes for the average new home fluctuate with the economy. When times are good, buyers can afford bigger lots. In recessions, builders respond to leaner budgets with smaller sites. Hence, in the recession of the early 1980's, lot sizes for new homes were in the 8000 to 8500 square foot range. When economic fortunes improved in the 1990's, the average lot expanded to nearly 10,000 square feet. Home builders expect the average lot size to shrink again by 2010; this time, limited availability of land might force builders to cram more houses into a subdivision in the future (that is, even more than today's cramped standards).

## Questions to Ask

Some of these questions can be answered by a buyer's broker. Others require an expert opinion from an architect, builder, or engineer. A few questions are for you to ask yourself.

**1** **Are there any impact fees?** In our "money bomb" section we explain this new tax on home buyers. Impact fees for new schools, parks, or environmental protection range from $500 to $30,000 and are usually scaled to the home's square footage.

**2** **What are the property taxes?** A buyer's broker should be able to give you an estimate for property taxes, given a certain size home.

**3** **How much are association fees and annual dues?** If your lot is part of a homeowners association, you may have to pay "submittal fees" to submit your plan to the group's architectural control committee. Annual dues pay for any common amenities such as a pool or clubhouse, private police protection/security, or the association's administration.

## Email from the Real World: Get a Map!

A reader in Janesville, Wisconsin discovered her "dream lot" was more of a nightmare after paying for a survey. Luckily, she was able to back out of the deal:

*"We were just about to close on a beautiful wooded country lot here in southern Wisconsin when we finally got the survey (boundary map) and perc test we had contingencies for. Upon looking at the boundary map (done by a professional surveyor only weeks ago) we discovered that the acreage of the lot was actually HALF AN ACRE smaller than the 1.2 acres advertised by the seller! This, combined with the setbacks on an extremely irregularly shaped lot, left us with a very limited building area. When we pointed this out to the real estate agents, we were given every excuse in the book. When we told the bank why we were backing out at the last minute, they were appalled and thanked us for being so diligent. We would never have been so careful if I hadn't read your book and developed a healthy paranoia regarding the whole building market. I've been getting some rather poisonous looks from the builders, architects and designers when I ask them some of the questions in your book. I rather enjoy making them uncomfortable. Thank you for helping me feel empowered during the home building process."*

**4** **What school district is the lot in?** Which elementary, junior high (middle school), and high school do kids attend? How far away are they? What is their quality relative to nearby schools? Is there "open enrollment" where you can choose another public school?

**5** **Describe the lot's topography.** Most Multiple Listing Service listings will include a description—the lot could be flat, gently sloping, or severely sloping.

**6** **Is the lot insurable?** Some lots in a flood plain may require special flood insurance. In the town we live in, a municipal flood management office will tell you whether your home site is in a flood plain and give information on flood insurance. Another issue is fire danger: if your home site is in a rural area with no fire hydrants or full-time fire station, you may have to pay through the nose for property insurance. A home insurance agent will be able to give you details on these issues.

**7** **How much site preparation will be required?** Will trees have to be cleared? These costs should be estimated by a professional architect/designer or builder.

**8** **What's the zoning?** What uses does this allow or prohibit? Can you have a home office? Could you get a variance or a zoning change if the current zoning isn't residential?

**9** **Are there any easements?** An easement is the right or privilege of someone else to use your property. Common easements are for utilities to run lines across the back of the property. The phone company may have an easement to put a junction box at one corner of your lot. Most easements are marked on a subdivision map—ask to have any and all easements revealed to you before you buy. If you have a survey done on the property, make sure all easements are located.

**10** **What is the access to the lot?** Is there any legal "ingress" across another lot? You may have the right to share a driveway with a neighbor.

**11** **Is municipal water and sewer available?** What about electricity and natural gas? Will you have to use propane or heating oil?

**12** **Are there any building moratoriums?** Some communities restrict growth by banning a water/sewer tap for new homes. Others slow the permit approval process. Some cities like our hometown Boulder, CO actually string up new home builders at the edge of town to discourage development. (Only a slight exaggeration). Ask a buyer's broker for the latest news in your area.

**13** **What are the conditions of the trees?** In some areas, an infestation of pests or insects may have killed all the trees on your lot. Some trees may look healthy but still be infected. Call a county forester or a county agriculture department for information.

**14** **What's the soil condition?** A soils test tells you what you're building on—a crucial protection for you. Has the lot been tested for pesticides?

**15** **Do you really like the neighborhood?** This may be a tough question to answer, but go with your gut feeling.

**16** **Are there any restrictive covenants?** These can be put on the property by a previous owner or a homeowners association. If you have your heart set on a two-story home, but the association's height restrictions only allow one-level homes, you're going to be very disappointed. Know the facts before you buy.

**17** **Can you get clear title?** Make sure there are no liens on the property—in most states, you can purchase title insurance. This guarantees the title will be clear of any liens or other encumbrances. The title insurance company does a search to make sure you'll get good title. If title insurance is not used in your area, have an attorney do a lien search to make sure the property is free and clear.

**18** **If the land purchase is contingent on financing, can this be written into the contract?** Making the lot purchase contingent on loan approval gives you an out in case the lender says no. Adding the conditions that you can obtain "market rate" financing also protects you.

**19** **Is there a survey already done on the lot?** A survey that marks the property boundaries and/or topography can be very helpful—and sometimes may reveal problems the real estate agent "forgot" to tell you about. Ask the lot owner if they have such a survey (if it was done by a certified surveyor it should be accurate). If not, pay for a survey yourself—and include a contingency in the contract that will let you back out in case the survey turns up some nasty surprise. See the following Email from the Real World for a reader's experience with this very topic.

**20** **Was the lot ever used for farming?** If so, has the soil been tested for pesticide residue? More on this issue later in this chapter.

## The Hamburger Theory of Neighborhoods

A college real estate professor of mine once described the process of determining the right site for a home as "the hamburger theory":

# Email from the Real World: Lot Premiums

*"We're reserving a lot this weekend in a development of a semi-custom production builder and have a question concerning lot premiums. In looking at the street layout of the twenty-some homes going in, some of the sites are labeled 'BP,' or base price (of home); but most of the lots have 'premiums' on them. There are a couple of lots that are a bit wider than the rest, so I suppose the builder feels justified in jacking up the price, but the majority of the lots are exactly the same size . . . and they have different premiums on them, ranging from $3,000 up to $10,000.*

*"We've picked up from the builder's sales rep that these 'premiums' are somewhat negotiable. (It almost seems like, if you're dumb enough not to question it, they'll charge you for it.) Of course, the lot we really like has an $8,000 premium on it; after adding some square footage and options to the house, we really can't afford another eight grand. Do you have any negotiating tactics/suggestions to assist us in getting the premium waived?"*

While it would make sense that the "better" lots in a subdivision might have premiums (locations with better views, access to open space, etc), that may not be the case—sometimes it may just be the builder's whim. Or mistake. In a builder trade journal article in 2001, mystery shoppers in Tuscon, Arizona found one builder who charged a $15,000 "view" premium for a lot that actually looked *away* from a nearby mountain. The lesson: if you are going to pay a lot premium, make sure the lot actually has the feature.

As for negotiating a lower price, it's rather simple: just offer what YOU want to pay for the home. Like any negotiation, any buyer that offers the best terms (a cash deal, quick closing or some other incentive), may sway the builder to forget the lot premium.

Different lots (just like cuts of meat) have different quality and prices.

Just like a side of beef, neighborhoods or subdivisions have various "cuts" of locations. There are the hamburger lots—these may have less-desirable locations such as on a busy street. Sites that back up to a highway or major thoroughfare are not much fun—traffic noise is a big negative for most folks. Low-lying lots that flood during rain storms are also definitely hamburger.

On the other hand are "filet mignon" lots. Depending on your tastes, such a location may be on a quiet cul-de-sac. The lots with the best views or nicest topography always sell for a premium. Locations that are next to golf courses or "greenbelts" (dedicated open space) are also top spots.

Of course, you may want a filet mignon location in the subdivision but you've only got a T-bone budget. The challenge for any new home buyer is to buy the very best location that your budget allows.

Nothing is black or white, either—many locations don't fall clearly in the hamburger or filet mignon categories. There are many different cuts of meat in between—ground chuck, rib-eyes, T-bones, etc. Such locations may be a mix of negatives and positives. A lot on a quiet cul-de-sac may be selling at a lower price since it doesn't have easy access from the subdivision's entry.

In a perfectly free market, the price of certain locations would be scaled to their attractiveness. Yet pricing is often part art, part science. Hence, some hamburger locations may be overpriced, while the filet mignon lots are under-valued. If you take the time to search, you may be surprised to find bargains.

## Money Bombs

### Money Bomb #1: Soil troubles

*"We bought a new home in Colorado and, six months later, the foundation began to buckle and heave—now tile pops off the walls, the patio has separated from the house and the deck lists to one side!"*

Yes, that's a true story from a Colorado new homebuyer who discovered his $234,000 new home suffered $100,000 in damages from a shifting foundation. And he are not alone. As reported in *Westword Magazine* (January 21, 1999), 15,000 Front Range homebuyers face similar catastrophes—soil problems cause $4 BILLION in damage nationwide each year. The result is a flurry of class action lawsuits against builders and developers.

The culprit in this mess? "Expansive" soils, made of sandy clay and claystone. Common in Colorado and other parts of the West, expansive soils swell when wet and can exert tremendous pressure on foundation walls. The result: cracked walls, floors and foundations. The above homebuyer told a reporter "at night he can lie awake and hear the house creaking and cracking. His home isn't settling. It's rising, like the accursed undead in some half-baked horror flick."

So, what are the builders' excuses for this? Some admit their own geotech engineers warned them about expansive soils . . . but they built the homes anyway. Now these builders find themselves on the business end of expensive class action lawsuits demanding compensation.

What can homebuyers do? First, ask for a copy of the soils test or report for your lot. If you don't understand the results and risks of building in a certain spot, get help (from an attorney, a geotech engineer, etc.). If you want to build in an area with problem soils, there are a couple of solutions: first, your builder can remove the swelling soils and replace them with more stable dirt. This "structural" fill dirt is compacted to provide a base for the foundation. If this is the case in your area, ask to see a copy of the "density test." This test, done by a qualified engineer, confirms the soil is appropriately compacted. Second, if the clay content in a soil is small, the builder can build the home with a "structural wood floor" that resists soil movement. This adds an additional $2500 or more to a typical foundation..

Of course, problem soils extend beyond Colorado's treacherous geology. In the mid-Atlantic and New England states, high seasonal water tables can wreak havoc with new homes. These water tables can flood crawl spaces and basements during heavy spring and fall rains.

The bottom line: investigate the soil under your dream home. Don't just take a builder's word that "everything is fine"—ask to see the reports and tests. If there are serious concerns about expansive soils or high water tables, build elsewhere.

### Money Bomb #2: Sins of the farmers

*"Our lot used to part of an apple orchard. After we bought the lot, we discovered the soil was contaminated with pesticides and will cost $50,000 to clean up!"*

Buying a new home in a subdivision that used to be a orchard or farm might sound romantic, but there is a dark side to that could turn an agrarian dream into a real-life nightmare: pesticide contamination.

How serious is the problem? The National Association of Home Builders raised the alarm about pesticide contamination in new home communities in an article titled "Sins of the Farmers" in a May 2001 article in *Builder* magazine. The article first noted how many subdivisions are being built on former farmland—in several Midwestern states, 50% to 70% of the total land developed for new homes from 1992 to 1997 was once farmland. The states with the highest percentage of farmland converted to housing include Illinois, Indiana, Louisiana and Iowa. While one would expect those Midwest states to be suspects, other states you might not think of (like Delaware, New Jersey, Ohio) have also had significant problems with this issue.

The key problem: almost all farmland has some level of pesticide contamination. In some cases, farmers used DDT and arsenic (among other long-banned substances) on their crops. The state of New Jersey has done the most research on this topic—the NJ Department of Environmental Protection in found that almost 5% of the state's entire land mass is polluted by pesticides from farms.

Anecdotal evidence suggests this topic is a huge potential liability for builders and home buyers—in Long Island, owners of million dollar homes that used to be part of a potato farm are suing a developer because of pesticide contamination, according to the *Builder* article. In Hayward North Carolina, the EPA declared a new 400 acre subdivision a Superfund site after discovering the soil was badly contaminated by a former farm.

So, what can you do to protect yourself? First, if you suspect your lot or subdivision is converted farmland, make sure the soil is tested for pesticides. Unfortunately, only a handful of states actually mandate such testing: California, Oregon, Idaho, Texas, Minnesota, Iowa, Illinois and South Carolina. A handful of other states only require "conditional testing" (that is, soil testing might be required, depending on the county or development): Arizona, Montana, South Dakota, Michigan, New York, Pennsylvania, Connecticut, Alaska and Delaware. Missouri has a "voluntary" program (one can imagine how effective *that* is).

Scary fact: 31 states require no testing at all for pesticides; that includes states like Indiana, Louisiana and Ohio that have large percentages of new homes built on converted farmland.

You'd think builders and developers would be rushing to sign up for soil testing, to avoid the huge potential liability of selling homes in subdivisions dubbed "Arsenic Acres" or "Lead Estates." Sadly, builders have actually fought testing requirements tooth and nail. The Builders League of South Jersey actually sued a local municipality over their strict testing rules. Fortunately, there is one party that is insisting on testing: lenders. Banks are now requiring builders do the soil tests for pesticides before they can get a loan.

What does a soil pesticide test cost? The minimum cost is about $600. Big sites (like a 100 acre subdivision) might cost a developer $7000. But those costs pale next to remediation—the bare minimum is $10,000 and those costs can soar into the six figures depending how much clean-up is required.

The big unknown with this issue is just how much contaminated farmland is out there. Fruit orchards (especially apple and peach orchards) seem to be high on the list of suspect properties. But other farms (sugar cane plantations, potato farms, golf courses) all might have had high doses of banned substances. One tip: if you suspect your lot or subdivision was a former farm, contact your local Department of Agriculture. They might have records as to what (and how much) pesticide were applied.

## Money Bomb #3: Impact fees

*"We were looking at land in a fast-growing community. Wow, we were shocked to learn that we would have to pay a $10,000 impact fee to build there."*

Impact fees are an insidious tax on new home buyers. The theory goes that new home buyers put extreme pressure on schools and other public services (parks, etc.). "Impact fees" are allegedly used to build new schools to accommodate an influx of newcomers. And they aren't insignificant amounts of money—in California, impact fees for a single new home can top $20,000 or $30,000.

Governments have grown fond of impact fees as a "painless" way to raise revenue without raising taxes on everyone. It's easy to tax a new home buyer, who has yet to even move to the area. It's also taxation without representation—how can you voice an objection to a tax when you're not around? Builders simply pass along impact fees in the form of higher sales prices for new homes.

Does the new home buyer solely benefit from new schools or parks? Of course not—existing citizens will also use these facilities, essentially for free since they don't have to pay any impact fees. What if you don't have children? You still have to pay an impact fee for local schools.

Impact fees also tend to raise the price of existing homes, a boon to those property owners. The simple fact is that impact fees are taxes to restrict growth. They also have the dual effect of making housing less affordable. An impact fee of $1700 on a $120,000 home prices 11,000 people out of the housing market.

Unfortunately, courts have upheld impact fees as constitutional. The result is that home buyers must pay if they want to live in a certain community.

Along with impact fees, consider all the "red tape" you must go through to build a home. Look back at the chart in Chapter 1 (Intro) which broke down the costs of an average new home. You'll note many of these expenses are for shuffling paper.

## The Bizarre World of Homeowners Associations

If you don't think the process of building a house is complete insanity, you probably haven't encountered a homeowners association yet.

Just what are these creatures? When subdivisions or communities are established, the developer may incorporate a series of "covenants, conditions and restrictions" (CCR's) on the lots. Most covenants are there to ensure a quality residential neighborhood. The rules may establish everything from how far you can build from your property lines (set-backs) to the minimum square footage allowed for new homes.

But who will enforce these rules? Enter the homeowners association. The association establishes a review board to look over future home plans to make sure they square with the rules.

Now, in a perfect world, this would work wonderfully. Covenants would be there to protect your property value—to prevent your neighbor from opening a truck stop. Benevolent associations would work diligently to enforce the covenants in a fair and consistent manner.

Unfortunately, this isn't a perfect world. The problem usually starts with the covenants—rules that are sometimes quite hysterical. Here's a sampling:

◆ Pornographic films, books or magazines in your home are prohibited by a Phoenix, Arizona, homeowners association.

◆ "Fat dogs" are outlawed in a Huntington Beach, California, community. Only pooches under 20 pounds are allowed.

◆ Basketball backboards must be the same color as the house, according to a Mission Viejo, California, association's rules.

As you'll note, California is a prime example of homeowner's associations run amok. "Orange County, CA has the distinction of having more homeowners associations than any place else on earth," said a recent article in the *Orange County Register*.

But the phenomena isn't limited to California. An estimated 47 million Americans live under the rules of homeowners associations, which are growing like a weed out of control—at last count, the U.S. had 231,000 associations. (In 1965, there were only 500.) New home buyers are more likely to fall under the spell of homeowners associations; about 50% of all the new homes sold today in major metropolitan areas fell within community associations.

When you build a home, you may enter the world of the association's "design standards." These are enforced by the omnipotent architectural review board or control committee. Fasten your seat belt—here's what you might expect to encounter:

◆ **Ambiguous design rules:** Here's an actual rule from a Colorado homeowners association's design standards: "A house must be in harmony with itself and its surroundings." Now what the heck does that mean? The ambiguous nature of many design rules may mean your home is rejected because it is not "harmonious." To comply with the above "rule," the association often asks home buyers to put in windows in their garages—at your expense, of course. How garage windows make a home in harmony with itself is beyond us.

◆ **Arbitrary enforcement:** With all those ambiguous rules, the door is left wide open to arbitrary and capricious enforcement of the covenants. In one case, an architectural board rejected a home because a board member didn't like the realtor involved in the project. The sheer volume of rules can sometimes lead to inconsistent decisions. Unfortunately, special exceptions to the rules are often granted to those with political pull.

◆ **Volunteer "control":** Most associations are run by volunteer homeowners, not paid professionals. This volunteer nature leads to high turnover of association officials. One result: inconsistent decisions on which houses are approved or rejected. Depending on the current political climate, your home could be rejected because of the roof color—despite the fact that a similar home was approved one month earlier. The reason? The new board has decided to enforce an obscure provision in the design standards. In some cases, the architectural review board has wide latitude to interpret the covenants.

How can you survive this process? First, find out what the covenants (sometimes also called declarations) are *before* you buy. You can get a copy from the homeowners association. Since these are also recorded with the county clerk, your buyer's broker can get a copy, too.

In addition, make sure you get a copy of any design standards or rules for new homes. At least that way you know what you're getting into before you invest money in a lot and design. Another wise move: Get a copy of the association's budget (usually available from the association's board members or management office). Is the association operating in the red? Are there proper reserves for emergencies? Associations that are losing money or have little or no reserves could be problematic.

Work the association like a smooth politician. Schmooze with the association's board members. Find out who's on the architectural review board and introduce yourself. Make sure they realize you're a nice person. Tell them you decided to build in the community because their covenants are a good protection for homeowners (they love hearing this).

Do some homework—if the association has a reputation for turning down homes (your buyer's broker should have some intelligence on this), ask the board the most common reasons why homes are rejected. Make sure your architect/designer understands the rules and the potential pitfalls—this lowers the chance of a rejection and the expense of revising your plans.

Despite the fascist and draconian tendencies of some homeowners associations, the fact is most buyers like communities that are governed by some type of covenants and restrictions. If you plan to resell your home sometime in the future, potential buyers may be reassured that their big investment will be protected to some degree.

Unless, of course, the buyer has a fat dog. But at least they'll like your garage windows.

# The Ugly Truth About Agents: Helping Hand Or Scum of the Earth?

**A** *ttention new home shoppers: want to raise the price of your home by $7650? And get nothing in return? All you need to do is make one simple call: to your friendly local real estate agent! Yes, they are dumber than a stump but that doesn't stop them from raking in a fat commission at YOUR expense!*

It's doubtful you'd ever see THAT ad in a glossy real estate magazine, but judging from the feedback we get from new homebuyers that is the ugly truth.

Dealing with real estate agents top the list of complaints we get from new homebuyers. When we open our email for this book (and trust us, we get a metric ton each week), the tales of woe involving agents who've wronged consumers flow like the business end of a fire hose.

To sum up, our readers tell us that FAR TOO MANY real estate agents are _____ (choose one):

**a) ignorant.**
**b) overpaid.**
**c) all of the above.**

Yep, the answer appears to be "C"– it seems like this country is overrun with real estate agents who are exceedingly stupid and paid far in excess of their worth.

So, you ask, just how ignorant are real estate agents? Let's take a look at a survey of agents who were trapped in their natural habitat (model homes of local builders), measured against the IQ of a rutabaga and then released harmlessly back into the confines of their leather-upholstered Lexus's. Don't worry: no agents were harmed in the making of this book.

The survey shows: three out of four Realtors NEVER graduated from college. Yes, you may be about to trust the biggest purchase of your life to someone who couldn't even figure out how to work his or her way through some back woods junior college.

Okay, to be fair, we should note that 87% of Realtors have had "some" college education but, as you can see, most never made it to graduation day. Yet, somehow, your average agent still manages to pull down $43,500 a year. So, we ask you: how many jobs out there pay over forty grand with only a high school education?

Now, we realize that you don't have to have a college degree to succeed in life and God bless those agents for finding a way to work for more than minimum wage. BUT, as agents like to point out, they are PROFESSIONALS. Like lawyers. Or architects. And they are here to help you with a VERY COMPLEX financial transaction (or so they constantly remind us).

The only flaw in this logic: all other professionals like lawyers or architects actually have to graduate from college. And then earn an advanced degree. And then study some more before they can become licensed to practice their specialty.

No wonder why they say the only license that is easier to get than a real estate agent license is . . . a driver's license.

# The Trolls of Real Estate

Now, we realize we probably just got crossed off the Christmas card list of the National Association of Realtors for that chapter intro, but we do have to thank NAR for one thing: they are the ones who did the above survey. Yes, Realtors (what agents who are members of NAR are called) did this random survey of 40,000 agents in 1999 to point out how smart their membership is. Since NAR only represents perhaps one third of the country's agents, we assume those non-Realtor agents out there might be even more intellectually challenged.

We think this survey speaks volumes—and it probably explains why we get are so many complaints about agents. The simple fact: there are MANY agents running around there that don't have a clue. And it's more than just a lack of a college education: agents seem to have a shocking lack of knowledge of the product they are selling (that is, homes).

Ask a real estate agent a simple question about new home construction and you're likely to get a blank stare. What are the pros or cons of a certain exterior finish like synthetic stucco? What brand of windows is the builder using? Should you upgrade the heating and ventilation system? The sad fact is that far too many agents have no understanding of the new home building process or even of rudimentary construction practices.

So, you might ask how did the Jar Jar Binks of real estate become so entrenched in the new home marketplace? After all, the vast majority of ALL homes sold in the U.S. and Canada involve one or more agents, eagerly awaiting their fat commission check at closing.

Agents would tell you it is their VAST knowledge of real estate that helps guide consumers through the maze of home buying. That's why they are so popular!

Guess again.

Our theory: agents are the trolls of real estate.

Like the hairy beast in the children's book that demands a toll to cross a bridge, Realtors control the INFORMATION that links sellers and buyers: the listings of homes for sale in a particular market. This information is locked away in the Holy Grail of real estate: The Multiple Listing Service (MLS). The MLS is the Realtors' exclusive database of homes for sale in a particular area. Want to find a home for sale? Well, you could search the classifieds or drive for hours in neighborhoods—but that MLS is such a quick and easy list of what's available! Conversely, as a seller, you could market your home yourself. But since 90% of all homes that sell are through the MLS, good luck.

Realtors guard the MLS like it is the Arc of the Covenant: they make sure the unwashed heathen (that is, you and me) can NEVER see it without help from the blessed (you guessed it—Realtors).

It's not so much that Realtors are indispensable to buying or selling a home—they've just rushed out there and built a toll bridge between you and that new home. Want to cross? You pay the fare—the $7650 in average agent commission that is added to EVERY new home.

# The Internet Battles the Troll

Fortunately, there is a way around the troll. What if you hopped in a helicopter and flew right by that hairy beast? Yes, your savior is a helicopter by the name of the World Wide Web.

The 'net is slowing revolutionizing in real estate—it holds the potential to directly connect buyers with sellers, eliminating the costly middlemen (that is, agents). Thanks to the 'net, Realtors' tight grip on listing information is starting to loosen.

Now, most agents don't have a clue about this oncoming tidal wave. They insist they do much more than just give buyers access to the MLS. And its true that the best agents do more for buyers: they negotiate contracts, troubleshoot problems and help close the deal. But the Internet shifts the balance of power to the consumer, since they will have instant access to listings, mortgage rates and even (eventually) online closings—and, hopefully, this will drive down the agent's sky-high commissions. The Realtors' days as gatekeepers to the American dream are numbered.

Sensing this reality, the National Association of Realtors has rushed onto the Internet to lay claim to this new frontier. That's because while individual Realtors may be one taco shy of a combo plate, NAR is incredibly shrewd: they launched Realtor.com as a way to corner the online listings market.

Yep, you read right—NAR is trying to make sure the ONLY place you can find new home listings is on THEIR web site. Which, of course, directs you to a friendly Realtor, ensuring their flow of big commissions will continue.

How has NAR done this? By "encouraging" their local boards to sign

EXCLUSIVE contracts to give their listings to Realtor.com—and no other web site. In some cities, like Dallas and Denver, if you want to look at listings of homes for sale, you can only find them at Realtor.com.

## So, what are the Realtors afraid of?

Two words: Bill Gates. When Microsoft started its Home Advisor web site (homeadvisor.msn.com), the Realtors feared Bill was going to horn in on their lucrative commission trade. While Microsoft's web site has been able to garner some listings, many local Realtor boards have blocked it. (Another NAR competitor, HomeSeekers.com, also has battled the Realtors for online listings).

The resulting fracas has caught the attention of the Federal Trade Commission, which in 2000 launched an investigation of NAR (and its online partner, HomeStore.com, which runs Realtor.com). The FTC ended its investigation in 2001 without filing any charges, but the Department of Justice put all parties on notice that it is watching the situation closely.

So, what does this mean for you, the homebuyer? Not much—no matter how much NAR schemes, moans and groans about the 'net, the digital Genie is out of the bottle. Information on the 'net has a funny way of squirting out in places you don't expect. Translation: the Realtors attempts to corner the home listing market are doomed to fail.

## Who really needs an agent?

Since most new home listings are available on the 'net, you may ask, "Who really needs an agent anyway?" Good question.

We think the following three categories of homebuyers may need the help of a real estate agent:

◆ **First-time buyers.** Yes, if you have never bought a home before, this can all look very scary. The "hand-holding" function of agents may be most appropriate here.

◆ **Out-of-state or relocating buyers.** As you remember from this book's introduction, we think this group of buyers should NOT buy a new home because of the scams and rip-offs that can trip up even the most experienced out-of-state buyer. Yet, if you insist, this would be another case where you would need the experienced knowledge of an agent to help out.

◆ **Folks who have no time.** Yes, we realize some professionals who are pulling down 60 or 70-hour workweeks have little time for this real estate stuff. Delegating this task to an agent may be the only way to accomplish the deal.

Yet, in ALL these cases, we don't think homebuyers should hire just any agent. Nope, we recommend an EXCLUSIVE buyer' agent. What's that you ask? Don't all agents work for a buyer? Ah, you've stumbled upon the biggest myth of all about real estate agents. Let's take a closer look at this.

# Biggest Myth about Real Estate Agents: The Agent Is Working for You.

*Myth: "We looked for a new home with a local real estate agent. She asked for our price range and income level. Later, when we found a house, we were shocked when we learned that the agent had disclosed this personal information to the builder! Wasn't the agent representing our interests?"*

NO! In almost all cases, real estate agents do NOT work for you, the buyer. Their boss is the seller—the builder in the case of a new home. The builder pays their commission.

So what does that mean in the real world? Despite how sweet the agent is to you, they are LEGALLY and ETHICALLY required to do the following:

◆ Negotiate the highest price and best terms for the *builder.*

◆ Disclose all known financial information about you to the builder. If you tell them you can really afford a $275,000 home but you'd like to bid $265,000, the agent must tell the builder. If you tell the agent your annual salary or net worth, that information is also passed right to the builder/seller.

◆ In some states, the agents are not required to tell you about any defects or negative aspects about the home. While most agents are required to be "fair" to both builder/seller and buyer, they don't have to tell you that a school down the street is about to close. Or that the home's foundation was designed without an engineer. Or that the builder has lost several lawsuits over defective construction.

Were you unaware of this? You're not alone. A 1980's study by the Federal Trade Commission revealed that 71% of new homebuyers thought "their" real estate agent was representing their interests. A Consumer Federation of America survey in 1990 showed that "only 30% of American adults know that real estate agents usually legally represent the seller only." That means two out of every three homebuyers are being duped into thinking the agent is working and negotiating for them.

As one observer told the *Wall Street Journal* recently, working with a real estate agent is "like working with an attorney who represents the defendant—and you're the plaintiff!"

# The Dangerous Consequences of This Myth

Believing this myth is hazardous to your health for two reasons:

**1** **You may disclose sensitive financial information to the agent.** Only a fool would reveal information that could damage your effort to negotiate effectively with a builder. But that's exactly what millions of Americans do when they talk with real estate agents. Reveal your income to the agent (who relays this to the builder) and the builder may hold out in the negotiation because he thinks you're loaded.

**2** **You may be duped into spending too much for your new home.** As we'll explain later, if you use a typical real estate agent, you'll add $7650 to the price of the average home and get absolutely nothing in return. The agent has an economic incentive (a higher commission) to get you to pay the most amount of money possible for the new home.

## How This Myth Spread

The myth that real estate agents are on your (the buyer's) side has become entrenched in consumers' psyche for several reasons. To understand why 70% of consumers misunderstand this crucial point, here's some background on how this sorry situation developed.

◆ **First, for all practical purposes, there are two types of traditional real estate agents: a listing agent and a selling agent.** The listing agent does just that—lists the property. It's his or her name on the sign out in front. This agent works with the seller/builder, getting all the information on the home and perhaps providing a few marketing tips, pricing advice and so on.

Of course, getting a house listed is just half the battle. The goal is to sell it. Enter the selling agent. That's the agent who finds and "works" with the buyer. He or she may show you several prospective homes. If you decide to buy, the selling agent presents the offer to the builder's listing agent and helps with the paperwork.

The selling agent is often called a "sub-agent" or "cooperating agent": that's because the selling agent is "cooperating" (a nice euphemism) with the seller/builder. That cooperation isn't voluntary—agency law in most states MANDATES whom an agent must work on behalf of. Unless otherwise agreed, the agent is ALWAYS working for the builder/seller.

You may note at this point that the score is 2-0. The seller has two agents working for him. You've got zip—no one to negotiate on your behalf and look out for your interests.

Both agents essentially split the commission on a new home, which runs a whopping 5% to 7% of the sales price. On a $300,000 home, that commission in real dollars is $15,000 to $21,000. (We should note that some builders do not use listing agents; instead they offer to pay the agent who finds a buyer a 3% commission). What does all that money buy you? We'll tell you later in this chapter. (Hint: not much.).

◆ **Law enforcement of disclosure requirements zaps consumers.**
Did you know that 43 states have laws that require real estate agents to disclose to you that they are working for the seller/builder? If this is so, how come only 30% of homebuyers know this fact?

The answer lies in the type of disclosure that a state requires. The Consumer Federation of America (CFA) recommends that agent disclosure requirements meet four tests:

◆ **WRITTEN.** "Verbal disclosures are not adequate because, among other reasons, their absence can rarely be proven, so that there is no way to ensure compliance with the requirement," CFA says.

◆ **ON A STANDARD FORM.** This "assures that a written disclosure is not made in complex legal language that is unintelligible to most home buyers."

◆ **SIGNED BY THE HOMEBUYER.** If you have to sign it, the theory goes that you might also read it.

◆ **MADE AT THE FIRST SUBSTANTIVE CONTACT OR MEETING.** If agents could wait until the closing or some later date to tell you they work for the builder, you may unknowingly disclose important information about yourself early in the game. Forcing agents to disclose their true allegiance up front is the only way to level the playing field.

So how many states require such "complete" disclosure as recommended by the Consumer Federation of America? Out of the original 43 states with disclosure laws, only seven meet that test: New York, Louisiana, Massachusetts, New Hampshire, Texas, Idaho and the District of Columbia.

The other states fall somewhat short. Some require written disclosure but no buyer signature. Others require disclosure but have no standard form. Hence, weak disclosure laws are often as much protection as nothing at all.

◆ **The propaganda war.** Real estate agents have been working overtime to convince homebuyers that they MUST use an agent to purchase that new home. Or else, they will catch the black plague and die a slow, painful death.

Agents spend vast sums of marketing dollars on slick advertising campaigns trying to portray themselves as indispensable. While these campaigns are warm and fuzzy, agents take a much harder line when it comes to pitching builders on listing their new homes: list with us or pay the consequences. The bottom line: builders are blackmailed into using agents. Many have told us so off the record. Negative comments about agents are always off the record, since builders live in perpetual fear of having the source for three out of every four customers dry up.

You can easily see the dilemma that builders face. If you have a spec home for sale and want to list it in the MLS, you must hire an agent. If 80% of new homebuyers are using agents, why fight it?

Of course, some builders openly court real estate agents to bring in homebuyers. How? Incentives and contests (read: bribes) are a common tactic today. For example, one homebuilder near Austin, Texas offered a free two-year lease on a new Mercedes E320 to any real estate agent who brought in the most sales. Other agents were offered $200 coupons for each prospect they brought to the builder's model—those coupons were redeemable for $1000 in cool cash if the prospect bought a home. And you wondered why that real estate agent is just dying to show you this great new home community?

Builders simply pass along the agent's hefty commission in the form of higher home prices. That translates into thousands of dollars "built" right into the home's price. But what does that money buy you from a consumer's perspective? The biggest rip-off of all new home rip-offs—the $7650 "taxicab ride."

## MONEY BOMBS

**Money Bomb #1: The $7650 taxicab ride.**
*Yes, it's the mother of all new house scams. The $7650 that you pay for what is essentially a taxicab ride.*

First of all, you might ask, where did that $7650 figure come from? That's how much a real estate agent is paid by a builder for selling the average $226,680 home (see chart from Chapter 1 for more details).

Most builders will pay a 3% commission to a real estate agent for "finding" a buyer for a new home. But that figure can go higher—if there are TWO agents involved (one to "list" the home and another "find" the buyer), the total commission could be 6% or more.

The numbers can be staggering. If you're buying a $300,000 home, the commission if one agent were involved would total $9000, Get two agents involved and you're out $18,000. Nearly all builders pass along every penny of those figures in the form of higher sales prices.

You may be asking, what exactly do real estate agents do for that money (which comes from your pocket)? Good question.

Do they negotiate with the builder to get you a better deal? Nope, the traditional agent is bound by law to get the highest price for the builder, not for you, the homebuyer. Does the agent make sure the home is designed and built with quality materials? No again. Most agents have absolutely no knowledge of new construction—they couldn't tell a floor joist from a roof truss. Is the foundation designed correctly? Who knows? Agents wouldn't know a proper foundation if it hit them in the face. Do agents visit the site to check or inspect the construction? No way. The only time you see an agent is at the closing—to collect the commission check.

The only thing agents really do for you is give you a ride to meet the builder. The agent may give you a tour of the builder's model home or show you some of his previously built homes. Whoopee. If you can drive, you don't need a real estate agent to find a builder. Take the real estate agent's bait and you've just spent $7650 for a taxicab ride.

## The Free Upgrade Dance

Astute readers at this point may wonder, "If I don't use an agent, will builders lower their price accordingly?" The answer is yes and no. Savvy builders will want to keep the agent's commission as extra profit. You obviously want all the commission—either in a lower sales price or in "upgrades" that equal the commission. And there's another factor—if word gets around town that builders are selling directly to consumers at lower prices, they will be history. Agents will collectively string up these builders and leave them for dead at the edge of town. And for the average builder who gets 80% of his buyers through agents, openly giving consumers discounts is a risky move.

So enter the Free Upgrade Dance. This is most relevant for buyers of semi-custom homes or partially built "spec" houses by custom builders. If you're going the pure "custom" route (buying the land, hiring an architect

## AGENTS CLAIM THEY AREN'T LIVING THE HIGH LIFE

When we complain about the fat commissions that agents earn for selling a new home, many agents pitch a fit. They point out that just because a builder may pay a 3% commission that doesn't mean the AGENT actually gets all that money. Nope, some agents must split that commission with one or more brokers at their home office. Other agents must pay franchisee management fees (the RE/MAX company works that way). If there is a "listing" agent on the property (which adds ANOTHER 3% commission to the list price), they have to pay to advertise the property, host open houses, etc.

We say "big deal." Just because real estate agents must share their bounty with head brokers in their office doesn't mean squat—the entire system of home buying is set up to enrich brokers and other bit players for very little work.

And one thing many real estate agents don't advertise is the side deals they get to fatten their paychecks. You might be surprised to learn that the special mortgage broker your agent recommends is giving a kickback to the agent. Or that the title insurance/escrow company who is closing your deal just so happens to be owned by . . . your real estate agent—and the agent (or his company) gets a cut of closing fees and title insurance payments. So, we find it hard to cry for agents. They aren't hurting for cash.

and a builder), it's doubtful you'll have a real estate agent involved.

The first "step" of the Free Upgrade Dance is to learn the "creative accounting" maneuver. Since a builder can't lower the price, perhaps he could give you $7650 more house? That way the builder still sells you the house for the "list price," albeit with nicer stuff inside. Now you've started what we call the Free Upgrade Dance.

A builder may offer you a series of "free" upgrades. Essentially, this is a cat-and-mouse game where you haggle over possible options—upgraded carpeting, a garage door opener, ceiling fan, etc.

Be careful. Shrewd builders may try to take advantage of your naivete. If you don't know how much a basic ceiling fan costs, they may try to convince you the ceiling fan is worth $400. This becomes like a bizarre version of "The Price is Right." If you do your homework, you know the average ceiling fan costs about $175. Unless the builder is giving you an expensive brand such as Casablanca (these cost $300 or more), you should haggle the price down closer to $175.

Oh, sure, the builder may say his price includes "installation." While this may be true, you might want to check to see if this is a good deal. Contact local stores to find out not only what items cost but also what delivery and installation may run. You may discover you can get several "builder options" installed less expensively on your own.

It's easy to determine the true costs of some upgrades. Programmable thermostats are available at any hardware store, for example. Other upgrades are more difficult to estimate—if the builder offers to finish part of the basement, how much does that cost? This common upgrade costs about $15-$20 per square foot—hence a 1000 square-foot basement would run $15,000 to $20,000 to finish. Of course, finding out these prices is a little tricky (you may have to call other builders or remodelers for cost estimates).

Would you like to move a wall to make a bedroom bigger? This is even fuzzier in terms of costs.

What if a builder REFUSES to give you any upgrades? Yes, in some markets, builders won't do the upgrade dance—if you don't bring an agent to the table, they'll just take that money for themselves, thank you very much.

If this happens, then we recommend hiring a BUYER'S agent and having them negotiate the transaction for you. Our philosophy: if the builder won't budge on upgrades, then he'll have to pay a 3% commission to a buyer's agent who will negotiate the best price and terms for you. The builder will wish he did the upgrades for free.

The bottom line: NOT using a real estate agent when buying a new home could mean free upgrades worth thousands of dollars. We believe that $7650 belongs in your new home, not an agent's bank account.

**Money Bomb #2: Builders who use "exclusive" contracts with agents.**
*"We saw a 'spec' home that is under construction. Can we approach the builder directly and save the real estate agent's commission?"*

## Email from the Real World: The $9000 Cup of Coffee

*"The other day I ran into a real estate agent at a coffee shop. She was having lunch with a builder, who introduced himself and asked about our project. Over coffee, we discussed the home and hit it off. After hiring the builder, however, we discovered the agent was demanding the builder pay her a 3% commission or $9000 since she "introduced" the builder to us. We hadn't ever hired this agent! All we did was speak to her ONCE over the phone—we never looked at any homes with her! She didn't negotiate the contract nor do anything else on the deal. We feel like we just spent $9000 on a cup of coffee!"*

Yes, that's a true story from North Carolina. In the strange world of real estate, a mere introduction at a coffee shop makes some agents believe they are entitled to a HUGE commission. Crazy, eh? Unfortunately, most builders simply pass this along to the home-buyer in the form of higher home prices. The lesson: if you do NOT plan on using an agent to find a builder, don't accept ANY advice or referrals from them. And pass up the opportunity to have "coffee" with any agent and a builder.

Well, yes and no. While the Free Upgrade Dance sounds easy to master, there is another hidden "money bomb" in the process: the "exclusive" contract some builders have with real estate agents.

Basically, an "exclusive right to sell" listing means the agent gets a commission even if the builder sells the home directly and the agent plays no role. The listing agent rakes in the entire commission, since there is no "co-op" or selling agent involved! Isn't that a great deal? Now you see why many real estate agents steer buyers toward their own listings—big-time profits.

The key to avoiding this money bomb is to simply contact the builder directly (the building company sign should be in front of the home—if not, check the building permit, which must be posted on the job site). If the builder gives you the bad news that the home is under an "exclusive" contract and he can't sell it to you directly with free upgrades, move on to Plan B.

Offer to buy the house with the agent getting a lower commission, say 3%. Keep the price the same, just have the builder throw in upgrades to equal the other 3% of the commission. (Ask what the commission rate is—it can range from 5% to 7%.)

This is a fair compromise since that's about what the listing agent would get if you were a "standard" buyer who came with another agent. Of course, the real estate agent will probably squeal bloody murder. "How can you do this?" they'll shout with arms flailing wildly.

Reasoning with the agent may be difficult, depending on the market. You might point out that if the agent would like, you could go out there and find another agent to share his or her commission. If all else fails, use a "buyer's agent," which we'll describe later. If you must pay full commission, you should at least have someone on your side of the negotiating table.

We should note that not all builders have "exclusive right to sell" deals with agents. A few builders use "exclusive agency" deals. "What's the difference?" you might say. "They sound the same."

Actually, there's a big difference. "Exclusive agency" contracts give the builder the right to sell the home directly to consumers and pay no commission to the agent. A small semantic difference, but a big difference to you. "Open listings" also let the builder sell the home directly to you. Frankly, these arrangements are quite uncommon—agents must be rather desperate for business to go this route.

### Money Bomb #3: Illegal kickbacks.

*"We used a real estate agent to purchase a new home. He strongly recommended we use a certain title company and mortgage broker. Later, we learned the agent was getting a kickback. The result was we got bilked out of $2000."*

Ever wonder why real estate agents "strongly recommend" you use a particular title company, mortgage broker, or inspector? Agents love to tell you that they have "special" relationships with lenders and title companies that will speed a mortgage application or get your home special attention.

Federal authorities and scammed consumers are now discovering just how "special" those relationships are. Illegal kickbacks to real estate agents are bilking consumers out of thousands of dollars in "under the table" deals.

According to a recent *Washington Post* column by Kenneth Harney, "institutionalized kickbacks are so blatant, according to one federal official, that [illegal payments] are the accepted way of doing business at some (real estate) firms."

Here's how they work. Mortgage brokers face "routine demands ... to split a portion of their fees with individual realty agents who recommend them to home buyers." The agent gets one-half to one percent of the mortgage as a "referral fee." For a $250,000 mortgage, that could mean a $2500 kickback to the real estate agent. Who pays for this extra "point"? Who do you think?

Of course, these kickbacks never show up on settlement or truth-in-lending disclosures—a blatant violation of federal law. Another version of the scam is agents who demand kickbacks from title companies. "In one case, a title company admitted paying $120,000 to $130,000 under the table to the head of one real estate brokerage firm over the last several years. The [title company] explained that 'It was the only way we'd get the title work', according to the investigators."

How widespread is the problem? Well, federal investigators have uncovered so many violations in one area (the Philadelphia/Washington, D.C. corridor) that they issued over 100 subpoenas to real estate agents and others. "Loan brokers in California, the Southwest and the Midwest have reported similar, aggressive [kickback] demands."

Consumers pay for these kickbacks in higher fees for mortgages and title company services. Does every agent get kickbacks? Of course not. But the widespread disease of kickbacks by shady agents has one clear message for consumers: do not solely follow the advice of the agent when it comes to a loan, inspection, or title/closing service. Shop around and compare to make sure you're not getting taken for a ride.

And the problem is more than just with kickbacks. Any home inspector who is "too honest" in his or her reports about homes may soon find themselves on the unemployment line. Example: Surety Property Inspections, a Riverside, California home inspector, was driven out of business by angry real estate agents who thought the inspectors told buyers too much about the homes they were buying.

### Money Bomb #4: Creeping commissions

*"We hired a buyer's agent to find an empty lot in Northern Virginia. When we found the right spot, she drew up a contract and slipped in a two page document with a clause that said 'the broker is entitled to three percent of the sales price plus any improvements.' She claimed this was for her 'advice and expertise' she will be offering throughout the construction. But we never intended to use her advice in the building phase! When we asked if this an optional service, she reluctantly said yes but she wanted the full commission."*

We call this "commission creep"—when you hire a real estate agent to do Task A and they suddenly expand the work that needs to be done. Why does this happen? Well, if the agent makes a 3% commission on a $100,000 lot, that's $3000. BUT, if you build a $300,000 house (for a total purchase price of $400,000), the agent would earn $12,000. So, what would you want to earn—$3000 or $12,000? The answer is the reason why some agents want to do much more than just search for raw land for you to build a house on.

## Our Recommendation: Use a Buyer's Agent

If you're going the "power home buyer" route (buying the land, hiring a design professional and then choosing a builder), we do recommend you use a real estate agent for one part of the process—purchasing the lot or building site. Also, if you feel uncomfortable dealing directly with large, production builders, using a real estate agent may put your mind at ease.

Of course, we don't recommend just any agent. You should seek out a "buyer's agent." What the heck is that, you say? A buyer's agent is a real estate agent who is working for you, not the seller. He or she is legally responsible for the following:

◆ Negotiating the best price and terms for the *buyer*.
◆ Identifying any negatives of the property or neighborhood—beyond what a seller must disclose.
◆ Offering to do a comparative market analysis to compare this property to others in the area.
◆ Possibly negotiating for properties that are for sale by owner or not even on the market.

Who pays the buyer's agent's commission? It might surprise you to learn that, in most cases, it's the seller or builder. The typical commission on a home sale (that is paid by the seller) is split between the listing agent and the buyer's agent—just like a standard transaction. Some buyers actually prefer to directly pay the buyer's agent a flat fee. This completely eliminates the conflict of interest so apparent in many real estate deals: the higher the sales price, the higher the agent's commission.

We recommend a buyer's agent in the following situations:

**1** If you're building from scratch and are purchasing a lot, a buyer's agent is probably the best source to find available land. A buyer's agent can dig for facts that might provide valuable negotiating tools—such as what the seller previously paid for the lot. Finding out how long a property has been on the market and how desperate a seller is also will give you an advantage.

**2** If you're moving into a new area and want to buy a new home, a buyer's agent may tell you the truth about certain neighborhoods and builders. In Tucson, Arizona, a buyer's agent told a retired couple to pass up a certain home after he found out that the neighbor's teenagers enjoyed loud rock-and-roll music at 2 a.m. Moving to a new town makes you extremely vulnerable to unscrupulous seller's agents who will take advantage of your naivete regarding neighborhoods, traffic and anything else they can think of. A buyer's agent evens the odds.

**3** Say you want to purchase a new home, but don't have the time to wait. Construction on a new home can take three to six months or longer—and that doesn't include the time to design the plans, buy the lot and so on. If you're in a hurry, a buyer's agent can show you new "spec" or production homes that are nearing completion.

## Buyer's Agents: What Will It Cost You?

In the old days (that is, the 1980's), buyer's agents used to charge consumers a retainer or flat fee to search for a home. That's just about disappeared today. Instead, most buyer's agents get paid the same way "traditional" agents get paid: the commission paid by the seller or builder. Yes, a few (perhaps less than 1%) of builders or sellers refuse to pay a buyer's agent commission, but it is a rare occurrence.

So, the short answer to the "What Will It Cost You?" question is:

### Going It Alone: Home Listings on the 'Net

If you plan to forgo an agent, there are several good web sites to find builders and new home listings. The first (and most obvious) is the National Association of Home Builder's site, Homebuilder.com. The site lets you search for new home listings, lots, builders, planned communities, custom builders and more. There are also more general sites (see Fig. 1 on the next page) for home listings: Realtor.com (as mentioned at the beginning of this chapter), Microsoft's Home Advisor (homeadvisor.msn.com) as well as HomeSeekers (www.homeseekers.com). The last one is a dark horse in the home listings race, but has an impressive search function.

**Figure 1:** No you don't have to use a real estate agent to find new home listings. The 'net can be a big help—these three sites (HomBuilder.com, HomeSeekers.com and HomeAdvisor.com) each offers a plethora of listings.

nothing. Buyer's agents add no additional cost to a new home—as long as the builder was planning to pay a commission to an agent anyway. And that's the rub: if you approach the builder without an agent, you may be able to do the free upgrade dance (as explained earlier in this chapter).

## Sources to Find Buyer's Agents

Unfortunately, real estate agents that exclusively represent buyers are not on every corner in the nation. A recent survey by the National Association of Realtors put their numbers at about 56,000. While that sounds like a big number of buyer agents, remember that there are some 700,000 real estate agents trolling around the U.S. Odds are, out of 100 agents you run into, only eight would be exclusive buyer agents.

And there are isolated pockets of resistance, where traditional agents still try to fight the concept by blocking buyer's agents from advertising in local publications or (at the very worst) actually sabotaging deals, as you'll read later. Here are some sources for finding an exclusive buyer agent in your area:

**1** **Buyer's Resource** (800) 359-4092 (web: www.buyersresource. com) This Denver-based company has 70 offices in 25 states that specialize in buyer's agents. If you don't live in one of those states, they also have a referral network of over 4000 buyer's agents across the country. There's no charge for a referral and the company will answer any questions you have about the buyer's agent process.

**2** **The National Association of Exclusive Buyer Agents** (NAEBA) will give you a local referral to a buyer's agent. Their number is (800) 986-2322. NAEBA's web site (www.naeba.com) is reviewed in the next section.

## Email from the Real World: Double Dealing

**A reader form North Carolina tells how a real estate agent undercut his efforts to buy a lot**

*"I recently visited a golf course community in North Carolina. I found a lot on the 18th hole I really liked and went to the on-site real estate office to discuss it with their agent. The agent and I went back to the lot to discuss how a new home could be sited on the lot; I asked what the procedure was for holding the lot. He said it would take a $500 deposit and there were seven builders to choose from. The agent informed me that one of the builders has an office in the clubhouse and is there daily. I told the agent I'd think it over and return the next day.*

*Upon my return, I went to look at the lot again. While I was looking around, a man drove up and asked if I was interested in the any of the lots. Turns out this is the builder who has an office at the clubhouse. Here's the kicker: he told he just bought the lot I wanted that morning! The agent had tipped him off that I was seriously considering it and he wanted to make sure he was going to be contractor!"*

This story points up why you should be very careful when discussing any property purchase with an agent. Some will scheme behind your back, double-dealing by tipping off a builder to your interest. It's best to hold your cards very close to your chest.

**Figure 2:** NAEBA's web site provides an easy way to find local buyer's agents in your area.

# New Homebuyers in Cyberspace: What's on the Web?

### National Association of Exclusive Buyer Agents

**Web:** www.naeba.com, see Figure 2 on the next page.

**What's cool:** In the old days, finding an agent who exclusively represented buyers took some detective work. Now, with a few mouse clicks on this web site, you can get several names in seconds. NAEBA's web site may not have extensive content, but the easy search function lets you select a city and state and then poof! Instant contacts, including agent's phone, email and web site address. We also like this site's list of questions to ask a real estate agent, as well as helpful links to related sites.

**Needs work:** Parts of this site are still unfinished, despite being live for several years. While there is some helpful material on finding an agent, we wish there were more. It's nice to read NAEBA's discussion of its legal battles with the National Association of Realtors over "dual agency," but no explanation in layman's terms of what the fuss is all about.

## Questions to Ask

**1** **How long have you been a buyer's agent?** While buyer's agency is still a relatively new phenomenon, some agents have more experience than others do.

**2** **Do you ever represent sellers?** The best buyer's agents are those who do this exclusively—they don't represent buyers on Mondays and sellers on Tuesdays. Exclusive buyer agents don't accept listings nor do they ever accept "sub-agency" commissions, thus representing the seller.

**3** **Does your firm take listings from sellers?** Ideally, the best situation is a buyer's agent who works for a firm that only does buyer's brokerage. The reality is that some buyer's agents work within "traditional" firms that also take listings from sellers. The problem, as is often the case with traditional agents, is that the agent might only push the firm's listings. The conflict of interest is obvious, and you should steer clear of anyone who claims to be a buyer's agent and then pitches you on his or her firm's seller listings.

## Email from the Real World: Beware of "registration" cards

*"I just found out that because I looked at a few model homes myself a few months ago and signed an 'information card' to get a brochure and the floor plans, the builder's sales representatives may refuse to share the commission with any future buyer's agent for a period of six months! The builder claims: why should he pay a finder's fee if I came in on my own? I wasn't even serious about buying a house then!"*

Yes, you've stumbled on a subtle rip-off with some builders—the innocent looking information or registration card. At many model homes, salespeople ask you to sign their guest book or fill out a card before you can see their models. While that sounds simple enough, watch out! By doing this without a buyer agent present, the builder may refuse to pay a buyer agent's commission if you later buy a home. That means you might have to pay for buyer representation out of your OWN pocket. The best course: don't sign ANYTHING when you visit a model home. Or give the salesperson a bogus name and address.

**4** **Can I have a written agreement?** True buyer's agents will provide a written agreement covering compensation and their responsibilities to you. Get in writing the agent's commitment to renounce sub-agency commissions (in which the agent represents the seller).

**5** **What are the pluses and minuses of a certain neighborhood?** If you've already identified a few potential locations for your new home, ask the agent about the pros AND cons of certain areas. A true buyer's agent will candidly lay it on the line.

**6** **Can you recommend a good inspector who is familiar with new construction, the local building code, and common defects?** This is a trick question—a good buyer's agent should give you not just one name but several possible candidates. Be aware that finding a good inspector who knows what he or she is doing is a very difficult challenge for many buyer's agents—there are so many inspectors who are used to rubber-stamping homes in order to curry favor with seller's agents.

**7** **What type of negotiation training do you have?** The fact is you're hiring someone to negotiate a very expensive purchase for you—it'd be nice if that person had some professional training in negotiation. Another good question: what training did you have in general as a buyer's agent? Any training in identifying the negatives of a property as well as the positives? Sure, it's easy to talk up the amenities of a piece of land or new home. The real pros are trained to spot weaknesses and talk frankly about them.

**8** **What designations do you have?** Yes, just about anyone can get a real estate license . . . but the best agents also have earned special designations like "Graduate Realtor Institute" (GRI). This requires agents to go through 90 hours of classroom instruction on residential real estate subjects. Another designation to look for: CRS (Certified Residential Specialist) or ABR (Accredited Buyer Representative). Asking about an agent's designations (they are usually noted on the agent's business card) is a good way to weed out part-timers and others who are just "dabbling" in real estate as a hobby. Only one out of four agents holds a GRI, according to a recent survey by the National Association of Realtors.

**9** **Will you keep my financial information and price range confidential?** Of course, this is a trick question. Any true buyer's agent is legally bound to keep this information confidential. However, traditional agents MUST disclose this to a seller. Any alleged "buyer's agent" who says he or she must disclose your information to the seller is not really a buyer's agent. They're frauds.

**10** Could I have the names of three to five of your most recent customers? Call these past customers to see whether the buyer's agent is fulfilling his promises.

**11** Is there a way to cancel our agreement? Some buyer's agents try to lock you into a long-term contract for their services. Why? They want to make sure that if you buy a home (with their help or on your own), they get a commission. That's nice, but there should be an "out" or cancellation clause. If you are unhappy with their efforts in finding a home or lot, you should be able to give them fair notice (a week or so) and cancel the agreement.

## CONTROVERSY: WHERE SHOULD THE MONEY COME FROM?

There is a split opinion in the buyer's agent ranks as to "where" the money should come from for their services. If you buy a $200,000 home and the buyer's agent wants a 3% commission, who pays it? Does the seller pay this out of the home's proceeds? Or does the buyer write out a separate check?

Philosophically, all the money comes from you, the homebuyer. So, we're less concerned with reality than with the semantics. And those semantics are crucial because they have important financial and tax considerations.

In the real world, the seller pays the buyer's agent commission about 99% of the time. That means your purchase of a $200,000 home is contingent on the seller paying your buyer's agent a 3% commission. This is good for a couple of reasons:

◆ **Most sellers don't mind.** Interestingly, more than 80% of sellers think all agents who work with buyers are "buyer's agents"! And, of course, they're used to paying for the agent who finds a buyer. The reality is most sellers are happy to talk with any agent (even a buyer's agent) who finds a qualified buyer.

◆ **If the commission is part of the purchase price, you can finance it with your mortgage.** If you pay it out of your own pocket, you can't. Detractors of this practice say it builds a "conflict of interest" into the deal—the bigger the price, the higher the agent's commission. But isn't he supposed to negotiate the lowest price? Shouldn't the money come from the buyer's wallet, instead of the seller's proceeds?

The reality is that buyer's agents make their living from representing buyers—if they don't do a good job (say, not negotiating the best price), they don't stay in business long. A good buyer's agent would rather trade off the slightly lower commission and get new client referrals from that buyer.

Flat fees and "target price" commissions paid by the buyer are nice but rarely used in the real world. Most buyer's agents work on a "traditional" commission of the actual purchase price—that comes from the builder/seller. If you find one that offers a flat fee or target price option, that's fine as well.

Granted, you also may be in an area where buyer's brokerage is so new that builders/sellers and their agents are balking at sharing or paying commissions to a buyer's agent. Most nettlesome are greedy "traditional" agents who want the entire 6% to 7% for themselves—refusing to pay buyer's agents the typical split. They argue, "why should we pay someone working against our interests?" Fortunately, this is the exception and occurs only in a few places.

By the way, there is one exception to the rule of the seller paying the buyer's agent commission: In northern Virginia, buyer's agents must be paid out of the selling agent's commission (not from the seller, directly).

## Money Bombs with Buyer's Agents

**Money Bomb #1: Dual agents.**
*"We hired a buyer's agent who then tried to pitch us on a listing by another agent at his firm. He said he couldn't act as our agent on that property—he could only be a dual agent. Is this a rip-off or what?"*

We believe it's a definite rip-off.

What the heck is a dual agent, anyway? Think of a spy thriller—the dual or double agent was always working for BOTH sides. In the end, they owed their loyalty to no one. While double agents might add some spice to a James Bond movie, they are nothing but trouble in real estate.

A "dual agent" is a new euphemism used by real estate agents when they pitch you a property listed by a fellow agent in their firm. Dual agents (also known as "facilitators," "designated agents" or "transactional agents,") allegedly represent BOTH the seller and the buyer. Are they kidding? This is a hostile negotiation in which the seller wants to get the highest price and to disclose the least amount of negative information. A buyer wants the lowest price and needs to know all the flaws. How can an agent play both sides? Dual agency is just an easy way for an agent to keep that fat commission and represent no one (except, perhaps themselves).

Dual agency is a cancer that's spreading fast in the new home market—a recent survey by the National Association of Realtors (NAR) revealed more than HALF of all agents (53%) are "switch hitters." These agents practice seller agency, buyer agency and dual agency. (Not so coincidentally, NAR has been lobbying state legislatures to let agents practice more dual agency, a practice most consumer advocates find harmful). It seems like agents want to have their cake and eat it too, representing buyers only when it is convenient for them. Interestingly, that same survey revealed a paltry 8% of agents practice EXCLUSIVE buyer agency. The message: when an agent says they represent buyers, ask them if they exclusively represent buyers 100% of the time. Given the statistics, it may take a little extra effort to find an exclusive buyer's agent, but just do it.

## Email from the Real World: Agent Fails to Present Offer

*"We offered to buy a new home for a few thousand under the $263,000 list price, plus we wanted the builder to seed the lawn. The builder accepted our offer, but refused to do the lawn. We told the agent we had to have the lawn. Our agent goes back to the builder and says we can't afford the home! We decided to fire her the next day!"*

*"We didn't use a buyer's agent, but just the regular real estate agent who represents the builder. We had wanted to put in an offer $3000 less than we did, but the agent said she would not submit it because it was too low! So, we offered $3000 more and were accepted. Later we were told it was illegal for the agent to not submit our offer. Is this true?"*

Yes, the agent broke the law. Real estate agents MUST submit all offers to builders, no matter how low or ridiculous the terms. If this happens to you during your home search, we would immediately fire the real estate agent and look for another. We'd also file a complaint with your state's real estate commission. The agent could lose their license over such misconduct.

In the first case, this agent's behavior was appalling. NO buyer's agent should EVER refuse to negotiate a counter-offer. Nor should they make any statement about your ability to afford a home to a builder.

We should point out that agents and salespeople might have an incentive to twist your arm into offering more money. Some builders practice something called "Profit Sensitive Compensation." Basically, if the agent or salesperson sells the home for full price, they get their commission PLUS a bonus. If the agent writes the offer for LESS than full price, they don't get the bonus—plus their commission may be cut substantially.

The bottom line: don't let an agent or salesperson pressure you into offering a certain price for the home. Bid what YOU think it is worth and insist the offer be presented.

## Money Bomb #2: Turf battles

*"A buyer's agent found us a wonderful new home—we decided to make a bid. The builder's agent discouraged the builder from taking our offer, saying that our buyer's agent was unethical and a sleaze-ball! What happened?"*

Welcome to the turf battles in the real estate business. Some traditional agents have resisted buyer's agents to the point of trying to sabotage deals. This can range from small-time harassment (such as accidentally forgetting an appointment to meet with a buyer's agent) to major damage—actively encouraging builders or property owners to reject bids from consumers who use buyer's agents.

The fact is that many real estate agents have been working overtime to try to kill buyer's agents. National trade associations have made concerted efforts to "stymie, suppress, and mislead" consumers' knowledge about buyer's brokerage, a leading proponent of buyer agency told us. This attitude filters down to the front line, where a few agents carry this turf battle to absurd ends.

Builders also work to stop buyers from having protection from construction scams. While some agree to pay the buyer's agent's commission, builders refuse to sign documents that acknowledge the agent is representing the buyer. This effectively helps kill any deal.

## Money Bomb #3: Counterfeit buyer's agents.

*"When we searched for a new home, we found a buyer's agent who was willing to work for us. After four weeks, we discovered the agent was refusing to look for lower-priced homes on our behalf. He also pitched us on listings from his firm. We fired him."*

And you should. The recent surge in popularity of buyer's agents has flooded the field with "counterfeit" agents who claim they're working for buyers. The reality is that some of these folks have no idea what representing the buyer really means—they just want a quick commission. You can usually spot fake buyer's agents when they fail to look hard for lower-priced properties. Others will not "dig for the dirt," failing to provide you with potential pitfalls about certain homes. Most counterfeit buyer's agents will not put your agreement in writing and refuse to renounce sub-agent commissions (they may be working other deals where they're representing sellers).

## Money Bomb #4: The shortage of land "specialists."

*"We're having a devil of a time finding a buyer's agent who knows anything about local building sites. No one seems to specialize in vacant land."*

Buyer's brokerage is still in its infancy and, in some places, it may be hard to find an agent who is familiar with vacant land or building sites. Of course, it's sometimes hard to find a buyer's agent at all—those that are out there may only specialize in existing houses.

Another problem is the fact that many building sites or open lots are not listed in the Multiple Listing Service (MLS). Lazy agents just rely on this book as a one-stop shopping alternative for their clients—hence you may miss some of the best properties. The best agents network with builders and developers who may have land available that is not listed in the MLS. Other lots may be for sale by owner—and these take some effort for an agent to identify. Some of the best deals may be for lots that aren't even on the market—the best buyer's agent should have no problem in approaching property owners about the possibility of selling.

That's the secret to the power of buyer's agents—they can negotiate for property that is invisible to the radar scopes of the MLS. Sure, a regular real estate agent can ask property owners whether they want to sell their house or lot—but this agent must require that the seller pay the agent's commission. This is a major negative for the seller. Buyer's agents are assured of being paid by buyers, freeing them to go out there and negotiate with any seller.

The bottom line: even though it may be a hassle, you should still try to find a buyer's agent. If you're purchasing a lot or building site, this may be a long search. If a partially built "spec" house is your goal, it still pays to have a buyer's agent despite the roadblocks some builders will try to throw in your way.

**Money Bomb #5: Relocation programs with "exclusive" agents.**
*"My company is relocating us to a new city. The relocation firm assigned to help our family insisted we use a certain agent that was NOT an exclusive buyer's agent. This agent refused to look for lower-price homes for us and insisted we needed to buy immediately."*

Corporate relocations are big business—many so-called relocation specialists "help" consumers by hooking them up with agents, movers and the like. The problem: the agents they INSIST you use are probably NOT exclusive buyers' agents. Nor are they necessarily the best and brightest agents in a particular area. Nope, these agents are often just folks who have offered to give the biggest kickback to the relocation company for their business. In the age of the Internet, you can easily find an exclusive buyer's agent in any town. We'd pass on the relocation company's "suggested" agents and hire your own.

# The Model Trap and Other Sales Sins Of Builders

Here's an interesting trivia question: what's the number one reason buyers of new homes cite for not recommending their builder?

If you said the quality of the home, guess again. Sixty-eight percent of new buyers said the humiliating sales process soured them on the whole experience, according to a Minnesota market research firm.

And who can blame them? Whether you're in Maine or Oregon, walk into any new home community and the sales pitch is frighteningly similar. Even *Builder* magazine, the official mouthpiece of the National Association of Home Builders, recognized this problem in a recent article and described the typical sales process like this:

"The hostess or sales associate greets the customers at the sales office door. Then, like it or not, the prospects are led to the topo table, the office's centerpiece, to get a bird's-eye view of the community, hear a spiel on the project's benefits and (to instill the first twinges of urgency) see all the little red 'sold' dots. Next, the buyers are delicately grilled ('pre-qualified') about their housing needs and pocket depth, then steered to the wall-mounted floor plan the sales staffer judges they'd like best. Then the prospects are released (or, if it's a slow day, accompanied) to the models."

"Back from the models (assuming they didn't climb over the model trap's fence), the prospects are intercepted, steered to the wall-mounted 'builder's story' for another canned spiel, then directed (or accompanied) to a lot. Finally, the sales associate eases the prospects into a cramped closing room to 'work up some numbers'—and to extract a 'be-back' promise or contract."

Sound familiar? After five minutes in a builder's model, you feel like cattle. That's what it's all about, after all—manipulating you both physically (why do think the model with a fence attached is called a "model trap"?) and psychologically. Builders are control freaks, who think the only way to weed out tire-kickers is to treat all buyers like a side of beef that's waiting to be processed.

There are some ways you can take control of the sales process as a buyer. Here are some tips:

◆ DO YOUR HOMEWORK **BEFORE** YOU STEP IN A MODEL. Don't rely on the canned "builder's story." Instead research the builder at the local library—all public builders will leave a trail of newspaper articles, both good and bad. Another good source if you have access to the Web: check out Hoover's Online at www.hoovers.com. This site includes profiles of 8500 companies, including their latest SEC filings and reports from analysts. Also: check to see if a builder has been sued by surfing a web site called KnowX.com (www.knowx.com)—this nifty site lets you search public records to uncover any lawsuits by angry past customers or unpaid suppliers. You can see whether the builder has declared bankruptcy, been sued or has any recent liens or judgements against them. The cost is $1.50 to $6.95 for a search and then $2.95 to $6.95 for a "detail record." It's a steal for the peace of mind.

◆ ASK FOR THE PRICE LISTS AND BROCHURES UP-FRONT. Instead of being led by the nose through the builder's model, insist on seeing these documents first. That way you can tell if you're truly interested or merely wasting both your and the sales associates' time.

◆ SHOP AROUND. Not all builders are blind to this problem—some actually have tried to make the sales process easier to swallow. For example, at Willow Lake in North Aurora, IL, United Development has life-sized plans on waterproof tarps—buyers can walk through the plans to get an idea of different layouts or to merely figure out how large that closet really is. Other builders are making their models more interactive, with freestanding displays of plumbing, windows, and other details. By revealing what's going on behind the walls, you can get a better read on the builder's quality.

# House by Design

Considering how expensive houses are today, it would sure be nice if the home actually suited your needs, wants and lifestyle. The process of designing the right home can be challenging.

Of course, houses don't just appear on command—there must be a plan. And somebody must draw that plan. This chapter focuses on the different design choices that face new homebuyers today.

First, let's point out that a "design" for a new home is more than a sketchy floor plan that says the kitchen goes here. Actually, a design is a series of plans and documents—from exterior elevations to framing, electrical, and plumbing/mechanical plans to a complete list of the specifications and materials to be used in the home.

Basically, new homebuyers have four options when it comes to home design: the "pick a floor plan" designs, plan books, designer/drafting services and professional architects. The key differences are the level of detail you get in the design and how finely tuned the design is to your lifestyle—plus you also diminish the chance of falling victim to the scams and rip-offs mentioned later in this chapter. Of course, the more detail and customized the plans, the higher the cost.

## "Pick a floor plan" design

Large production builders have boiled the new home buying process down to these four simple steps: walk into a builder's model, look at floor plan layouts on a wall, pick your colors and poof! You get an instant house! But just like instant coffee, you can't expect your house to be a gourmet blend of custom features and amenities.

The "pick a floor plan" model of home design does have a couple of advantages, of course: first, many of these production homes are in the "starter home" price range. In markets where land is scarce, this might be the only option open to homebuyers who want to spend $200,000 or less. Another advantage: you don't have to make many decisions. The production homebuilder has allegedly simplified all this by distilling all the choices into several simple plan options.

Yet, in the real world, it can be more confusing. We recently visited a large new home development and discovered the production builder offered a mind-numbing 37 different floor plans! Hello? That's like McDonald's having 37 value meals—no one can really handle all that much choice.

And speaking of McDonald's, that's exactly the downside of the "pick a floor plan" design method—you basically get a McHome, a cookie-cutter design stamped out by the hundreds or thousands by a production builder. Left to their own devices, many builders would plaster the country with look-alike homes decorated in mind-numbing earth tones. If you look at many of the "home-in-a-box" subdivisions that dot this country, you'll discover why builders should be banned from designing.

The "pick a floor plan" design method often extends to smaller builders as well. You can pick a standard design or have the builder whip something up himself. This would work fine, except for the fact that most builders aren't trained in design. A simple drafting course does not make them a designer or architect, just as strapping on a tool belt doesn't make you an expert carpenter.

Many builders simply rely on past homes they've built for design ideas ("It worked the last time—let's do it again"). This inbreeding of design perhaps leads to the sorry shape of home design today. Builders may pitch you their own design services more for their convenience than your benefit. First, it's easy for lazy builders. Second, there's no architect working for you who's looking over the builder's shoulder. No architect means no design elements (such as a fancy archway) that require extra effort on the part of the contractor.

If you go this route, consider the following precautions:

◆ **Ask for all the details.** There's much more to a home's design than a sketchy floor plan—ask the builder for copies of the ENTIRE set of blue prints, elevations, and a list of specifications and materials. These are important protections for you the consumer. Reality check: some

## Customization Is The Craze

The production home appears to be a one-stop shopping alternative where the builder has decided for you what the design will be. But, the hip trend with big builders now is to offer you the ability to "customize" the house. Customizing might include changing the size of rooms or adding higher-end options, such as a home theater.

One builder told us he is willing to change anything in his houses (except load-bearing walls) to offer customers a choice. A word of caution, however: there is ALWAYS an additional charge for these changes and options—be sure to check on this before you make any agreements and get all changes in a written contract.

builders refuse to give out this much detail, fearing you'll know too much. We'd avoid hiring these contractors.

◆ **Dimension plans are a nice start, but dig deeper.** Some builders who do their own design may give you a blueprint of your new home design—but instead of the detail you get from an architect or professional design, the plan is "dimensions only." You get a rough layout of the rooms and that's it. For example, there's an opening specified for a door, but no mention of what type and quality of door you're getting. Dimension plans often are missing separate framing, electrical, and plumbing/mechanical plans—making the prospect of dangerous and costly field changes more likely. The lack of specifications (what exact windows? doors? faucets? trim?) opens you up to the biggest rip-off of all: substitution of cheaper materials. Want a nicer faucet? Well, there's an "upgrade fee" that you usually find out about late in the ball game.

◆ **Be wary of field changes.** When the builder does the design, one risk are contractors who wing it "in the field." They actually think it's possible to take an empty lot and create the perfect house—all from vague sketches or no plans at all. Once they get a crude set of plans approved by the building department, they then make dozens of "field changes" that could dangerously affect the structural integrity of the home.

## Money Bombs with "Pick a floor plan" design

**Money Bomb #1: Omission by design.**
*"The builder on our $280,000 semi-custom home implied we were to get top-of-the-line plumbing fixtures and faucets. Unfortunately, the plans had no mention of the exact brand. We later found out the builder put in cheap, builder-grade fixtures."*

As is so often the case, the plans provided by many builders are so incomplete that consumers aren't quite sure what they are buying. Often missing are the "finishes," those items that make a home special or just another tract home. Finishes include such items as plumbing fixtures, trim, flooring, paint and more.

Do builders intentionally leave such details off their plans? In many cases, new homebuilders have a "don't ask, don't tell" policy. A complete list of specifications and materials is probably sitting in a file drawer in the builder's office. Yet, many buyers never ask for these documents—and most builders don't volunteer them.

Think of it this way: you wouldn't buy a new car without looking at the window sticker first. Does it have air bags? Anti-lock brakes? At the same time, many homebuyers will buy a new home without ever asking the builder for a list of the "standard equipment." Only by looking at the "window sticker" (the complete plans and specifications/materials list) will you know what you're really buying.

## Money Bomb #2: Charging for changes.

*"We got charged $200 for a goof our builder made—he failed to draw the furnace ventilation system correctly on the plans. Halfway through the construction, we got billed for an extra soffit. Ouch!"*

This is a real-life story that happened to us. While the $200 didn't bankrupt the project, it certainly ratcheted up the frustration level. The lesson we learned: the more detail you have in your plans, the harder it is for the builder to make "field changes." Field changes are just what they sound like—changes to the house made after building starts. Because subcontractors may charge builders for such spur-of-the-moment changes to the house, this cost gets passed on to you in the form of a higher sales price.

Complete and detailed plans (we'll discuss what makes plans complete later in this chapter) greatly lower the opportunity for this rip-off.

## Money Bomb #3: Paying for a builder's new Lexus.

*"A production builder presented us with a long list of 'options' that we can add to their stock plan. But how do we know what options really add value instead of just lining the builder's pockets?"*

Tough question. And we're not sure there is one right answer to this, but there are a couple of things to consider. First, realize that options that enhance areas like the kitchen and bathrooms appeal to a wide audience. That doesn't mean you should nix optional built-ins in a home office if you need them—just realize that many future buyers may look at that $5000 "extra" as unnecessary.

Production builders make the fattest profit on so-called "designer" options, like upgraded flooring, wall/window coverings and the like. If possible, skip the builder's offer to sell you mini-blinds and do this after you move in.

## Money Bomb #4: Look ma, no plans!

*"Our production builder says we can't get a copy of the plans to our new home. What do we do?"*

First, consider whether you should even buy a home from any builder that refuses to give you detailed plans. But what if you already signed a deal and now the builder refuses to give you any blueprints? First, realize that builders MUST submit detailed plans and drawings to their local building department to get a permit. Those documents are public record and available for you to copy and take home.

# PLAN BOOKS

Visit any bookstore or newsstand and you'll probably encounter house plan books. Basically, these publications are page after page of home

# The 9 Biggest Design Goofs in Production Homes

Some people collect stamps. Other folks do woodworking. Our hobby is to visit new home models to collect examples of the Worst Home Design in America. And we've seen it all. After travelling all around the country to promote this book, we've collected a list of the 9 Biggest Design Goofs of Production Homes. Here we go:

**1. Garage swallows house!** No, it's not a tabliod newspaper headline but an all-too-true story for many new homes. Instead of a house with a garage, many builders seem to think a huge garage with a small, attached house is what every buyer needs. The design solution to this problem? Pull the garage back from the facade. And what ever happened to the good, old-fashion rear-access alley? Hiding a garage in the back or side of a home does wonders for its character.

**2. The commode view.** Walk in the front door and what do you first see? A lovely view of the toilet in the powder room.

**3. Honey, I shrunk the driveway!** Nothing is more frustrating than a driveway that's too small. Even though sport-utility vehicles have been hip for years, builders still design driveways that are far too narrow for any vehicle bigger than a Beetle. Experts say a 35-foot wide driveway pad is needed for a three-car garage with posts between each bay. The driveway should be at least 14 feet wide at the curb (or street).

**4. Failing the grocery bag test.** How long does it take to go from the garage to the kitchen? Bad design forces you to make a long trek, or even worse, go up a set of stairs to get to the kitchen with an armload of groceries.

**5. Traffic flow nightmares**. A common design goof in homes we've viewed puts the breakfast area in the traffic flow between a kitchen and living room.

**6. The closet is alive!** Ever hear an upstairs toilet flush while you're downstairs? Thank a builder who used non-insulated drainpipes (or PVC pipe instead of cast iron). Another common goof is designs that tuck mechanical systems (hot water heaters, furnaces, and laundry areas) into closets right near living areas.

**7. Furniture twister.** Watch out for windows that make furniture placement impossible. For example, windows in a master bedroom often dictate where the bed goes. In one model we visited, the only logical place for a bed blocked access to the master closet.

**8. Doors that swing into each other.** While this sounds like an obvious no-no, you wouldn't believe the number of kitchens we've seen with this problem. Another example: doors that swing the wrong way in the bathroom, whacking a person standing at a sink.

**9. Lost in space.** Many homes have plenty of space—it's just lousy design that makes storage under-utilized. For example, many homes have attics above garages, yet builders fail to provide access. Under-stair storage is also often overlooked. The flip side of the space problem: narrow hallways only a laboratory rat would love. Designers maximize open space in great rooms and master bedrooms, only to make hallways incredibly small.

designs. Each design gives you a picture of what the house is supposed to look like, plus rough layouts of the rooms.

The publishers of these publications don't make their money selling books or magazines—the real bucks come from selling the plans, which cost $500 to $900 a pop. But what do you get for that money?

Basically, you receive "complete" blueprints (usually five sets) for a new home. This includes designs for a foundation, floor plans, "exterior elevations" (the outside views of the house), interior elevations and cross sections, roof plans and schematic electrical layouts. You may also get a list of general specifications. On the plus side, these plans provide a quick and cheap way to get a home design. You can typically order a hard copy of the plans (on vellum, which can be reproduced) or a digital version that can be altered in computer programs like SoftPlan (a software program used by designers). As you'd expect, the digital version is preferred if you plan to modify the design.

Critics point out that the quality of these plans varies dramatically—some are more complete than others. If you decide to go this route, make sure you get a money-back guarantee. Charge the purchase to a credit card, as well. If you discover the plans are defective or incomplete and the plan book company refuses to refund your money, you may be able to reverse the charge on your card.

Beware of hidden charges with plan book designs: while most companies will sell you a set of blueprints, there are extras . . . like materials lists ($50), a color rendering of the plan ($100), a mirror reverse of the plan ($50) and more.

## New Homebuyers in Cyberspace: What's on the Web?

Just pop "home plans" into search engine and you'll come up with dozens of sites. Here's a quick overview of some of the best places to surf (see Figure 1 on the next page for samples):

◆ **Home Planners** (www.homeplanners.com) boasts it has the largest collection of home plans on the net (it is part of the ePlans web site). You can search by various criteria and come up with a list of homes that might work. Each plan has a front elevation and floor plan, plus description. Plans run $600 to $1000, depending on how elaborate the house and many copies of the blueprints needed. Unfortunately, that doesn't include "extras" like materials lists which run another $60. Neat features included "virtual tours" to provide a "reality walk-through" of plans and "The Planner" which lets you create a construction schedule calendar.

◆ **Home Plan Network** (www.homeplan-network.com) offers a "Home Building Survival Kit" for $30 that includes various forms like a construction specification worksheet, bidding comparison sheet and lien waiver forms. Their site's plan search function is provided by HomePlanFinder. The

**Figure 1:** A sampling of the better home plan sites onilne.

site's graphics are excellent; we saw color renderings of plans and good detail on the specs and layouts. Plans run $400 to $600.

◆ **Homestyles** (www.homestyles.com) has a whopping 10,000 plans online and a well-designed site to boot. Another cool feature: a $99 planning seat that includes the home's exterior elevations and floor plans. You get full credit for the set if you decide to purchase the plan. Most plans are $500 to $700.

◆ **Residential Technologies:** (www.residential.com) is a publisher of home plan magazines that has a web site which lets you search for home plans. Yes, the site is ugly but it does have 600 plans (front elevation and floor plan) online for you to preview for free. A toll-free number lets you order the plans.

◆ **United Designs** (www.designconcepts.com) has an excellent site with an extensive "plan library." Each plan features a sharp graphic of the exterior elevation and floor plan, plus a nice description of the amenities. Symbols call out handicap accessible plans. This site offers a "pre-construction package" for each plan that includes blueprints, a cost estimate and a materials list for about $100. Coolest feature: some plans have "client photographs," actual photos of the house built by one of United's customers.

◆ **CD-ROM:** In addition to web-based home plan sources, we also found several on CD-ROM. Among the best: AbbiSoft's "Home-Plan Finder" ($29.95, call 800-345-HOME to order; web: www.abbisoft.com). This CD-ROM has 3600 plans from 57 designers. Instead of sifting through all the designs, you can target your search using the CD-ROM's search capability—tell the program what you "must have" and what you "want to have," which lets you prioritize architectural elements and features. You can search by bedrooms, square feet, building site area and more. We think this CD-ROM is among the best on the market, despite the fact the search criteria (65 categories at last count) can be somewhat overwhelming. One other drawback: this is a Windows-only product (there's no Mac version). AbbiSoft's web site with online plans is www.homeplanfinder.com.

## Money Bombs with Plan Books

### Money Bomb #1: One Size Does Not Fit All.

*"It was love at first site—we found a great design in a plan book that was to be our dream house. Our hearts sank, however, when we discovered the plan needed to be adapted to our sloping lot. The builder offered to 'fix' the plan—for a hefty sum."*

Most plans are designed for flat lots. In the real world, lots are rarely perfect. The plan may show the house with a window in what looks like a perfect location, but when placed on your lot, it looks onto an ugly, neighboring home.

Also, note the fine print in the plan book's sales pitch. If you want to make changes to the design (such as modifying the foundation to fit a sloping lot), the publishers urge you to consult only with an architect for "major changes or alterations." The fact is most buyers who use plan book blueprints end up modifying them in both major and minor ways. This seems to defeat the plan books' major selling point that they're saving you all this money in architectural fees.

In the real world, we found few architects who modified these plans. Who does the changes? It's often the builder, whose entire design "experience" is basically limited to rudimentary drafting skills. This exposes the buyer to major risks if the builder goofs. And builders often charge you $500 to $1000 for their time to modify the plans. Given these facts, it may make more sense to forget the plan books and just hire a real architect or designer to design a house that fits you and the lot.

### Money Bomb #2: Plan book catch-22

*"One item my wife and I have struggled with is the gray area between the amount of financing we can afford and the actual amount of house that will get you. To get a reasonable bid (or attention for that matter from a builder) we need to have a set of plans. The plans can run up to $700! Of course, who wants a plan only to find out you can't afford it to start with?"*

Yes, this can be a catch-22—which comes first, the plan or the budget? A solution to this is to ask to meet with the builder and tell him your target budget range ($200,000, for example). Then show him the plan book with the rough layout of the plan (it shows square footage, bedrooms, etc). Ask if that's in the ballpark—if the answer is yes, only then order the plans. Yes, there is some risk that the actual plan will still be more than your budget, but you can always trim things a bit here and there.

An alternative: ask a buyer's broker for recent sales data for the area you want to build in. What does $290,000 buy you? Since your new home will be worth approximately what other recent new homes have sold for in the area, you will have an idea what kind of square footage, bedrooms and finishes you can buy. Remember: the TYPE of finishes you pick can dramatically affect the final price of any new home.

# Designer/Drafting Services

What is a designer? How does this person differ from an architect? To understand this, you should first realize that an architect must be licensed by the state in which he or she practices. The licensing requirements vary, but most states require certified training and several years of experience.

Yet, architects aren't the only individuals allowed to design houses. In most states, anyone can design homes and call himself a house "designer" without having a license. The only prohibition is that such designers cannot refer to themselves as architects.

The experience of home designers can vary widely. Some are newly minted architectural graduates working toward certification. Others have taken a drafting course and have grand delusions of being great designers. Occasionally, designers join forces to form a drafting service firm. Such companies usually offer "limited" architectural services—they basically just draw the plans. It's up to you to find and negotiate with a builder, as well as to monitor the construction.

The chief advantage to these companies is that they're much cheaper than hiring an architect—designers' fees to design a home are about one-quarter to one-half of what an architect charges. Critics point out that you get about one-quarter of the quality that a professional would deliver. And there's more to building a home than just drawing a blueprint—negotiating with builders and monitoring the construction (services most designers don't offer) are key elements as well.

In a few states such as California and Florida, design services are popular alternatives to architects. In Florida, there is actually a state registry for home designers.

Some states require an architect and/or engineer to stamp a designer's plans with their professional certification to ensure that the home is structurally sound. Designers get around this requirement by having an architect or engineer "friend" provide the stamp. Some of these architects will look at the plans carefully, while other simply "rubber stamp" them for a fee.

## Money Bomb with Designer/Drafting Services

**Money Bomb: Over promise, under perform.**

*"We hired a designer who just moved to North Carolina from Massachusetts. She charged us $1800 for the plans and another $6000 to supervise the construction. Yet, when problems cropped up during the construction of the house, the designer just shrugged her shoulders and said, "Well, that's not how we did things in Cape Cod, but I guess that's how it's done here."*

That's a true story from Columbus, North Carolina where this unlucky homeowner is now saddled with a whopping $100,000 in repairs for a defective home. What happened? After viewing a videotape of the house, it was painfully obvious that the designer knew little about construction customs and procedures in North Carolina. In this case, you had the worst combination of factors: an inexperienced designer and an incompetent builder.

# Architects

All of the above options (builders, plan books and designers/drafting services) are poor substitutes for the real thing: the residential architect. After investigating all the alternatives, it's our opinion that the best person to design your home is an experienced residential architect. In a nutshell, here are the key reasons:

◆ **Experts at design.** This is perhaps the biggest reason people give for using an architect—and it should be. After all, architects go to school for years to learn how to design a functional living space. When you walk into a house designed by a good residential architect, you'll know it. Don't forget about resale value as well—we often see ads for existing homes that tout they were "professionally designed by an architect." These homes typically sell for a premium.

◆ **Complete Plans.** In contrast to some blueprints provided by plan books, a trained, residential architect will provide a complete set of plans including specification/materials lists, inside and outside elevations, cross sections, etc. The level of detail is often extensive—instead of just drawing a fireplace symbol, an architect will draw the exact fireplace, complete with mantel. Exact door types will be provided instead of just "rough opening" sizes. With most architects, this level of detail is standard procedure. Also, as we mentioned above, complete detailed plans help limit the number of field changes (and change orders), saving you time and money.

◆ **Consultation with structural engineers for the foundation and structural elements.** This is crucial to ensure a proper foundation for your house. Faulty foundations are at the core of many defective construction horror stories—hence, the more careful the design, the better. Most architects will consult with an engineer to ensure your foundation is designed properly. Some architects have engineers on their staffs and still others have engineering backgrounds themselves. Don't underestimate the importance of a proper foundation—forget about the kitchen cabinets or decorator tile. If the underpinnings of your home are crumbling or improperly designed, you're sunk.

◆ **Periodic inspections of the construction to ensure that the builder is following the plans.** The work of most full-service architects doesn't stop at drawing the plans—many continue to work with you to monitor the construction. Inspections when the footings/foundation are poured, framing is finished and interior finishing is completed are most common. The exact number of inspections varies from architect to architect. Some don't offer construction monitoring at all; others offer the service but, unfortunately, don't have a lot of experience. Depending on the cost of the house, you may want to hire a private inspector to double-check the construction as well.

## Money Bombs with Architects

**Money Bomb #1: The occasional house designer.**
*"A friend of ours is a commercial architect who designs office buildings. He offered to design our home, but the results were disastrous! The home fell way short of our expectations."*

Architects who do mostly commercial work and an occasional residence can be trouble. If an architect's business is more than 50% or 60% commercial, look somewhere else. Frankly, unless an architect spends at least half her time working with residential clients, she is going to be out of touch with costs, techniques, technology and trends in residential housing. As a result, the "occasional house designer" may not be able to suggest which materials/designs are cost-effective and within your budget.

Interestingly, architectural schools tend to emphasize commercial work over residential. Some of the brightest architectural talents are steered away from residential design. Other architects find commercial design (schools, shopping centers and the like) to be more financially rewarding and less frustrating than the tumultuous world of residential real estate. As a result, there are a limited number of good and experienced residential architects in most metro areas.

### Money Bomb #2: Architects from the Planet of Unrealistic Costs.

*"We instructed our architect to design us a $300,000 house. A design was completed and sent out to bid with several local builders. We were shocked at the result! The bids all came in at $400,000 or more!"*

What happened? You've encountered an architect who spends too much time on the Planet of Unrealistic Costs. Unfamiliar with local costs and trends, he or she whips out a lovely design that's way over your budget. The resulting plans must be redrawn ... a considerable waste of time and money for everyone involved.

Of course, understanding local construction costs isn't as easy as it seems. Staying up-to-date on residential construction trends and materials is quite a task. Nonetheless, such experienced architects actually exist and are obviously worth searching out.

We recommend you ask the architect how long he's been designing homes in your area and about his experience in estimating costs. How close do the architect's designs hit the budget mark when costed out to builders?

As a professional, an architect has a responsibility to stick with a budget (plus or minus 8%). If an architect blows it and designs you a Taj Mahal, the plans should be redrawn at his expense. Any reputable architect should agree to this in writing.

Other problems consumers have with architects can be chalked up to miscommunication—and a fundamental misunderstanding of the architect's role. A recent article in the *Wall Street Journal* on new home problems commented that "architects and construction lawyers agree that while shoddy or even dangerous design mars some projects, most conflicts stem from crossed signals. Owners don't appreciate design and structural issues at the core of the architect's profession. Architects don't fathom how deeply personal the experience of building a home can be for clients."

## Email from the Real World: $930 for stock plans

Don't assume that just because a builder is giving you a "stock" home plan that there won't be a charge, as this homebuyer in Vermont found:

*"I noticed our builder has included a charge of $930 for plans even though he has built this home before and is making no changes! When questioned, he said he uses the money to pay for additional plans to increase his 'library'!"*

Our general opinion is that the builder should not charge you for plans he has built from before. If you make substantial changes, however, there should be a reasonable fee for this.

### Money Bomb #3: The out-of-towner.

*"We live in a small town and are thinking of building a home. There is one architect in our town and he does nice work ... but, we heard great things about another architect who lives 80 miles away. Are there any problems with hiring an out-of-town architect?"*

Most architects live in large metro areas. If you aren't planning to build in or near a large city, you may find the architectural pickings slim. Hence, some buyers hire an architect who lives out of town—some even contract with professionals who are outside the state.

The problem: A Boston architect may be an expert at building customs, codes and prices in Massachusetts, but may be a fish out of water trying to do a vacation home in Maine. The skill and knowledge level required to pull this off are rather high.

Some architects get around this problem by consulting with local experts. For example, a local engineer who's familiar with soil conditions can help design the foundation plan.

Obviously, monitoring the construction is much more difficult when you're long distance. We have noted this problem in several cases. For example, a Florida homebuyer we interviewed hired an out-of-town architect to design her $600,000 beachfront home. When problems cropped up, the "local" builder convinced the buyer that the architect's design was flawed. Since the architect was 100 miles away, he couldn't adequately defend himself or his design. So the buyer fired the architect.

Big mistake. The builder turned out to be a con artist, whose incompetent construction led to a nightmare. When he finished the home, 19 of the home's 23 windows leaked. The roof was defectively installed causing more leaks. Giant cracks appeared in the exterior, thanks to a faulty foundation. Total bill for repairs: $300,000.

Not all consumers who hire out-of-town architects have such disastrous results. Hiring a local private inspector (such as a licensed engineer or retired contractor) to monitor the construction lowers the chance of problems (the above homeowner didn't do this). However, our first preference would be to hire a "local" architect before searching out of town. The key advantage to a local architect: they know the builders in your area and steer you toward the right contractor for your project.

## What Will It Cost You

An obvious question that confronts every homebuyer: how much will the design of my new home cost? Here are some guidelines:

**Builder/designers** will charge anything from $0 to $1000 to develop plans for a new home. If you use a "stock plan" the builder has already designed, the cost can be zero. Modifying the plan may incur additional costs for redrafting, etc.

Plans purchased from **plan books or web sites** run the gamut: from $400 to $1000, depending on the number of prints you want. You will probably need to purchase several sets—one for the lender, three for the builder, two for the building department, and one for your own use. (Ask your builder for recommendations on this.) If you plan to do significant alterations to a plan, purchase a "digital" version of the plan in a computer format that can be altered by CAD (Computer Aided Design) programs.

One negative about plan books is the extra costs. For example, if you want an itemized list of materials, that's an extra $50 to $60. There are also "surcharges" if you want a reverse or mirror image of a plan or if you want "how-to" diagrams for suggested framing and wiring. Add up all the costs (including hefty shipping charges) and plan books are less of a bargain.

**Designers and drafting services** charge in the range of $500 to $2000 for a set of plans. **Architects** run about 5% to 20% of the home's cost. The lower figure is for "bare-bones," design-only services. In the most expensive housing markets, a full-service architect could run 12% to 20% of the home's cost. However, the average for full-service (design through construction supervision) runs 8% to 12%. For a $300,000 home, this would cost $24,000 to $36,000.

One cardinal rule to remember about new home design is that you're paying for the design one way or another. Even production builders who have "stock" plans are charging you for the design—they've just built the cost into the price of the home. Granted, many production builders spread the cost of one design over 50 or more homes. That's how they can sell production homes for comparatively lower prices than true custom homes.

Remember, however, that the quality doesn't necessarily correspond to the price, especially with builder/designers. In one case we researched, a builder wanted to charge a homebuyer $600 for a bare bones, dimensions-only plan. Only by shopping around for several alternatives will you be able to understand the quality differences. And don't forget the hidden costs of trying to go cheap—the money you might save could be far out-weighed by future surprises.

## Step-by-Step Strategies: Designing the House

If you're designing a house from scratch and are planning to use an architect or other design professional, here are the steps in the design process.

**Step 1: Ideas.** Before you meet with a design professional, it's a good strategy to get some ideas of what you like. Home and decorating magazines are excellent sources. Floor plan designs from plan books are too limiting—most designers and architects prefer you to think in terms of "spaces," not boxes. Hence, a magazine picture of a bay window or the perfect kitchen is more helpful than a floor plan. Also, put together a list of "needs versus wants" to help the architect key in on your requirements.

**Step 2: Getting to know you.** At the first meeting, discuss briefly what your project will be, answering any basic questions. Most design professionals should ask you for a budget. Try to get a feel for the architect's style by asking a few key questions (listed earlier in Chapter 3) and looking at some past designs. Also, ask about the services offered and the corresponding prices.

**Step 3: Show and tell.** Look at homes the architect/designer has recently completed, as well as homes under construction. Remember that some cosmetic details are often the owner's choice, not necessarily the architect's. Focus on how the spaces in the house are arranged. Is traffic flow logical? Are the rooms pleasant to walk through? How did the designer utilize natural light? From the outside, do the different exterior elements look in balance? How is the "curb appeal," the first impression you get when driving up?

**Step 4: Check references.** This step is extremely important—don't skip it. When talking to a reference, ask simple questions like: Did the designer meet your deadlines? Did he or she stay within your budget? How familiar was the architect with local builders? Did the monitoring of construction meet your expectations? Add any other questions that relate to your project.

**Step 5: Get a bid.** Ask the designer to give you an estimate on the cost of his or her service, including all the necessary construction documents. Extra services such as bidding/negotiation to builders and supervision of construction should be clearly delineated. Ruminate on the bid for a week or so before making a decision.

**Step 6: Hire the designer.** Our recommendation is to use the contract from the American Institute of Architects (AIA) with certain modifications (see Chapter 8 for a discussion). Architects who are members of the AIA (and even some of those who aren't) should have copies.

**Step 7: Lifestyle questionnaire.** The next step is a detailed discussion (called programming) of your ideas about the new home. Many architects will give you a questionnaire to help you focus on your "needs and wants." Heidi Richardson of Richardson Architects in San Francisco has an excellent lifestyle questionnaire. Here are some sample questions:

◆ SITE DESIGN: What views are important? What do you **not** want to see? What's the home's relationship to neighbors in terms of view, noise and privacy? Any outdoor activities such as hot tub, garden, play areas, entertaining?

◆ KITCHEN/DINING ROOM: How much cooking is done at home and who does it? What kind of entertaining do you do (small or large groups)? Focus on where you are going to eat (nook or dining room) plus whether the use of the dining room is casual or formal. How much storage is needed for food in the kitchen?

◆ LIVING/FAMILY ROOM: What will happen in the living/family rooms? Separate rooms? What furniture do you have that you want to accommodate?

◆ MAIN/MASTER BEDROOM: How private? How much time do you spend in it besides sleeping? Should master bath/dressing areas be directly off it? How large should the closets be (compared to your current situation)?

◆ MASTER BATH: Separate shower, tub or special features like bidets? Separate sinks for his-and-her use? Do you use the bathroom just for washing and cleaning or do you spend time in it? Should the closet be off the bath or off the master bedroom?

◆ OTHER BEDROOMS/BATHROOMS: How many extra bedrooms and who are they for? Size of beds and needed storage? Home office? Does each bedroom need its own bath? Separate powder room near main living areas?

◆ STORAGE: Will everyone's belongings fit the proposed closets/cabinets? Do you need storage for linens, luggage, valuables, coats, brooms, etc.? (Note: There are regional variations to the storage issue. For example, in Texas, few homes have basements, so storage is usually under staircases or in an attic.)

◆ LAUNDRY: Do you need a separate laundry room? Where should it be? Near the garage, kitchen, bedrooms?

◆ HEATING/VENTILATING/AIR CONDITIONING: Do you need air conditioning or will passive cooling methods such as shading or ventilation work? What type of heat source is available? Do you have a preference for forced air, wall radiators, or radiant floor (hot water) systems? Any interest in active solar system or passive solar design?

◆ **PLUMBING:** Sewer or septic system? Well or city water? How much hot water do you use each day?

Richardson's lifestyle questionnaire is substantially longer than the questions listed above. The questionnaire is perhaps the most complete of all the architects we interviewed, but most professionals will have some sort of questionnaire to help determine your needs. The goal of this step is to develop specific ideas about what you want and don't want in this new home.

**Step 8: Rough sketches or "schematic designs."** Schematic designs are intended to give the homeowner some idea of how the house would sit on the lot and how the rooms of the house would be arranged. Also, a good designer will be able to give you a preliminary cost estimate at this time.

**Step 9: Design development and refinements.** The designer begins to develop a specification (spec) list and provides more detailed drawings of your house. Cost estimates also will be refined at this stage. Give yourself a month to really think about the design. If you have any questions, consider paying for a three-dimensional model or drawings to help you visualize the design better. (Some designers now use 3-D design computer programs that let clients "walk through" a design on a computer). Remember that change orders are expensive later, so nailing down any changes before construction is a cost savings.

**Step 10: Construction documents.** Once you have given the designer all your input and have come to an agreement on the design, he or she will prepare the detailed drawings that the builder will (hopefully) follow during construction. A detailed spec list is also provided. Keep in mind that to prepare these documents, you will have to make decisions on minute details including light fixtures, trim colors, cabinet finishes

## GET A BIG SAMPLE.

**I**f there is one tip we could give new homebuyers, it would be go BIG. Big samples, that is. When deciding on countertops, paint or carpet, don't rely on small samples or swatches to make a decision. Instead, get a large chunk of countertop or paint large piece of drywall to get a better idea of what you are really choosing. Take these samples into your home and look at them in different light (direct sunlight, dusk) before you make a decision.

and more. Expect to spend some time with the architect or at a home center looking at sample books.

With builder/designers, you may receive an allowance for certain items. For example, the builder will tell you can spend $25 per yard on carpet. You won't have to pick the carpet immediately in this case—but it is smart to visit a carpet store to make sure the allowance meets your expectations.

**Step 11: The bid process.** An optional service offered by many full-service architects, bidding and negotiation involves sending the construction documents to several qualified builders. (More on finding a builder, in Chapter 7.) Builders will, in turn, get bids from their subcontractors and suppliers—this could take a couple of weeks. Once the builders' bids come in, the architect negotiates with them to arrive at a final deal (subject to your approval, of course). As a side note, if the architect is experienced at estimating costs, the bids should closely match your budget (plus or minus 8%). If the bid comes in way over your budget, the architect will have to redraw the plans at his expense, incorporating any money-saving suggestions the builder provides.

**Step 12: Decision time.** At this point, we assume the bids are in line with your budget. Basically, you pick a builder and take the plunge. But the architect's or designer's work isn't quite over—many pros offer construction monitoring. This involves visiting the site at several key inspection points to make sure everything is proceeding correctly. More on these inspection points in Chapter 9.

## REALITY CHECK

◆ **Too-Many-Cooks syndrome.** Anyone who's ever attempted to cook a holiday meal with several well-meaning relatives knows this pitfall. One homebuyer we interviewed experienced this firsthand. The original design meetings for her home included her architect, the builder and an interior designer. The result was chaos and the process dragged on for months.

Houses are not designed by committee. You and your architect or designer should really meet one on one. While you should seek the input from a builder or interior designer, they should not be present at every meeting. Designing your home shouldn't be a democracy—it's your house, so make it your choice.

Input from your builder is important when it comes to costs—any cost-saving suggestions are obviously helpful. If the builder spots a problem with an early drawing (such as a proposed roof line that might leak), he should have an opportunity to comment. But allowing too many people to cloud the design process with too many voices is counterproductive.

◆ **Resale vs. your own quirks:** Is it your dream to own a purple house? What about having a chartreuse master bath with matching tile and carpet? You may decide you want a chartreuse master bath, and, since it's your house, you should have one. But . . . what if you plan to sell your house in five years? Chartreuse is not in the Top 10 Colors Preferred by Most Buyers.

Here's where many new homebuyers face a dilemma—they want to customize the house to their tastes, but they worry about "resale potential." The average homeowner lives in a house for just seven to ten years—after that time, it's on to another home.

OUR ADVICE: Use restraint. While we don't advocate doing everything in a non-offensive beige, we do think staying away from shocking colors is a good idea. One strategy is to choose neutral fixtures (like white or almond toilets, tubs and sinks) and accent them with color. For example, you could put a white sink into your powder room, but use an exotic wallpaper to add zing. That way, if a buyer doesn't like your choice of wallpaper, she can come through and put up something else. Ripping out a bright purple sink is another matter.

The goal is not to box future homebuyers into a corner with your color or design choices. The home should reflect your personality, but not in such a way that it destroys any resale potential down the line. An architect or buyer's broker will give you hints on what's in and what's out.

For example, when we built our home, every other home in the neighborhood had a three-car garage. Did we need one? Not really. But we spent the money anyway and now we have a three-car garage. The reason is simple. If we go to sell the home in a couple of years, only having a two-car garage would be a major negative. Most buyers today like the three-car garage for the extra storage space.

◆ **Don't forget practical issues like fire safety.** When designing a new home, you can get carried away with aesthetic details while ignoring important design elements—like fire safety. While it is impossible to design an entirely "fire-proof" home, there are some basic concepts. First, if you are building in a heavily treed area at risk for forest fires, make sure your home has a "defensible" space. This is an area free of trees and brush which firefighters can use to fight off a fire. Ensuring the driveway is wide enough for emergency vehicles is also wise. Of course, building with as little wood (asphalt/composition shingles for a roof; stucco instead of cedar siding) is wise.

◆ **Make sure your home design is climate approriate.** It sounds obvious: homes in extreme climates (the cold of Minnesota or the humidity of Alabama) require designs and construction techniques that are climate appropriate. But what's appropriate? We found an excellent web site with the answers: BuildingScience.com. This Boston-based architecture and science consulting firm has a fantastic web site with "climate specific building details." Click on any region of the U.S. and you get specific recommendations for design considerations, roofs, mechanical systems and so on. Their "Builder's Guide" book series (one for each of the four different climate regions) are an excellent resource as well. Check out the web site at www.BuildingScience.com or call 978-589-5100.

## Getting Started: How Long Is This Going to Take?

A builder/designer may have a stock plan or design ready to go—this convenience may be a major advantage. If you want to make modifications, this could take one to four weeks, depending on the extent of the changes.

Plan books require at least a week or more for shipping. Overnight shipping is available, but at a premium. If you need time for a builder or designer to redraw these plans to your tastes, add another few weeks.

The average custom or semi-custom home designed by a designer or architect will take about two to three months, while a high-end, luxury home designed by an architect can take as much as six months to a year. And that's before a single shovel-full of dirt is thrown.

Making all the decisions required to design the house that's right for you takes time. Be sure to allow yourself plenty of time to consider each decision—don't be rushed by a proposed moving schedule.

The bottom line: plan ahead. If you want to be in the house by September 1, recognize that construction may take six to nine months (at a minimum). Add on top of that the time required for your design method. Many homebuyers find they must start designing the home one to two years before they plan to move in.

## Design Trends: What's Hot and What's Not.

Let's be honest—you're not building a house that's going to sit in some museum. If you plan to sell your home in the future, it'd be nice if it contained some of the items that other buyers want.

To determine just what's hip, we interview homebuilders and buyers nationwide. So, what's hot and what's not? Here's a rundown.

### The Top Eight Trends for New Homes

**1** **Less frills, more space.** Homebuyers are forgoing the ornate marble foyers and cherry kitchen cabinets. What do they want instead? More space. More "value." Forget those fancy cathedral ceilings—it seems folks would rather have bigger bedrooms. Buyers walk into two-story entryways and think, "Gee, that space could be a spare guest room." Parents with giant master bedroom closets are perhaps feeling guilty that their children's rooms are tiny boxes.

**2** **Storage, storage, storage.** That's the key word for new homebuyers. This trend is probably driving the "three-car garage" as a standard amenity in some areas. It's not for a third car but for all the important junk folks seem to acquire. In parts of the country where basements are rare, storage areas in inventive places (such as under staircases) are hip. For more tips on this topic, check out the box "The Storage Squeeze" below.

## The Storage Squeeze

The average new home built in America today is 2500 square feet—that's DOUBLE the figure of homes built a generation ago. With all that room, you'd think today's homes would have tons of storage, right? Wrong. The fact is that storage is sadly lacking in many new homes and there's one clear culprit: bad design. In order to cut corners, many builders waste valuable space or miss the opportunity for storage altogether.

Smart storage doesn't happen by accident. Check out these tips to squeeze more storage out of your new home:

◆ Expand the garage by a few extra feet to provide a wonderful space for storage or a worktable. Another idea: build a storage space on the back of the garage that's accessed from the outside to house lawn and garden items.

◆ Use the attic space over a garage for storage of bicycles, holiday decorations, etc.

◆ In the master bedroom, extend cathedral ceilings into a master closet. Pulling these tall ceilings into the closet will provide all kinds of storage. Add a couple of shelves for storage of items like luggage or extra clothes. Another idea: extend high ceilings in the kitchen into the pantry as well.

◆ Finish off the attic space under eaves or over a garage.

◆ Add closets or pantries under stairs.

◆ Squeeze storage out of breakfast nooks. Window seats should lift up for storage of linens and other kitchen gear.

◆ In showers, build shallow shelves into tub walls for bath supplies.

◆ Put a low shelf or drawer in a kid's closets to provide toy storage—children can also use this shelf as a stepping stair to reach hanging clothes.

◆ Go direct. Direct vent fireplaces eliminate the need for space-hogging chimneys—instead put in bookshelves, cabinetry or other storage above the fireplace.

◆ Add cookbook shelves in the kitchen. The island (or below an eating bar) are smart places for this storage.

◆ Tuck bench seats into bedrooms with flip-top lids for storage.

**3** **That's entertainment.** Media rooms have replaced dens, as many new homebuyers go for big-screen TV's and home theaters.

**4** **Real home offices.** Whether you work full-time at home or just occasionally bring back a little homework from another workplace, the home office is becoming a standard amenity. Obviously, multiple phone lines and electrical outlets are a necessity. For serious home offices, counter space and storage is a must. And the location of the home office is important to consider as well—the old days when home offices were crammed into a secondary bedroom or a small space off the front foyer are gone. The best home offices offer views or have lots of natural light.

**5** **Mom, can I get an iBook?** You can't be a kid today if you don't surf the 'net. And most kid's bedrooms today need to be larger to accommodate all the computer equipment. Instead of the standard 10x10 size, consider adding at least two to four feet to each dimension. Don't forget the wiring–if you want broadband Internet access for your kids, make sure the secondary bedrooms have the appropriate ports/connections.

**6** **One word, flexibility.** Rooms that do double duty (such as a sitting room that converts to a guestroom) are hot. Another hip trend: "accessory dwelling units," a fancy term for a separate nanny's quarters, or apartment over the garage for a live-in grandparent or adult child. These spaces often have private entrances and kitchenettes. "Accessibility" is another key issue—designing homes with accessible or "universal" floor plans for the wheelchair-bound is a growing trend. Check out the American Association of Retired People's web site (www.aarp.org) for free advice on this topic.

**7** **Relaxing on the porch.** Many communities are trying to make neighborhoods more "pedestrian-friendly." Designers have responded to this trend by including six-foot front porches on many new homes.

**8** **The all-purpose kitchen.** The plain kitchen desk has morphed into a "planning center" complete with computer and storage. The widely reported death of the formal dining room has given rise to plush "casual eating spaces" that function both for everyday and special occasions.

## Eight Inexpensive Thrills

Not everything in your new home has to be expensive. Here are several fun, yet inexpensive options that add a little pizzazz to your new home.

◆ **Built-in ironing board.** Ironing probably doesn't top anyone's list of Fun Things to Do, but it's slightly less of a hassle if you don't have to drag out and set up an ironing board. Adding a built-in ironing board for $100 to $400 is quite a space- and time-saver. Most designs have an unfinished oak cabinet that hides the ironing board. High-end models also have an electrical outlet, light, and a sleeve attachment. We recommend putting your built-in board in the master bedroom closet or your laundry room—think about where you do your ironing before choosing a location.

◆ **Laundry chute.** Staying with laundry for a minute, we recommend putting a laundry chute in any two-story house. You have unlimited options as to where you can locate the chute, as long as it ends in the laundry room. No more lugging baskets of dirty clothes downstairs. The cost: $100. Another smart design idea for two-story homes: put a laundry area upstairs.

◆ **Motion-sensor lights.** These are a neat idea to help protect against theft and to shed a little light when you come home late. For about $20, you can attach a motion sensor to your garage lights or any outdoor lights. When something (even as small as a neighborhood cat) approaches within 50 feet, the light turns on. Another nice feature: the sensor automatically turns off the light after a preset time period.

## Don't Buy a Lemon on the Info Highway

Even with all the buzz about super-fast cable or DSL modems and a future with 500-channels, many builders are still wiring new homes with cheap co-axial cable and inadequate phone wire. The result: when high speed 'net access rolls into your neighborhood, you may have to spend big money re-wiring to achieve the bandwidth promised by tech-heads.

The solution: purchase a "structured wiring package" and have it installed in your home. Some builders are now selling upgraded wiring and connectors that allow your home to go hi-tech at a cost of $1000 to $2000. These systems include a central distribution hub that lets you parcel out video, phone and Internet to each room of your home. Our advice: install better wiring now (when you're building a home) so you won't have to pay later.

Another option: consider a wireless computer network. Apple's "Airport" technology, for example, allows several computers to share one high-speed Internet connection. Similar wireless technologies also exist for the PC. While a discussion of these options are beyond the scope of this book, it's wise to consider the design of a computer network (wireless or wired) when you are constructing a new home.

◆ **Wiring for house-wide stereo.** Here's something you can do while the walls are going up, even if you don't have all the equipment for a house-wide stereo system. In a living room, you can wire for a home theater system. You can always hook up speakers later (keep a plan of where the wires end, so you know where they are). The cost: only $30 to $70 per pair of speaker wires, depending on the distance.

Another neat option to consider is a remote-control stereo. In our office, we have a remote-control sensor and set of speakers that are connected to an Onkyo stereo receiver downstairs. The remote control allows us to change stations, fiddle with the volume, and even play CDs—all without going downstairs. Cost: $80 for the sensor and $200 for the extra speakers. Beats having to buy a separate stereo.

◆ **Pet door.** If you have a pet or expect to have one in the future, install that pet door now while the walls are still going up. Framing a hole for the door is much easier now than later. Cost: $50 to $100.

◆ **Gas log fireplaces and grills.** Many people want a fireplace in their house, but don't want to fuss with buying or chopping wood and cleaning up ashes. Gas log fireplaces have become increasingly popular in the past five years. They require no maintenance and only need to be switched on—some even have remote controls! And for you eco-conscious folks, gas log fireplaces don't contribute to air pollution and can be burned on "no-burn" days in high-pollution areas.

A great idea to consider: new, high efficiency (80%) gas log fireplaces that are direct vented. Forget the expensive chimney—the smoke goes right out the wall through what looks like a dryer vent from the outside. One benefit: you can put a picture window right over the fireplace. The cost for one of these designs is $900 to $2500, but remember you save by omitting the chimney. You can add a fan (to disperse the warm air from the fireplace) for another $100 to $200. Basic gas log models start at $500 but aren't as efficient.

Another fun option to consider for folks who like to grill outdoors is a natural gas grill. First, you need a gas spigot on your patio (or wherever you want the grill). This costs about $50 to $100 and is usually installed by the plumber or a licensed gas contractor. Then you buy a natural gas grill, available from your local utility company or appliance store. Prices start at about $250 for a basic model and go up to $500. No more charcoal or filling up propane gas tanks.

◆ **Master bedroom refrigerator.** How many times have you been settled in bed and then decided you wanted a late-night snack? You get out of your warm bed, trudge out to the kitchen, and fix yourself a plate of cookies and a glass of cold milk. But, hey! What if you had a mini-refrigerator in your bedroom? This inexpensive option costs only about $100 to $200 and can be built into a bookcase or hidden in a walk-in closet. If you have a baby on formula or medicines that must be kept chilled, a fridge is a great idea.

◆ **Weather station.** For all those weather nuts who simply have to know the temperature, humidity, wind chill, barometric pressure, wind speed and direction, and rainfall, a weather station is a great toy to install. Since it has several external sensors that need to be mounted on a roof, an ideal time to buy one is when you're building a home.

The best bet for weather stations: Davis Instruments (800-678-3669; www.davisnet.com). A complete station like the Weather Monitor II gives you all the basic current conditions for $395. A "wireless" version of this station (the Vantage Pro) is $595.

# The 4 Things They DON'T Tell You About Living on a Golf Course

Memo to Bill Murray: Perhaps you were right. Living on a golf course can drive you crazy.

For millions of Americans, buying a golf course home sounds like the epitome of the American Dream: a beautiful home, bordered by lush green grass that will never be built on. And someone else does all the mowing.

Yet like all dreams, this one can turn into a Caddyshack nightmare quicker than you can say "Four!" Just ask John and Rebecca Zellick* (*not their real names). This couple bought their dream house on the end of a fairway in Louisville, Colorado in 1995. Shortly after they moved in, they quickly discovered their home was on the firing line: thanks to the way the course was designed, their living room was the approach for the golf equivalent of a busy runway at O'Hare airport.

Two lawsuits and $90,000 in legal fees later, the Zellicks prevailed in court and forced the developer to buy back the house. Their experience may be extreme, but it points out a cruel fact of golf course home buying: this isn't as easy as it looks. If buying a simple home is complex, then buying a golf course abode is a half-gainer with a triple twist.

To help, here are the **The FOUR Things They DON'T Tell You About Living on a Golf Course:**

**1** **Two words: "Landing Zone."** If you can, it's best not to put your house in the middle of the landing zone, quite simply the place where most golf balls land after being hit off the tee.

So, where exactly is the landing zone? Well, on a typical par 4 or 5 hole, most golfers can hit the ball 200 yards with a wood club. If your home is that distance from the tee, guess what? You're in the middle of the landing zone.

Of course, how CLOSE your house is to the course also determines the number of golf balls that might come whizzing in your living room window. Experts say buyers should consider the distance between the midpoint of the fairway and your lot line. The minimum distance is 150 feet; 180 feet is better; 200 feet is best. Unfortunately, in their zeal to sell more lots, some developers are shaving that distance to the bare minimum. By cramming more houses into golf course developments, the distance between you and the landing zone may be very short indeed.

The best golf course developers warn potential buyers about landing zone issues. Since no state laws mandate disclosure, it's up to the consumer to ask. Another clue: landing zone lots are the least expensive ones in the community. Lots near the tee or green have much fewer "golf ball conflicts" and are more pricey.

**2 The type of hole you live on can make or break a home location.** Not all golf holes are created equal, at least as far as home-buyers are concerned. Par 3 holes are better for homes. Why? Golfers are more likely to use a high loft-angle club to attack these holes. A simple fact of golf physics: these clubs produce shots that come down at a steep angle. As a result, there's less danger of out-of-control balls on par 3 holes. So should you only buy a home on a par 3 hole? Well, it's not that easy. Unfortunately, most golf courses are designed with lots of par 4 and 5 holes—and only a handful of par 3 ones.

Another quirk: homes on the left side of the fairway are safer than those on the right. Why? Most golfers are right-handed. As a result, their golf shots tend to curve in that direction. In recognition of this fact of life, some new golf course developments are designed with homes only on the left (and open space on the right).

**3 Golf is NOT a quiet sport.** Those glossy brochures handed out in the sales offices of golf course developments sure look serene. And calm. But be careful of what you can't see. Or hear.

Anyone who's actually lived on a golf course can tell you this fact of duffer life: golf can be a very loud game. Golfers whoop it up when they hit the perfect tee shot. Or sink that impossible putt. Sometimes the most noise comes from golfers chatting while waiting to tee up.

And golf isn't just played from 9am to 5pm. Golfers hit the links early in the morning. Some play late into the evening. In Florida, the busiest times are in the winter months. Thankfully, golfers are limited by the short daylight hours in those months. But remember that the sun is up until 9pm in June in most parts of the U.S.—and that means you could have folks playing through way into the evening.

Another source of noise: grounds keeping equipment. Some courses fire up the mowers early in the morning (5am wake-up call, anyone?) to get the grass cut before the links open. Add in edge trimmers and leaf blowers and you've got some industrial strength noise, all out your bedroom window on a Sunday morning.

In order to speed play, some courses require golfers to use carts during peak periods. While some courses use quiet electric carts, others still cling to the noisy gasoline models. Check into this as part of your due diligence.

Ask the developer what their projections are for golf course use. When will be the busiest times? Slowest? When is the maintenance time? Do they have any strategy for mitigating the noise and disruption of grounds keeping efforts?

**4** **Privacy? What privacy?** Golf courses seem like idyllic places to live, but ask the developer this simple question: how many golfers will be passing your house each day? You might be surprised that during peak periods, that number could be 200, 300 or even 400 golfers.

Imagine 400 people walking by your backyard each day, peering in your living room windows and you can see why privacy issues can be a thorn in the side of the golf course homeowner.

Of course, there are ways to mitigate the peeping toms. The best way: site your home a few feet ABOVE the course. If your house sits five to ten feet above the green, golfers won't be able to easily peak into your windows. You maintain the pretty views, yet may not even see the golf carts as they whiz by.

Clever architects and designers can use tricks to maximize privacy. A strategically placed glass block wall in a bathroom or a bank of narrow windows that sit high in the wall still let light in, without the privacy concerns.

Nonetheless, still expect to spend a fortune on window coverings. One new idea to explore: solar screens. These black screens (either interior or exterior) block out glare and heat gain from big picture windows, yet still preserve the view. And, best of all, no one can see in from the outside.

Another issue to ask the developer about: security. By day, golf courses are islands of grass. By night, the same courses are islands of unlit open space—a perfect hangout for wayward teens or troublemakers. Since most courses forbid fences, your house is exposed to all comers. While no statistical data exists that shows golf course homes are more prone to burglary, anecdotal evidence points up that security isn't a mere passing issue to such homeowners.

Inquire about the community's security plans and strategy. A gate at the front of the community might give a false sense of security—such barriers are easily foiled. The best communities have a proactive strategy that includes on-foot patrols and education programs to address security issues.

## Eco-Houses: They're Not Just for Granola-Heads Anymore

Drive by any ex-hippy community (like the one we live in) and you'll spot 'em: 1970s-era versions of "environmentally-friendly" homes. They also had an additional feature: they were god-awful ugly. The same people who brought us tofu and natural childbirth were also responsible for the ultra-eco-conscious geodesic dome. And they were always brown.

Of course, today these folks don't seem as crazy as they did in the days of Jimmy Carter. We called them "health nuts" then, but later discovered, to our horror, that Big Macs and Ding-Dongs were not extending anyone's life span.

So, it is the Revenge of the Granola Heads that today we put "environmentally-friendly" houses right up there with Mom and apple pie (as long as the apples have not been sprayed with Alar). Fortunately for today's homebuyers, the eco-house has undergone a metamorphosis into something much more palatable than the geodesic dome. Many of today's eco-houses are cleverly disguised to look like real homes. From the exterior, they are normal. Look under the roof, however, and you'll note a few changes. In Chapters 9 and 10, we highlight several eco-friendly building products with our "eco-alternative" symbol.

And those products are just the beginning. Many new products are flooding the "green" market every year. How do you find out the latest eco-news? Ask your architect/designer or builder if he or she has a copy of the Environmental Resource Guide published by the American Institute of Architects (www.aiaonline.com). Another possibility is the Sourcebook for

## 5 ways To Make a Small House Seem Spacious

If you have champagne tastes on a beer budget, consider the following tricks to make a "cute" house seem like a mansion (or at least, feel not as cute):

**1. Go see-through. Install a fireplace that is see through from one room to the next.** The same goes for kitchen cabinets—see-through cabinets between a kitchen and eating area make the space seem bigger. Kill the formal dining room to save space.

**2. Use window tricks.** Lots of windows can make a small space seem much bigger. Use corner windows to frame views and lower the sills to add light.

**3. Raise the ceiling.** New nine-foot drywall sheets give you an extra foot at very little cost.

**4. Keep the flooring simple.** Going from a tile entry to carpet in a living room breaks up the space visually. Staying with one flooring option gives the illusion of more space.

**5. Low walls and less hallways.** Use low walls to separate rooms like the dining area and living room. Hallways are a big space-waster—keep them to a minimum.

Sustainable Design, a catalog of eco-friendly building materials published by the Boston-based Architects for Social Responsibility. (There is also a web site listed below with additional green building information and links).

If you would like to use tropical hardwoods in your home (trim, cabinets, doors, etc.), consider using wood with the "Smart Wood" logo. This certification comes from Green Seal or the Rainforest Alliance (www.rainforestalliance.com), who certify "approved" tree harvesters and make sure the harvesting does not have a negative environmental impact on the species.

◆ **A great source for eco-friendly products.** Planetary Solutions of Boulder, Colorado (303-442-6228, www.planetearth.com) is a one-stop shopping source for "environmentally sound building products." The business offers many interior finishes such as paints, wood trim, tile, carpets and even some more esoteric products—like wall board made from straw waste. Many of the eco-friendly products we mention later in this book are available from Planetary Solutions or you can hire them as a consultant for a per hour fee (the company credits back the money if you purchase products from them).

◆ **Newsletters, sourcebooks and guides.** Environmental Building News is a bi-monthly, 20-page guide to sustainable design and construction. Since it takes no advertising, look for more hard-hitting articles on controversial topics like steel versus wood framing. A one-year subscription costs $79; call (802) 257-7300; www.buildinggreen.com.

The publication's web site (buildinggreen.com) has a plethora of green building resources, including excellent product reviews.

## Drawbacks to the Eco-Home

◆ **Unskilled laborers must learn new tricks—at your expense.** Many eco-products require special installation methods. Unfortunately, this can be beyond the skill level of many subcontractors. As a result, there may be time delays and cost overruns as they learn steel framing or the installation of plastic wood.

◆ **A few of these products are still in the experimental stage.** All the bugs haven't quite been worked out from some eco-friendly products. In the real world, the distribution of these products is spotty—in some areas there may not be a local source. Call Planetary Solutions (mentioned above) to track down a hard-to-find product.

◆ **Some eco-products don't work.** It's the dirty little secret environmentalists don't want to advertise: some of their vaunted eco-products simply don't work well. Or not at all. Take low-volume toilets, which only use half the water of older models. Sounds great, right? Congress thought so and mandated their use in the early 1990's. The only problem: low-volume toilets didn't have enough water volume to wash waste down. So, what do folks do who have them? They flush TWICE, negating any water savings! There's also a black market that's developed in old (high volume) toilets, which are in great demand.

The same thing goes for "eco" wood floor finishes that don't contain harsh chemicals. Great idea, but in practice they don't wear as well as traditional finishes—and require significantly more upkeep and maintenance.

Of course, every eco product isn't a failure. BUT, the lesson here is to clearly understand the trade-offs and do some homework BEFORE you go the eco route.

# Manufactured Homes: Logs, Panels, Modular, Post & Beam

Let's be honest about the new home process: it's darn expensive. Whether you buy from a production builder or hire an architect to design a home from scratch, the cost for a new home today can easily top $200,000, $300,000 or more. So, it's not too surprising that many folks look to money-saving design options like pre-manufactured homes.

Now, if the words "manufactured home" bring to mind trailer parks hit by tornadoes on the evening news, guess again—many of today's manufactured homes look strikingly similar to "site-built" homes. The only difference: manufactured homes are built in factories and then trucked out to the home site. And the cost? Most are about $20 to $30 per square foot; compare that to a site-built house that can start at $60 and soar over $100 to $150 per square foot to build. The average price of a manufactured home: $43,600.

There are about 280 manufacturing facilities that churn out 250,550 homes each year. That means about one out of four new homes started each year are "pre-manufactured." A good place to find more info on this topic is the Manufactured Home Institute's web page at www.mfghome.org. Check out the "Consumer's Corner" which includes several useful publications and links to local associations of manufactured home builders.

Log homes are probably the most popular example of the "pre-manufactured" category, but there are several other options including panelized homes, modular designs and dome homes. Here's a brief description of each type, along with some sources for further exploration.

**1** **Log Homes.** Hey, it worked for Abe Lincoln. Many companies offer a complete log home packages with all the logs, studs, joists and beams pre-cut and numbered for easy installation. You get drawings, an instruction manual and even a visit from a company representative to help you put it all together. A few companies have dealers who can recommend reputable local contractors or you can do it yourself.

A good place to find info on log homes is the Log Homes Council, a 50-member subsidiary of the National Association of Home Builders. You can reach them at 800-368-5242 to get a referral or surf their web page at www.loghomes.org. You can read articles on log home

## Top Ten Manufactured Home Builders

*Here are the biggest players in pre-manufactured home building.*

| Company | Phone | Homes Sold in 2000 |
| --- | --- | --- |
| 1. Champion Enterprises | (248) 340-9090 | 52,442 |
| 2. Fleetwood Enterprises | (909) 351-3500 | 42,123 |
| 3. Oakwood Homes | (336) 664-2400 | 25,933 |
| 4. Horton Homes | (706) 485-8506 | 12,600 |
| 5. Skyline Corp. | (219) 294-6521 | 11,719 |
| 6. Palm Harbor Homes | (972) 991-2422 | 11,589 |
| 7. Cavalier Homes | (256) 747-9800 | 11,478 |
| 8. Southern Energy Homes | (256) 747-8589 | 5,504 |
| 9. Four Seasons Housing | (219) 825-9999 | 5,000 |
| 10. Cavco Industries | (602) 256-6263 | 4,332 |

*Source: 2000 sales as reported by Manufactured Home Merchandiser*

building, check out designs and get a referral to a company near you.

There are several purchase options when it comes to log homes. You can buy a do-it-yourself kit or a complete package of a partially assembled home. Some companies also just sell the logs a la carte. Whichever way you go, most log home manufacturers recommend you buy the windows and doors locally.

One caveat to the log home: there is periodic maintenance that can be a hassle. The logs must be washed, cleaned and stained every five years. For most homes, that will run about $2500 to $3000.

**2 Panelized Houses.** These companies provide factory-built wall sections, in some cases finished with insulation and drywall. Most designs include floors, trusses, windows and doors—just add a foundation and sub floor and poof! Instant home. Most panelized home companies enable you to make small changes in stock designs for a fee; a few even offer custom design services. A good web site to get more info on panelized homes is The Building Systems Council from the NAHB (www.buildingsystems.org).

**3 Modular Homes.** Modular home companies take the pre-manufactured concept one step further—instead of finished walls, you get entire sections of the home that are 90% complete when they arrive at your home site. The sections (or modules) include insulation, electrical, cabinets—even carpeting. Place it atop a foundation, hook up the utilities and you've got a home. The Modular Connection web site (www.modularconnection.com) has more info on this concept, along with modular house plans, a FAQ , links and more.

**4** **Domes.** Interconnecting triangles create this version of the pre-manufactured home. Most dome homes come with framing, sheathing, and connectors plus hardware. A good web site with links to dome manufacturers, as well as general info on this type of pre-manufactured home is at: www.dnaco.net/~michael/domes/domes.html

**5** **Post & Beam (or timber frame).** The revival of craftsman-style design has renewed interest in these pre-manufactured homes. Large posts and beams are connected together to form a freestanding frame that doesn't rely on load-bearing walls or exterior sheathing for structural integrity. Most post & beam homes have large, open floor plans. One of the key manufacturers of post & beam homes is Timberpeg (603-542-7762; www.timberpeg.com). Their well-designed site provides excellent information on timber frame homes.

*For further reading, check out the The Timber-Frame Home, by Tedd Benson (2<sup>nd</sup> edition, $34.95, 1997, Taunton Press; www.taunton.com). This 240-page book features excellent illustrations and photos.*

# Design Tips for Kitchens & Baths

You don't have to have a doctorate in architecture to know this truth about new homes: it's the kitchen and baths that can make or break a home. Invest more time in thoughtfully designing these areas and you'll get back big dividends—both in higher resale value and in simply enjoyment of your new home. Here are our 27 tips for the best kitchens and baths:

## Kitchen

◆ THE PLAN IS KEY. "The first step toward a flawless kitchen is a flawless plan" goes the saying in the building business and we have to agree. A perfect kitchen is not something you can wing out in the field. Of course, you can't even draw the plan without first making some other important decisions: specific models of appliances and plumbing fixtures (i.e., the sinks) must be selected and rough-in dimensions for electrical, ventilation and other plumbing details must be determined first. Since designing a good kitchen is a complex task, you should insist on seeing a separate plan for the kitchen with detailed elevations, cabinet layouts, etc. Details like special trim, decorative shelves and other specialty items should be clearly spelled out.

◆ PRACTICAL PLACEMENT OF APPLIANCES IS CRITICAL. For example, the dishwasher should be next (or as close as possible) to the sink.

◆ KITCHENS IN CYBERSPACE. Any desk in the kitchen should be large (and deep) enough to accommodate a home computer. And if you want a copy of a hot recipe you find on the Web, make sure you leave enough room for a printer.

◆ **Two words: dramatic lighting.** A kitchen is a great place for splashy lighting—an investment that may pay off later in resale value. Under cabinet lighting helps in food preparation. Lights above cabinets add flair.

◆ **Calm the kitchen traffic.** No major household traffic pattern should cross the work triangle.

◆ **Someone's knocking at the door.** Entry and appliance doors should not interfere with work center appliances or counter space. Consider a pocket door in the kitchen to solve this problem.

◆ **Natural light is a key element**—even if it's a sliding glass door near the nook. If you look onto a neighbor, consider an opaque window option (such as glass block).

◆ **Mix and match colors.** Mixed tile colors usually cost the same as a single color—and add visual pizzazz.

◆ **Add functionality to islands.** For example, an electrical outlet is a must. A mixer cabinet is a nice plus as well. If the island is large enough for a sink, make it full-size so clean-up is easier. (A dinky sink isn't much help in food preparation or clean-up). Another idea: put the microwave below the countertop so kids can more easily access it.

◆ **Hide the dishes.** A raised eating bar should be high enough to hide the view of kitchen clutter from an adjoining living space.

◆ **If you like entertaining, double up.** Not only are double ovens convenient, consider double dishwashers as well.

◆ **Here's a neat idea: refrigerated cabinet drawers.** Sub-Zero's "Integrated 700 Series" (call 800-200-7820 or 608-271-2233 for a dealer near you) lets you put refrigeration anywhere in the kitchen. Say you want to have some veggies handy near the island. Install a vegetable crisper drawer cabinet in your island and you'll have them handy right near the prep area. Sure, this is a pricey option (a two-drawer base unit is $2000) but the exteriors are designed to match your cabinets for a seamless look. You can also mix and match refrigerator and freezer compartments to your heart's content.

◆ **Go for a snazzy range hood.** That lowly fixture of kitchen design is slowly coming into the modern era. The snazziest range hoods on the market are made by Berkeley, CA-based Cheng Design (510-549-2805; www.chengdesign.com). Yes, they cost $6000 to $8000 a pop, but these hoods are really a work of art.

◆ **Equal access.** Three cheers to General Electric for introducing the "Real Life" design series, a special line of kitchen appliances, fixtures and accessories for people with physical impairments. A mechanized sink raises or lowers to accommodate wheel-chairs and other cabinets are specially designed for easy use. Call GE at (800) 626-2000 or web: www.ge.com for more info.

◆ **Schedule and be happy.** For a builder, a kitchen can be a scheduling nightmare. Cabinets must be ordered just on the right schedule and even basic items like appliances and plumbing fixtures must arrive at just the right time. And then you've got to make sure the subs show up—in the right order. Communication is key. Your builder must take a hands-on, proactive stance on this issue to make sure delays don't plague the project.

If space is tight:

◆ **Do double duty.** Make counter space play multiple roles—for example, a serving bar could double as a clean-up space.

◆ **Combine areas.** In one model we viewed, the eating nook and desk space shared the same area.

### Baths

◆ **Don't slip up.** Slip-resistant flooring is a smart move. Instead of high-gloss tile, go for a matte (or textured) finish.

◆ **Single steps.** Tubs should have no more than one step.

◆ **Watch the door.** Shower doors should always swing out, not in.

◆ **Make the shower practical.** Consider a seat in the shower, if you have the room. A shelf to store shampoo and soap (instead of a puny soap dish) is also a great shower amenity.

◆ **Separate the sinks.** Split sinks (separated by a foot or more) are easier to use than side-by-side options.

◆ **Watch the waterworks.** Position the showerhead to keep water from spraying outside the shower when you turn it on.

◆ **Raise the vanity.** A 36-inch high vanity saves back strain.

◆ **Make the lighting recessed.** Recessed cans offer better light than strips above the vanity. Another plus: with recessed cans, you can run the mirror all the way to the ceiling, giving the bathroom a more spacious feel.

◆ **Kid-friendly design.** For kid's baths, consider lowering light switches and vanity heights.

◆ **Think twice about clear glass shower doors.** In areas with hard water, these doors can be a nightmare to keep clean.

## The Not So Big House

If you buy one book during the design process of your new home, make it this one: *The Not So Big House: A Blueprint for the Way We Really Live* (by Sarah Susanka, Taunton Press, $30, 1998). Packed with 200 color photos and illustrations, this book explodes the myth that to have a great house, it must be HUGE. Susanka, a Life magazine Architect of the Year, shows you how to build "smaller, more personal spaces" into your new home design by creative use of nooks, built-ins and more. If we were king, we'd decree that every home builder and architect in America be strapped to a chair and forced to read this book before ever building another cavernous big box on a hill.

# BRING ON
# THE BUILDER

**P**op quiz! Today's question is: in many states, you need a license to:

a) Cut hair at a beauty salon.
b) Teach in a public school.
c) Build a home.

Pencils down! Yes, if you answered "A" or "B" you'd be correct. But what about "C"? In 17 states (including Texas, Missouri, New York and Pennsylvania), you do NOT have to have a license to build a new home. That's right, the persons cutting your hair, teaching your children and cleaning your teeth all must get a license to do their jobs—but home builders are truly an "equal opportunity employer." Have a pulse? You can be a homebuilder too!

And what about the rest of the states that license homebuilders? In many cases, the licensing of contractors is more a tax than consumer regulation—state and local governments rake in license fees but pay scant attention to whether the contractor is actually competent to perform his or her job.

Hence, it doesn't take a rocket scientist to recognize a simple rule of new home construction: The quality of your home will be directly related to the builder's competence. A perfect site and expert design plans are worthless if the builder is an idiot.

So how do you "idiot-proof" your new home's construction? The answer: homework. Only by checking out the builder thoroughly will you be able to separate the talented from the pretenders. It probably wouldn't shock you to know that very few home buyers really check out their builder—instead of a thorough examination of the builder's past homes and reputation, many home buyers spend all their time ruminating on carpet colors or kitchen cabinet finishes.

First, recognize the three truths about new homebuilders today:

**1** **You're hiring a builder "team," not a single person.** Looks are deceiving—it may appear that you're dealing with just one person. Actually you're hiring three groups:

◆ **The builder's crews:** Larger builders may have their own crews who do some or all of the framing and finishing work. These crews work solely for that builder and may construct dozens of homes from the same basic design. Smaller builders may have a foreman or site supervisor who manages the project on a day-to-day basis.

◆ **Subcontractors:** Many builders farm out the production of their homes to "subs," independent workers/companies. For example, few builders install the heating/cooling systems with their own crews; a plumbing or HVAC contractor does this work. The quality of the subs your builder uses is directly related to whether you get a quality home or a lemon. Later we'll offer some tips on determining the quality level of subs.

◆ **Materials suppliers:** Builders may have certain sources for building materials. If the builder has "contractor's discounts" with suppliers for such things as kitchen cabinets, light fixtures and other materials, you will want to know this information. Identifying the suppliers gives you an indication of the builder's standard of quality. Take kitchen cabinets, for example. It's obviously more impressive if the builder has an account with a custom or high-quality cabinet manufacturer than with a lower-end, tract-style cabinet supplier.

**2** **Caring craftsmen were long ago replaced by number crunchers.** Years ago, homes were built by builders who were craftsmen—they tended to build homes one at a time. Sadly, "merchant" builders whose main skill was number crunching and slick marketing long ago replaced many of these caring craftsmen. Craftsmanship was replaced by "volume" in the push to build more homes at a faster pace and lower cost. Builders are tripping over one another to do things faster and faster. In a recent article in a building trade journal, U.S Homes trumpeted the fact that it just completely built a 3600 square foot home in Lowes Island, Virginia in a mere 29 days. Whoopee. We'd rather have a builder take three times as long and build it right, not fast.

Today many builders seem more skilled at marketing than construction. More emphasis is put into slick ads, brochures and model homes than making sure things are built right in the field.

Sadly, even smaller builders—who focus less on volume and somewhat more on quality—can get caught in this trap. When times are good, some get greedy and take on far too many homes to supervise carefully.

The decline in craftsmanship can also be traced to another big problem: a shortage of skilled labor. A recent study by a management institute in Colorado found that "two-thirds of all builders reported more difficulty finding skilled craft labor now than five years ago," reports the *Wall Street Journal.* And the problem may just get worse: "According to the Home Builders Institute, an education arm of the NAHB, some 340,000 skilled construction workers will be needed annually over the next decade—but only 170,000 trainees actually enroll in apprenticeship programs each year," the article said.

As with many problems in the construction industry today, the arguments quickly become circular. Builders say the shortage of labor is the root cause of quality problems in new homes. Tradespeople say the shortage is the builder's fault— in the builder's rush to cut costs and build homes faster, many skilled workers are discouraged from entering the business.

**3** **Quality control is tied to the level of supervision by the builder.** Even if you can find skilled tradespeople, an unsupervised crew or subcontractor is an invitation to disaster. We've seen many new home fiascoes that were built by allegedly quality-conscious builders. The reason for all the defects? The builders spread themselves too thin and couldn't supervise the homes properly. The best builders watch their workers like hawks, personally staying on site for long periods of time. If the actual builder isn't there, a qualified foreman or supervisor should be. Subcontractors should also supervise their workers carefully.

In the real world, however, supervision ranges from the merely adequate to the barely there. The builder may be called away from the construction site on the afternoon that the furnace is installed. The sub botches the installation by putting the furnace in the wrong place. Or the wrong trim materials are delivered to the site and are installed by a crew that couldn't care less.

Therefore, one of the best ways to screen for a quality builder is to determine the level of supervision you're buying. And you don't want to just take the builder's word for it—visit actual job sites to see what's happening. We'll discuss more details on evaluating the builder's level of supervision later in this chapter.

## Sources to Find a Quality Builder

◆ **Architects.** An experienced residential architect has seen which builders have been naughty or nice. The architect will also have some idea of which builders are best for your particular house—while they rarely admit it, builders often specialize in certain types of homes or price ranges. A builder may be able to build a quality $250,000 three-bedroom "basic" home, but may be a fish out of water on a $550,000 "executive" home. The degree of difficulty in executing the architect's design is also an important factor in choosing a builder.

A good architect should offer bidding and negotiation services with potential builders. Even if you go with more bare-bones service from an architect (say, design only), he or she should be able to pass on the names of several reputable builders. BE CAREFUL: An architect's recommendations should not be taken on blind faith. You must still screen the builder thoroughly.

◆ **Recent homebuyers.** Ask your friends and relatives if they know anyone who has recently built a home. A satisfied customer of a builder is a very important find. Later we'll talk about questions to ask such previous customers.

◆ **Driving around in new home communities.** If you drive around areas where new homes are being built, you'll no doubt see builder signs. You may also see a builder sign on a vacant lot the builder owns. Of course, just because a builder is building homes in a certain area does not mean they're actually doing quality construction. But at least it gives you the names of several possible candidates.

## Not-So-Good Sources

◆ **Professional Associations.** Nearly every state has local home builder's associations (HBA), which are affiliates of the National Association of Home Builders (NAHB). What does it mean if a contractor is a member of a so-called professional homebuilder's association? Do they screen for quality contractors? Are you kidding? Membership in such an association means they've paid dues to the association. That's it. Big deal.

Oh, sure, there's lots of propaganda from the builders that these associations help consumers. Please. An ethics pledge or a requirement that members be licensed is not very meaningful.

In Kansas City, a consumer's group (Homeowners Against Defective Construction or HADD) uncovered some disturbing facts about their local HBA's "Certified Master Builder" program. The home builders there have long been touting their status as Certified Master Builders in their advertising, but HADD discovered the program was a sham. The group's investigation found the HBA had "grandfathered" in all its members to the program (which allegedly has strict standards for membership) with no background checks. Only in the home building industry does the words "Certified" and "Master" have so little basis in reality.

In Florida, we read a newspaper article about a builder who was touting the local homebuilder's association's ethics committee. "If a builder screws up, we'll throw them out of our group. And that means they can't participate in the local Parade of Homes." We're sure the scam artists are quaking in their boots at that threat. Frankly, we've found no evidence that homebuilder's associations ever "police" their members or protect consumers. In North Carolina, the *president* of a local homebuilder's association was accused of building severely defective homes,

. . . . . . . . . . . . . . . . . . . . . . . . . . . . . .

according to a television documentary. Despite the overwhelming evidence against him, he was never censured by the association.

What these groups are good at is political influence. Local homebuilder associations are big political contributors—this money "buys" off local politicians from enacting tougher consumer protection laws. Watering down enforcement of building codes is a major "non-public" goal of some associations.

◆ **Real Estate Agents.** Few agents would know a quality home if it landed right on them. What an agent is good at is ferreting out builders who offer bigger commissions. Others steer you to new homes they have listed—that way they get the whole 6% to 7% commission to themselves.

Even honest agents are hobbled by their own ignorance—most have no clue about sound construction. Just like unsuspecting consumers, they may equate cosmetic details like six-panel oak doors or cherry kitchen cabinets with "quality." Is the foundation engineered correctly? Did the builder use energy-efficient construction methods? Too many agents are often clueless.

◆ **The Newspaper.** Most newspaper real estate sections are pure advertising for builders. Articles disguised as editorial copy are really puff pieces about how "wonderful" and "talented" certain builders are—and the builders pay for this. They may even write their own copy.

Sadly, many newspapers are intimidated by powerful developers and builders, who fill the paper's coffers with big advertising bucks. Most papers are scared to death of offending these big clients. Not only can builders buy positive coverage, they can also kill negative articles at some papers. Complaints about defective homes are buried or not even reported at all.

On the plus side, at least newspaper real estate sections point out neighborhoods with new home construction. Of course, many new homes or available lots are never advertised, but it's a start.

## New Homebuyers in Cyberspace: What's on the Web?

**Homebuilder.com**
**Web:** www.homebuilder.com
**What it is:** The mother of all new home sites.

**What's cool:** Designed by the same outfit that did the Realtor's slick site, HomeBuilder.com is a massive compendium of new home builders. You can search for a contractor, new home listings, planned communities, lots or custom builders. Easy navigation makes surfing this site quick and effective.

**Needs work:** While this site aims to be comprehensive, sometimes it is a mile wide but an inch deep. A click on custom home builders in Denver yields just six contractors—and instead of getting a quick profile on each, all you see are links to the builders' own sites. The site's listings are often limited to major metro areas and some states are devoid of content—a search for new homes in the entire state of Montana produced just nine listings. Nine?

### New Home Network
**Web:** www.newhomenetwork.com; see Figure 1.
**What it is:** The best-designed new home site on the web.
**What's cool:** This site was our favorite. You start at a graphic of the US to target your search; then you go to a city level and then finally to new home communities. A quick listing tells you about each community and what models are available. You can add a certain plan to your list of favorites and even calculate a mortgage payment for each house!
**Needs work.** Well, no site is perfect. We'd like to see more floor plans and pictures of actual homes; instead you get vital stats like square footage and number of bedrooms. Some of the graphics (like community maps) are so small, they're rather useless.

## Other sites of interest:

◆ **American Builders Network** (www.americanbuilders.com) says it screens builders to make sure they have been building for at least five years AND they are licensed in the states they build. Nice concept, but the site was rather thin on listings when we last visited. And after searching for a certain area, all you basically get are links to builder's homepages.

**Figure 1:** The NewHomeNetwork.com is our pick as the best site for finding builders and new home communities.

◆ **BuildFind** (www.buildfind.com). This site isn't pretty to look at, but the search engine of "500,000 pages of home improvement information, resources and links" is rather impressive. It kind of helps to know what you are looking for before you dive in, but we liked the site's massive listings of new home forums, chats, newsgroups, and more.

## GETTING STARTED: HOW FAR IN ADVANCE?

When should you hire a builder? If you're buying a production or "spec" home, this is a moot point. Your search for location and builder are one in the same.

However, if you're building from scratch or doing a "custom" home on a lot you've located, there are three different ways to go:

**1** Hire a builder BEFORE you hire an architect/designer. Some folks recommend this path, but we see several big problems. If you don't have a home design yet, how can you get a price estimate? How do you know that the builder is really skilled at building your design? What incentive does the builder have to bring your project in at a certain cost? Going this route implies you must trust the builder—and have faith in his or her ability to execute a design no one has yet seen. Frankly, finding someone who you can put that much trust in is a 9.0 on the 10-point difficulty scale.

**2** Hire a builder at the SAME TIME you find an architect/designer—but before there is any design yet. This method requires extreme faith in your architect—they must have a rough feel for the best builder for you even without doing a design yet. The advantage is you bring the builder on board early in the process—he can contribute to the design effort by suggesting cost-saving ideas. The disadvantage is there is no "competitive" bid process—you've committed to a builder even before you've gotten a price estimate. Sure a good architect should design a home that's within your budget range—but not all architects are experts at construction costs. Hence, you may get a design that is way over your budget. And you're stuck with a builder who does not have an incentive to hold down costs.

**3** After you complete the design, bid out the house to two or three builders. Hire the one who gives you a good bid and seems most interested in your home. This method offers a "competitive bidding process" that provides a builder with an incentive to hold down greed—the competition will get the job if he gets too pricey. The key to making this process work is having an architect draw plans that completely spec out every detail—that way you get "apples-to-apples" bids. What are the disadvantages? In hot markets, builders may not want to go through the hassle of submitting a bid. Also, if you bid the home out to more than three builders, this sends the signal that you're just price-shopping (such a negative in the builder's mind that he might not even want to bid). By not having the builder in at the beginning of the design process, you may miss out on cost-saving suggestions and other insights.

What's the best course? It's up to you. We think the last method is probably the best in most cases. If you are lucky enough to find a talented architect who is very experienced in residential design and construction cost estimating, method two is certainly acceptable. Unless you're convinced you've found the very best builder, hiring a builder first without an architect or design seems least preferable.

## THE FOUR TYPES OF BUILDERS

There's no "IBM" of home building—most home builders are local contractors who build less than 25 homes a year. The nation's largest homebuilder, Pulte, built just 27,781 homes in 2000. We say "just" because even though that was a record for Pulte, it was less than 3% of all the single-family homes built that year. According to sales reports, the nation's top ten builders in 2000 accounted for 165,000 home sales/—or less than 15% of the total. Even though big builders' share of the market has doubled in the last five years, they still account for a small part of the new home business. Put another way, eight out of every ten new homes are built by smaller, local builders.

As far as we can tell, most contractors come in four flavors. Here's an overview of who you will encounter on your new home journey.

**1** **The Dog and Pickup Truck Builder.** As you might expect, these guys' basic assets include a pickup truck and a dog that follows them to work. No fancy office or plush model homes. They tend to build one home at a time. This builder is the sole employee and supervisor of the project.

Some of the best homes we've seen are built by dog-and-pickup-truck builders. And some of the worst homes we've seen are built by them as well. Most small-time operators build between one to five homes a year—in good times, they could double that volume.

## THE BID: APPLES TO APPLES

You take your plans to two builders for bids and you get back one that's $40,000 under the competing bid. What's up? Ask yourself—are you getting an apples to apples comparison? Make sure the bids contain detailed specifics, from the type and brand of windows spec'd to the allowances for flooring, appliances and more. You might discover the lowest bid is based on lower quality finishes in the home. That's OK if you want to make those trade-offs . . . but don't automatically assume the cheaper bid is the best.

Unfortunately, they rarely have the skill or staff to supervise more than one home at a time.

**Best For:** Semi-custom homes designed from a plan book. Lower cost homes (less than $200,000 depending on market conditions). If the builder is bold, he may try a few "semi-custom" spec homes. Most other homes they build are "pre-sold" to customers.

**Worst For:** Architect-designed homes—most don't know how to work with or understand architects. Don't expect wonderful design skills from these folks—most have limited drafting skills and churn out plain vanilla homes.

**Used To Be:** A framer or other subcontractor who recently "promoted" himself into being a builder. While he may have knowledge in one area (such as framing), he might be clueless about plumbing, roofing, etc. Hence, it's difficult for this builder to judge the quality of certain subcontractors.

**Watch Out:** Most dog-and-pickup-truck builders are poorly capitalized—if they fail financially, they could take your home down with them. Lack of adequate insurance looms as another major risk for you—it's rare to find a small-time builder with "errors and omissions" (E & O) insurance. Others lack worker's compensation insurance—another negative.

**2** **The Mini-Tycoon.** This builder has grown beyond the pickup truck and now may have a small office. While this contractor is still the primary supervisor of homes, he has one to four other employees who help with site supervision, materials purchasing and so on. Most build between 3 and 15 homes in a typical year—up to 25 homes during boom periods.

Quality tends to be a little better since this builder has slightly more experience than the dog-and-pickup-truck builder. At the same time, the emphasis on bigger volume can drag down the quality. Some mini-tycoons specialize in the custom home market and build spectacular homes.

**Best For:** Move-up homes in the middle to upper price ranges. Some build small communities of semi-custom spec homes, while others concentrate on the custom, pre-sold market. Occasionally works with architects/designers. The larger mini-tycoons may do both custom homes and "production" homes in a hot subdivision.

**Worst For:** Challenging designs or complex plans. Difficult sites may also pose problems. With some successful homes under their belts, mini-tycoons may have an over-inflated opinion of their design skills. They still haven't learned that the best thing for them to do is build, not design.

**Used To Be:** A dog-and-pickup-truck builder but now has more money. Other mini-tycoons may have worked for a subcontractor or materials supplier and wanted a bigger piece of the action. However, just because he's worked for a kitchen cabinet manufacturer as a rep does not necessarily make him a talented builder.

**Watch Out:** These folks still have money problems—they often use the profit from the last home to build the next one. Foolishly, they go out and buy land in hot markets to do spec homes, then get caught with no cash and lots of dirt when the market turns sour. Lack of insurance still haunts mini-tycoon builders—while they probably have liability and worker's comp, E & O is beyond their financial grasp. Despite the increased chance of better supervision, these builders must be watched like a hawk on quality issues.

**3 Top-Gun Builders.** These builders have taken home building to the next logical step—forming a professional company with a focused emphasis on a certain market. Usually, that market is either pure custom homes or communities of semi-custom executive homes.

The president of the company has "retired" from field supervision—that's left to teams of project supervisors and site foremen. An in-house estimator does nothing but estimate and bid projects, holding down construction costs. The general contractor focuses on administration and marketing. As a result, these folks can crank out 25 to 100 homes a year.

Surprisingly, some of these builders are willing to do custom homes in most price ranges. However, most of their customers are building expensive homes designed by architects—hence they get used to building for a certain clientele.

**Best For:** Move-up and luxury homes. Experience working with an architect makes this builder a preferred choice for home buyers.

**Worst For:** Starter homes—top-gun builders rarely take on these projects, except in slow markets when they are looking for work. If you don't want to hire an architect, these builders may not want to work for you. They've realized that what they do best is build, not design.

**Used To Be:** Successful small-time builder—but with financial and managerial skills. They didn't take risks by locking up all their money in vacant land—instead they let clients take that risk in buying the lot.

**Watch Out:** Since these companies are bigger, the risk of bureaucracy headaches increases. There may be several layers of management between you and the company president. While these builders tend to produce the best quality, they still must be watched by private inspectors and architects to insure unsupervised subs don't botch complex or difficult plans.

**4** **Production builder.** These are the builders you see advertised in the newspaper—the builders of large communities of cookie-cutter homes. Many falsely promote themselves as semi-custom builders since you have the choice of "customizing" the carpet color. The reality is that a production builder's main emphasis is just that—production. Quantity over quality. As a result, the largest crank out 20,000 homes a year. Smaller production builders may build "just" 100 or more homes a year.

**Best For:** Starter homes and townhomes. If you don't have the time to invest in going the semi-custom or custom route, this may be a viable alternative.

**Worst For:** Anything with creativity. You basically pick from one of several stock plans. The builder owns all the lots.

**Used To Be:** A faceless corporation that wanted to diversify into real estate. Or, it is remotely possible that these builders did quality homes at one time. Eventually, that quality-conscious builder sold out to number-crunchers who, with the backing of lots of Wall Street money, built the company on savvy marketing and luck.

**Watch Out:** Remember, the goal for the production builder is quantity, not quality. Frankly, you can't do a quality home in just 29 days—corners are cut and worse. Look out for the production builder's contract—a team of lawyers may have worked late nights to find ways to limit your rights.

## Questions to Ask a Builder.

**1** **What do you think about architects or designers?** Here's a loaded question that probes for builders with problem attitudes. A typical knee-jerk response is, "Architects design pretty houses but they know nothing about costs." A better answer: builders who say they appreciate an experienced residential architect, but also add how they can contribute ideas to the design process. You may ask the builder if he's ever worked with the architect you are considering.

**2** **How long have you been in business? How many "pre-sold" versus spec houses have you done?** Builders who do lots of spec homes may not know how to work with custom buyers—they're used to making their own decisions, not having an architect or consumer call the shots.

**3** **Have you or any partner in your company built under any other name?** This question hits at the heart of a scam that has bilked home buyers out of thousands of dollars in defective construction rip-offs: builders who change their names and move to another state to avoid angry customers. Be suspicious of newly formed corporations or companies. Later, we'll discuss how to probe a contractor's background to make sure they haven't ripped off home buyers under other names.

## The Square-Foot Price Myth

One of the biggest potential mistakes you can make in searching for a builder is to shop by "square-foot price." How does this method work? Well, if Builder A has a 3500-square-foot home that costs $455,000, then the price per square foot is $130. However, Builder B down the street is charging $360,000 for a 3000-square-foot home—the per square foot price is just $120. Is Builder B a better deal than Builder A?

The fact is you can't tell just by the square-foot price. Builder A might use expensive granite kitchen countertops, top-quality windows and better insulation. Meanwhile, Builder B has cut some corners, using cheap carpet, builder-special faucets and inexpensive doors. The point is that expensive, quality materials will push up the price per square foot of any house. The builder with the lowest prices may be giving you bottom-of-the-barrel quality.

Another problem is location. If the lot value is included in a builder's square foot price estimate, it could bias the calculations. A big part of a home's price is the land—up to 30% and even 45% in some parts of the country. Lots in bad locations (on a busy street, for example) are definitely cheaper than prime location lots on golf courses, with views, on a quiet cul-de-sac, etc. Homes in less exciting locations will probably have lower prices per square foot. Separate out land value to get a better read on a builder's prices (in industry jargon, the home's cost less the land value is the "hard cost.")

Don't forget that it's also cheaper per square foot to build "up" than "out." Hence, two-story homes are often less expensive (per square foot) than one level, ranch-style homes. Comparing the prices of these two home types is like comparing apples to oranges.

Basically, per square foot prices are only helpful on a large scale. When you analyze such prices on a community, city or county-wide basis, you have a more meaningful comparison to other communities. Therefore, all the regulation and high land costs in California make their homes cost $200 to $400 per square foot in some cities. On the other hand, homes in North Dakota may be closer to $50 per square foot.

One builder we interviewed best summed up the "price per square foot" myth by saying that he can build you a home for anywhere from $5 to $200 per square foot. Five bucks buys you a tent, while $200 gets you the Taj Mahal.

**4** **Could you provide me with a copy of your contractor's license and insurance coverage (both liability and errors & omissions)?** Any legitimate contractor should give you a license number to check out. (Unfortunately, 17 states such as New York, Texas, Illinois and Pennsylvania don't license builders. These states may license subcontractors like plumbers, but homebuilders or general contractors are exempt). It's not enough to get a promise that the builder has insurance—you must get written proof. As a side note, many insurance companies are dropping builder coverage after a rash of defective construction lawsuits. Hence, only the most reputable builders will probably be able to maintain coverage. Of course, insurance is no guarantee—it's just one piece of the puzzle.

**5** **How many projects do you currently have going?** Is the builder spread too thin? If a dog-and-pickup-truck builder has ten homes currently under construction, it's not a good sign. At the same time, a builder who's been sitting around doing nothing for several months is suspicious as well. If they aren't working, is it because their reputation is scaring off new customers?

**6** **Can I see several of the homes you are working on?** Paranoid builders may not want you poking around, but the most reputable contractors have no problem at all. They're proud of their work. No apologies. Ask if you can visit the homes without the builder to get a more objective look-see.

**7** **Would you be willing to look at my plans and provide cost-saving suggestions?** Do you see any mistakes or missing elements in my design plans? This is crucial to getting an accurate bid. A real pro should spot potential problems—such as a poor roof design that might lead to leaks. Alternatives to expensive materials should be discussed. You can really tell a builder's experience level if he can answer this question well.

**8** **Can I have a copy of your contract? What level of warranty is offered—can I get a copy of the warranty?** In the next chapter, we'll talk about contracts. You want a copy now to see what terms and warranties the builder offers. A builder with an anti-consumer contract loaded with clauses designed to severely restrict your rights is a major red flag.

**9** **How will the construction be supervised? Is the supervisor the builder himself, a foreman, or a site supervisor?** This is a critical issue—while you can't expect the builder to be at your site 24 hours a day, there must be a strong commitment to quality supervision or you're in trouble. Unsupervised subs will run amok. Ask for a commitment here—builders who are spread too thin will be nervous about this issue.

**10** **How much are change orders?** Odds are that you'll want to change something during construction—it's a fact of human nature. If you want to add a window, how much does it cost (for the window and installation)? Is there one charge before construction begins and another set of fees afterward? Are there any "administration charges" for changes? If a builder has to track down the price of an added item, this takes administrative time. A small fee ($25 or a small hourly rate) is alright, but a massive charge is questionable.

Change orders also can be initiated by the builder. When the builder discovers a problem with the plans, he may want to charge you to change it. Watch out: some builders make a killing charging customers "change" fees. These builders nit-pick the plans and charge you for every extra screw and nail. A good way to sniff out this scam is to simply ask the builder how many change orders normally occur. A couple of change orders are expected—20 change orders initiated by the builder are excessive.

Some builders are more innovative than others when it comes to managing change orders. Lonergan Homes in Columbia, MD (www.lonerganhomes.com) has an excellent web site that lets buyers sign on (with a password) and view all their change orders. Homebuyers can modify or delete any change order, view the new total price and even track the project's completion date. We wish more builders viewed their web site as business tools instead of toys.

## THE SITE SUPERVISOR: A KEY CONTACT.

**M**ost large production builders (and even mid-size contractors) assign a site supervisor or foreman to oversee your home's construction. This person is the guy in the trenches—his job is a bit like the air traffic controller at La Guardia, overseeing the entire project and juggling various schedules. When shopping for a builder, ask to meet the site supervisor for your home. Ask these questions:

**1. How long have you been supervising homes for this builder?** At least five years experience is a must.

**2. How many homes do you supervise at once?** There is no one correct answer, but one person can only be in so many places at once—or their work (or supervision) suffers. Most foremen can only watch 3-4 homes at once. A supervisor keeping tabs on 10 homes at once is stretched too thin.

**3. How do you feel about us hiring a private inspector to visit the home during construction?** A pro shouldn't have any problem with that at all.

**11** **Who are your subcontractors? Materials suppliers?** Can I have a list of all the subs' and suppliers' phone numbers and addresses? Let's say you talk to a previous home buyer who complains about the plumbing. If you know the sub who did that plumbing job and the prospective builder's plumber, you'd be able to steer clear if the two names match. Getting a list of all the subs will help you confirm that they've been paid prior to your home's closing. This helps lower the chances you'll get stung in a "mechanic's lien scam:" the builder takes your money but doesn't pay the subs, who then promptly file liens on your new home. A wise tip: before you close on any new home, call the subs and suppliers to confirm they have been paid.

**12** **Can you provide me with a bank reference? A business reference (a supplier, for example)? Personal credit report? Financial statement?** The more information they supply, the better you will feel about entrusting tens of thousands of dollars of your money with them. Most builders will at least provide a bank reference. It's fair play for you to turn the tables and ensure that the builder is financially qualified to build the home. Those who get nervous at these requests or say it's "none of your business" may be trying to hide shaky financial footing.

**13** **Could you provide me with references of buyers with comparable homes?** Get names of three to five previous customers who have bought from the builder between now and three years ago. Make sure at least one or two references have been in their homes more than one year—by that time some construction defects will be more than evident. Also, the glow of new home ownership has worn off.

By the way, we realize that if you get four references from each of three builder candidates, this means 12 interviews. But we know of no other way to find out whether a builder is worth his asking price. All the sales talk is meaningless if customers aren't satisfied—and you can't tell if you don't ask them.

An alternative to this would be to ask the builder for a list of all the homes he has built in the past five years. Will you contact all these buyers? Of course not. You can pick and choose among several prospects. The goal here is to prevent the builder from giving you a list of just the most trouble-free homes.

"But won't the builder just give me happy customers as references?" This is a reasonable fear. However, by asking for home buyers who have built similar or comparable homes, you're cutting down that risk. The builder can't just pick happy customers at random. Also, by limiting the search period to three years, you prevent the builder from finding happy customers from the 1980's.

You don't have to rely on the builder's list of customers, of course. Your real estate agent should be able to do a search of public records to come up with a list of the builder's previous sales. Look up the owners' phone numbers and presto! You have a reference list.

# Step-by-Step Screening Strategies

**Step 1: Decide on the design "strategy" for your new home.** Will you hire an architect? Use a plan from a magazine or book? Or go with a stock plan from a builder?

**Step 2: Identify three to five potential builders.**

**Step 3: Set up an interview appointment with each candidate.** Leave a good hour or more to ask the above questions. Talk about the builder's past projects.

**Step 4: After the interviews, narrow your list to two or three final candidates.** Call them back and ask for the following:

◆ A list of current projects you can visit.

◆ The names of recent customers (1 to 3) who have bought homes in the past year.

◆ Other recent customers (3 to 5) who have been in their homes for more than one year and less than three years.

**Step 5: Before you go looking at homes, check out several "home inspection" books from your local library or bookstore.** Familiarize yourself with some basic construction aspects—you're not expected to be an expert engineer, but get a feel for "good" versus "bad" construction methods.

**Step 6: If possible, visit the construction sites without the builder.** This gives you uninterrupted time to evaluate the home. But remember to stay out of the way of workers. As an alternative, you can visit the home in the evening after the workers are gone and before the sun sets. If the builder wants to be present, don't let him distract you. Take time to look at basements, attics and other nooks and crannies. If you have any questions, don't be afraid to call the builder on certain problems you notice. See the box "Visiting the Other Homes: Evaluating Construction on the Fly" for more tips.

**Step 7: Call the previous home buyer references.** See the following box for more tips on finding a builder's past customers. Ask the builder's past customers a series of simple questions to get just the facts, such as:

◆ Was the house built on schedule and on budget? Did it start when the builder promised? Were there any delays?

◆ Were there any problems that the builder had to come back to fix? Did the builder fix these problems quickly? To your satisfaction?

# Finding a Builder's Past Customers

Ask any contractor for a list of references and you're sure to get happy clients. But how can you get a list of ALL the builder's past customers? Since most contractors won't divulge that to you, there are several clever ways of uncovering this info:

◆ **Check county deed records.** Go to the county where the builder has constructed the majority of his or her homes. The county clerk's office typically has a computerized database of real estate transactions. Search for the builder (called the "Grantor") and note the names of the home buyers (referred to as the "Grantee"). Remember to search under the builder's personal name and any company names. Realize that there may be several variations of the builder's name in the public records (Smith Construction, Smith Development, etc). Go back as many years as possible (10 is a good bet). You should have an extensive list of past customers and their addresses. Simply cross reference this with a local phone book (or try the web site Bigfoot.com) and you'll have contact numbers.

◆ **Has the builder been sued?** Again, the county clerk's office will be useful. Court records in these matters are public and you can easily search for the builder's name (again, personal or business name) to see if he appears as a "defendant" in any suit. Determine the case number and find out if the lawsuit deals with defective construction. Another item to check: mechanic liens. If the builder doesn't pay his bills, subcontractors and suppliers may have filed mechanic liens against the builder. Again, the county should have these records for you to access as well. Any liens indicate a builder with financial difficulties. You can also do this search on the web at KnowX.com. For a small fee, you can look up lawsuits or liens filed against ANY builder.

◆ **Local building departments.** Your city or county building department may have additional intelligence on your home builder. Since you know the builder's previous homes' addresses (see the first bullet in this box), you can look up their inspection records. Check to see if the builder repeatedly failed inspections. How long did it take to fix the problems? Cross reference several home projects to see if the builder is making the same mistakes over and over again.

◆ **Secretary of state.** All corporations in a state must register with the Secretary of State. You can typically access a builder's records with a simple phone call. If a builder has financial problems, he might "forfeit" his corporate status and start under a new name. This is also a strategy to avoid liability in lawsuits—a builder simple closes up one company and starts a new one. Treat any irregularities you find in the Secretary of State's records as a major red flag.

Special thanks to Homeowner's *Against Defective Dwellings (web: www.hadd.com) for these ideas. Their publication "Managing the Home Construction Team" is an excellent primer on hiring builders.*

◆ Did the builder initiate any change orders? How many?

◆ Does the roof leak? If you have any skylights, do they leak? Is there any water problem in the basement? Are any rooms hot/cold or drafty? (Add your own questions to this list, given the home you're building.)

◆ How is the "warranty" service? Does the builder promptly respond to warranty repair requests? Did the workmen show up when they promised?

**Step 8: As you visit each reference, make notes about the quality of construction and craftsmanship that you see.** After each visit, make more notes to yourself in the car about the interview.

## 10 Clues To Quality Builders

Every builder says he builds quality homes, but how can you really tell? On your trip to evaluate homes under construction, take with you a flashlight, pocketknife, marble and this list of 10 quick construction items to check:

**1 Smart drainage.** When you walk around a new home, look at the ground. It should slope away from the house so no rainwater collects near the foundation. Downspouts should have black plastic pipes to move rainwater far away from the home. Another tip: look for a foundation drain in the basement or crawl space. All these drainage items aren't required by code but the best builders should do them at no extra cost.

**2 Ugly backsides.** Sure, all builders try to make the fronts of their homes attractive. But be sure to check out the sides and backs of new homes. To save money, some builders omit exterior wood trim from windows in the back or sides of a home. While you are checking out the window trim, see if it has been caulked with a thick bead of caulk to prevent air and water infiltration.

**3 Roof ventilation.** Every roof needs adequate ventilation. Look at the roof—you should see several vents to allow for ventilation. Additional screened air vents under the eaves are wise as well.

**4 Concrete cracks.** Yes, small hairline cracks can occur in any concrete driveway or patio. But anything over 1/16th of an inch could be a problem. One quick test: see if a knife blade fits in the crack. If it does, it's a concern. Concrete cracks are a sign of sloppy construction—either the concrete has too little reinforcement, was watered down to reduce strength or is settling due to poor soil preparation underneath the slab.

**5 Framing tips.** If you can view a home during the framing stage, you don't have to be an expert carpenter to spot good (and bad)

**Step 9: Confirm the builder's license and insurance coverage.** Call your state contractor licensing board (the local building department should have this number) to confirm the builder's license status. Ask the board whether the builder has had any complaints and/or license suspensions. If the builder built in another state in the past five years, call that state's licensing board as well. Call the builder's insurer to make sure any liability, workers compensation or errors/omissions coverage is in place. Don't just take the builder's verbal assurances about insurance coverage.

**Step 10: Do the financial "screens."** Call the bank reference and ask about the builder's account. Any bounced checks? When was it opened? Any other information they can give you? Check the supplier references—what type of credit does the builder have (net 30 or

construction. Look at where the framing meets the foundation—is everything flush and square? Check where joists are nailed together—lots of hammer marks may mean a sloppy crew.

**6** **Roof overhangs**. Look up at the roof overhang at the end of a home (called the gable end). The best builders use two-by-fours to support the roof and extend this back into the house. Called "bargeboard' supports, these keep a roof from sagging in the future. Once again, these are not required by code but the best builders do this.

**7** **Siding.** If the siding is wood, check for cracking or excessive knots. Also look at the paint: if you see the wood grain bleeding through, it probably needs another coat. The best builders use at least two coats of paint.

**8** **Cleanliness.** Take a look at the job site of a home under construction. The best builders are neat and clean; trash should NOT be strewn around the site. Another place to check: the crawl space (if the home has one). Sloppy builders stick all sorts of trash down there; take a flashlight to ferret out problems.

**9** **Do the marble test.** Take a marble and set it on the home's floor. If it rolls in one direction, it could indicate problems (severe settling or a home that's out of plumb). If you see the floor before the carpet or tile is laid down, make sure the builder has screwed the subfloor down (instead of just nailing it). This prevents floor squeaks.

**10** **Feel that drywall.** The best way to evaluate a builder's wall finish is to use your hands. Run your hand along the walls, millwork and trim—it should feel smooth. Gritty or rough textures indicate sloppy construction. To get a smooth finish with millwork, you need to paint it twice and lightly re-sand it between coats. Sloppy builders cut corners on this. If you see drywall tape or nails after a wall has been finished and painted, that's a sign of bad construction.

C.O.D.)? Has the builder been current with payments?

**Step 11: Have your attorney do a judgment and mechanic's lien search on the builder.** If the builder has worked under another corporate or company name, search it too. This will determine if he has any unpaid bills or outstanding judgments from lawsuits. The fact is bad builders leave a trail of such liens and judgements behind them—sniffing out this information is extremely important. Another tip: have your attorney run a "D&B" on the builder—this credit report from Dun & Bradstreet may also turn up credit problems. As mentioned earlier in this chapter, you can do much of this yourself at web sites like KnowX.com.

**Step 12: Call your local Better Business Bureau and your area's consumer affairs department**. Most new home complaints don't go to the BBB, but it's worth a shot. Consumer affairs departments (which may be separate agencies or part of a district attorney's office) may have a record of past complaints.

**Step 13: In areas with high utility costs, ask your local utility company for a print-out of utility bills (gas, electric, etc.) for the builder's previously-built homes.** So the builder claims he builds energy efficient homes? See if it's true—some utilities provide this information for free or a nominal charge. It's the best way to see whether the builder's promises match reality.

**Step 14: If the builders pass these tests, get cost estimates for your project from the winning candidates.** Have them break down the bid by trade-area/subcontractor. Any options should be clearly spelled out in terms of costs. Suggestions for lower costs should also be listed (an asphalt shingle roof is $3000 less than the specified cedar shake shingles, for example). If you've hired an architect, she may assist you in preparing the "bid package" to get an apples-to-apples cost estimate from each builder. Some architects also offer negotiating services.

**Step 15: Cross your fingers and pick a builder.** We know this sounds like a major commitment of time, but your new home will be your biggest life investment. Only by thoroughly checking out builders will you prevent yourself from falling into a scam. Remember, the key is to hire the best builder, not to be seduced by the best sales pitch. We realize that you may not have time to do all the steps we outline above. That's fine, just do as much as you can.

## Money Bombs

**Money Bomb #1: No insurance.**
*"We built a home last year that ended up with serious structural problems—the foundation walls cracked and*

*water damaged our basement. The problem was a 'math error' by the builder when he was calculating the foundation's strength. We sued but found we couldn't collect since the builder had no insurance and had just declared bankruptcy."*

"Errors and omissions" (E & O) insurance covers just such problems. Unfortunately, few builders have it. And even if they do, it's no guarantee—you may have an expensive legal battle with the insurer to settle the problem. Nonetheless, it's worth the time to ask about E & O. Another type of insurance required for builders in many states is workers compensation—in case someone gets hurt working on your home. Small-time builders may try to skirt these rules—it's basically your risk, however. If someone falls off your roof and dies, the building department may pull the site's permit if the builder was improperly insured. An expensive lawsuit also could drain the builder of cash. All of these possibilities imperil your home. What about warranties? We'll discuss the in's and out's of builder warranties in the next chapter.

**Money Bomb #2: License loopholes.**
*"A builder in our neighborhood recently built a $300,000 home without a license. How can that happen?"*

Loopholes, in a nutshell. Some states don't require builders to be licensed. Others have loopholes you could drive a truck through—in North Carolina, for example, builders who do a home for less than $30,000 don't need a license. As you might expect, some contractors fudge their numbers to exploit this loophole. Other states let unlicensed builders construct homes they intend to live in—many builders just turn around and sell them a few days after completion. The result: Some new homes slip through the "safety net" system of licensing, permits and inspections. Due to lack of oversight, the homes are often riddled with defects and poor construction.

A similar problem: states with such weak licensing laws that they might as well have no laws at all. In Colorado, the builder's licensing exam is a 20-minute open-book test. On the other hand, Florida has a grueling five-day exam that is one of the toughest. But builders in Florida have invented creative ways around this—those individuals who pass the test are hired as "front men"—the ace student holds the license but doesn't do any actual building. The building is done by less-than-caring individuals who are still mastering their multiplication tables at press time.

If that weren't enough, some con-artist builders use another contractor's license to get a building permit. Incompetent bureaucrats in some states don't even check to see if the builder is legit before they issue him a building permit.

# Visiting Other Homes: Evaluating Construction on the Fly

L et's say you try to follow our advice and visit a few of the builder's existing construction projects. So, what are you looking for? Here are the clues:

◆ **Supervision.** Is there a supervisor or foreman on the site? Are the subs working unsupervised? Does the supervisor just drive by from time to time and wave from his truck?

◆ **Beer bottles.** It always amazes us to walk around in a new home under construction and find beer bottles and cans lying about. How exactly can you install a window properly or align something in a straight line if you just quaffed six Bud Lights? Any builder or sub-contractor who employs workers who drink beer or booze on the job is amazingly stupid. One homeowner we interviewed found an empty Jim Beam whiskey bottle in the basement—it belonged to the plumber, who had just botched the home's plumbing installation.

◆ **Trash and "stacked materials."** Materials and supplies should be stacked neatly, not strewn around the job site. While most construction sites have some amount of trash, you can tell if it's accumulating.

◆ **Supplies and materials left exposed to the weather.** Expensive products like windows and fireplaces should be protected from the elements. Floor joists should not be left in the open for more than a few days since they can warp. Sadly, we see many job sites where expensive materials and supplies lie exposed to rain, wind, vandalism and worse.

◆ **Foundations.** Girders (the main beams under a home) should be centered on the foundation piers that support them. If they aren't, big problems can result. Are anchor bolts installed? These hold the house to the foundation in severe wind storms or earthquakes.

◆ **Particle board or plywood exterior sheathing?** Particle board is made of pieces of wood glued together, while plywood is a single sheet of wood. "Tongue-in-groove" plywood is the best choice for exterior sheathing, but once again it's cheaper to use particle board. Another note: while small gaps between exterior sheets are acceptable (to accommodate swelling due to rain/moisture), large gaps are not.

◆ **Plumbing.** Here's one good sign of a quality plumber: wiped joints. When two pieces of copper pipe meet, a soldered joint holds them together. See if the plumber wiped the solder to form a smooth joint—that's a pro job. Amateurs don't wipe and leave globs of solder behind.

◆ **Drywall.** 'Sheetrockers' are a peculiar bunch who work at lightning speed. Pros screw and glue the drywall to the walls instead of nailing.

◆ **Paint.** For the interior, professionals can be distinguished from amateurs by their equipment—heavy drop cloths, quality brushes and paint. Also, pros do a lot of prep work such as patching nail holes. Exterior painters who are pros always use a coat of primer before putting on the actual paint—builders often cut out this step to save money, and it's a major money bomb (as we'll explain later). A good paint job means no paint on the trim work or window glass and no visible brush marks.

◆ **Brick work.** A quality brick mason makes sure the mortar is of even depth between the bricks. Obviously, any cracks or gaps in the mortar are a telltale sign of problems. In areas where concrete block and masonry foundations are common, check to make sure mortar is between each block or brick.

◆ **Trim work with no gaps.** Look at the corner of the molding that lines the floors—any gaps? Real pros don't do gaps. Good molding or trim work is evenly stained and painted . . . and installed without any hammer marks. Filled in nail holes indicate quality—many builders rushing to complete a project may "forget" to do this.

◆ **"Seamless" carpet.** Good installation of carpet is almost as critical as the type of carpet itself. If you see a seam, it's not a good sign. Look at the corners, doorways and walls to see if the carpet was professionally installed.

◆ **Windows.** Most builders install windows and leave the name brand sticker on for a little while. This gives you a clue as to the quality level—ask a local window supplier or home center for information on the brand.

◆ **Gutters and "smart" drainage.** Downspouts should be extended at least five feet from the home. Even better: black plastic pipe that connects to the end of the downspout and moves water far away from the home. The ground near the home should be graded to drain water away—sadly, most builders pay scant attention to these details. Contractors think that once they have finished the inside of the house, they're done. And the home buyer doesn't notice bad drainage until water washes away dirt under a concrete sidewalk, causing it to crack and collapse, or until water floods a basement or garage.

◆ **Decks.** Most deck posts are placed in cement footings—make sure the post is in the center of the footing (as opposed to off-center, which causes "eccentric loading.") Ask the builder about the grade of deck lumber. For redwood or cedar, two-inch decking is better than thinner options.

◆ **Driveways.** Check out older driveways from the builder's previous customers—see how they've aged. Proper drainage off the driveway is important—you don't want water pooling near your house. Expansion joints for concrete are critical as well. Does the builder reinforce the driveway by use of steel re-bar, mesh or fiberglass-impregnated concrete? Is the soil under the driveway compacted before the driveway is poured? If these steps aren't done, the chances of driveway cracks increase.

As you can tell, professional subs tend to have professional equipment—trucks, extensive tools, large crews, etc. We urge you to visit homes under construction and look at the subs as they work—you'll either confirm that the builder you're going to hire is professional or you'll be forewarned about potential problems.

## Money Bomb #3: Inflated subcontractor bids.

*"On our custom home, we hired an architect who helped us bid our house out to three builders. Each one broke down the bid by trades or subcontractor area. To our horror, we found that one builder padded each sub's bid with extra profit. Then he added another 15% profit onto the bottom line."*

We heard this story from one home buyer who noticed part of the bid was for pricey custom kitchen cabinets. In trying to negotiate a better price, the architect called the cabinet maker to confirm their $18,000 bid. "$18,000?" the cabinet sub said, "We only bid $14,000." When confronted, the builder admitted to padding the subs' bids with extra profit.

While there is nothing wrong with builders making a fair profit on a new home, the subs' bids should be free of "extra padding." The builder can add profit on the bottom line, but nickel-and-diming the home buyer on every sub's bid for a custom home is a cheap shot. This "double dipping" in such a deceptive manner should never happen—but it does. Notice that the architect in the above story discovered the fraud by calling the subs to confirm their bids.

Of course, if you structure the home purchase so the construction loan draws (that you approve) are based on the actual sub's bill or invoice, you also can stop this. In the above case, the builder was in charge of paying the subs' bills directly. Hence the home buyer would never have known what hit him.

## Reality Check: Builder/Architect Tension

In a perfect world, builders and architects would work together as teammates on your new home. In the not-so-perfect world of new home construction, there is often tension between the architect and the builder.

Occasionally, home buyers don't have to wait until construction begins to witness this phenomenon. Nope, some builders and architects square off right at the beginning, during the design and bidding process.

Some builders balk at bidding on a home they think is a "leaker." That's defined as any home they think might leak because of an unusual roof design. If this happens to you, you should meet separately with that builder and discuss his opinion of the design flaw. A frank discussion with the architect should follow and he or she should justify the design and make doubly sure it won't leak.

Other builders think the architect's blueprints are just advisory—if they need to adjust things out in the field, what's the big deal? Of course, design professionals will have a major problem with that.

Why is there all this tension between builders and architects? A lack of any contractual relationship is part of the problem: the buyer has a contract with the architect and a separate agreement with the builder. Notice what's missing? The architect has no agreement with the builder and vice versa. This can lead to all sorts of miscommunication. As the *Wall Street Journal* pointed out recently, "architect and construction lawyers agree that while shoddy or even dangerous design mars some projects, most conflicts stem from crossed signals. Owners don't appreciate design and structural issues at the core of the architect's profession. Architects don't fathom how deeply personal the experience of building a home can be for clients." And some builders get caught in the cross-fire.

# Choosing a Production Builder

In many parts of the country, a production builder may be your only option when it comes to buying a new home. And many large, corporate builders make it seem so easy—just pop into the model, pick out a lot and poof! You're a homeowner.

Yet purchasing a home from a production builder has its own challenges. Here are our tips:

**1 Beware of bait and switch.** Production builders are famous for advertising a SUPER LOW PRICE for a new home model, then trying to switch you to an "upgraded" version of that home that costs significantly more. Yes, it's the old deceptive marketing practice known as bait and switch—lure you in with a promise of a low price and then "upsell" you on all those extras.

On a recent visit to a production model home, we noticed the following "fine print" in a model's description that was posted in the kitchen:

*"This model has been professionally decorated and landscaped. Items such as wall coverings, custom paint, upgraded flooring, drapes, extra mirrors, built-in furniture, shelves, decorator items and furnishings are for display only. Back yard landscaping is also an optional feature. The front yard landscaping will differ from what is shown in the models. The following items are shown in the home and are available for an optional charge . . . ."*

The disclaimer then goes on to list a whopping 19 items, including such extras as a "3 car garage," "air conditioning" and "decorative light switches." Then there is this caveat at the end of the option list: "Additional options may be shown in this model. Please see your sales consultant for further information."

Translation: your home will definitely NOT look like this model. It will be a stripped down, ugly version of this house. That is, unless you'd like to add thousands of dollars to that SUPER LOW PRICE you saw advertised.

After we walked through this model, we asked for a printed options list. This apparently took the salesperson by surprise. Their first response to us is "We work out a final price for your home after we have a 'planning' session with you on the options." That's nice, but we persisted—can we see the options list? Pretty please? After some arm-twisting, we finally got the list. Here are some sample "extras" and their costs:

| Option | Price |
|---|---|
| 3 car garage | $5700 |
| Air conditioning | $4200 |
| Decorative switches | $300 |

And it went on. We noticed some options were grossly overpriced (a whole house humidifier, $775, garage door opener with two controls $550)—you can easily compare those prices with local suppliers and hardware stores. Other items gave you a choice of "doing-it-yourself"—you could get a ceiling fan installed for $350 or just a pre-wire for a fan for $125. That assumes the fan itself would be worth $225. Unfortunately, the builder didn't specify the fan brand, which makes us think it is some K-Mart special for $75.

Now, we expect certain decoration in a model to be fluff—the furniture, the wall coverings, etc. But we were amazed at the number of permanent features like fireplaces, three-car garages, and rounded dry-wall corners that were in the "extra" category. Production builders undermine their credibility when they advertise low prices and then load model homes with "optional" items that should be standard.

Options are such high-profit add-ons for the builders that many contractors are erecting huge "design centers" to encourage more option business. While seeing all 40 faucet options in one place is convenient for buyers, remember to not get carried away. According to *Builder* magazine, design centers can add 3% to 10% to a home purchase price and some builders manage to add 20% in upgrade sales!

Our advice: get the upgrade list UPFRONT before you walk into a model. Also, ask the salesperson to point out any additional "extras" that may not be on the list. Of course, you can always negotiate these items—some builders might throw in an extra option for free if you buy two, for example. As always, compare "real world" prices with the builder's inflated price list. Decide what you really need, what can be installed later and what is in the category of "would be nice if we win the lottery."

**2** **Entering the Model Trap.** Did you know that production builders actually call those model homes "model traps"? That's because they're designed to trap buyers—first you visit the sales office to view a map of the community (as we mentioned before, to notice all those "red" sold dots, which scream "buy today or you're toast!") Then you exit by another door that leads you to the model home.

You'll first notice the "driveway lawn," one of the funnier tricks of the model trap. Instead of installing a big concrete driveway to the garage, builders plant grass to make the front yard seem oh so spacious. We've even seen builders put shrubs and other landscaping in front of the garage door, as if you'd drive over the azaleas in order to back the Explorer into the garage.

The pathway to the model home is designed by scientists to make sure you have the perfect (and most unblemished) view of the exterior of the house. Inside, you'll find the ideal specimen of caring construction—every corner is perfect, every detail is right. The furnishings are designed by an interior designer in such a way as to bamboozle you into thinking the rooms' sizes are just right. Not too pretentious and not too Wal-Mart, the furniture and window treatments are calculated to maintain the illusion that "this could be your home" (if you had a live-in maid). Mirrors are strategically placed in rooms to make them seem larger.

After you finish visiting the model home, a fence keeps you from

## Email from the Real World: Pricey Brick Upgrades

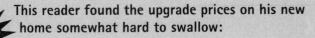

**This reader found the upgrade prices on his new home somewhat hard to swallow:**

*"We were recently confronted with (what we thought) were extremely high prices for our upgrades on the new house we are thinking about buying. We were told that the front brick siding upgrade for our new house was going to be $18,000, including $7,000 for a brick fireplace and $3,000 for a side entrance garage! We about fell out of our seats at these prices but accepted the front brick siding only and declined on the brick fireplace and side entrance garage. You say in your book that a 10-15% markup is fair for builders to add on to what the contractors have done. What about options/upgrades on windows, kitchen cabinets, ceiling fans, garage door openers, etc.? We know that everything is negotiable but, without going or calling a brick siding contractor, what would have been a ball park percentage discount for us to offer for the $18,000 front brick siding? Is the 10-15 % discount fair in this case? Some friends of ours say they only paid $7,000 for their front brick siding! What about the options/upgrades? How do you price them fairly?"*

Well, that is one of the mysteries of life: how builders price upgrades. Yes, they are a BIG profit center for many builders, but it's hard to determine whether you're being taken. As you've discovered, some items are hard to comparison shop for (brick work, for example ) while others are simpler (you know what a ceiling fan would cost, etc.). Everything is negotiable, so you can always offer the builder less. The other option: with some upgrades, you can decline the upgrade and get a credit for the item (the ceiling fan) and then install it yourself. The bottom line: look at the TOTAL price of the house and make sure you are not paying MORE for what similar houses have sold for lately.

returning to your car. You must walk back into the sales office to be pitched by the cheery salesperson. Despite the fact that this salesperson really knows less about the home than your cat, she will endlessly try to get you to buy. Today. Right now. This is the "trap" part of the model trap.

But you're smarter than this, aren't you? There are several ways to defeat the model trap, as you'll read next.

**3** See "real homes." These could be partially finished homes under construction in the community. Or, even better, check out real homes lived in by real people. If you visit the community on a weekend, chances are you'll find neighbors out doing yard work. Say hello and shoot the breeze—about the neighborhood, the builder and their home. It's amazing how different homes look when they're decorated by real people, not interior decorators. You may be impressed ... or you may run away as fast as you can.

**4** Check out the "model variances." That's jargon for the fact that models aren't reality. The builder doesn't guarantee that your home will look that good. If you don't believe us, check out the production builder's contract—it usually says in the fine print that your home may vary "significantly" from the model. Grill the salesperson and any other builder representatives for concrete examples of such "variances." Is the trim always oak or do they substitute a cheaper wood? Do they always use that name brand (window, furnace/air conditioning, carpet, flooring)? What warning do you have of a possible "substitution"? If they can't give you a straight answer, don't buy. Get brand names and features IN WRITING to prevent misunderstandings.

The bottom line: you don't have to get trapped in the model trap. By taking a few steps, you can eliminate those unpleasant surprises.

## THE 48-DAY EMAIL RESPONSE

**J**ust about every home builder these days has a web site, from the biggest production builders to Joe Schmoe & Brothers Construction in North Dakota. Many of those sites have email links ... so you might think as a customer, you could email the builder a query about their homes and get a response, right?

A hilarious article in *Builder* magazine in July 2001 actually tracked response times for email queries sent to builders nationwide. Their findings? It took Washington DC builders a mere 48 *days* to answer email queries. California builders were a bit speedier, answering emails in just 7 to 10 days. Atlanta builders clocked in at 14 days. The article also noted: "(we) sent dozens of emails to Florida builders and is still waiting for responses." Adding insult to injury: 60% of builder web sites forgot to list a phone number to local sales offices.

# The Top 10 Biggest Builders

Who are the top builders? Here's a list of the biggest production builders in the U.S., based on 2000 sales figures (the latest available). "Closings" refers to the number of homes closed or sold in 2000. Top markets are where the builder has the biggest market share; many of these builders construct homes in multiple states. Web sites are abbreviated, omitting the http://www. prefix.

| Builder | '00 closings | GPM* | Top markets | Web |
|---|---|---|---|---|
| Pulte** | 27,781 | 9.8% | Atlanta, Dallas, Las Vegas | PULTE.COM |
| Centex | 26,627 | 11.9 | Dallas/FW, Southwest | CENTEX.COM |
| K B Home | 22,847 | 20.4 | West, Southwest | KBHOME.COM |
| Lennar/US Home | 22,560 | 12.4 | Northeast, South | LENNAR.COM |
| D.R. Horton | 18,942 | 21.6 | Denver, Dallas, Austin | DRHORTON.COM |
| Ryland Group | 11,418 | 19.7 | Austin, Carolinas, Houston | RYLAND.COM |
| NVR | 10,055 | 21.1 | Washington-Baltimore | NVRINC.COM |
| Del Webb* | 8,419 | 9.8 | Phoenix, Las Vegas | DELWEBB.COM |
| Beazer Homes | 8,088 | 18.7 | Washington, Phoenix | BEAZER.COM |
| MDC/Richmond | 7,484 | 15.1 | Denver, West | RICHMONDAMERICAN.COM |

*GPM: Gross Profit Margin
**In 2001, Pulte merged with Del Webb.

# Insider info

Builder's web sites are nice and slick, but wouldn't you like to know the unfiltered truth about the big builders? Check out a web site like Hoovers.com—you can search for any public company for free on this site. Once you find them, click on the company's SEC filings (10K, 10Q, etc). Yes, these reports can be dry but revealing—companies explain to Wall Street how they are doing, whether they are being sued, etc. Very interesting.

◆ **Attack web sites:** Pop any major builder's name in a search engine and you might find something the builder would rather you NOT see: a protest site about the builder that's put up by angry past customers. These "attack" web sites provide a fascinating view into the world of homebuilding. An example: John Cobarruvias, an unhappy Ryland home owner in Houston, TX. John has posted a web site (http://users2.ev1.net/~johncoby/ryland/) that is quite revealing—you can read newspaper and magazine articles about homebuyers problems with Ryland in Houston, San Antonio, Dallas, Austin, Baltimore and California. This amazing site has links to other consumer groups' web sites (described below).

◆ **Grass-roots consumer groups.** Each of these groups was started by consumers as a response to home building problems in their area. These groups can provide valuable intelligence on area builders, communities and other local issues.

1. HOMEOWNERS AGAINST DEFECTIVE DWELLINGS (HADD) www.hadd.com; see Fig. 2 below.. HADD is focused on the Kansas City metro area; their web site includes homebuyer stories, links and news articles. HADD also has authored several publications to help consumers which are for sale on the site. In recent years, HADD has added chapters around the country.

2. HOMEOWNERS ORGANIZATION FOR MEDIATION AND EDUCATION (HOME): (817) 861-7000; www.flash.net/~carlton2/home.htm. This group is based in Dallas, Texas. Formerly called Sick of Bad Builders, HOME is now working to license homebuilders in Texas (currently one of the states that does NOT do this). The web site features an FAQ, pictures of bad construction and links to other related sites for Texas homebuyers.

3. HOMEOWNERS FOR BETTER BUILDING (210) 402-6800; www.hobb.org is based in San Antonio, TX. One of this group's goals is to warn homebuyers about the pitfalls of binding arbitration clauses in new home construction con-

**Figure 2:** HADD is a great source for links to local homeowner sites.

tracts. Their excellent web page is easy to navigate and is updated regularly.

4. HOME BUYER BEWARE (www.charlotte.com/observer/special/house/) is a six-part series by the Charlotte (NC) Observer on home building problems in North Carolina.

## MONEY BOMBS WITH PRODUCTION HOMES

### Money Bomb #1: "Builder-grade materials."

*"We paid $320,000 for a semi-custom home only to discover we got tract-home quality. Everything from the windows to the garbage disposal is 'builder-grade' cheap and has caused us nothing but problems and repair headaches. How did this happen?"*

There's not one single building product out there that someone hasn't figured out a way to lower the quality of, in order to sell at rock-bottom prices. And what do manufacturers call these super-cheap materials? "Builder grade." Makes you wonder.

Many companies that make everything from windows to siding to carpet have three grades—the quality stuff for professionals, medium quality for do-it-yourselfers, and the lowest of the low, reserved for your friendly builder.

The problem is most of the "builder-grade" materials aren't built to last much longer than the warranty period on your home (usually about a year). Cheap carpet wears quickly in traffic areas, cheap paint fades fast and builder-grade appliances break down with alarming regularity. You end up replacing the cheap stuff and spending thousands of dollars in the process.

How do you avoid this ultimate money bomb? First, forget about the builder's stock brochures and sales materials, filled with warm and fuzzy references to their great quality. Instead, get brand names/grades on materials used in the home—everything you can think of (especially the big ticket items like windows, siding, roofing, and the like). Even better: ask for a complete list of specifications and materials used in the entire home. Some of this information is in plain view, while for some items you may have to ask the builder to provide this information.

Investigate the quality by going to a home center or calling a professional. For those faucets you suspect are cheap stuff, call a plumber and ask. Ask a home center or roofing supplier about the quality of the shingles. Beware of builders who use obviously high-quality items in very visible areas like the kitchen or bath, only to turn around and use builder-grade stuff for not-as-sexy items like windows, furnaces, shingles, etc.

### Money Bomb #2: Deceitful decorating.

*"A model home that we saw the other day was quite slick. In the living room, there was just a love seat. When we got home, we realized our six-foot couch may not fit there."*

You've just discovered what we call "deceitful decorating." Clever builders use all kinds of tricks to make their model homes more attractive. One favorite: using undersized furniture to make a room seem larger. A love seat creates an "optical illusion" of a bigger room. Mirrored walls also make dinky rooms seem cavernous.

Don't be fooled—bring along a tape measure and take actual measurements of rooms. Also ask to see real houses under construction and measure those rooms. Don't rely on the builder's information: they often "forget" to put room measurements on floor plans or fudge the figures to boost square footage.

## Money Bomb #3: Ten-year warranties.

*"The builder who sold us our home pitched us on this 10-year warranty program. He said only quality builders can participate and the warranty company will stand behind his work. Later, after we discovered a structural problem specifically covered in the warranty, we got an endless run-around from the warranty company. They refused to fix our home unless it was falling down."*

Welcome to the world of 10-year warranties, the biggest rip-off of all with new homes. In the next chapter, we'll tell you how thousands of complaints like this prompted congressional hearings in 1991 on this insidious scam. The bottom line: production builders love to pitch these warranties, but the evidence shows they're worthless. The best "warranty" on your home is confirming the quality of the builder and then subjecting the actual construction to a series of inspections by a private inspector (who works for you).

## Money Bomb #4: Customization confusion.

*"Our builder promised they could customize our plan with all kinds of extras—nine-foot ceilings in the living room, oversized windows and hardwood flooring. Yet, all this customization just seemed to confuse the sub-contractors. Numerous delays and the wrong materials delivered to our job site meant our home ran two months late. To add insult to injury, the workers spilled Coke all over our unfinished hardwood floors!"*

It's the hot buzzword in the world of production builders today—customization. While builders will promise you anything, many are still trying to figure out how to deliver on those promises. As a result, crews who are used to building three basic plans now must actually think about special options and requests. The reality: many builders botch custom requests, thanks to inexperienced crews, a lack of supervision and other logistical problems. Many home buyers find they have to closely watch to make sure custom requests are not omitted during crucial construction phases.

## Money Bomb #5: Pumped up electrical bills.

*"The builder recommends we put an electric heat pump in our new home—he says it's much more efficient than a furnace that runs on heating oil. Yet, I've spoken to other homeowners who say just the opposite. Who do I believe?"*

That's a true story from a home buyer in Pennsylvania, who soon discovered why her builder was "strongly recommending" an electric heat pump. It turned out the local electric company was giving builders a $500 cash rebate to install electric heat pumps in new homes. After doing some checking, the homebuyer realized her utility bills would be 50% higher with this option.

While it's impossible to say exactly what heat source option is most effective for every part of the country, it's wise to do your homework before being sold a particular "solution." Ask neighbors for their experiences, check average bills and quiz heating contractors about different options.

## Money Bomb #6: The incomplete contract / low-ball allowance game.

*"We got hooked on a semi-custom home and signed a contract. It turns out that the one-page contract gave us no details on our new home. First we found out that the nice oak trim in the model was an option— the standard was ugly pine. Then the allowances we got for lighting and carpet were pitifully low. We ended up shelling out $8000 more to get the quality we thought we were buying in the first place."*

It's shocking to see the actual contracts of many production and semi-custom builders. Lots of legal mumbo-jumbo about deposits and payments due to the builder. What's missing? The "specs and materials." This list tells you exactly what you are buying—the type of trim, brand of windows, type of fireplace, type and size of doors, etc. Very few consumers ask for this and most regret it later.

Not seeing the specs and materials list (in some cases, it's a small book) is like buying a car without seeing the price sticker. Do you get a manual or automatic transmission? Air bags? Air conditioning? The last thing you want to do is first buy the car, pay the money and then discover what's in there. Sounds silly, but that's exactly how many production and semi-custom homes are bought today.

Another twist on this scam is the "low-ball allowance game." Many semi-custom builders give you an "allowance" toward purchasing flooring (carpet and vinyl), tile, appliances, light fixtures, landscaping, brick selection, and other items. The allowance is money the builder pays for the items—anything over is your responsibility.

As you might guess, the low-ball allowance game rip-off occurs when the money really doesn't pay for anything. Here's a sample allowance from a real semi-custom home:

| Lighting fixtures | $500 |
| Appliances | $2000 |
| Tile, carpet, and vinyl flooring (installed) | $8500 |

Now, $500 sounds like a lot of money for light fixtures ... but have you priced light fixtures recently? Basically, $500 might pay for *one* dining room fixture. Don't forget about outside fixtures as well—one of those nice carriage lamps can easily run $100. And you need two of them for most garages. Even if you buy the bare bones, cheapest light fixtures on Earth, you'll be hard pressed to spend less than $500. We fell victim to this scam and ended up spending another $600 out of our own pockets to get semi-decent light fixtures—and that was after scouring discount stores and catalogs.

Be aware of lighting allowances that include "recessed lights." The builder may give you $1000 for lighting, but that might include recessed cans. A basic, no-frills recessed can is $30 to $50. Ten cans could set you back $500 and then you'd only have $500 more for other lights.

How about $2000 for appliances? Of course, the first question you should ask is, "which appliances?" Does the builder assume you already own a refrigerator? Trying to stretch $2000 to buy a refrigerator, range/oven, microwave, dishwasher, disposal, washer and dryer is impossible. You can easily end up spending $3500 to $4500 (on the low end) or up to $10,000 to $20,000 (on the high end) for all the above. Just walk into an appliance store and start taking notes on prices to determine whether the builder is really offering you a deal.

Here's another good question: does the builder have any "contractor discount deals" with local suppliers? For example, an appliance store may give your builder "contractor prices" that are 5% to 15% below retail. Any reputable builder can qualify for these discounts by simply filling out credit forms to get an account.

However, beware of builders who might be getting kickbacks from certain suppliers, who then jack the prices you pay. One builder we knew also owned a carpet/vinyl store and "heavily recommended" that his buyers shop there. The prices were quite high. The best tip: shop around to sources not recommended by the builder to make sure you're not getting fleeced on the price. Despite the pitfalls, seeing whether the builder has such discounts or accounts with suppliers is a good money-saving tip.

## Tips for saving on production homes

Wouldn't it be nice if buying a new home or townhome would be as easy as buying, say, a new car?

You could read consumer magazines to check up on the latest models and the best deals. Laboratory technicians in white coats would "road test" several home designs and report back on which models had the best floor-plans, energy efficiencies and future appreciation. After

# Is the builder overcharging for your new home?

**B**id out any new home to a contractor and you'll liable to wake up one night and wonder aloud: am I overpaying for this new home? While there is no one way to know the true value of a new home (short of a full-blown appraisal), there is one solution: find out the sales prices of OTHER similar homes in the neighborhood where you are building. The theory goes that your house will be worth what a similar, nearby house sold for. But how do you find such info? Check out the web site "Home Price Check" by CBS MarketWatch (http://homepricecheck.marketwatch.com/). Just pop in a range of addresses (all the homes that sold in 1100 to 1200 Maple Street) or a single address, and poof! You can valuable data that can tell you whether you are getting a deal. Another cool feature: you can find homes sold between a certain price range (say $300,000 to $350,000) in a specific town during the last year. That way you can tell what that amount of money would have bought you in another neighborhood.

test-driving several models, you'd haggle with the builder for a big rebate and other freebies.

Ah, if only life were that easy.

With all the look-alike subdivisions, cookie-cutter models and big corporate builders, is it still possible to get a good deal on a new production home?

Of course it is.

One key point to remember: builders are loath to cut the price of new homes—it displeases their shareholders, not to mention the buyers of last year's models. So, instead they offer "incentives" such as cut-rate mortgages, upgraded carpeting, free landscaping, and money toward closing costs. That way they still technically sell the house for full price, even though they're giving you $5000 in closing costs and another $5000 in "designer options."

Of course, being a smart new home shopper entails much more than just getting free carpeting. Here are seven tips to getting a good deal on a new production home.

**1** **When's the best time to get a deal on a new home?** Public builders need to pump up sales numbers to impress Wall Street near the end of their fiscal years. Hence, many wheel and deal on closing costs, options and landscape packages in the days before the end of that month. While some builders' fiscal years follow the calendar (Pulte, for one), others end during odd times of the year (Kaufman & Broad is November 30, while Beazer Homes is September 30). Be prepared to close escrow before their fiscal year ends to get the goodies. Check with your local library or online at Hoovers.com to find the fiscal year-end dates of public builders in your area.

**2** **Avoid the Specialized Room Trap.** Builders today are selling model homes with all kinds of "specialized" rooms, from home offices to exercise areas. But don't get trapped by a specialized room that can't convert back to another common use, like a bedroom—it's better for resale to maintain the flexibility. For example, don't remove the closet from a home office. Wire an exercise room for cable so a future owner could convert it to a media room.

**3** **Beware the "designer packages."** Builders charge huge mark-ups on so-called "designer packages" for plush carpeting and window coverings—sometimes as much as 25% to 50% over cost. A better bet: shop around for the best deals on these items and see if you can beat the builder's price. Then negotiate for a credit from the builder and hire another company to install the items. The only down-side to this tip? Some builders will only give you a fraction of the designer package as a credit. Still, you may come out ahead.

**4** **Nearly new homes may the best deals of all.** In many large subdivision still under construction, you may find "nearly new" homes that have been lived in for a year or two and are great deals. Why? Owners of such homes have usually invested in landscaping, window coverings, flooring upgrades, built-ins and other goodies. Yet these sellers can't sell their homes at a premium because they're competing with the builder's sparkling new homes and special incentives—and many sellers are more willing to haggle on price than builders.

**5** **Avoid flooring overkill.** Here's a common mistake made by new home buyers—upgrading the flooring in a new home beyond what is appropriate in that home's price range. For example, in California, a limestone entry-way in a $400,000 home is appropriate. In a $200,000 starter home, it's overkill. While that may seem obvious, many home buyers who fall prey to flooring overkill often sink money into fancy finishes that they may never recover on resale. Another money-loser: upgrades in mid-price homes of all-wood or tile on first floors can rarely be recouped later upon resale.

**6** **Carefully consider the choice of windows.** Some builders offer wood casement windows as an upgrade, but think carefully before doing this. Wood windows require periodic painting or staining to avoid water damage—this could add hundreds if not thousands of dollars in maintenance over the life of a home. A better option: newer vinyl clad windows with wood-like finishes provide the aesthetic look most buyers want, without all the maintenance headaches. Another wise idea: check out how the builder's windows rank in energy efficiency. A window industry trade group, the National Fenestration Rating Council, publishes a "Certified Products Directory" with energy performance ratings for over 16,000 windows, doors and skylights from over 120 manufactures. You can access this directory via the NFRC's web site at www.nfrc.org. The directory is also available in CD-ROM.

**7** **Act quickly for bargains on "standing inventory."** Big builders employ armies of economists, financial advisors and accountants to guess the number of homes they need to built to meet demand. Sometimes they goof. The result? Unsold homes known in the biz as "standing inventory." Each day a new home stands unsold is painful to builders, who must eat huge interest costs on construction loans. If you look for communities with standing inventory, you could get great deals, such as thousands of dollars in closing costs, landscaping packages and more. The only disadvantage: you may have to move quickly. Such "sales" only last for a week or less. The amount of standing inventory can vary widely from one area to another—and from month to month. Yet, when it happens, the deals can be huge. For example, in San Diego, one builder offered a package of goodies including a washer and dryer, fridge, mini blinds, landscaping, upgraded flooring—plus a below market rate mortgage. The catch? You had to close quickly, within a two-month window.

## Strategy for Production Homes: Use That Salesperson

Many salespeople who work for production or semi-custom builders have a vested interest in making sure you're happy—many are given bonuses based on "customer satisfaction" surveys.

Hence, you can often get the salesperson to act as your advocate when things go sour. One home buyer we interviewed had just such an experience. The supervisor on her semi-custom home was an . . . let's, just say "not a very nice person."

The supervisor would lock the home buyer out of the home to keep her from snooping around and finding problems with the construction after hours. Even though the home buyer had a key to the garage, the supervisor would jam the door with a piece of wood. When the home buyer did get inside, she noticed lots of problems. Some of the workmanship was poor, in other cases, the buyer's paid for "semi-custom" requests were being ignored.

The home buyer discovered the salespeople at the development were sympathetic to her plight. One salesperson left windows of the home open so the home buyer could crawl inside. By complaining directly to the president of the company, she got action. It was the president himself who accompanied her on a final walk-through inspection that lasted two hours. The supervisor no longer works for the builder.

Another lesson from this debacle: make sure your rights to visit the home under construction are spelled out in the contract. You should have a key and the right to visit the home any time without notice or warning. Common sense says you shouldn't get in the way of the workers, of course. Another related point: your contract should also allow access for a professional home inspector to visit the house during construction.

Some builders are quite nervous about letting home buyers into their homes under construction. Their official reasons for denying consumers access: "construction sites are dangerous places and our insurance company forbids anyone but workers from being there." Ask a contractor for a copy of this policy provision to verify this claim; you might be surprised to find no such provision exists.

The real reasons: some builders fear that if home buyers see the actual construction, nothing but trouble (for the contractor, that is) can result. You may find out that the options you paid for are not being installed. Or the workmanship is not up to their promises. A few builders worry that consumers will want to make lots of costly and time-consuming changes as well.

We believe total access to a new home under construction is a fundamental consumer right. You are the one who's put down a substantial deposit and it's all your money on the line. You're on the hook for the next 30 years to live with the thing. And, sad to say, the quality of many production homes just cannot be left to chance.

## Translating Builder-speak to English

**G**ood morning, class. Today we're going to study the homo-habitatus, that sub species of human beings who builds new homes. Unlike normal folks, this species has a language all their own. Here are some utterings you'll hear when you talk to builders—and the easy builder-speak-to-English translation.

**1. No problem.** As in, we'll fix this, no problem. Translation: it's a BIG problem that will cost you your life savings and take three times as long to fix as we estimate.

**2. It's on order.** Translation: we totally forgot about this item and are currently trying to find the scrap of paper with the supplier's phone number to place the order. Another definition for the phrase "it's on order" came from free-lance writer Ruth Squires in *Builder* magazine: "I forgot to order it because it was written down on a doughnut box that was jammed into a heat duct the day the crew decided to clean up the job site." Ruth is married to a builder.

**3. We'll get right on it.** Translation: after we get back from vacation and if it's not raining, snowing, sleeting or the sun is shining too brightly, it will be the seventh item on our to-do list.

**4. I'll be working in my shop this day, so we won't be on the job site.** Translation: After sleeping in to 10am, I'll be bidding another job and then leaving at lunch for an extended three-day hunting trip.

**5. The sub is scheduled to be here today.** Translation: Whoops! I forgot to schedule the sub and I doubt he'd show up anyway since I haven't paid him yet for the last job. I think I'll call my brother who's a part-time electrician/dry-waller/plumber/roofer.

# THE PAPER TRAIL: PROTECTING YOUR RIGHTS WITH A GOOD CONTRACT

## CHAPTER 8

**W**hen you sign a contract, you might as well consider that pen in your hand to be a stick of dynamite. Over the next several months, you will have to live by what is and—equally important—what is not in the contract.

In a perfect world, there would be "model" new home purchase contracts that would give equal footing to both builder and consumer. The builder would have to disclose the final home price and agree to a schedule for delivery. Each party would have clear responsibilities and requirements to complete the deal.

Fast forward to the real world: you have more consumer protection when buying a toaster than a new home. Contracts for new homes run the gamut, from those written on the back of a napkin to elaborate, lop-sided agreements drafted by $300 per hour lawyers. After looking at many new home contracts, we've noticed three ways bad contracts zap good buyers:

**1** **Generic real estate forms.** Surprisingly, many new homes are bought with just the generic real estate "Contract to Buy and Sell." While this might be fine for existing homes, new home construction is another ball game. Although this generic contract does identify the buyer and seller and the amount to be paid, no mention is made of exactly what you're buying or when it will be completed. Some builders get around this problem with a "new construction addendum," which is nice but runs into the next problem.

**2** **Omission of details.** Even contracts written for new construction are often devoid of critical details. For example, it's rare to find a completion date and any penalty clause. No specs or materials are promised—just vague wording that says the home will be built in accordance with the "drawings and design plans." If the builder drew those plans, the plans may still omit many details. For example, a door opening is drawn on the plans but no mention is made whether it's an expensive, six-panel, solid oak door or a cheap, masonite hollow-core door. And it's like that all down the line: heating/cooling systems, windows, faucets—the plans give you no clue as to whether you're getting quality or trash.

**3** **Verbal promises.** The final straw of these bad contracts is verbal agreements. The builder may promise a brick fireplace at the beginning, but having no written agreement makes it easier for the builder to say later he never promised that. If you order a change but fail to put it in writing, the builder may fail to make the change. Or the change will be made and you'll be charged twice the "verbal" price. Near closing, you may be shocked by huge bills for items you thought were more affordable in earlier conversations.

We do have a prescription to avoid bad contracts. But first, here are three reality checks on this process.

## REALITY CHECK

◆ **In most cases, the type of contract is not your choice.** With production homes, the builder will insist you use *their* written agreement. There won't be much discussion about contract terms. At best, you can negotiate an addendum that specifies a few more details in writing. Many production and semi-custom homes are sold with this "take it or leave it" attitude.

Custom homes are slightly different. In some cases, you (or your attorney) may be able to draft your own contract. Some builders will insist on their own contracts while still others will use a neutral third-party contract such as the American Institute of Architects' standard form (more on this later).

We suggest you pass on a builder who refuses to use a fair contract. Such an agreement includes many of the clauses discussed later in this chapter. One home buyer we knew walked away from a deal on a new home when the builder balked at putting the "specs and materials" for a $355,000 home in writing. Without knowing exactly what you're buying, you're almost assured of disappointment. In the worst case, you might be a victim of a major rip-off when that $355,000 home turns out to be loaded with cheap materials and poor workmanship.

◆ **Market conditions will affect your ability to negotiate.** Most contracts are negotiable. You can delete clauses you object to and add to the contract in an addendum. However, you're ability to do this is tied to whether the local housing market is "hot" or "cold."

In cold markets (where there are many sellers but few buyers), builders are begging for work. Hence, they may agree to a penalty clause that fines them for each day the home's construction runs late. They also may remove or modify clauses that limit your rights—such as the right to inspect the home prior to closing. In their desperation, builders may negotiate on many "non-negotiable" items and throw in free upgrades.

Hot markets are another story. In areas that are booming, builders can get very arrogant. It's a take-it-or-leave-it world and they're the gods of new home construction. "If you don't like it, go live in an apartment," is the basic attitude. Sure, some builders will be willing to make a few concessions, but most might tell you to take a hike when you want contract changes.

Of course, in the real world, most housing markets are neither extremely hot nor cold when it comes to new construction. In a lukewarm market, you'll find some builders willing to make concessions while others are intransigent. Your (or your attorney's or buyer's broker's) ability to negotiate will greatly impact the outcome of the contract negotiations.

Another factor that affects your ability to negotiate: the home's purchase price. Generally, the more expensive the home, the more willing most builders are to negotiate on the contract. Conversely, builders of entry-level houses may stubbornly insist that their contract is the "law"—no matter how hot or cold the real estate market is.

So, how do you negotiate the best deal with a builder? There are no secrets to this. The best you can do is to draft an "offer" for the new home that includes your terms and conditions (price, contract clauses, etc.). The builder can say yes or no—and then you negotiate from there.

◆ **Builders have expert lawyers and take extensive classes all designed to limit your rights—and their liability for problems.** One reason you need an experienced real estate attorney to review your contract is because the builder has one. In fact, many builders (especially the large production builders) have battalions of high-paid attorneys who stay up late at night tweaking new home construction contracts to favor the builder as much as possible.

Builders also take seminars and read books designed to "limit their liability" (translation: strip you of your rights). For example, the National Association of Home Builders actually has a publication that advocates builders use contracts that "disclaim implied warranties in states where they are permissible." What's an implied warranty? As you'll discover later, this is court-mandated consumer protection for new homes (which builders loathe). Some states allow you to sign away your rights for implied warranties and builders know it.

The result: contracts that are loaded with land mines that strictly limit the builder's liability for goofs or problems. Other clauses restrict your rights for redress. If you're not careful, the deck could be stacked against you even before the first shovel of dirt is thrown in the air.

As a side note, builders' sneaky and covert attempts to zap consumers with clever legal maneuvering belies the "trust factor." Many builders implore their customers to "trust" them and claim that they are acting on the customers' behalf. One builder we know actually wrote the trust factor into his contract, stating:

*The contractor accepts the relationship of trust and confidence established between he and Owner by this agreement. He (the builder) covenants with Owner to furnish his best skill and judgement in furthering the interest of Owner.*

Gee, that sounds nice. But this same builder on the next page strips the consumer of important rights like implied warranties and redress of grievances in a court of law. Instead, the contract mandated "binding arbitration" to address disputes (more on this later). We'd be more apt to believe the trust propaganda if the builders stopped trying to limit implied warranty rights and stopped setting up bogus 10-year warranty companies to dupe consumers.

# A Special Warning

We do not intend to give legal advice in this chapter, but instead to provide a general discussion of several contractual issues as they apply to new construction. You should always seek professional counsel before signing any legal document—especially one that obligates you to pay big bucks, such as a new home purchase.

As a side note, there is no federal law for real estate. Essentially, every state (its legislatures and courts) has established different real estate laws. This patchwork quilt of 50 state laws and requirements is another reason to have a real estate lawyer look over your contract. What is a consumer protection or requirement in one state may be completely absent in another.

Some readers have asked us to put a sample "good" new home construction contract in this chapter. While we see how that would be helpful, we decided against it for one simple reason—given the variety of state laws and court cases that cover these contracts, we feel it would cause more confusion than provide guidance. And, as we've noted, very few consumers ever have a choice of new home contracts—it is the builder who often dictates the terms and conditions.

That said, we think there should be a "model" new home construction contract that balances the rights of both builder and consumer. If there are any attorneys out there who would like to take on this project on a pro bono basis, contact us via email at feedback @YourNewHouseBook.com.

Despite the fact that no "model" contract exists, there are a couple of sources for sample contracts. Among the best is the American Institute of Architect's documents, described in the next section.

## Sources for Sample Contracts

**1 American Institute of Architects (AIA) form contracts.** The AIA has standard form contracts for both architects/consumers and builders/consumers that have become the standards for the industry. The AIA acted as a semi-neutral third party in developing these contracts, with input from both builders and consumers. Copies are available from any AIA document distributor, member architects, and the AIA headquarters in Washington, D.C., by calling 1-800-365-ARCH; web: www.aiai.org. Non-members may have copies as well. Architects can also buy these documents in electronic form.

Specifically, the AIA has the following agreements:

- A101    Standard Form of Agreement Between Owner and Contractor
- A201    General Conditions of the Contract for Construction
- B141    Standard Form of Agreement Between Owner and Architect
- G701    Change Order
- G702    Application and Certificate for Payment
- G704    Certificate of Substantial Completion

Despite their fairness, critics say the contracts give the architect lots of authority, but very little responsibility if things go wrong. For example, the AIA contract doesn't require the architect to perform continuous on-site inspections, only to be "generally familiar with the construction" and to "endeavor to guard against defects and deficiencies." Gee, that's nice, but we suggest you get more specific about the architect's oversight and supervision responsibilities. The AIA contract also doesn't hold the architect responsible if the design doesn't work.

Also, the contract mandates arbitration, which precludes your right to sue in the case of a dispute. Ownership of documents such as blueprints is also an issue. As we mentioned earlier in this book, you may also want to negotiate the ownership of the final documents and designs. Most owners don't realize that the architect typically retains ownership, but this is negotiable.

**2** **Contracts and Liability for Builders & Remodelers** (Home Builder Press, 1-800-368-5242, www.builderbooks.com, $45). Published by the National Association of Home Builders publishing arm, this 52-page book gives you an interesting insight into contracts—from the builder's perspective.

You learn how all kinds of creative clauses can be used to limit your rights. Note "Chapter 3: Environmental Liability in Real Estate Transactions," which provides a fascinating discussion of how builders can avoid liability for homes built on hazardous waste sites. Builders also learn how to avoid responsibility for new homes that are contaminated by high levels of radon gas.

Wading through all this as a consumer may be somewhat challenging since the legalese is thick and the jargon can get rather technical. Nonetheless, reading this book puts you on equal footing with builders in negotiations. You also may gain an insight into why certain provisions appear in your contract.

# New HomeBuyers in Cyberspace: What's on the Web?

## REprofile
**Web:** www.reprofile.com

**What it is:** A real estate news web site with an extensive legal database.

**What's cool:** You can get an update on real estate legislation state by state as well as read the latest articles on legal matters with this well-designed site. We liked the national map that let you zero in on your state. There are also numerous links to other related sites.

# Key Clauses to a Good Contract

Remember, the basic ingredient of a good contract is that it's written. Also, any changes, letters or notices regarding the contract should be written. Verbal agreements are an invitation to trouble.

## 1 Work Description

Will the builder construct the entire home? Or will you do some of the work, such as painting, landscaping, etc.? You must clearly specify what each party (you and the builder) will do, including any authorization for the builder to purchase materials for the job.

We spoke with one homebuyer who ran into a big dispute with his builder over this issue. The buyer and builder agreed verbally that the buyer would paint the exterior of the home—but both failed to write

**Figure 1:** You can find the latest on real estate law and legislation on REProfile.com.

this down in the contract. As the project went on, the builder failed to do several other tasks, claiming that the buyer had agreed verbally to take care of them. Since there was no written contract, it was hard to figure out who agreed to do what.

## 2 The Money Stuff

How much will the home cost? What's the deposit? Will the deposit be placed in escrow? How (and when) will the builder be paid the balance? If there are draws off a construction loan, what is the procedure for payment? Is the deal contingent on financing? Must there be any proof or evidence that the buyer has obtained permanent financing?

We STRONGLY recommend that any deposit should be placed in ESCROW. This is a special account administered by your buyer's agent or a title company. The builder does NOT have access to the money until closing (that is, the home is completed according to the agreement). Some builders will balk at this and require the deposit be placed in their bank account. Why? Two words: cash flow. Builders on shaky financial footing may want your deposit money to get started (or, worse, finish paying for their last job).

Another area of concern may be change orders. Does the builder charge a fee to process a change order? How is such a charge calculated? Are there any allowances? When do change orders have to be paid—during the job or at closing? Each change order should be in writing, specifying an exact cost of the item and indicating any time delay as a result of the change order.

## 3 Fixed price or cost-plus?

When it comes to settling on a price for a new home, builders typically give you one of two options: fixed price or cost-plus.

Most homes are built on a "fixed price contract." This means you pay X dollars for the home. The only exception to this could be soil conditions that increase excavation costs—some builders won't lock into a specific figure for this on custom homes.

The alternative to the fixed price contract is a cost-plus deal, also called "time and materials." Here you pay for the "cost" of the home, plus a fee (usually a percentage of costs) to the builder as profit. In rural areas or difficult to build sites, builders may tell you this is the only option since estimating costs for a fixed price contract are difficult. The problem with cost-plus is, what exactly are the costs? Are they just the materials and labor? What about rental charges on equipment needed for excavation? How about sales taxes or impact fees? Don't forget travel expenses—some builders try to tack this onto the "costs" category.

It's this difficulty in defining "costs" that makes fixed price contracts more attractive for homebuyers. If the only option is cost-plus, you might want to have an architect, attorney or buyer's agent help you negotiate a fair definition of costs. If you aren't careful here, the builder could include everything under the sun as costs, driving your final price through the roof.

# Email from the Real World: Cost-Plus Nightmare

**A reader in Utah ran into the pitfalls of a cost-plus contract.**

*"My partner and I are having a house built and picked a long-time builder to do the construction. He gave us an estimate as to what the house would cost, but the contract says we have pay to the "actual" costs beyond the estimate. We were worried about this, but the builder assured us he would be 'very frugal with our money.' Four months later, we are getting bills for lumber and other items that are DOUBLE the estimate! When we express our concern over this with the builder, we get a flip answer that they can always stop work when the money runs out! Now, they are telling us that some of the things we wanted to have in the house need to be cut to reduce costs! Help!"*

**Cost-plus puts all the risk of a building project on the consumer, not the contractor. If the builder fails to manage the project professionally (including the initial estimate of costs), the consumer is on the hook. As you can see from the above example, this leads to nothing but trouble.**

One suggestion for cost-plus deals: try to negotiate caps on critical expense areas like framing, plumbing, electrical, etc. That way builder's must receive your written approval before exceeding a certain cap.

No matter what method you choose, your contract should spell out details on the final payment to the contractor. Define "substantial completion" and specify the conditions under which you can withhold monies for uncompleted work. You should be allowed to escrow a reasonable amount of money at closing to account for unfinished items. The builder only gets the money after all the work is completed.

## 4 Difficult Sites

As mentioned above, some builders like a provision to cover themselves in the case of difficult soils or site conditions. Especially for semi-custom or custom homes, this can be an expensive clause for the buyer.

Insist the builder give you a specific budget for excavation and back fill. (Back fill is explained in the next chapter.) For our home, this came to $5000. Now, if the soil under your home is nice and soft, the allowance should cover the costs of basic excavation and back fill. But...what if they hit bedrock? Rock-hard limestone? Clay? A high water table?

All these cases almost always mean higher excavation costs—and you're on the hook here. In our case, we ran into limestone and the excavation costs went through the roof (or the floor, more accurately). Final tab: $7000. Ouch. There went an extra $2000 we had planned to spend elsewhere. This points out a major rule in home buying: LEAVE AN EXTRA 10% FOR EMERGENCIES. If you're building a $300,000 home, make sure you budget an extra $30,000 for little surprises like this and other cost overruns (your desire for an extra window here, nicer tile there, etc.). Even if you don't need the entire $30,000, it's nice to know you're prepared in the worst case.

A good way to spot difficult soil conditions is to do a soils test *before* you buy the lot. Make the purchase of the lot contingent on a satisfactory soils test. If you're purchasing a yet-to-be-built production or semi-custom home in an existing community, the builder may have already done a soils test on your lot. Insist on seeing the test results and consider consulting with a soils engineer or geologist to get an opinion about the ease/difficulty of building on this lot.

Make sure your contract defines just what a "differing site condition" is. You also should have a certain number of days to inspect and confirm the condition if one is discovered. If everyone agrees this is a problem, a specific amount of extra compensation to the builder should be identified. While some builders like an extra percentage of the sales price, we think the best course is the actual bill from the excavation company. The buyer would pay any actual documented amount over the original excavation and backfill allowance.

## 5 Contingencies and Other Fun Items

Do you want to make your purchase of this new home contingent on selling an old one? (Good luck—most builders won't agree to this condition, but it won't hurt to ask). Your contract should specifically define a time period to sell the old house, including a refund in case the contingency falls through.

Many builders insist on contingencies regarding financing—that is, you, the buyer, must get a commitment or qualification letter for a permanent mortgage. You may be required to diligently search for financing within a certain time period—30 to 90 days is typical. If you can't get the money, the deal is off. Whether you get all your deposit back or whether the builder should be reimbursed for any out-of-pocket costs should be negotiated in this section of the contract.

Another good tip: ask the builder to pay for an "extended coverage" title policy that gives you mechanic's lien protection. In some states, title companies offer this extra coverage that protects you against the builder who doesn't pay his bills (and then the subs come back and file liens against your home for their unpaid invoices). The cost is a mere $100 to $300—a wise buy even if the builder won't pick up the tab. As you've noticed in other parts of this book, we strongly advise you to include in your contract that the builder will provide lien releases from all subcontractors, suppliers and workers before you close. Basically, these forms indicate that all the workers have been paid in full.

Personally review these documents before closing; don't just take the word of the lender or builder that they are "taking care of the releases."

## 6 Time, Time, Time

When will the construction start? When will the home be finished? These seem like simple points, but like everything else in the world of home building, it's not as easy as it looks.

The start of construction may be contingent on you getting financing, the plans being finished on a certain date, all the permits being pulled, surveys and other tests on the lot being completed, and so on. Your contract should state that assuming all the above are accomplished (and weather permitting), construction should start on month/day/year.

Instead of specifying a completion date, some builders like to use a more fuzzy method—estimating a total number of calendar days. Most production houses are slapped up in 80 to 120 days, while semi-custom and custom homes can drag on beyond six, nine and even twelve months for the most complex homes. Be careful of loopholes in this process—the contract could call for 90 "working days," which is a lot longer than real calendar days. One contract we viewed had the builder giving himself "up to 729 days" to complete the home—yes, that's a mere TWO YEARS.

And what exactly defines the word "completion"? Is it when a certificate of occupancy (CO) or final inspection from the building department is given? Or when the buyer takes possession and moves in? Or is it some other point in time, such as the final stamp of approval from your private inspector? We prefer the last two methods—too many corrupt building departments have been known to give out certificates of occupancy on defective or unfinished houses. In the worst cases, government inspectors take bribes from builders and never inspect the homes they "pass." As a result, you should trust only someone working directly for you (an architect, engineer, or private inspector) to give the final stamp of approval. If you don't, the builder (with a bogus certificate of occupancy) may declare the home "completed" despite serious flaws or omissions.

Amazingly, we also discovered cases of new homes that were sold WITHOUT final certificates of occupancy. According to an investigation by ABC's 20/20, builders who sold such homes were only subject to minimal criminal penalties (such as a $100 fine)—that is, if they were prosecuted at all. It's hard to decide which was worse in these cases: buyers who closed on new homes without checking to see if the home was legal to occupy . . . or city/county building departments that let builders exploit this loophole.

Let's put this into bold caps: DO NOT CLOSE ON A NEW HOME WITHOUT A CERTIFICATE OF OCCUPANCY. Don't settle for excuses or a "temporary" CO, which some building departments issue to builders as a stopgap measure before a home is completed.

As a side note, we've seen some states and/or municipalities that issue an Improvement Location Certificate (ILC) on completed homes.

This document shows all improvements, a foundation survey, where the home sits on the property and so on. Lenders and title companies may require this as "proof" that your home is completed.

In a perfect world, builders would never fudge start or completion dates. Conscientious builders would be honest with their appraisals of work length: "Gee, Mr. Smith, I'd like to start your home June 1, but another home is running late and it looks like it might be June 15 before construction begins."

Back to reality. Some less-than-honest builders intentionally mislead you as to a start date just to get you to sign a contract. Since all the wheels are in motion by this time, it's hard to turn back when the builder announces a "two-week delay" after he takes your deposit. Most homebuyers just grin and bear it.

Holding a builder to a completion date is another quagmire. Do you want to pressure the builder into crashing the schedule, causing sloppy workmanship as subs rush to finish? While a little deadline pressure is healthy, too much may cause more problems in the end. Forcing the builder to pay your out-of-pocket expenses (such as hotel or storage bills) is probably enough incentive to get the home finished on time. Another realistic compromise: get a specific completion date, plus or minus 45 days. This gives the builder a reasonable amount of time for delays, problems, etc.

Here's the bitter reality: most builders give overly optimistic finish dates. They know it's really taking 120 days to build a home, but they promise 100 to get your business (knowing full well they'll probably miss the deadline). As a result, you should build extra time into your moving schedule. If your home is "promised" October 1, make sure you can lease that rental on a month-to-month basis until November 1 or later just in case. If you're selling an existing home, it's better to put the closing off an extra month than to be surprised about a delay. In case the builder actually finishes the home on time, you can seek to move up the closing on the older home (which is sometimes possible).

## 7 Defaults and Delays

What if the builder fails to build the home in accordance with the plans and specifications? What if you, the buyer, refuse to buy the home? How about delays—what if the builder intentionally delays completing the home?

This section of the contract should define what constitutes a delay and a default (on your or the builder's part). The builder will want a broad interpretation of "delay" including such fuzzy language as the "failure of the architect to cooperate." Of course, the architect could be balking at the builder's request to use cheaper materials or deviate from the plans.

As a buyer, you want a more limited definition. While bad weather always delays construction, builders like to blame the weatherman for everything. Sure, a driving rainstorm or sudden blizzard makes it difficult to pour a concrete foundation. However, just because it is 25 degrees outside doesn't mean framers can't frame a house. One builder we know ran two months late on a home because he was too lazy to shovel the snow out of a basement to complete the plumbing and heating rough-ins.

"Acts of God" is another fun heading. What exactly is that? Does a strike by workers count? How about the unavailability of materials? What if the wrong materials arrive (because the supplier goofed or the builder ordered the wrong stuff)—what about subsequent delays in getting the right materials to the job site?

Once you arrive at the definitions of defaults and delays, the next step is to allow for "liquidated damages." If the builder goofs and delays the completion date, should he pay for your storage cost for your furniture? The extra rent (or hotel bills) you incur during that period? Travel costs? Frankly, the builder should pay these and any other reasonable expenses you incur because of the builder's default. An alternative to this method would be a penalty clause that docks the builder a certain amount of money per day that the home is late. On the other hand, you may include a bonus payment in the (unlikely) event the builder finishes the home early.

As you might expect, your ability to get the builder to agree to a penalty clause/expense clause reimbursement depends highly on the market. In slow times, builders may go for it. In hot markets, your chances are diminished.

A reality check: most builder contracts are loaded against the consumer when it comes to defaults. If you back out of the deal, many contracts say the builder can not only keep your deposit, but also sue you for more damages, legal fees, your first born child and so on.

What if the builder defaults? When the shoe is on the other foot and the builder can't (or won't) sell you the house, all the buyer typically gets is the deposit back, which is his money anyway. That's it! Sorry to inconvenience you for the last six months! We've decided to sell the home to another buyer for more money—so here's your deposit! Don't let the door hit you on the way out! This exact scenario happened in Denver in the 1990's, when greedy builders in a hot market suddenly "cancelled" contracts, sometimes just days before the home was to be completed. Deflated buyers were left scrambling while the builders sold the homes to new buyers who were willing to pay more money. The best advice: if you can, negotiate stiff penalties (including specific performance, which lets you sue the builder to force him to sell you the house) if the builder defaults.

## 8 Termination of the Contract

What if the whole deal falls apart? What if the builder balks at fixing a problem your inspector identifies? Does the builder have any time to "cure" such a problem? What if you fail to pay the builder?

Clear wording should define both your and the builder's rights in the case of termination of the contract. Remedies should also be spelled out— and that's where the fur may begin to fly. What if you want to fire the builder? It's generally fair that you should be required to reimburse the builder for all work done to date. But what about the profit? If the house is 33% completed and the builder has breached the contract (leading to termination), does the builder deserve one-third of his profit?

What if the builder is incompetent and makes several mistakes that will cost you $30,000 to fix? If the builder has already done $50,000 worth of work, what do you owe? If the builder owns the lot, do you get all of your deposit back? If you own the lot, how much money should the builder get?

All these questions must be answered. We believe if you default on the deal, you should pay the builder's profit to date (in addition to any other out-of-pocket expenses the builder incurred). If the builder defaults and you own the lot, you do owe the builder for any actual costs incurred—but no profit. If damages occurred because of the builder's negligence or default, the amount of damage (as confirmed by estimates from another contractor, architect, or engineer) should be deducted from any amount owed for work done. If the builder owns the lot, you should be entitled to an entire return of your deposit.

Reality check: if you have to sue a builder to cancel a contract (or any other reason), it will get ugly. We've interviewed homebuyers who've sued their builders and they often say there were victimized twice: first by a contractor and second by the legal system. Huge legal bills may outweigh any judgement you get from the builder. So, just because your contract says you are entitled to X if the builder defaults, you may face an expensive legal battle that is a no-win situation.

## 9 Arbitration

More and more lately, builders have been slipping mandatory arbitration clauses into their contracts. If a dispute develops, the contract may call for binding arbitration, in which a third party sits down with both sides, hears the dispute, and makes a decision to solve the problem. Proponents of arbitration say it lowers legal costs and keeps minor disputes out of the clogged court system.

There is a darker side, however. Just listen to what the National Association of Home Builders says about arbitration in their guide to contracts for builders:

*"Arbitration provides a mechanism for resolving disputes without the publicity, and probably the cost of litigation. Arbitrators, generally experts who may be more likely than a jury to understand the technical aspects of a construction controversy, may provide a more impartial forum for a dispute than a courtroom. Additionally, the mere existence of an arbitration provision may deter potential lawsuits. Builders should suggest arbitration or mediation procedures early in a dispute, before a buyer begins to suffer 'mental anguish' that a jury might find compensable in a damage award."*

Now you see some of the builder's ulterior motives in promoting arbitration. Negative publicity is one of the few tools available to consumers fighting a builder—a protracted legal battle in the public spotlight that points out shoddy practices by the builder may cause significant harm to his reputation. Even the thought of this may drive some builders to fix the problem or settle the case. Arbitration limits bad publicity by moving the dispute process out of the public spotlight of a court trial.

Furthermore, arbitrators sometimes aren't the "expert, neutral" parties that proponents claim. Some are former contractors who are quite sympathetic to their peers and not so to the homebuyer. Others are idiots with little knowledge about construction that may be swayed by the builder over the consumer. Personally, we'd rather have a jury of 12 good citizens decide a defective construction case than a tainted arbitrator. And frankly, there really is "mental anguish" when the home you spent so much money on collapses, cracks, or in some other way fails. Choosing a route that eliminates mental anguish awards is bad for the consumer.

Nonetheless, you are bound to run into arbitration clauses in the paper chase for your new home. Here are a couple thoughts on the process:

◆ **A third-party arbitration** service such as the American Arbitration Association (AAA) should be specified in the contract. The AAA has special "construction industry arbitration rules" that it follows. Be forewarned: this can be rather expensive since you and the builder will have to pay both the AAA and the arbitrators of the dispute. Another group that does arbitration is the National Academy of Conciliators (NAC). Builders think the NAC is less expensive and faster than the AAA.

◆ **An alternative to picking a service** such as those above is to have each party choose their own arbitrators. Those two arbitrators then choose a third arbitrator. Obviously, three arbitrators instead of one will cost more as well.

One thing you can say about arbitration: it isn't cheap. The American Arbitration Association (AAA) charges a variety of fees for their service. Initially there is a filing fee of $500 to $3500, depending on the dollar amount of the claim. You then have to pay hearing fees, processing charges and more. All this can add hundreds of dollars to the process.

Given the complaints we've heard about binding arbitration from consumers, we do NOT recommend this contract clause for new homes. If you can, strike any binding arbitration clause from your new home purchase contract. If the builder insists on an arbitration clause, make it VOLUNTARY, not mandatory.

## 10 Inspections

As you probably have noted in this book, we are big boosters of private inspections during the construction process. There are two types of inspections for new homes that should be guaranteed in the contract:

◆ **Informal inspections by you.** We believe you should have complete access to your new home at all times. While you should pledge not to interfere with workers or get in the way, this does not preclude your right to visit the home (especially after hours, when the work has stopped for the day). Guaranteeing this right in writing is smart, as well as making sure you are entitled to a key once the home is locked up at night.

◆ **Formal inspections by a private inspector.** Specific inspection points should be clearly spelled out in the contract. Examples include foundation/footings, framing rough in (plumbing, electrical, and mechanical), as well as finishing work prior to closing. Decide on these times with your inspector before drafting your contract.

The builder should be given a reasonable period of time to fix any problems found during the inspections. Prior to closing, a punch list of "minor repair items" also has to be given to the builder. A period of 30 to 45 days to fix these items is standard.

Be forewarned: many builders deny any responsibility for fixing any problems that are not listed on the signed punch list. The exception may be "latent defects" (those not visible at the time of closing), which are covered in the builder's warranty. As a result of these provisions, you'll want to make darn sure the punch list inspection is thorough—now you can see why having a private inspector at this point is so important.

## 11 Mistakes in the Plans

Whether the plans are supplied by your architect/designer or by the builder, most builders will absolve themselves of any liability for mistakes in the blueprints.

If an architect draws the plans, expect the builder to make sure *you* are on the hook for any delays or costs caused by any defect in the plan. On the other hand, some designers put statements on their plans that they cannot be held liable for problems with the design. We wouldn't buy a home if the plans were stamped with this clause, nor would we hire a designer who wouldn't take responsibility for his work.

In a classic case of "having their cake and eating it, too," builders also like to absolve themselves for any goofs in their *own plans*— except for protection provided by the builder's limited warranty (which might be quite limited indeed).

As a side note, it's probably a good idea to have a copy (or several copies) of the plans if the builder is providing them (as is usually the case for production or semi-custom homes). This provides you ammunition in case the builder deviates from them without your permission—you can't tell what's missing if you don't have the plans.

What if your builder refuses to give you a copy of the plans? Yes, this does happen and it can be frustrating. A solution: get a copy of the plans from your city/county building department. While these plans may lack detailed specifications, it's better than nothing. Another plus to this strategy: approved plans may vary from the builder's stock plans. Why? Building departments routinely require builders to modify the plans to comply with local codes. You'll want to know what these changes are.

Another good tip: make copies of inspection comments (these are noted on the building permit, which is posted on the construction site). Obtain copies of any letters or documentation on your home held by the city inspection department. One expert told us "it's amazing how many times these documents disappear" after problems with the home arise.

Finally, it is wise to include a statement in your contract that the home must meet all local and state housing codes. If no local code applies, you might want to specify the home should be built to one of the nationally accepted building codes (like the Uniform Building Code). Another idea: have the contract state that all materials will be installed according to manufacturer's instructions.

## 12 The Model Trap Revisited

Remember when we told you that those gleaming models aren't all they're cracked up to be? Well, you begin to get the picture when you read the fine print in many production builders' contracts. The bottom line: what you see in the model ain't necessarily what you get.

Many builders rather arrogantly reserve the right to change certain items in the home. What are those certain items? Building dimensions, room sizes, appliance brands ... just about everything. The "decoration and style" of the home also may change.

Basically, some builders want you to sign away your life in these clauses. Sample passages we've seen: "Buyer acknowledges and agrees that he/she has not relied upon the accuracy of any representations made by the builder with respect to the square footage of the home." Translation: the builder may show you a 3000-square-foot model and then deliver you a 2800-square-foot home. And that's just tough.

Here's another whopper: "Builder reserves the right to make changes or substitutions of materials of equal or greater quality than those shown in the model or specified on the plans and specifications." Translation: a home version of the bait-and-switch scam. Note that any written approval or even verbal notice is NOT required—the switcheroo takes place and you just have to trust the builder.

Furthermore, how many consumers can tell whether a substituted material is of "equal or greater quality"? Unless you have intimate knowledge of building materials, you could be hoodwinked. We urge consumers to insist on written notice of any "substitution" or change in square footage—you should have time to confer with an expert (your private inspector, for example) and the right to reject any proposed substitution. (Even if you can't negotiate the right to reject changes, at least you'd be informed of the substitution). The builder also should document, for example, that those different roof shingles are actually better than the ones he originally promised.

Now, we're not saying that your home should be an exact clone of the model, down to the last atom. Small changes (due to the characteristics of the lot, for example) are okay, provided you're given notice. However, the switch of an appliance brand or type of sink faucet is suspicious. The natural reflex of most builders is to make a substitution that's cheaper in order to make more profit. As a result, signing away your rights on this subject is dangerous.

## 13 Environmental Liability

All the recent warnings about radon and other environmental contaminants have builders' attorneys working overtime to draft contracts that protect contractors.

Some builders have been bold enough to try to avoid liability for hazardous materials previously on the site (such as homes built over landfills, toxic dumps, and other fun locations). Whether builders can truly exempt themselves from this is a matter for the courts. However, it brings up one good point: doing an environmental search of your property (as described in Chapter 4) is your main line of defense.

Be sure to confer with your attorney regarding any environmental clause. He or she might want a modification in the wording to protect you in the case of an environmental problem.

## 14 Gag Rules & Forced Closings

Here's an exciting new trend: some builders have "gag-rule" provisions in their contracts. If you're unhappy about the quality of your home, some contracts prohibit your right to post protest signs or picket the builder. Can you believe this?

Obviously, the constitutionality of these provisions is seriously in doubt. Recently, the Pennsylvania State Supreme Court struck down a gag rule provision in a home purchase contract as a violation of the First Amendment.

These gag-rule contracts point up how touchy builders are about bad publicity. Instead of building quality homes and not cutting corners, it appears it's easier for some builders to intimidate their customers into signing contracts that eliminate the right to free speech.

If you come across this type of provision, we strongly urge you to ask the builder to remove it. Consult with your attorney regarding your state's latest court decisions about gag rules.

Almost as insidious as gag rule provisions are "forced closings:" in Texas, we found some builders put clauses in their contracts that say the homebuyer MUST close on a home within THREE days of a "final inspection." In southeast Michigan, another reader said their contract stipulated they must close "within 10 days after a certificate of occupancy has been issued EVEN IF THERE REMAIN UNFINISHED OR DISPUTED ITEMS." Or else, the buyer has to pay the builder a $100 per day penalty. Amazing, eh?

Obviously, we have serious concerns about buyers agreeing to any such "forced closing" provisions. If the home is NOT completed or there are items in dispute, you should not be penalized for not closing (that is, giving the builder ALL his money and hoping some day he'll fix/finish the items in dispute). One buyer we interviewed felt pressured to close even though the builder had not installed the home's air conditioning compressor, doorknobs, sinks and other items. Watch out for contracts that have vague wording with respect to your responsibility to close after a "final inspection." We recommend escrowing money for any unfinished items valued over $500—that way the builder doesn't get all his money until you get ALL your house.

## 15 Cleaning

You might assume that if you are buying a new home, it would be a clean home—but think twice. Many homeowners we interviewed were forced to move into filthy "new" homes. All that construction activity leaves tons of dirt, dust and other fuzzy creatures everywhere. The carpet may be soiled with the mud from workers' shoes; the bathrooms may be covered with all kinds of dirt; the windows may be splattered with paint.

The solution: you should specify that the home should be clean at time of delivery. Even specifying the extent of cleanliness you expect is fine. Most builders omit any mention of this in their contract and some use this omission as proof that all they were supposed to do was build a house—cleaning isn't included.

Reader Dale Williams e-mailed us a funny note about this issue. He and his wife bought a $300,000 home in Euless, Texas and had a devil of a time trying to convince the builder to clean the home before the carpet was laid. "Since my wife has constant problems with allergies, we wanted to make sure the builder didn't slap down the carpet over the leftover tacquitos, cigarette butts and dust bunnies." Their request that the contractor damp mop the slab before carpet was laid was met with howls of protest, in which the builder explained that it a) will cost extra, b) delay the process and c) could damage the integrity of the floor. Dale prevailed in the end, but it points out that most homebuyers probably need to have such details in writing before construction starts.

## 16 Specifications and Materials

Finally, the exact materials and specs should be included with your contract. If an architect generated the plans, you should already have this as part of the construction documents. However, if this is the builder's design (as it is with semi-custom and production homes), you must ask for it.

Production builders have told us that they have entire booklets filled with specifications and materials—and guess what? Most consumers don't ask for them! In a box later in this chapter, we give you an idea of what "specs and materials" really cover.

Reality check: some builders REFUSE to divulge their specifications/materials lists. Others may only give you a partial list. We realize that in a perfect world, all contractors would have to disclose this information. Absent that, get as much info as you can.

# Getting Specific: Finding Out What You're Really Buying From a Production Builder.

**B**ack when you were shopping for a builder, we strongly suggested you get the builder's specifications and materials up front. But what does that cover? How can you tell when a builder gives you a good list or one that is missing a few items? Here's a quick primer to the world of specs and materials—the following items should be clearly spelled out on a spec list:

1. **Water and sewer.** Where's the water coming from (city tap or well)? If there's a well, who drills it and to what depth? What type of pump? For the sewer, is it a city tap or septic system? The specs for any septic system done by the builder should be clearly outlined.

2. **Excavations.** How deep is the hole? Which trees will be removed and how will they be marked? Will any unmarked trees remain? What steps will the builder take to protect trees near the construction site?

3. **Footings.** The exact type and dimensions of the footings should be identified. A description of the concrete to used (strength, additives, etc.) would be prudent as well.

4. **Foundation.** As with the footings, the thickness (expressed in weight or pounds in the mix) for the concrete should be specified. How will the foundation be built (concrete block or poured concrete)? For poured concrete, what type of forms will be used (metal or wood)? Will you or your architect be able to approve in advance any additives put in the concrete? Will any reinforcing steel rods be needed? (The need for steel re-bar depends on the soil. This points up the need for a soil test and, in many cases, a professionally designed foundation/footings by a certified engineer.)

5. **Waterproofing of the foundation.** What type of water- or damp-proofing will be used? How will it be applied?

6. **Perimeter drain.** This drain is usually a black pipe that snakes around the foundation and empties away from the house, down a slope. The exact type and installation of drain should be specified. Where and how will it be "day-lighted" (or emptied)? A structural engineer provides this information.

7. **Back fill.** What type of back fill material will be used? How will it be put in? To what depth and how far will back fill extend from the foundation? Will it be tamped down or left to settle naturally?

8. **Sills, girders, and columns.** The sills sit on top of the foundation and should be pressure-treated lumber. How will they be attached to the foundation? What type of columns and girders will be used? For the columns, will they each have a separate concrete footing?

9. **Joists.** What type, size, and installation will be used?

*Continued on the next page*

*Continued from the previous page*

10. **Framing.** What type of floor sheathing will be used? How will it be glued and nailed to the joists? How will the walls be framed (the exact grade of lumber and installation)? What type of wood will be used for door and window headers and how will these be done? Exactly what type of wall sheathing will be used? Will the roof be made from pre-fab trusses or rafters? Make sure all these details are spelled out.

11. **Siding.** What type of siding will be used? How will it be installed? Confirm the quality of siding and make sure enough nails are used to secure it in place.

12. **Roofing.** The exact shingle type should be specified. What type of flashing will be used to prevent leaking? What type and weight of felt will be used?

13. **Insulation.** The type and installation of insulation for the floor, walls, ceiling and roof should be specified.

14. **Chimney.** A specific plan should be identified for chimney construction, including any necessary footers, materials (bricks, concrete blocks, etc.), and height above the roof line.

15. **Windows.** The exact brand, type, and color of frames should be specified. Will they be low-E (a more energy-efficient window)? Will they be flashed to prevent water damage? What about the screens?

16. **Attic/roof ventilation.** Another often overlooked item, adequate ventilation of attics/roof areas is important in all climates. A specific plan for ventilation and the location of vents should be identified.

17. **Exterior painting/finish.** What type of primer will be used? How many coats of paint? How will it be applied? Confirm that an experienced painter with the appropriate tools will do the exterior painting—not some high school kid with a power sprayer.

18. **Exterior doors.** What type of doors do you get? The type of locks? The brand name and size should be listed.

19. **Interior doors.** What type of material (wood vs. Masonite)? Finish? Type of wood jambs? What brand/type of door hardware is included?

20. **Inside walls/ceilings.** How thick will the drywall be and how will it be installed? What type of finish will the interior walls and ceilings have? Don't merely assume you're getting a certain type of wall finish (orange peel versus a smooth plaster).

21. **Trim.** The exact wood should be specified, as should the finish/stain. Installation at doors, windows, and other openings should be called out.

22. **Cabinets, countertops, vanities.** Do you get plastic laminate or Corian countertops? Most buyers get a cabinet allowance, which must cover both the cabinets and installation. Be careful of the low-ball allowance game here.

23. **Stairs.** A stair plan should clearly identify the type, materials, banisters and handrails. Any finish or stain also should be noted.

24. **Flooring.** What are the allowances for carpet, vinyl, or hardwoods? Does this include installation? Sub-floors also should be mentioned.

25. **Plumbing.** Make sure allowances for faucets, sinks, toilets, and other stuff are identified. If a specific bathtub is included, make sure the brand and model number(s) are spelled out. Fixtures (including brand and color) should be identified if no allowance is given. Don't forget about shower doors or sinks in the utility room (plus the location of the washer/dryer connections). Most other plumbing details (such as pipe locations, materials) are spelled out on the plans. Confirm any exterior water spigots—the number and location. What type of drain lines are used? Be aware that if plastic (PVC) lines are used on the second floor for toilets and these lines are not insulated, you will be able to hear the toilet flush throughout the home. A solution is to use cast iron drain lines or insulate the areas around the waste lines.

26. **Bath hardware**. We realize this sounds trivial, but what type of toilet paper holders are specified? Towel racks? Towel rings?

27. **Interior paint.** As with the exterior, confirm the brand and application method. Color options should be spelled out. How many coats?

28. **Electrical.** This includes many items. Starting with the outside, how many exterior outlets are there? Can you specify the location? What is the fixture allowance? Does this include doorbells, ceiling fans, exterior lights, or range hoods? How many interior outlets are there? What type of light switch is included? Most electrical outlets and switches should be noted on the plans— what flexibility do you have in changing this?

29. **Heating/cooling.** What type of furnace or air conditioner is included? Confirm that adequate ventilation for each room is specified.

30. **Telephone jacks.** How many lines are in the home? The number and location of phone jacks? If you plan to have high-speed internet access, consider a hub for either a digital subscriber line (DSL) or cable modem—and that all rooms have access to this wiring.

31. **Gutters/downspouts.** What color? Type (aluminum or other; seamless)? Where will the downspouts dump the water? As mentioned, water should be deposited at least five feet from the house. Even better: use plastic pipes attached to the downspouts to move water to the perimeter of the property. This prevents pooling and settling.

32. **Finish grade**. An often-overlooked item, final grading smoothes out the dirt near the home. A nice gradual slope away from the home is preferred. This can be done with heavy equipment and/or a rake. Any disturbed areas may be re-seeded. Additional topsoil may have to be brought in—this comes out of your excavation allowance.

33. **Other items.** Is there a security system? Central vacuum? Home automation system? Window treatments? Appliances? Landscaping? Retaining walls? Any and all other deals you make with the builder should be specified to the same level of detail as the above items.

# Money Bombs in Contracts

### Money Bomb #1: The pressure to move in.

*"We signed a contract to move into a partially built spec home on January 1. Well, the lease on our rental expired December 31 and the new home wasn't ready. We were forced to close and move in early! Much of the work was unfinished and the house was a filthy mess!"*

Obviously, one of the truths about new homes is that they always seem to take longer than expected. Some of this is dumb luck—weather delays may push back the finish date. In other cases, builders intentionally lie about the completion date or their own incompetence delays closing.

The pressure to move in can be a powerful weapon . . . for the builder. If you have to close early and the builder gets all his money, the incentive to finish your home in accordance with the plans and specs goes way down. We've seen cases in which builders have turned on the "move-in pressure," forcing homebuyers to make concessions or accept substandard work.

The obvious tip: don't put your back to the wall. Make sure you can lease that apartment/home another month if need be. If you've sold a previous home, put the closing date off beyond the alleged finish date of the new home. If the new home is to be "finished" August 1, set the closing on the old home September 1. In the worst case, the builder finishes on time and you pay an extra mortgage payment on the old

# Email from the Real World: Spec Struggle?

**A reader in Tennessee asked how many builders readily hand out specs:**

*"We were seriously looking at a house and asked for the specs beyond the two-page glossy marketing brochure they hand out. Not only did they REFUSE to disclose the specs, but also they wanted to know WHY we wanted this! The builder said if we don't trust them, perhaps we should NOT buy from them. So, we have to ask, what percentage of production builders actually provide extensive specs to buyers?"*

**While we don't know the exact percentage of builders who provide this info upon request, we realize there are quite a few "tight-lipped" contractors out there. But we're going to stick to our guns here. If a builder refuses to disclose the detailed specs on this very expensive purchase, we'd shop elsewhere. It has NOTHING to do with trusting a builder.**

home. (You may try to move up the old home closing at the point you know you can safely move into the new house.)

Moving from another town is tricky. If you arrive in town with all your furniture, what can you do if (or when) the home runs late? It's probably a hotel stay for you and a storage facility for your stuff. And, of course, in all cases you should make sure your contract says your builder will reimburse all these costs.

Even if you try all the above tips and you still have to close on the home before all the work is finished, remember this one word: escrow. Instead of giving the builder the full contract amount, escrow monies to cover the remaining work. That way, if after the closing, the builder "forgets" to complete your home, you'll have these funds available to finish it. Ask a title company and/or your attorney for advice on how to set up an appropriate escrow for unfinished work.

## Money Bomb #2: The low-ball allowance game.

*"We were given a carpet allowance of $20 per square yard. This seemed all right—until we actually priced carpet and found out anything decent that we liked costs at least $30 per square yard installed! Help!"*

As you noticed in our discussion of contracts, you may get several "allowances" on your new home's construction. Everything from the excavation to the light fixtures may have a figure attached.

The obvious scam is the low-ball allowance—the builder knows darn well you can't buy an entire house full of light fixtures for $500. How do you know you're getting low-balled? Do your homework—ask an architect, an inspector, previous homebuyers, anyone. Visit home centers and take notes on prices.

The worst case is to agree to an allowance first, and then discover later it's far from adequate. This money bomb can set you back hundreds if not thousands of dollars on your new home purchase—another good reason to leave a "buffer" figure of at least 10% in your target budget, as mentioned above.

One custom homebuilder in Austin, Texas has taken the low-ball allowance game to a new extreme—he now charges customers a 15% penalty fee on any allowance overages. This seemed ridiculous to us, since it's the builder who often sets the allowances in the first place. Not only do his buyers have to pay for any overages, now they must pay the penalty fee as well! While the builder does this because he claims allowance overages eat up his time and overhead, we find these policies to be a good example of why the new home construction process is so crazy. Our advice: stay away from builders who charge these penalty fees. Even better: do away with as many allowances as you can by selecting specific items/amenities *before* you start construction.

While these money bombs are common in contracts, the most prevalent problem is the lack of any agreement at all. In the research for this book, we were shocked to find consumers whose entire contract to buy or build a new home was merely a generic real estate "buy and sell" agreement—no plans, specifications, materials . . . nothing but the home's address and price. We also found custom builders who gave out skimpy details about their new home—far from adequate protection for a consumer.

In the case of production-type homes, many builders have "specs and materials" lists that gather dust in a file cabinet because no one asks for them. Granted, many builders don't tell consumers about this information, nor do they include it in the slick brochures they hand out. It's there if you ask, but many builders figure what you don't know (or ask for) can't hurt them.

# The Wild World of Home Warranties

Buy any new home today and you're likely to be given a glossy brochure on the builder's warranty. Like any other product, you'd expect this warranty would cover any problems you have with the new home. Right?

Wrong.

Like many other aspects of the new home purchase, so-called "buyer protection plans" aren't what they seem. Somehow, these warranties have morphed into BUILDER protection plans, not buyer. In fact, of all the sleazy and dishonest practices we've seen in this business, we'd have to give new home warranties the top prize.

And don't just take our word—so many consumers complained about these warranties that Congress held formal hearings on the matter in the early 1990's. The government's 455-page report is a shocking indictment of the questionable practices of the companies that sell and service these new home warranties.

Before we get to the dirt, however, let's go over a few points about these warranties. First, realize that most builders (big or small) don't give you an option as to warranty coverage. Many contractors simply purchase "insured warranties" for ALL their new homes (at a cost of a few hundred dollars per home). These so-called insured 10-year warranties are "guaranteed" by companies like Home Buyers Warranty (HBW), Residential Warranty Corporation (RWC) and HOME of Texas. Instead of just having your builder promise to fix things that go wrong with your home, these companies are supposed to INSURE the home will be repaired whether the builder is around or not. But does that really happen? Let's take a trip into the wild world of new home warranties.

# The Three Ugly Truths about New Home Warranties

**1** **Warranties are worthless.** Surprised? But you have a document that says the builder will fix any problems during the next X years! The first lesson all homebuyers must learn is that a warranty is only as good as the builder who's standing behind it. If the builder is honest and cares about his reputation and product, your warranty has value.

But what if something breaks and the builder doesn't care? What if he ignores your calls and letters that plead for help? Forget all the fancy wording and wonderful promises in your warranty. To enforce the warranty, you've got an expensive court battle looming: attorneys who charge big hourly fees, experts called in to verify the problem at hefty costs—the bottom line: you lose. We've spoken to many homebuyers who spent $20,000, $30,000, and even $50,000 fighting a builder in court—even if they "win" a judgement, the legal costs usually negate any victory. And the amount of time involved and emotional torment is even worse.

Even the so-called "insured" warranties offered by HBW or RWC offer very little protection for the consumer. And it's more than the numerous "exemptions" listed in their warranty brochures. One look at the numbers and you'll realize why these warranties cover so little—builders pay $200 to $1500 per home for a "limited" 10 year warranty on a $250,000 house. You don't have to be an insurance expert to realize that those tiny premiums aren't going to cover much in the way of repairs on a home.

**2** **Builders load their warranties with fine print.** Even if you have a reputable builder who is willing to do warranty repairs, many warranty deals are loaded with so much fine-print that they're rendered useless.

One builder's "limited" warranty we saw listed 23 exclusions that went on for ten pages. The most common fine-print problem: builders who ask you to sign away your rights to any "implied warranty." As you'll see later in this chapter, this is a whopper.

**3** **The best "warranty" to ensure a quality new home has nothing to do with the formal, written warranty.** That written warranty by the builder is nice, but what you should really count on is the "consumer warranty." That's the peace of mind you get if you follow the paper-scissors-rock strategy outlined in this book.

Start by quizzing the builder's references about warranty experiences. Did the builder respond quickly to warranty repair requests? Ensure you get good "paper" from the builder that includes thorough plans, specifications and materials. Hire a private inspector (engineer, architect or construction manager) to be a "scissors" for you—poking and prodding to make sure the home is built as promised. Finally, control the "gold," paying the builder the profit after he's fulfilled all the promises.

A good tip is to ask the builder for a list of all the homes he has built in the past five years. You should be able to contact any of these buyers, if you wish. This prevents the builder from giving you a list of just the most trouble-free homes. Whether you're building a $75,000 two-bedroom cottage or a $600,000 luxury estate, going the "smart" consumer route will be more insurance than any so-called warranty you get from the builder.

# The Saga of "Insured 10 year warranties"

You might think that homes built 40 or 50 years ago were better quality than the homes built today. And you may be right, except for one point. Until 1957, there was no warranty protection for homebuyers. If you bought any home and the builder offered no warranty, the home was "as is." Find a problem that was covered up by the builder? Tough. The buyer was stuck. Shady builders were able to wave their hands in the air and speak the only Latin words they know: caveat emptor—let the buyer beware.

The switch to consumer protection did not come from Congress or state legislatures. The powerful builder lobby throughout history has effectively blocked any legislation that protects consumers. But what about the courts? Judges, in most states, are not elected, nor influenced by the builders' lobby.

Therefore, the first rays of hope came from the courts. In 1957, a court in Ohio held that if no written warranty exists, builders must give an "implied" warranty that the home is of good quality. This was taken a step further by Colorado, where the state supreme court became the first court in the U.S. to say an implied warranty for a new home means it is suitable for habitation, built in a workmanlike manner and meets all building codes. This became formally known as the "implied warranties of habitability and good workmanship."

This was a bombshell. Builders could no longer slap up a defective house, sell it without a warranty, and expect to get off scot-free.

States across the country rushed to adopt the Colorado decision. As of this writing, most states recognize implied warranties with new homes. Georgia is the only exception—there is no implied warranty protection there.

The court's reasoning for this action was quite simple—how could homebuyers tell whether a home was defective? If the walls are all sealed up, could you really tell that the wiring or plumbing is dangerous? How many homebuyers are experienced enough to determine the quality of construction? The courts reasoned it was the builder's responsibility *not* to sell a "lemon" house.

As you can imagine, builders by this time were squealing like stuck pigs. To add insult to injury, many courts held that builders must honor an "implied warranty" on homes for 10 years. "Ten years! That's outrageous!" the builders screamed. After several months of cursing, homebuilders decided to get even.

The first tactic was to try to put disclaimers into contracts saying a new home was sold without any implied warranties. Of course, this was usually in the fine print, readable only with a magnifying glass. Naturally, the courts frowned on this. In Texas, a court ruled that any disclaimer for an implied warranty must be "accomplished by clear and unambiguous language, which is narrowly worded and specific." Basically, it has to be in all capital letters and buyers must be made aware of it (usually done by having the buyer initial the clause).

Not all states went along, however. Several ruled that such disclaimers were illegal. Other states followed Texas' lead and required adequate notice. Since the issue is decided on a case-by-case basis in each state, you probably need to ask your attorney about the current status of implied warranties and disclaimers in your state.

By this time, however, the genie of consumer protection was out of the bottle. Builders feared that many states would actually adopt laws that required all new homes to be sold with written warranties. Yipes! (Actually, the builders were right—many states did just that. These include Connecticut, Maryland, New Jersey, Virginia and West Virginia.)

So the builders went back to the laboratory and cooked up a monster. In a burst of ingenuity, they decided to "regulate" themselves. If they set up their own warranty system and pretended to police themselves, builders figured they could head off the impending flood of regulation.

Hence, on a bright, sunny morning in October 1973, the Homeowner's Warranty Company (HOW) was born. The proud parent was the National Association of Home Builders (NAHB). HOW was first a subsidiary of the NAHB, but was later spun off in 1981 as a separate company. (Actually, HOW and the NAHB still shared strong family ties. One of NAHB's executives served on the HOW board of directors.)

To show their belief in the free enterprise system, the NAHB also encouraged other companies to get in to the builder warranty business. Hence, Home Buyer's Warranty Insurance (HBW) based in Denver, Colorado, Residential Warranty Corporation (RWC), and other companies sprung up as "competitors" to HOW.

### "A builder-owned warranty company designed by builders for builders."

That's how HOW described itself in a brochure pitching builders to sign up. And it's an apt description. But just what is the mission of all these warranty companies? Basically, it is to provide insurance to protect builders from lawsuits over defective construction, in our opinion. As HOW put it in its builder brochure, their warranty was "designed to help you (the builder) avoid costly and time-consuming court battles. HOW protects your good name and reputation."

How is this done? Basically, warranty companies offer "2-10 insured warranties." The builder takes care of any problems outlined in the limited warranty (faulty workmanship and structural defects) for the first two years. Then, as HOW says, "for the next eight years—when major problems can often occur—HOW insures you (the builder) against the cost of repairing specified major structural defects. We take care of these repairs for you (the builder)!" (As a side note, if the builder skips town in the first two years, HOW claimed it is responsible for the "builder's performance.")

You'll note the warranty period is 10 years—by sheer coincidence, the same period many courts have assigned for implied warranties. By now, you may be thinking that HOW should be renamed BW, for builder's warranty, since the protection really applies to them, not the home buyer. Given the true nature of these warranties, how could the builders ever convince homebuyers they should pay (in the form of higher home prices) for this builder protection plan?

Slick marketing is the answer. The builders tried to market HOW as consumer protection. This was truly a deceptive marketing milestone in American business history. Here are some of the things HOW specifically promised consumers in their literature:

◆ **Quality checks on builders.** HOW promised to be selective about the builders allowed to offer their warranty. "HOW evaluates (builders) in three fundamental areas: construction competence, financial stability, and customer service. Even after a builder has been accepted, HOW has a staff of trained construction investigators throughout the country who selectively monitor new home construction for acceptable construction practices." The message: if you see the HOW logo, the builder is reputable, has been checked out, and is monitored for quality.

◆ **Written, approved quality standards.** "The (HOW) warranty is in writing, not simply a vague verbal promise to 'take care of everything for a while.' You'll note, for example, that the warranty incorporates Approved Standards, developed by HOW, which outline minimum performance standards and tolerances to which the home must be built and maintained." Sounds tough, right?

◆ **"Unique, no-cost dispute settlement."** "If you and your builder disagree on any issue of coverage under the Builder's Limited Warranty, HOW arranges, at no cost to you, for an independent dispute settler to review the facts with both of you and render a decision on

## A Lemon Law for New Homes?

As we were going to press on this edition, a rather amazing trend was happening with consumer protection and new homebuyers—some states were actually considering "lemon laws" for new homes. Similar to the protections afforded to car buyers, some states like Texas and Massachusetts were talking about new laws that would force builders to buy back defective new homes if they failed to fix them. Don't get too excited, however. The bill in Texas died in committee in 2001 (although San Antonio state senator Leticia VandePutt will re-introduce it in 2002). And Massachusetts is just talking about legislation at this point.

But the ball is rolling, and that's an encouraging sign. There's no doubt that the recent spate of articles and TV specials about defective new housing is spurring interest in new home lemon laws. In April 2001, the Boston Globe did a major investigative piece ("Luxury by Design, Quality by Chance") that exposed problems with Toll Brothers homes. And DATELINE NBC in 2001 took on Pulte's warranty claims, which some Pulte buyers said fell far short of Pulte's promises.

While the homebuilder's lobby promises to kill any such consumer laws, it might be a good fight. Stay tuned.

the responsibility for repairs." Wow, that sounds neat. But just how independent is the dispute settler?

If you thought the above stuff was attractive, you're not alone. HOW and other warranty programs were very successful. HOW alone sold more than 2 million warranty policies. 7,000 builders participated in the HOW program. At one point in the early '90's, more than one out of every four new homes sold was "covered" under a HOW warranty. When you add in the other home warranty companies, government experts estimate 75% to 80% of all new homes are sold with some type of insured warranty.

Everything was going fine for the warranty companies, until a trickle of complaints from consumers about HOW turned into a flood in 1991. The man consumers turned to in Washington was Henry B. Gonzales, then chairman of the Congressional Committee on Banking, Finance and Urban Affairs. The builders had met their match.

## Truth Squad

All of those aforementioned benefits sound wonderful—except the congressional investigation found most of them to be false. Witness after witness testified to Congress in October 1991 about the reality of homeowner protection plans. Here's what the committee heard.

◆ **Builder quality checks?** Don't bet on it. A report by a Virginia insurance regulator revealed that HOW's "Level 1 builder program [a HOW-member builder who has been in business for a short time] does not require screening for customer service reliability. This appears to be misleading and contradictory as the advertisements state the builders are screened for [this]."

Furthermore, according to congressional testimony, HOW had only 12 inspectors nationwide in the mid-1980s. These inspectors were supposed to inspect 1.4 million homes a year built by HOW's 11,500 builders. A San Antonio, Texas, consumer who successfully sued HOW for failing to fix his home discovered that no HOW inspector had ever visited his home—or any other home the builder built once he had been accepted into the HOW program.

◆ **Written, approved quality standards?** The fine print in these homeowner warranties defines a structural defect as "actual physical damage to a load-bearing element of the home which makes the home unsafe, unsanitary or unlivable." Translation: Unless your home is falling down, you're not covered.

That's what consumer after consumer complained about at the hearing. When they discovered a major problem, the warranty company refused to cover it unless the home had collapsed or was "unlivable." As you might expect, many defective homes didn't quite meet this tough standard—and many claims were denied.

The Virginia state regulator called HOW's advertisements "misleading." While HOW promises to cover major structural defects for 10 years, the reality is that only those defects that make the home "unlivable" really qualify. Just because you've got a giant crack in your foundation doesn't mean the house is unsafe or you can't live there, right?

Consumer advocates charge that the warranty companies only settle large claims when it appears the consumer will hire an attorney. Small claims, they allege, are allowed to wallow in a bureaucratic limbo. The warranty company balks at settling and tries every delaying tactic imaginable.

◆ **Unique, no-cost dispute settlement?** Well, unique is a good description. However, HOW's promises of an "independent dispute settler" were open to debate.

The Virginia regulator disagreed with HOW's claims here as well. It turns out the dispute settler is actually paid by HOW—regulators questioned how independent this person really is.

HOW and other warranty companies promise the dispute settlers will be experienced in the construction industry (retired contractors, architects, and the like). However, one New Jersey couple found out their expert dispute settler was a landscaping salesperson with little building experience.

No "expedited dispute settlement" was offered to the San Antonio, Texas, homeowner either in this chapter. A jury found HOW guilty of violating the Texas Deceptive Trade Practices law. "The jury ruled that HOW had engaged in fraudulent practices . . . by misrepresenting the degree of protection provided by their warranty."

So what was the warranty companies' defense in the face of this onslaught of evidence? Would you believe the warranty companies (HOW included) didn't even show up for the congressional hearing? That's right, HOW and the other companies refused to testify.

According to a source on the committee, congressional staffers met with the warranty companies before and after the hearings to discuss the charges. The companies basically told the staffers there was no problem and they planned no corrective action. Rather arrogant, huh?

In the industry's defense, the National Association of Home Builders testified that everything was just fine. The president of the NAHB said no further regulation of home building is required because there are already "a number of checks and balances in place." He claimed that local building codes are "strictly enforced" (please!) that, "most states already require a one-year warranty" (but what about the later years when serious defects come to light?) and that "legal channels are always open" to home buyers (but at what cost?).

Builders raised the specter of higher home prices to "justify" why this disgusting situation should not be remedied. "Unnecessary restrictions or requirements on warranties will merely create increases in the price of housing, resulting in a product that will be less affordable and less available to the buyer who needs it most." Translation: We shouldn't be held to the same standards as other industries.

Well, Congress didn't take this lying down. Or at least Henry B. Gonzales didn't. The committee proposed forbidding the government from insuring mortgages on houses covered under these warranty programs. Since over one-fourth of HOW's business comes from FHA- and VA-financed mortgages, this action stung.

Unfortunately, the builders' lobby went into overdrive. It seemed every builder in the country called Congress and, under pressure, a compromise was reached. Congress ordered the Dept. of Housing and Urban Affairs to do a one-year study about eliminating these warranties. That study was never completed, despite the Congressional mandate.

## The Death of HOW

HOW's past behavior came back to haunt it on October 14, 1994. That was the day that the State of Virginia placed HOW in permanent receivership. HOW was bankrupt. Why? The official reason was HOW didn't have enough reserves to cover anticipated claims. Translation: juries were dishing out so many punitive damage awards against HOW that it was only a matter of time until the company collapsed from it's own wretched practices. Insurance authorities estimated HOW's inadequate reserves left the company insolvent by more than $100 million.

So, HOW is dead. Yet, it's hardly smooth sailing for other new home warranty companies. Home Buyer's Warranty (HBW) barely avoided bankruptcy in October 1995, when a Colorado state judge delayed an effort by state regulators to get HBW to increase reserves. It turns out that HBW only has a meager $10 million in reserves to cover claims from a whopping 800,000 policies.

A simple bit of math indicates why Colorado state insurance regulators want HBW whipped into shape. If a mere one-tenth of one percent of HBW's policy holders file claims, that's 800 claims. And since the average claim for structural damage can be substantial (say, $50,000 in repairs), HBW would need to come up with $40 million—four times its current reserves.

Of course, you could argue that HBW will never have to pay $40 million, since it was never their intent to pay on claims in the first place. Brent Limon, a Dallas attorney who specializes in litigating home warranty cases, claims that a check of HBW's files revealed that an amazing 86% of all claims filed with HBW are denied. And Limon says those that are accepted are then subject to endless bureaucratic and legal maneuvers to delay pay-out.

In the wake of HOW's failure and HBW's stumbles, several new warranty companies have entered the market. Among these are Residential Warranty Corporation (RWC) and HOME of Texas. Each offer insured warranties similar to HBW. Yet, we've seen no evidence that these new home warranty companies are any different in than HOW or HBW.

## Why These Warranties are Dangerous

Most warranties for other products are rather benign—if you get a lousy one, you have a few headaches, but no major problems. However, these "homeowner protection plans" offered by builders are dangerous for several reasons.

◆ **Skipped inspections.** Believe it or not, the warranties let the builder skip inspections on some houses! For new homes financed by FHA or VA loans, there are usually three inspections by government inspectors. Obviously, since the government is insuring your mortgage, they want to make sure the new home meets certain standards.

However, if a builder buys a HBW or other "2-10" warranty for the home, two of those three inspections are WAIVED. Amazing, no? The government inspector just comes at the end of the project—after the walls have been sealed up. The bizarre reasoning is that the government doesn't need to look closely at such homes since warranty companies allegedly have done such a good job of screening builders.

Builders love this since they save time and money—two fewer inspections are a major windfall for them. In fact, that's one of the big selling pitches the warranty companies use to sign up builders.

While you should never rely on any government inspector (from the FHA or the local building department) to ensure you're getting a quality home, the fact that these warranty companies (and, hence, the builders) have negotiated such a sweet deal with the government is rather shocking. While it is more expedient for the builder and the government, we're at a loss to explain any potential benefit to consumers.

◆ **A false sense of security.** Warranty companies advertise heavily in home magazines. Over and over, they try to convince you that the best quality choice is a home that's covered by these warranties.

All this lulls the home buyer into a false sense of security. Why hire a private inspector if HBW is already monitoring the builder for quality? Why even check out the builder—hasn't HBW already done this for you?

◆ **Waiving "implied warranty" protection.** What all these builder-sponsored warranty companies have done is gutted the implied warranty protection granted to consumers by the courts, plain and simple.

Instead of builders building quality homes and taking responsibility for structural defects that show up down the road, the builders have created a bureaucratic monster to swallow consumer complaints. It's a black hole where claims go in and they never come out.

All of this gives some shady builders a perfect excuse to pass the buck. "Oh, there's a major problem with your house in year three, Mr. Smith? Well, you'll have to talk to the warranty company about it. Oh, you filed a claim and the company is refusing to fix this $10,000 crack because your home is not falling down? Gee, that's too bad, but there's nothing we can do."

**Our recommendation:** Ignore the pitch on the "2-10" warranty from the builder. While most buyers get this warranty whether they want it or not (the warranty companies require builders to enroll all their homes), you should still pay close attention to the builder's limited warranty. Ask the builder to explain any fine print. Realize that a warranty for one or two years by a quality, reputable builder is more than adequate. If a major structural problem develops in seven years and the builder refuses to fix it, the courts in your state may allow you to recover damages under an implied warranty.

PART 2

GO!

BUILDING THE HOME
AND OTHER
TRAUMATIC EXPERIENCES

# Key Inspection Points: Part One The Skeleton House

**C**hapter **9**

**I**t would be nice and infinitely simpler if there was some giant "New House Machine" that plopped out a complete new home in one swoop. Just push a lever and zap! New home.

In reality, building a new home is comprised of hundreds of small tasks. Some can only be done in succession, while others are accomplished concurrently. While we don't expect you to become experts in new home construction techniques, it is generally helpful to understand the different phases your new home will go through.

In this and the next chapter, we outline most of the major steps. Special attention is given to suggested "inspection points," critical phases when you should have a professional inspector or architect make sure everything is on track. We also throw in money bombs that unlucky homebuyers have encountered on this journey. In addition, you'll note eco-friendly alternatives to traditional building products and materials. These "green" alternatives are sprinkled through the next two chapters. Here we go!

## Permits and Approval

Before you can begin building a house, your builder must apply for permits and approval from the local building department. In some cases, the builder will also need approval from the zoning department, the health department (if you plan to use a septic system), a local environmental authority, and even a homeowners association (HOA). Some HOAs have architectural control committees that will review your plans to make sure they meet any community covenants covering height restrictions, style, color, position on the lot, and whatever other insane rules they can dream up. After your plans are ready to go, the permit and approval stage can eat up a month or two in your schedule. Add more time if you need to redesign the home to gain approval from a HOA or local government agency.

## Money Bomb with Approvals

**Money Bomb: Bogus engineer approval.**
*"In order get a building permit, the county required an engineer's stamp on the foundation plans. My builder told me I didn't need to hire an independent engineer—he had one he worked with who would make sure the foundation was sound. Apparently, this engineer just rubber-stamped the builder's plan. This was no problem until giant cracks appeared in my home's foundation. Another engineer we consulted said the builder's plan was woefully inadequate. Help!"*

Some counties allow builders or developers to hire their own engineer to certify structural soundness of the plans. The city/county building department approves the plans by taking the word of the engineer for structural soundness. The problem stems from corrupt or inept engineers who will put their stamp on any plan as a favor to the builder. Florida had this system until a flood of complaints about defective construction and design surfaced from home buyers who purchased homes that were "certified" by corrupt engineers.

**Solution:** The point is, just because the builder found an engineer to say your home's plans are sound is no guarantee—have your OWN engineer certify the plan's soundness. Yes, it's easy to cut this corner, but resist.

## Foundations

We realize it's a cliche, but a home really is only as good as its foundation. Get a lousy foundation and forget all the money you spent on nice carpeting or fancy trim. Your home's value may go to zero. Zip. Nada.

Given this fact, it's important to understand just what makes a good foundation. First, note that there are three different types of foundations: slabs, crawl spaces and full basements. Basically, a slab-on-grade foundation is a flat concrete floor poured directly on the soil with no crawl space or basement. A crawl-space foundation is just as it sounds: There is a space between the foundation floor and the first floor of the house just big enough to crawl around in. Basements can extend under the entire first floor of the house or just part of it. Ceilings in basements range from seven feet to nine feet high.

Slabs are the most common foundation type—about 40% of all homes were built on slabs, according to the U.S. census. Full or partial basements came in a close second, with 38%. Only 21% of all homes had crawl-space foundations. However, as you might imagine, this varies dramatically by region. Basements are rare in Texas, crawl spaces are most popular in the Carolinas and so on. One architect we interviewed told us that basements are common in colder regions because the climate requires the foundations be dug below frost line. If frost line is four feet down, it isn't much farther to dig a full basement.

A hot trend with basements: not calling them basements. Builders have discovered that finishing off basements and re-christening them as "entertainment zones" with home theaters is a big and profitable business. Some production builders are adding "teen quarters" or "guest suites" downstairs, for prices that range from $15 to $25 per square foot. That makes most finished basements cost $12,000 to $35,000, depending on how luxurious the finishes. The trend has even caught on in such basement-rare areas as Georgia.

Whether the basement is finished or not, it's important to understand some basic construction methods. Foundations can be made from concrete blocks or poured concrete. Regardless of the method, footings are required underneath the concrete walls or blocks to support the weight of the walls. Most foundations also require the installation of piers or columns made of brick, concrete blocks or steel beams to hold up the main support beam of the house.

During our research for this book, we read a number of books written by the National Association of Home Builders (NAHB) for builders. One book we read, Production Checklist for Builders and Superintendents, made this astonishing statement:

*"It is not uncommon for a foundation to be laid out and poured on the wrong lot, or placed too close to the property line. Occasionally, the front elevation is built facing the rear property line, or the building footprint is reversed. The wrong or unapproved plan can even be applied to the right lot. Sometimes the house just does not fit on the lot."*

Note that this book says, "It is not uncommon" for such major screwups to occur—just one more reason to have an inspector on your side. (By the way, the book does point out that "Such mistakes cannot be justified. Not only are they costly, but also very embarrassing." No kidding.)

## Key Inspection Point

Your inspector or architect should inspect the site at several points in the foundation process. First, after the hole for the foundation and footings has been dug, an inspector can check for proper depth and layout. After the walls and footings go up, another inspection might be done to make sure everything is correct.

**Tip:** Get the "ticket" from the concrete subcontractor to ensure the correct mix of concrete was poured. If an insufficient amount of concrete is delivered to the job site, the builder may water down the concrete—a dangerous situation since this greatly reduces its strength. Another issue is the outside temperature when the concrete is poured. If it's too cold, chemicals may have to be added to the mix. If it's too hot, the concrete may cure too quickly and sometimes crack.

## Email from the Real World: Cylinder Tests

A reader in South Carolina had this smart idea to make sure the concrete poured as part of his new home's foundation is the correct strength:

*"I am having 'cylinder tests' done on the concrete that was poured for the footings and foundations. My engineer takes two cylinders from every concrete truck as the concrete is being poured. The first cylinder is sent to a lab and is "cracked" after seven days. The lab applies pressure to the cylinder to see at what PSI (pounds per square inch) it will destruct. Since concrete gets stronger as it cures, you may not reach the nominal value until after seven days. In my case it was high enough that the engineer felt it would meet or exceed its nominal value as it cured. If we were not sure, we could then send the second cylinder to the lab after 28 days for another test. At $60 per test (plus engineer's time) I felt this was a cheap price to make sure the concrete was up to snuff. For me, the only sure way to make sure the pour was good is to test the stuff coming out of the truck. For peace of mind some of your other readers may be interested in this test."*

## Step-by-Step: Constructing the Foundation

**Step 1: Stake out the foundation.** Basically, staking the foundation allows you to see exactly where the house will sit on your lot—if you don't like it, theoretically you can move it at this point. However, if you want to move it, check to see if your homeowners association (if you have one) has to be notified. Staking also helps identify which trees need to be removed and tells the excavator where to dig. Some builders mark trees that will need to be cut down while others mark the ones that will stay.

**Step 2: Site preparation.** At this stage, your builder will have the site cleared of trees and graded so trucks and heavy equipment can access the site. Beware of tree cutters who are not professionals. In the case of our home, the builder offered to let some amateurs cut and remove the trees from our lot (in return, they got to keep the wood). That was fine, except the tree removal crew almost took out their own truck with a falling tree during the process. This "wrecking crew" also damaged several other trees we wanted to keep.

Some homeowners choose to save a little money on site preparation by removing trees themselves. However, a chainsaw and "do-it-yourselfers" are not necessarily a good mix. Frankly, we recommend you bring in a pro. If you do it yourself, there's a lot more to it than just chopping down the trees. Stump and branch removal can be challenging. Best leave this to someone with the right equipment and courage.

Occasionally, the utility trenches are also dug at this time. If you're not on city water, a well is another item that may be dug at this point.

**Tip:** Make sure the well-drilling contractor is a Certified Pump Installer or Certified Well-Driller. Even better, see whether they're members of the National Ground Water Association (800) 551-7379, (614) 898-7791; web: www.ngwa.org. The best well diggers are the ones who have been in business the longest period of time. You can't survive long in this business if you can't find water. Instruct the well digger to stop when he hits an appropriate amount of water, instead of digging to a depth specified in a contract. This will save you money in case you discover water sooner than expected. One issue to consider is whether to dig the well deeper in order to provide more storage capacity. Discuss this with the well driller.

**Step 3: Excavation.** Here's where dirt starts to fly, literally. Excavators bring in the heavy equipment and dig the hole slightly larger than the area marked by the stakes. Excavation is not a precision science—some over-excavation or damage to nearby trees may occur.

**Step 4: Footings.** Footings are what the foundation walls sit on. They form the bottom edge of the walls and, as such, should extend out beyond the walls on both sides to spread out the house's weight.

Typically, most builders use concrete to create the footings. A trench is dug around the exterior of the foundation and then filled with concrete. Again, it is vital that the footings extend at least three inches beyond the edge of the foundation walls on either side.

Footings also may be poured as the base for piers or columns that will be used to support the upper floors. Again, the footings must extend beyond the piers or columns they are intended to support.

Footings are also used for masonry fireplaces. If you will be including a brick or stone chimney, be sure footings are poured properly. In one case we investigated, the builder did not pour proper footings for a large fireplace. What happened? In one short year, the chimney began separating from the house and was in danger of collapsing.

**Step 5: Foundation and waterproofing.** Foundations can be made of either poured concrete or concrete blocks. If it is common in your part of the country to use concrete blocks, be sure your builder will be using steel reinforcing bars extending through the blocks. Concrete should fill each block and they should be bonded together with mortar. The exception are two-story homes with no basement and minimal foundation walls. In this case, the blocks often are not required to be filled solid with concrete.

As for poured foundations, the process begins with the setting of temporary "forms" into which the concrete will be poured. The forms are either wood or metal, although a new "eco-friendly" alternative called an insulated concrete form system (ICF) is also available. See below for more details.

Once the concrete dries, the forms are removed. Depending on the soil condition, steel reinforcing bars are sometimes used in poured foundations.

After the walls of the foundation are poured or built, the outside wall will be waterproofed with some black gunk called asphalt compound. If you live in a very wet part of the country, you may even get asphalt-treated felt or plastic to cover the foundation walls.

Also at this stage, the builder will install a French drain or perimeter drain around the outer foundation walls. The drainpipe is made from clay or perforated plastic—the goal is to divert water away from the foundation. Ideally, the French drain should be completely encased in gravel to allow water to enter the drain and to prevent the drain's holes from clogging.

**Step 6: Septic system.** If you are required to have a septic system, we hope you had a "perc test" completed before you even buy the lot. The perc test will help you determine what type of septic system is needed and its proper location.

Trenches will be dug to lay the septic pipes from the house. These connect to another trench into which the collection tank is laid. Yet another trench is dug from the tank to the septic field where the solid waste will eventually leach out.

**Step 7: Back filling.** Once the foundation is completed, the excavator will come back and "back fill" around it with the dirt left over from the excavation. If you have a basement, the window wells will be added before back filling. The back fill should be tamped down to prevent settling.

## Eco-Friendly Alternative

◆ **Arxx High Performance Wallsystems** (800-293-3210; www.arxxbuild.com) and **SmartBlock** (800-CON-FORM; www.smartblock.com) sell rigid foam insulation boards that form the walls of your foundation. Unlike standard forms that are removed after the concrete is poured, these stay in place and provide R-20 insulation. You can get more info on this topic at the Insulating Concrete Form Association web page (www.forms.org).

## Money Bombs with Foundations

**Money Bomb #1: No soils test.**
*"I had to pay an extra $3000 to have the foundation of my house excavated because the excavator hit limestone.*

*What could I have done to either avoid this or at least be prepared for it?"*

A soils test, plain and simple, would be the solution to a problem like this. Whether you have rocky, sandy or clay-filled soils, you can't tell just by looking. The soil can even very from one lot to the next. Insist on a soils test before you even buy the lot. If you're buying a spec house that is already under construction, ask to see a copy of the soils test.

In some areas of the country, "open-hole inspections" take the place of soils tests. This inspection occurs after the foundation is dug—an engineer checks the soil condition and recommends any foundation modifications.

Some builders intentionally "lose" the soils test or fail to do one altogether. That's because some homes are built on dangerously inadequate soil like loose fill dirt, landfill debris and worse—we've heard all the horror stories. Basically, if you don't have good soil, your house could "settle" to Peru. Cracked walls, disintegrating tile, destroyed concrete—you can avoid all of this by simply getting a copy of the soils test or open-hole inspection on any new home you're buying.

As we mentioned in Chapter 4, homeowners in a subdivision near Denver found out about this pitfall the hard way. The developer and builders didn't do soils tests on each lot and slapped up woefully inadequate foundations on very expansive soils. Several class action lawsuits later, the homeowners recovered some of their damages. A word to the wise: don't assume that just because you're buying from a "big builder" that all the correct soils tests and foundation designs have been done.

**Money Bomb #2: Undercut footings or none at all.**
*"I've been in my house for about a year and we have begun noticing severe settling in my house's walls and foundation. We hired a private inspector to find out what was happening. After he excavated the foundation, he found that the footings under our piers were 'undercut' and causing the house to sink on one side. What happened?"*

Here is a situation that can be devastating: undercut or no footings. Footings are the basis of the support for your house—if they're not installed properly, your home may become unlivable. Repairs are astronomically expensive.

In the situation above, the builder did not pour the footings to create straight-sided "square" blocks. Rather the footings were undercut—curving under or rounded. The result is a "ball-and-socket" effect—this may be nice for hips, but it's hell for houses. That's because the house can move, causing major damage in the process. If the piers or foundation walls are sitting on an undercut footing, you've got big trouble.

**Solution:** The only way to ensure that you don't have missing or undercut footings is to have a licensed structural engineer or experienced inspector inspect the forms for the footings. Also have him attend the actual pouring of the footings and inspect them again afterward.

Can you do this after the home is bought? No, unfortunately, you can't. That's because the foundation and footings are "back filled," which basically means they're covered with dirt. Only by excavating the foundation or footings could you tell—an impractical solution to say the least.

### Money Bomb #3: No mortar between the concrete blocks.

*"When I visited the construction site of a friend's new home, we noticed that the concrete block piers had no mortar between the blocks. My friend was outraged because the builder had told him the piers were completed and they were ready to move on to the next stage. Is this a common problem?"*

It may sound rather elementary, but we've seen several cases of builders who merely "dry stack" concrete foundation blocks in order to save time and money. As you might imagine, a wall of anything without mortar or glue isn't the picture of stability. Drystacking is an obvious code violation in most parts of the country.

Perhaps the most vivid example of this we saw was in a PBS documentary about North Carolina building practices. In the documentary, an independent inspector took the reporter out to a building site and proceeded to push over piers that were dry stacked, illustrating the poor building practices of that builder.

**Solution:** Once again, here is where the inspector comes in. The builder should not be allowed to proceed with the next phase of construction until your inspector determines that the job is done to code.

### Money Bomb #4: Incredible shrinking concrete.

*"I can't believe I've only been in my house for six months and I'm already starting to see huge cracks in my foundation. The inspector I hired claimed the problem could have been caused by watered-down concrete. Is this true?"*

Yes, your foundation could be suffering from extreme shrinkage due to too much water in the concrete. This may happen if the concrete company is unscrupulous, or your builder may have been trying to cut corners and eke out a little more profit. By adding water to the concrete, the builder can save money (since he has to buy less of it). Unfortunately, when you add water to concrete, you dilute its strength.

As a result, watered-down concrete may not even be strong enough to support the very walls of your house. (An exception: additional water may be added to the concrete to make it easier to place and finish the foundation.) Another rip-off: Some builders add rocks and dirt to concrete to reduce the amount they need and hence lower their concrete bill.

**Solution:** When the concrete is delivered, insist on getting a ticket for every load of concrete the subcontractor pours. The ticket should spell out the kind of concrete used, the "concrete (or cement) sack mix," and the water ratio. The architect or engineer who designed your foundation should have specified the proper mix.

How can you stop a builder who's intent on watering down the concrete to save a buck? Homebuyers who have been a victim of this scam say they should have paid an inspector to be on the site the entire time concrete was poured. Whether you want to go to this extreme will depend on how prevalent this problem is in your area—ask an architect or inspector for some advice.

If you discover the builder has used watered-down concrete, what do you do? If the builder can rip out the weakened concrete and do it again the right way, this is the best solution. However, such drastic action may not be practical. At that point, you've got a serious problem. Consult with your attorney—the builder may be in default for such a breach of your contract.

### Money Bomb #5: Shoddy waterproofing.

*"After a major rain storm, we noticed water damage in our basement. After we called in an expert to evaluate the problem, he determined that the builder failed to waterproof the foundation!"*

What causes most foundations to leak? Surprisingly, it's usually surface water from the roof or downspouts that are not properly drained away from the house. In a small number of cases, an underground spring or rising water table can cause damage.

Either way, shoddy waterproofing by a builder exacerbates the problem. In arid climates, most builders just use an asphalt compound to waterproof the exterior foundation walls. Felt or plastic treated with asphalt is more common in wetter climates.

Builders in a hurry may skip this important step—who can tell, anyway? After the back fill is brought in, you can't tell how much waterproofing you have or don't have. The foundation walls are all buried with dirt.

In Frederick County, Maryland, several homeowners have filed suit over flooded basements. The culprit? A "seasonal high water table" that floods the homes during the winter and spring months. The homeowners allege the builders knew (or should have known) of the high water table, yet built the homes with basements anyway.

Interestingly enough, about 16% of Frederick County is rated "severe" for seasonable high water tables by the federal Soil and Conservation Service—yet the problem area isn't confined to one particular part of the country. This is also true for other parts of the Northeast; you have to check on a lot by lot basis to discover this problem.

Here's the scary part: while most counties have regulations prohibiting building in floodplains, most have NO rules about construction in areas with high ground water tables. Some counties are now "studying" ways to deal with this problem. Proposed changes include banning basements in high ground water areas or new zoning ordinances to encourage builders to build in drier spots.

**Solution:** The only way to ensure you've got adequate water-proofing is to physically inspect the application of these materials before the back fill is done. When it comes to high water tables, the only way to detect this problem is with a soil test—always ask the builder for a copy of this test. Check with a local Soil and Conversation Service to see if this is a problem in general in the county.

### Money Bomb #6: Untreated wood used for supports.
*"I thought the wood support columns used in my basement were only temporary until steel beams are set up. However, the builder now says the untreated wood columns are permanent. Is this a problem?"*

You bet it is! Untreated wood should NEVER be used in a foundation for the support columns. The lumber for sills that sit atop your foundation walls should be pressure treated as well. Some states don't require this—a big mistake in our opinion.

Untreated wood is subject to deterioration, susceptible to termite damage, and is a major fire hazard. You certainly don't want your entire house to be dependent upon a foundation of untreated wood.

**Solution:** Obviously, if you have a house designed by a competent architect and/or engineer, the plans will call for the proper foundation supports and treated wood sills. This is your insurance against a builder who "wings it" in the field and uses inferior materials. Your private inspector should be right on top of this and not approve untreated wood columns as permanent supports. (We should note that some builders use untreated wood columns in a basement for *temporary* support, before permanent steel columns are put into place.) The bottom line: Never accept a home with such an inadequate foundation.

## Framing

Once the foundation is in, it's framing time! In a short time, you'll see the walls, floors and roof go up. Windows will be framed. Your new home will be a maze of two-by-fours and wood sheathing. At this point, the electrical wires, plumbing pipes, and mechanical systems (duct work, furnace, air conditioner) are installed or "roughed in", as the jargon goes.

### Key Inspection Point

When you have an architect inspecting your house, expect him or her to visit the site at least twice during framing, if not more often. A private inspector will visit the site at least once during the framing.

The first framing inspection should confirm that correctly sized girders (which support the home) are used. Proper installation of critical structural elements (joists, beams and so on) also is checked. An inspector may also note any warped or defective studs that may need to be replaced.

Another framing inspection may occur to check the electrical, plumbing and mechanical systems—more on this later.

## Step-by-Step: Framing

**Step 1: Floors.** When framing the floor of your house, the builder should attach wood sills to the top of the foundation. This can be done with an insulating foam adhesive—in areas such as California, anchor bolts set in concrete are used. (This helps prevent damage during an earthquake.)

Joists are then attached to the sills. Joists are sometimes prefabricated or can be made on site.

We recommend a quality prefabricated joist like the Silent Floor, made by Trus Joist Co. (800) 628-3997. Normal joists may be split or uneven; hence when a nail is driven into the joist to secure the subfloor, the nail can begin to work its way out. This causes squeaky floors. Silent Floor joists are engineered to resist warping and shrinking; nails can't work their way out, eliminating squeaks.

We have Silent Floors in our home and have been pleased. Some builders swear by them, while others try to get by with cheaper joists to save a buck. You can tell whether a home has Silent Floors since the name is stamped prominently on the joists.

After the joists are in, the subfloor is next. This is glued and nailed to the joists. In some parts of the U.S., gluing of the subfloor is not required. We suggest you insist on it and pay extra if need be.

The subfloor is usually sheets of plywood or "chip board" (wood chips formed into sheets with glue). To be honest, plywood sheets are much more expensive than chip board and aren't necessary to build a good floor in our opinion. Save your money here and use chip board.

**Step 2: Walls.** In a previous edition of this book, we recommended 2x6 wood studs over 2x4's (2x6 means that the stud is about 2" wide and 6" deep—the result are walls that are about 6" thick). We commented that the larger size stud/thicker wall cavity allowed for more insulation and, as a result, lower heating and cooling bills.

We've changed our mind, however. Thanks to high lumber costs and relatively low energy costs, the savings in energy bills do NOT outweigh the added cost. A recent study points out that even in areas with severe winters like Minnesota, the annual savings of 2x6 versus 2x4 construction is only $30. Yet, given the cost of lumber today, it costs 20% more to build a home with 2x6's instead of 2x4's. That would make the pay-back 75 years in Minnesota—much longer in milder areas of the country.

A better option: use rigid foam sheathing on a conventional 2x4 wall. This costs 10% less than a 2x6 wall, yet is more energy efficient. The rigid foam sheathing not only prevents heat loss but also acts as a wind barrier to prevent drafts from entering the house.

On tract and some semi-custom homes, the walls are fabricated in sections on the ground then "raised" to their positions along the ground floor. On custom homes, walls are built in place. Either way, this is the fastest part of building the house—some framers can frame a 3000-square-foot home in only a couple weeks. You'll probably be amazed at how fast your house is taking shape—but don't get out the moving boxes yet. The time-consuming finishing work is just around the corner.

By the way, if you or your inspector notices warped or uneven studs, insist on having them replaced with more sound pieces. Warped studs can cause "drywall popping," in which your walls separate from the studs—not a pleasant experience.

In the last few years, we've seen several new "wall systems" debut as alternatives to the standard 2x4 stud—these include steel framing, structural insulated panels and concrete wall systems. While a discussion of these new systems is beyond the scope of this chapter, you can find more info on this topic online. We found the Oak Ridge National Laboratory's "Building Technology Center" (www.ornl.gov/roofs+walls/) is a good sources for more details on these new methods.

While these alternative methods are attractive for their energy efficiency (and subsequent savings), there is almost always an additional cost. Insulating concrete forms run 7% to 10% more than wood. On the other hand, studies show heating and cooling bills in concrete homes can be 33% to 44% LESS than wood-framed homes. Of course, there are other benefits beyond energy savings: concrete walls reduce sound transmission, are easy to maintain and are earthquake and fire-safe. The same earthquake benefits apply to steel framing, which is more forgiving in tremors due to its "tensile strength."

**Step 3: Roof framing.** Two methods are used for framing the roof on a house. One is to manufacture the rafters, ridge board and collar beams on site. A ridge board is the board that makes the top point of the roof. Rafters are the side boards that form the "A" in a peaked roof. The collar beams are cross pieces that connect to the rafters.

The second (and more popular) method of framing a roof is to use prefabricated trusses. These wood structures look like "A's" of various sizes and are connected by metal brackets. The truss manufacturer makes the trusses and then delivers them to the site. Prefab trusses are usually put in place by a crane or by crazy framers who have a death wish.

Builders give the truss company a set of the house plans and the truss company's engineers determine what size to make the trusses. It can take as much as a month to get the trusses delivered; therefore your builder will need to order them early in the process.

**Finishing:** When building a spec house, many builders also finish off the roof at this time. Why? Because the house looks more attractive to potential buyers with the roof complete. First, the trusses are covered with wood sheathing. Next, a treated felt base is applied over the sheathing. Finally, the shingles are attached, starting from the bottom of the roof line. See the section on finishing for more details on roofing.

**Step 4: Sheathing.** The walls are typically sheathed on the outside with plywood, chip board, or "oriented strand" board, among other materials. The roof and floor are usually sheathed with plywood although chip board is also common.

Over the sheathing, some builders use a "house wrap" to help better insulate the home. Still others might add rigid foam insulation board (as mentioned above in the framing section). For house wraps, we recommend Tyvek by Dupont. Tyvek is an energy-saving air barrier that is literally wrapped around a house during construction. Made from polyethylene fibers, Tyvek keeps outside air from penetrating the walls of your home (although it does allow condensation to escape).

A local Tyvek dealer did a "House Energy Analysis" for a custom home in Denver, Colorado to demonstrate energy savings. The bottom line: Tyvek saved the home buyers enough money to pay for the installation in just 1.7 years. Total savings in energy costs over eight years ran $2322. For more information on Tyvek or to find a local dealer, call (800) 44-TYVEK; www.tyvek.com.

## Eco-Friendly Alternatives

◆ **Silent Floor's Performance Plus TJI Joists by Trus Joist Corp.,** (800) 628-3997; web: www.tjm.com. As described earlier, this flooring system uses pieces of aspen trees instead of rapidly disappearing fir. Also, the ends of the joists are laminated instead of solid wood. As the name implies, Silent Flooring systems aim to reduce squeaks.

◆ **Steel Framing** is becoming a more feasible replacement for wood. Although it was previously popular only in Texas and Florida, builders are giving steel framing another look as the price of lumber wildly fluctuated during the last 10 years. Two-thirds of the steel is recycled from scrap, old bridges, etc. For example, a 4000 square foot home can be built using six junk cars (contrast that with the lumber needed—cutting down 50 trees—to build the same size home). The only negative: In some cases, the steel members arrive unassembled and uncut. This tends to vex framing crews, who are more familiar with wood framing than steel. For more information about steel framing, contact the American Iron and Steel Institute's Steel Home Hotline at (800) 79-STEEL or (202) 452-7100; web: www.steel.org.

◆ **LO/MIT-1 by Solar Energy Corporation,** (609) 883-7700; web: www.solec.org, is a paint for the underside of roof decks. The reflective-surface coating forms a "radiant barrier," blocking heat from radiating into an attic. The result: Cooling bills are reduced by about 20%. The cost is reasonable, running 25¢ to 35¢ per square foot installed.

## Money Bombs: Framing

**Money Bomb #1: Warped joists and trusses.**
"When our house was built, the builder had the floor joists delivered to the site weeks before framing began. Unfortunately, it rained for days during that period. The joists weren't covered and we suspect they were warped. When we confronted the builder he said he would have the joist company replace them. However, our floor now has numerous squeaks—we suspect the builder never replaced the joists."

Warped floor joists (and roof trusses) may cause serious problems in the future. In our inspection of construction sites we have frequently found materials left exposed to the weather. Even worse are delivery men who seemingly throw the materials off the truck—expensive products are strewn across your site like match sticks. Improper

---

### Engineered Wood: Miracle product or time-bomb?

Watch any PBS home show like "This Old House" and you'll note the 2x4's are always long and straight. And the contractors only use solid-sawn beams and joists.

If only lumber looked like that in the real world. Today, if you grab a random 2x4 at most lumber yards, you'll see a twisted and knotted mess. To deal with this problem, contractors are turning to a new product: ENGINEERED lumber. But are these Frankenstein blends of wood a miracle cure or some mutant building product time-bomb waiting to explode?

First, it is important to understand just what an "engineered" wood product is. Made from wood by-products and scraps and then glued together with resins, engineered lumber is used in new homes in several ways. Perhaps the oldest engineered wood product is plywood, made from several layers of wood bonded with adhesive under heat and pressure. Another engineered product used for sheathing is oriented strand board (OSB), which is made from narrow strands of wood and costs about 30% less than plywood.

Sheathing is just one part of the engineered lumber market: in recent years, builders have started to use laminated veneer lumber (LVL) and I-joists (used as structural supports). To replace solid beams, contractors use Glulams (which stands for glue-laminated structural timbers) and Parallams.

Overall, engineered wood costs less and is more stable and reliable than the real thing—there is less shrinkage and (as a result) fewer problems like drywall pops. Another advantage: I-joists span much further than traditional beams. Longer spans means there is less of a need for load-bearing walls and supports; that enables homes to have more open floor plans.

stacking of wood also can cause damage.

Unfortunately, some builders don't return warped or weather-damaged wood products to the supplier for replacement and instead "make do" with what they have. The typical excuse: such actions are too time-consuming.

**Solution:** Insist that wood products (especially trusses and joists) be covered with plastic sheeting or tarps. And if they are just plopped any old place by the delivery truck, insist that they be stacked properly.

If your inspector notes that warped floor joists or trusses have been installed, have the builder send back the problem pieces and get them replaced. One manufacturer of floor joists, TJI (Silent Floors), told us they are happy to replace any damaged joists. Better to accept delay in the construction schedule than to install defective materials.

The best way to monitor this situation is to visit your home site every two to four days during framing. While you can't be at the job site 24 hours a day, an occasional visit will probably ferret out any problems

Builders also tout engineered wood's environmental pedigree. Since these products are made from scraps, lumber mills make more efficient use of each tree (and that keeps more trees from being used in new homes).

Of course, there are some problems with these products. First, some people may be allergic to the glues and resins used to make engineered products. While no studies have been done on the problem, some critics think these resins may be contributing to poor indoor air quality.

Even more troubling is the "experimental" nature of some of these products. The biggest failure of an engineered product to date is Louisiana Pacific's OSB siding. Since the 1980's, consumers have been complaining that LP's OSB siding or sheathing has deteriorated and failed, especially in moist or wet climates. In 1996, LP agreed to pay $275 million to settle claims from a class action lawsuit over the siding. Similar class action lawsuits have been filed against hardboard siding makers Masonite, Georgia Pacific and ABTco Inc.

Our concern: some of the companies are using deceptive marketing practices to hype their engineered wood products. For example, a federal judge in 1998 fined Louisiana Pacific $37 million for falsely labeling OSB siding as having been tested to meet the standards of the American Plywood Association. It didn't.

As a result of these cases, we do NOT recommend the use of exterior siding made from hardboard, Masonite, or OSB (LP's brand is called "Innerseal"). While most of the complaints about siding has come from moist climates like the Gulf Coast (Texas to Florida) and the Pacific Northwest, we've also seen problems in Midwestern states like Wisconsin. For more information on this problem, check out a Defective Siding web page (www.sidingclaims.com) started by a Houston homeowner who's struggled with this problem.

quickly. What if you're out of town and can't visit the site at all? If money is tight, have a friend drop by to give you eyewitness reports. Or consider spending the extra money to have your inspector drive by every few days.

### Money Bomb #2: Substitution of lumber grades.

*"I don't know that much about wood, but some of the framing studs look like poor quality to me. The builder told me he was going to use top-grade lumber for my house. How will I know if he is?"*

Lumber is stamped with various grades—trying to decipher these stamps is a science in itself. That's because lumber from different companies is graded in different ways. Often the salespeople at lumber yards aren't even aware of what all the stamps mean.

While grade is important, condition is critical. Lumber with the least number of knotholes is obviously preferred. Also, the best boards will not be warped or split.

How often do builders substitute cheaper grades of lumber? It's a common problem in some areas, several architects have told us, since it is hard to detect.

**Solution:** Leave it to a professional (inspector or architect) who's familiar with lumber grades and qualities to discover this money-bomb. If your builder promises you high quality oak molding, your inspector better be familiar with the differences between oak and birch, so you don't get snookered. Some good lumber yards will be able to give you advice, but don't rely solely on them to help determine the grades of wood used in your house. Also, a well-specified blueprint that clearly calls for certain grades and types of lumber is smart.

### Money Bomb #3: No "floating walls" in a finished basement.

*"Two years after moving into our new home, we discovered cracks in our dining room wall. The builder did a cosmetic fix, but the problem recurred. We called in an engineer, who discovered the problem was in our finished basement—the builder didn't use floating walls. What's this all about?"*

Concrete basement floors are not the world's most stable creatures—they may rise or fall slightly because of settling or other sub-soil problems. Hence if you want to finish the basement, the builder should use "floating walls." Floating walls allow for slight movement in the basement floor. Without floating walls, the wall studs are directly attached to the basement's ceiling—if the floor moves, the entire wall moves, which might crack the upstairs walls. Since "floating walls" are an invisible structural component (you can't see them after the drywall is put up in the basement), many builders omit them to save money. You may end up paying later for this tactic.

**Solution:** Make sure floating walls are specified in your plans. An inspector should verify their installation on site as well. A great discussion of floating walls (with diagrams and explanation) can be found online at www.asktooltalk.ca/home/qanda/faq/foundations/floatingwalls.htm.

# Rough-in: Plumbing, Electrical, HVAC, Insulation

As the framing progresses, the next step is the "roughing-in" of all the mechanical, electrical and plumbing systems. Insulation is added in the final phase of the framing.

## Key Inspection Point

Just before the walls are sealed up with drywall, an inspection should confirm the proper installation of plumbing, electrical wiring, duct work, and mechanical (heating and cooling) systems. Proper drainage of plumbing is verified as well. An optional inspection after the insulation is installed is also a possibility.

As you might expect, this phase is critical—you can't look at the home's wiring after the walls are up. No one thinks about his or her plumbing . . . until it fails. If you have a large or complex home, it may pay to have several framing inspections to ensure these "invisible" items are correctly installed.

## Step-by-Step: The Rough-in

**Step 1: Plumbing.** During this stage, the pipes that lead from the main water and sewer lines are connected to the house. A plumber will install the hot and cold water pipes, and the waste pipes from the toilets/sinks. If the plumber is also the heating/cooling subcontractor (as is often the case), this system and all duct work (supply and return lines) will be installed as well. Once the rough-in of the plumbing pipes is completed, the basement concrete floor (if you have one) can be poured.

**Step 2: Electrical.** The electrical subcontractor will run electrical wires throughout the house to each switch and outlet, as well as to all the light fixtures. You may go through the house with the electrician in advance to decide on the exact position of each switch—if you have an architect who supplied detailed drawings, this won't be necessary.

The electrician will also install phone lines and jacks and cable TV—you should confirm these are put at the correct locations. Now is also an excellent time to have the electrician run speaker wires throughout the house for a future stereo or home theater system. If you want to network computers in your home, now is the time for the electrician to run Ethernet cables to a hub location where you can plug in a high-speed modem.

**Step 3: Heating and air conditioning.** There are several heating options which are often put in by the plumber. The most common is forced air, where a furnace delivers hot air through a series of ducts to each room (cold air returns also are placed throughout the home to return air to the furnace). The main furnace for the house is centrally located, usually in the basement or crawl space. Heat pumps are another option; these provide both heating and air conditioning, but most operate on electricity, the most expensive energy option in cold climates.

One of the best methods of heating a house is hot-water "radiant" baseboard heat. In this system, pipes from a central boiler circulate hot water to baseboards or radiators throughout the house. While we recommend that type of radiant heat, we urge caution with radiant FLOOR systems—these use a system of hoses that distribute heat under the flooring of a home. There have been significant failures of several of these systems in recent years due to faulty hoses, prompting a flurry of lawsuits by consumers facing tens of thousands of dollars in repair bills. While manufacturers of such systems insist they've fixed the problem, we'd still urge caution. If you still want to go ahead, you can get info and tips on this topic from Radiant Panel Information Association (800-660-7187, 970-613-0100; web: www.rpa-info.com).

**Tip:** Don't have the furnace installed in the middle of your basement if you plan to finish it off at any time. Otherwise, you will have to locate rooms around the furnace instead of having a large, open space.

Also, if you're trying to compare brands of central air conditioners, check out Consumer Reports. Their June 1998 issue gives good advice and buying tips on central air conditioning.

Another new trend to consider: zoning your heating and air conditioning. Instead of having one thermostat control an entire house (and often leave one part too hot and another too cold), several HVAC companies are rolling out "zoned" systems. These systems use a series of dampers and thermostats to zone heating/cooling to provide more comfort. An example: Honeywell's zoning system; find info on this at honeywell.com (search for zoned heat).

**Step 4: Insulation.** You have innumerable choices of insulation types and brands. For example, most people are familiar with the rolls of pink fiberglass insulation. There are also blown-in fiberglass, foam or cellulose (which is made from recycled paper). One architect we interviewed doesn't like to use the blown cellulose because it settles unevenly and some people have an allergy to the Boron used in the product as fire treatment.

Talk insulation with anyone and you're likely to hear the expression "R-value" trotted out. Basically, an R-value is how resistant a material is to air infiltration (or heat flow). The higher the R-value, the better.

Depending on where you live, recommended R-values for the ceiling range from R-19 to R-49. Wall R-values range from R-12 to R-19 (most of them are R-19), while floor R-values range from R-11 to R-25. See the chart on the following page for the R-values recommended in your area. You can also call Owens-Corning at (800) 447-3759, give them your zip code and they will tell you the appropriate R-val-

# Recommended R-Values for Insulation

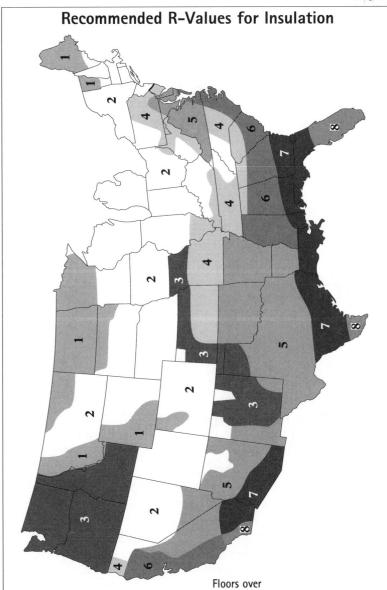

| | | Ceilings below Ventilated Attics | | Floors over Unheated Crawl Spaces, Basements | New Construction Exterior Walls† |
|---|---|---|---|---|---|
| | Resistance | Gas, Oil, or Heat Pump | | | All Fuel Types |
| 1 | R-49 | R-49 | | R-19 | R-19 |
| 2 | R-49 | R-38 | | R-19 | R-19 |
| 3 | R-38 | R-38 | | R-19 | R-19 |
| 4 | R-38 | R-38 | | R-19 | R-19 |
| 5 | R-38 | R-30 | | R-19 | R-19 |
| 6 | R-38 | R-30 | | R-19 | R-19 |
| 7 | R-30 | R-30 | | (††) | R-19 |
| 8 | R-30 | R-19 | | (††) | R-19 |

† The D.O.E. recommends R-19 for new construction exterior walls.
†† In these hot climates, additional insulation in the floor does not provide any cooling benefits.

ues for your area. The same info and more is available on their web site at www.OwensCorning.com.

Some people go for even more insulating value by using foam board. Most often used in basements and on cathedral ceilings, foam board is used with regular insulation for added R-value.

When your builder's subcontractor installs the insulation, be sure it is cut to fit snugly around pipes, trusses, ducts and studs. Any gaps will lead to future air leaks and higher utility bills. If the insulation in your house will be blown in, there is less of a problem; however, make sure there are no thin spots in the ceilings or walls.

**Step 5: Other details.** At this time, builders usually install windows, tubs and any other items that can't be installed once the drywall goes in.

## Eco-Friendly Alternatives

◆ GeoExchange (www.ghpc.org) is a consortium of geothermal heat pump manufacturers and installers. Their excellent web site has good info for those looking into this eco-friendly heat source.

◆ **GreenBuilders** (a web page: www.greenbuilder.com/sourcebook/insulation.html) has an excellent guide to "alternative" insulation products, including contact info for makers and distributors.

◆ **Copper piping** is also earth-friendly to a certain degree. According to the Copper Development Association (www.copper.org), about 65% of the copper used in new homes is recycled from used scrap. In addition to plumbing, copper can be used in the home's wiring and roof flashing.

As a side note, we found a web site by Eco Products (www.ecoproducts.com) that carries many of the eco-friendly building products at reasonable prices.

## Money Bombs with the Rough-In

**Money Bomb #1: Trashed out vents and pipes.**

*"We moved into our new home during the winter and immediately turned on the heat. We noticed that some vents in the house seemed to blow little or no air at all. What happened?"*

*"In our new house, the main sewer line to our basement from the street continually backed up. It took expensive visits from three different plumbers before we discovered what the problem was—trash was stuffed down the sewer during construction!"*

Construction sites aren't the cleanest places on Earth, to be sure.

Empty caulk containers, packaging, and other debris is strewn around the house. Krispy Kreme boxes, soda cans, whiskey bottles and other personal effects of the workers are also left behind.

Of course, workers are supposed to clean up after themselves during construction (yea, right). Unfortunately, some workers definition of "cleaning" entails throwing soda cans and cigarette butts down your heat vents or into your water/sewer pipes. Instead of getting disposed of properly (often there is a huge dumpster on the property that is ignored by crews), the trash goes down the nearest convenient hole.

Such debris can block hot air from making it through a vent, as in the first home buyer's case. The second story we cited, which actually happened to a neighbor of ours, was very expensive indeed. Once again the culprit was slovenly workers who disposed of trash down the homeowner's sewer pipes.

**Solution:** Insist that all heating vents on the floors be covered during construction, until the floor coverings are installed. This will keep stray trash from falling down them and encourage the crews to use the real trash receptacles. If you have any doubts about trash in your vents, bring a shop vacuum to the site and try cleaning them yourself. This is such a prevalent problem that professional "duct-cleaning" companies have sprung up to meet demand from new homeowners. They use industrial-strength vacuums to surgically remove those Burger King bags from your duct work—it might be worth the expense to have this done after you move in, especially if you have allergies.

In the case of the sewer line, you may not be able to catch the trash. However, if you make your builder aware that he will be responsible for any future plumbing bills related to such trash, you may be able to ward off this problem. Having the house locked up as soon as possible once the walls are up will keep neighborhood vandals from contributing to this problem.

A quality builder will insist that the construction site isn't a pigsty. Careful supervision of the subcontractors will also head off most of these problems.

### Money Bomb #2: No tub drain in the basement.

*"Our basement has two problems: the roughed-in plumbing for a future bath doesn't have a tub drain and the furnace was installed too close to the future bath's plumbing. To finish the basement, this means we either have to move the plumbing or the furnace. How could this happen?"*

Several possibilities come to mind as the reason for this money bomb. Often, subs simply don't read the plans, forget what they're doing from one day to the next, and/or aren't supervised appropriately by the builder. In this case, the builder should cut out the concrete and put in the tub drain at his expense. The builder should also move the furnace or the bathroom pipes—either way it's a big mess. In reality, the builder may balk at such extensive repairs and you may have an expensive legal battle looming.

**Solution:** Once all the pipes are roughed in, compare them to the electrical/plumbing schematic in your blueprints. Everything should be in the places specified in the plans. If not, you will have to insist that the problem is fixed before the basement floor is poured. Quick action here can prevent a costly fix later.

One couple we interviewed actually experienced the problem above and found themselves in quite a predicament. Unsupervised subs botched the location of the basement bathroom plumbing rough-in. Second, there was snow in the basement when the furnace installer arrived. Instead of shoveling the basement to find the correct location, the sub simply cleared a small space where he *thought* the furnace should go and proceeded with installation.

Note that the sub never looked at the plans to confirm that the furnace was in the right place—he later denied any responsibility for the mistake. The builder also failed to fix the problem, until the threat of legal action changed his mind. Even then, the builder didn't want to move the furnace. Instead he proposed chopping up the concrete basement floor to move the pipes. What a mess!

If you are buying a production home, check out the basement carefully before buying. If you plan to finish the basement, there should be plumbing pipes roughed-in for a tub or shower drain, a toilet, and a sink or two. Be sure they aren't located too close to the furnace or other mechanical equipment.

### Money Bomb #3: Furnace disasters.

*"In my house, there aren't enough heat registers. One room is so cold we can't use it in the winter."*

*"Our furnace worked fine for a couple days and then conked out. This happened several times before the furnace supplier finally admitted it wasn't calibrated for our high-altitude location. We had to have it replaced."*

*"We had the local gas company come out to our house after it was built to do a study of its energy efficiency and they told us our furnace had a problem. The cold-air return was too small for the furnace to operate at peak efficiency. All that money for the high-efficiency furnace was wasted, thanks to sloppy installation."*

The bottom line: it doesn't matter how energy efficient your furnace (or cooling unit) is, if it's installed improperly, you're sunk. Having too few heat registers (supplies), an improperly calibrated unit, or too small of a cold-air return can add up to higher energy bills and a very uncomfortable house.

**Solution:** The problem with too few heat registers (or cooling vents) is easily avoided during the design phase. Calculating the correct number of vents is best left in the hands of a professional. Make certain that your inspector counts the vents and notes their placement to make sure the builder follows the plans.

As for high altitudes or other extreme conditions, confirm you are getting an appropriate furnace. Check the invoice and paperwork to make sure you got what you ordered.

For forced-air furnaces, the cold-air return must be the same size as the hot-air vent leaving the furnace. If not, your furnace will not heat your home efficiently. Have your inspector check the size of the return before you close on the house.

In addition, a cold-air return in the home should NOT be installed near a fireplace. If a fire is burning and the furnace kicks on, the fire will "back-draft" toward the cold-air return—screwing up both the fireplace and the home's heating system. This is a common problem in some production home developments.

Finally, have your inspector pay close attention to the duct work installation for the heating/ventilation and air conditioning system. A common problem with duct work is crimping that restricts air flow.

### Money Bomb #4: Weakening the floor joists.
*"When the electrician came in to string the electrical wires, he cut big notches in the top of floor joists to string the wires through them. Now we have a basement full of damaged joists. Is this a problem?"*

In some cases, such damage to the joists can weaken their structural integrity. Notches at the top or bottom of the joist can diminish its load-bearing capacity. In plain English, this can be big trouble.

**Solution:** Some pre-fab joist manufacturers pre-cut small holes in the joists for pipes, wires, and the like. If your builder doesn't use these pre-manufactured joists, insist that the subs drill small holes near the MIDDLE of the joist to ensure the integrity of these supports. Have your inspector check this item to ensure correct procedures are followed.

# Key Inspection Points: Part Two
# Finally, Finishing

**S** o, you thought most of the time-consuming stuff was over for **your new house?** The foundation is poured, the walls are up, and the roof is sheathed—any day you'll be moving in, right? Hold the moving van, the fun has just begun. You've just entered the Finishing Zone.

While progress on framing the house was quite visible, you're now in for weeks, if not months, of finishing work that seems to move at a snail's pace. At the same time, the house is definitely crossing the line into becoming a home: the faucets are installed, light fixtures are added, and so on.

For simplicity's sake, we've divided this chapter into two parts: interior and exterior finishing. Outside finish work includes siding and roofing. Inside finishing includes drywall installation, painting, trim work, lighting fixtures, plumbing fixtures, cabinets, and a host of other items. In reality, some of this work is done concurrently—for example, your roof may be shingled at the same time the drywall is installed.

Here's an overview of the major milestones you'll pass:

## Exterior Finishing: Key Inspection Points

Finishing work is the icing on the cake. Now that you've made sure the home is structurally sound, the last thing you want is for the finishing work to be botched. As a result, it's prudent to have an inspector or architect out to inspect the finishing work. This can be done at several stages, culminating in the final walk-through where a "punch list" of problems to be corrected is created.

Specifically for exterior finishing work, inspectors are looking for proper installation of roofing materials, siding, and gutters/downspouts. Since these aspects typically come at the end of the building process, deadline pressure may cause the builder to make mistakes or cut corners—an inspector should be there to protect your rights on these critical and expensive finishing items.

# STEP-BY-STEP: OUTSIDE FINISH WORK

**Step 1: Roof.** Before the shingles are applied, a black felt sub-roof is first attached to the roof sheathing. Ideally, the shingles should be applied soon after—if not the felt may tear in the wind. Also, the felt sub-roof doesn't completely protect the interior from rain or melting snow.

Many choices are available for roofing material—all of them should be fire rated. The best fire rating is A, followed by B, and then C. If you're looking at ratings on shingles, don't assume the rating means it is the best shingle—it is just a gauge of fire resistance. Our discussion of shingles covers seven major options, from least to most expensive.

**Asphalt shingles** (also known as composite or fiberglass shingles) are often the least expensive choice. Asphalt shingles have life expectancies ranging from 15 years to 25 years or more. If you don't plan to live in your house for 25 years, consider buying a 15- or 20-year shingle. Because of their low cost, asphalt or composite shingles are often used on starter or production houses.

Some companies are now coming out with a thicker, three-dimensional asphalt shingle intended to look like cedar shakes.

**Metal** roofs are more expensive than asphalt, but offer longer life spans. Although not common, metal roofs are seeing a resurgence in popularity. Whether they are galvanized steel or aluminum, one neat aspect to metal roofs is their colored finishes. We have a neighbor near us who has a dark red metal roof that really adds some panache to his house.

Buyers who want a more rustic look often choose **cedar** shingles or cedar shakes. Cedar shingles have a smooth appearance, while shakes have a rougher look; both weather to a gray color. Cedar roofing material is highly flammable and, in some areas, can raise your home insurance rates. A few cities have even banned them for safety reasons.

A roofer in Mason, Michigan called our office with several good tips on getting a quality cedar shake roof. First, he pointed out that with correct installation, a cedar shake roof can last up to 40 years. Adequate roof ventilation (with gable vents or a fan) greatly extends the life of most cedar shakes. Hand-cut shakes (versus those that are machine cut) also have a longer life. In addition, he recommends cedar shakes, instead of those made from pine. For more info on this topic, you can call the Cedar Shake and Shingle Bureau (800) 843-3578; web: www.cedarbureau.org and request the publication on "New Roof Construction." Without proper installation or in areas with extreme climate (like the Rocky Mountain West), a cedar shake roof may only last 10 to 12 years.

For a roof that will last 30 years or more (some manufacturers claim they'll last "a lifetime"), **concrete** roofing tiles are quite hip, especially with Mediterranean-style homes. Available in a variety of shapes and styles, concrete is an excellent option for folks who can't afford tile or slate—concrete is about half the cost. It also comes in a wide variety of colors including such exotic designer options as adobe, bronze, and alpine blue. Concrete (as well as tile and slate) requires a more substantial roof structure due to the materials' weight.

One of the most expensive options for roofing material is **clay tiles**. Seen mostly on Mediterranean-style homes (especially in California), tile is available in a variety of colors from classic red to brown and even blue. Except for the occasional broken tile, they have a relatively long life and a good fire rating.

**Slate** is mined mainly in Vermont, Maine, and other northeastern states. Because it is limited in supply, this is the most expensive roofing option. However, your slate roof will probably be around long after the house below it disintegrates! Some slate roofs have lasted several centuries. The colors available depend on the area the slate comes from—the most commons shades are maroon and black. There are three different grades of slate, with life spans ranging from 20 to 40 years for low grades to 75 to 100 years for the top grade. Be careful to buy slate that has been graded—poor-quality slate is often ungraded.

A note about flat roofs: There are several new **"membrane roof systems"** on the market today designed for flat roofs. We recommend consulting a roofing specialist about these new roofs, since correct installation is paramount. Plus, membrane systems are designed for different situations; therefore, a specialist will be better able to instruct you before you make a decision. If you have a low-pitch roof, you may consider using asphalt roofing rolls. Similar to shingles, they come in rolls and are simple to install.

Besides the shingles that go on a roof, you will need to have flashing installed. Flashing is metal strips installed under the shingles around the chimney, in the seams where different roof lines meet, and around skylights and vents. Flashing helps keep water from leaking inside your house by channeling the water into the gutters. Good flashing is a must—if you have a roof leak, the first suspect is usually inadequate (or missing) flashing.

**Step 2: Siding.** The options for siding are at least as varied as those for roofing materials. They include wood, vinyl, aluminum, steel, fiber cement, cedar shingles, stucco, brick or stone veneer. Some homes combine styles, such as stucco accents on a cedar-sided home. Regardless of the type of siding you use, all openings (windows, doors, etc.) will need to be flashed to prevent water damage and air infiltration.

**Wood.** It pays to visit a local lumber yard or home center to see what options they offer for siding materials. Most have a display of various wood siding, including clapboard, weatherboard, drop siding, cedar shingles, etc. Plywood siding is also popular in many parts of the country—fiberboard is a close second.

**Vinyl and aluminum.** Vinyl siding is the most popular siding treatment for entry-level production homes and holds a 35% market share.

Vinyl's key advantage: it is affordable and requires very little maintenance. Vinyl has come a long way in recent years—the latest versions have more attractive finishes and improved pigments that resist discoloring.

We've always wondered if vinyl siding manufacturers have an inferiority complex—what else could explain why they stamp their product with a "faux wood grain" finish? It's an obvious fake—and the irony is that real wood siding usually has a smooth finish and doesn't show a wood grain when painted! Also, when inexperienced installers put up vinyl siding, it can look extremely sloppy, especially where long pieces are connected.

Vinyl siding does come in several grades—choose the thickest and you'll be happier. The best grades will also look much more natural. The biggest advantage of vinyl siding is that it doesn't have to be painted—ever. The color goes all the way through the vinyl and, except for some fading, will look as good as the day it was installed. Ask the builder if the vinyl siding is "VSI Certified." The Vinyl Siding Institute (VSI) initiated a quality inspection program in 1998 to insure the products meet a minimum standard. Check out their web page at www.vinylsiding.org (or call 888-FOR-VSI-1) to get a list of certified products.

Aluminum siding is another option, although most builders are using vinyl these days. Unlike vinyl, aluminum can be dented and scratched. No doubt the Tin Men image of siding salesmen as scam artists has contributed to aluminum's decline in popularity.

**Masonite, OSB or hardboard.** As we mentioned in the last chapter, we do not recommend these engineered wood products to be used as exterior siding on new homes. See the box in the previous chapter on engineered wood for details.

**Stucco.** Most commonly used in the West and Southwest, stucco can be either traditional concrete or a synthetic material. Traditional stucco requires expansion joints. Such joints help the concrete expand and contract without cracking, similar to the joints you see in concrete driveways and sidewalks.

Synthetic stucco (also known as exterior insulation finish systems or EIFS) was invented just after World War II but became the rage in the 1980's, when builders began using it as a more affordable alternative to the real stuff. Manufacturers of EIFS touted its aesthetic appeal (it didn't require expansion joints), durability and low maintenance. Yet, synthetic stucco ran into problems in the 1990's when a rash of consumer lawsuits claimed the product was defective. We'll discuss this in more detail later in the Money Bombs section of this chapter.

**Steel** is a niche product that is used in the drier, Western climates of the U.S. If you go with this siding, look for a galvanized rating of "G-90," which is necessary to resist rust.

**Fiber cement.** This product is engineered from 90% cement and 10% wood fiber. Its finishes give a realistic wood look at a lower price. Unlike other engineered wood siding products (Masonite, OSB or hardboard), fiber cement siding seems to have a better track record at withstanding the elements.

**Brick and stone.** Brick houses really just have a brick veneer, unless they were built prior to World War II. In other words, the brick is just a facade, like wood siding or stucco. Brick is very popular in the South, perhaps because it is less expensive there.

Brick requires a subcontractor familiar with masonry. This sub bricks the home's exterior, as well as any interior accents such as the fireplace. A less costly alternative to brick is a brick-faced plywood product, which "simulates" a brick veneer. Make sure that "weep holes" are installed in any brick veneer—this enables water trapped behind the brick to escape. A lack of weep holes may cause damage to the home's framing.

Stone is usually applied in the same manner as a brick veneer—by a masonry expert. Some composite or "cultured" stone options are less expensive than the real thing. We've been more impressed in recent years with the looks of cultured stone, which is cast in molds from real stones but made of cement, light weight aggregates and iron oxide pigments. The process replicates stone colors and textures, including vanishing resources like coral stone. A good source is the Cultured Stone Corp by Owens Corning (800-255-1727; web: www.cultured-stone.com). Best of all, cultured stone weighs and costs a fraction of real stone (about $7.50 to $12 per square foot installed).

Some buyers like to add a touch of brick, mixed with stucco or other siding. Be careful—a professional architect should design the combination of siding elements. We've seen many "builder-designed" homes that mix and match siding in such a haphazard way it would make your head spin.

**Step 3: Gutters and downspouts.** Made of galvanized steel, aluminum, or vinyl, gutters and downspouts are typically cut to fit your home right at the job site. On our house, the gutter subcontractor must have had the IQ of a house plant—he cut the metal gutters in our neighbor's driveway, leaving sharp metal pieces behind. Needless to say, when our neighbor experienced a flat tire, we were far from being the most popular people on the block.

Drainage is one of the most important parts of building a home—after all, if you end up with standing water you may have roof leaks or leaks into your foundation. Special attention needs to be given to make sure the design of the gutters and downspouts is correct; bad design can mean endless headaches.

A personal story on this front: our builder designed a main downspout to empty right next to the concrete front porch. Runoff from the roof washed away the dirt from under the porch and we had the fun experience of "severe settling." The result: part of the porch cracked and a set of concrete stairs separated from our home. While the builder made good at fixing the problem, it could have been prevented at the outset.

Here are some signs of well-planned drainage:

◆ Downspouts that empty at least 60 inches from the house—anything less could cause settling, water leakage into the home, or worse.

◆ Grading of the surrounding soil to drain water away from the house. Water only flows downhill—hence you must carefully design the drainage to keep it from damaging your home.

◆ Connect black plastic pipes to your downspouts to move water away from the home. These pipes can be buried underground, draining out 10 to 20 feet away from your house. Cover the end of the pipe with a wire mesh to prevent debris or small animals from blocking the pipe.

We eventually went with the black plastic pipe option and have solved our drainage problem. Unfortunately, most buyers only realize they have a problem AFTER major damage has occurred.

**Step 4: Exterior paint.** Primer and top-coat paints should be applied to your house as soon as the siding goes on. Don't allow the builder to put off painting your house for longer than a week or two, or the weather may begin to damage the raw wood. If you live in a rainy climate, the paint should go on as soon as the weather is nice—don't wait!

## Eco-Friendly Alternatives

◆ **TREX by Mobil Chemical's Composite Products Division,** (800) BUY-TREX; web: www.trex.com, is a plastic that also contains recycled wood fibers. Trex resists water damage, never splinters and is used in applications that normally require treated wood, such as deck planks and window trim. It costs $1.50 per lineal foot or about twice the cost of pressure-treated pine (or about the same as pricey redwood). One drawback to Trex: it doesn't look anything like wood, lacking any of the grain or character a wood deck has. Instead, it is rather bland with a gray, smooth finish. On the plus side, Trex requires much less maintenance than real wood, which requires periodic waterproofing and staining.

◆ **Eco-Shakes** by Re-New Wood (800) 420-7576, (918) 485-5803 are made from 100% recycled materials and have met the UL's highest standard for hail resistance. Running $180 per square, these shingles come with a 50 year warranty and class A fire rating. You can see this product online at web: www.ecoshake.com.

## Money Bombs with Exterior Finishing

**Money Bomb #1: Improper installation voids warranty.**
*"Our house has a great-looking roof made of tile. The problem is that the roof is leaking like a sieve. The roof manufac-*

*turer refuses to fix the problem because they say the builder installed it improperly. Can they do this?"*

Many manufacturers we spoke to told us they can't guarantee their products if the builder or subcontractor installed them improperly. If the builder balks at fixing the problem, the frustration level can reach a boiling point. You may end up in a ping-pong game, where the roofing manufacturer blames the installation (that is, the builder) and the builder blames the product.

**Solution:** An experienced private inspector or architect should be able to determine whether the roof is installed correctly. This monitor will need to visit the site while the roof is installed. Insist that your inspector get up there and take a look. If your inspector isn't familiar with your roof system most manufacturers are happy to provide literature that details the installation process.

What if you discover a defective roof too late (that is, after you move in)? Get to the bottom of the issue by discovering the root cause—you may have to call in an engineer, an inspector, or another roofing contractor to assign the blame. By presenting this "third-party" evaluation to the roofing supplier and builder, you may get some action. If you don't, a sharply worded letter from your lawyer may loosen up the logjam.

**Money Bomb #2: Overzealous painters.**
*"Just after moving in to our new home, we noticed we couldn't get the garage door open without the help of the Incredible Hulk. So we called*

## Eco Product Reports

How environmentally-friendly is that new green product you saw in the hardware store? How can you find more sources for eco products? We found a great web site that answers those questions and more: Environmental Building News (www.building-green.com) is both an online and print publication that covers the eco-product biz, complete with industry news, product reviews and detailed articles. Their web site has a "product" section with FREE reviews of energy and resource-efficient products, with manufacturer sources and more. Another good web site to check out: Center for Resourceful Building Technology ( www.crbt.org) which has similar online resources. If you live in Northern California, check out the Alameda Waste Management authority's informative web site, www. stopwaste.org. Their "Residential Green Building Guidelines" is available free online, as well as a Green Building Materials Resource Guide. The latter is a complete list of how/where you can purchase eco-products in the Bay Area.

*the subcontractor who installed the door. When he came out, we were informed that the house painter had painted over the vinyl strip at the top of the door, causing the door to stick. To make matters worse, the sub pointed out a tag on the garage door specifically directing painters to NOT paint the vinyl."*

Yes, it does seem as though painters' answer to a job is to slop paint on any bare surface. In this case, the paint actually caused a malfunction with the garage door. In other instances, it may mean painting over electrical outlets, wood that should be stained instead, and more.

**Solution:** Obviously, you need a builder on site to supervise these problems. In the case above, no supervisor was present during the painting of this house. It also would be nice if the painting subcontractor could or would read warning tags.

Barring all these intelligent checks on gung-ho painters, your inspector should check for painting problems during the finishing inspection. Make sure the inspector notes any improper painting and insists that the builder correct it.

### Money Bomb #3: No primer means painting again in a couple years.

*"When my builder painted my house a couple years ago, I assumed the paint would last at least five years. But here I am, two years later, painting it again. What caused this?"*

If your builder didn't use a primer coat on your house before painting it with top coat, the paint may not last very long. In fact, in the area where we live, most builders don't put on a primer coat—and many recently-built houses are beginning to show it. Builders here are simply trying to save a few bucks by not using primer. Their excuse is, "It wasn't in the contract."

Another similar scam: builders who use clear (or transparent) stains on cedar-sided homes. While those stains look great when first applied, they don't last. In a couple of years, it's time to re-stain (at a cost of a few thousand dollars). We've noticed this problem is prevalent in new home communities in the Rocky Mountain West.

**Solution:** Insist on having the paint subcontractor use at least one coat of primer before the final paint is applied. Once the primer is applied, have the painter do the top coat as soon as possible. Contrary to some painters' opinions, the primer does not need to "cure" or sit around in the sun. In fact, the longer the primer is exposed to weather and sunlight, the less effective it becomes, according to experts we've consulted.

### Money Bomb #4: Synthetic stucco woes.

*"The fake stucco on our new $300,000 is destroying our house! The stucco absorbs moisture, which is causing the sheathing in our home to rot and crumble. Now, we face a $40,000 repair bill."*

Exterior insulation finish systems (EIFS) have come under fire in recent years as consumers have claimed their synthetic stucco homes sustained major water damage. A raft of lawsuits came to a head in 1998 when a North Carolina court approved a class action settlement for consumers who had Senergy fake stucco on their home. Eight other stucco makers are part of the suit, which was covered in a recent DATELINE NBC episode (you can read the transcript in the DATELINE NBC story archive at http://stacks.msnbc.com/news/252454.asp). You can also read the industry's official position on this controversy at the EFIS Industry Members Association web site at www.eima.com.

Amazingly, synthetic stucco is still installed in 4% of new homes today, despite all the bad press. EIFS manufacturers point the finger of

## The Perils of Being Trendsetter

How can you spot a pioneer? Yes, they are the folks with the arrows sticking out of their backs, so the saying goes. The same can be said for new home construction pioneers—you might be a trendsetter by using a brand new product, but there might be a heavy cost in future repairs and headaches.

Each year, the construction products industry rolls out new "miracle" products made of space-age or recycled materials. While it may be tempting to be the first on your block to use one of these products, we urge caution. That's because MANY new products are never certified or code-approved—that is, tested by building code organizations to make sure they do what they claim. And, amazingly enough, many local building departments will approve these materials for use on new homes without such certifications.

Some of the failures of these products are the stuff of legend. Perhaps the best known is polybutylene pipe, which was used as a substitute for copper plumbing in the 1970's and 80's. These so-called plastic pipes (which are no longer made) led to a $1 billion nationwide class action settlement after the pipes leaked and broke.

As we mentioned in the last chapter, hardboard and OSB siding makers Masonite and Louisiana Pacific have faced a spate of lawsuits claiming their products are defective. A similar controversy is sweeping the synthetic stucco business, as reported earlier in this chapter.

Of course, it is somewhat less risky using a new product that is not critical to your home's structural integrity or mechanical systems. Example: plastic decks, which seem like a relatively harmless and allegedly more maintenance-free alternative to wood decks. But even here you must be careful: there are NO standards for these products. And manufacturers give little warning to consumers of the product's pitfalls, like many plastic decks become very hot in the summer and can sag under the weight of a heavy barbecue grill.

So, if you have a hankering to try something experimental on your new home, keep in mind the risks. Stay away from products that might require huge expenses to repair or replace if they fail.

blame at stucco installers, who they claim botched the installation by not using correct flashing or sealant. Many installers (small mom and pop operations) simply disappear into the night when troubles occur. The controversy has become so heated that recently a major window manufacturer (Marvin) put a special exclusion into their warranty—it warned homeowners with synthetic stucco that water damage to their windows would NOT be covered by Marvin's warranty.

If you still want to use this product, check with your window and door manufacturer to make sure you are still covered if you use an EFIS product.

# Interior Finishing

Interior finishing includes everything it takes to make your house livable: drywall, doors, windows, floor coverings, trim work, brick accents, etc. While we can't possibly detail every minute aspect of finish work, we will try to give you a good idea of the major components.

## Key Inspection Points

The finishing inspection can be one major inspection, or a series of shorter visits to check quality. Important points to consider are the hanging of the drywall and setting of windows, as well as installation of the floor coverings and the trim work. If you have a brick or stone fireplace, you may want to have this inspected as well.

## Step-by-Step: Inside Finish Work

**Step 1: Windows.** Windows come in every price range and size with every possible energy-saving option imaginable. We discuss the differences, advantages, and disadvantages of windows from leading manufacturers at the end of this book.

As for installing the windows, your builder's framing team will have framed out each window and door opening. We recommend requiring the framers to use a double thickness of "headers" (blocks of wood over the window/door opening) to protect against future warping.

Your inspector will be able to determine whether the windows have been anchored to the frame and are supported properly. All windows should be level (or "plumb") and most important, properly flashed. Flashing windows is similar to flashing a roof: galvanized metal strips or well-painted wood is used to guide water away from the window opening and down the side of the house.

We have actually seen the effects of having no flashing around the windows on a Florida home located near the coast. In a state like Florida, you can imagine that flashing would be even more critical, thanks to fierce thunderstorms that blow rain horizontally toward windows and doors. Unfortunately for this home buyer, the lack of flashing led to rotting of their windows as well as damage to the interior of the house. Your inspector must inspect the flashing before the siding goes up on the outside of the house.

**Step 2: Drywall.** Once the insulation has been installed in your house, the drywall can go up. Referred to as gypboard, wall board or sheetrock, drywall is a sheet of gypsum sandwiched between two pieces of paper.

Wallboard should be installed using drywall screws, which hold the walls to the studs better. The other alternative is nails, which can pop out if the stud is warped or the drywall is improperly installed. Be sure the screws are inserted roughly every 12 inches to ensure the board is secure.

Once the drywall is installed, the seams are covered with a joint compound (known as "mud"). Next, the seams are taped with a special paper tape and then spread with more compound. Any "dimples" from where the drywall screws are inserted should also be leveled out with joint compound. If your walls are going to remain smooth (as is common in the Northeast), a good taping team will come back after the compound dries and reapply a second coat. Then, after this dries, the crew sands the surface smooth.

In many parts of the country, smooth walls have been replaced with textures. In my parents' house (built in the 1960s) the designs were elaborate, including scalloped ceilings. Today, the most common texture is called "orange peel."

Textures are used since they save time and money. Only one layer of joint compound is used, and then the texture is applied over it. Texture will hide poor taping and sheetrocking jobs. If you plan to have textured walls and ceilings, have your inspector check out the sheetrock job carefully before the walls are textured.

**Step 3: Interior paint.** Once the drywall is completed, the walls can be painted. Most paint and hardware stores are happy to give you tips and pointers about the pros and cons of certain paints.

However, if you have children or pets, consider using a semi-gloss or gloss paint inside your house. This makes it much easier to clean the walls should you have a drooling Rover or a budding Rembrandt.

**Tip:** Be sure to keep extra cans of paint around the house after it's completed, so you can do any touch-ups. If there is no extra paint, get the names/codes of each paint color from your builder, buy a can or two and keep them in a safe place. This goes for the outside paint or stain as well.

**Step 4: Trim work.** Trim work includes doors, mantels, window frames, floor trim—anything that requires a little wood to finish it off. Trim is used to cover the bare ends of drywall, the tops of fireplaces, and the frames around windows and doors. We also include doors in the trim work because the painting or staining of inside doors is done at the same time as the rest of the trim work.

Trim work should be stained before it is installed. Once stained, door jambs and frames should be installed first, and then the doors are installed. After the stained trim has been completely installed, the finish crew should go back through the house and fill in the nail holes with putty approximately the color of the stained wood.

If you prefer painted trim, the wood should be painted after it has been installed (except for the doors). The nail holes should be filled before painting as well.

Trim work is a prime area for builder shenanigans. For example, on a house we examined, a subcontractor asked the builder where the redwood trim supplies were. Cheaper-quality cedar trim had apparently been delivered to the job site. The builder told the sub to put in the cheaper trim despite specific directions on the plans to use redwood.

Watch out for switches with doors as well. Specify the type of doors and trim (as well as the paint or stain) in your blueprints. Have the inspector verify this on the finishing inspection.

If you're building a custom home, all the trim work should be clearly called out on the specs and plans. If you're buying a production or semi-custom home, make sure the builder clearly tells you the type of trim work you're getting before you commit.

Another point: if you expect your trim to be flush with the wall, you will have to inform the builder in advance. A common problem is gaps between the trimwork and walls, caused by sloppy drywall work. This can be covered up at this stage with the infamous caulk gun (more on this later).

**Step 5: Floor coverings.** This stage includes the installation of carpet, tile, linoleum, and hardwood—finally, the house is beginning to look more like a home. Regardless of the finishing floor coverings you choose, you should insist on having an "underlayment" installed by the subcontractor. (The exception is hardwood, which can be nailed directly to the sub-floor.) Underlayments, usually made of plywood, smooth out any bumps in the sub-floor. Varying thicknesses will help level the different floor surfaces in your home. A good underlayment costs about $1.50 per square foot installed.

**Hardwood floors.** Most builders install hardwood floors first because it's much simpler to fit other types of floor coverings to the wood, rather than the other way around. We watched a little of our wood floor being installed and it was quite impressive. The subcontractor moved at lightning speed as he pounded the boards into place.

A cross-piece is used under a door or where the hardwood meets other types of flooring. Once installed, hardwoods are sanded and finished with several coats of a polyurethane stain. Polyurethane has made it possible for consumers to avoid time-consuming waxing that previous wood flooring required. Just a mild vinegar and water solution is needed to clean most hardwood floors today.

One hot eco-trend: cork or bamboo flooring. We'll discuss these later in this chapter under Eco-Friendly alternatives.

**Vinyl.** Used most often in laundry rooms or even in bathrooms and kitchens, vinyl is a cost-effective floor covering. Most vinyl is cheaper than tile, carpeting, or hardwoods. Vinyl runs about $6 to $20 per square yard—expensive "solid" vinyls can top $50.

Vinyl requires a smooth, strong underlayment—usually plywood. Once the underlayment is installed, the vinyl is adhered to the sub-floor using a latex adhesive. The actual type of adhesive depends on the brand of vinyl used.

One of the hottest trends in vinyl is to make it look like wood or stone—these finishes can look very much like the real thing, at a fraction of the cost of course. Some manufacturers have rolled out vinyls that look like marble or distress stone. Pergo (www.pergo.com) is one of the popular manufacturers of faux wood vinyl flooring.

**Carpeting.** Carpeting can range widely in price. Our best advice: get carpeting with the highest nylon content (or wool content if it's berber). The more nylon, the better the carpet. It doesn't snag as easily and it resists traffic patterns better. If you plan to live in your house for many years, invest in long-lasting carpet.

Carpet is installed over an underlayment, just like vinyl. Padding (preferably 3/8 to 1/2 inch thick) is laid on top of the underlayment and the carpet is then installed on top. Some people use carpeting that already has padding attached to it—a cost-saving advantage.

**Tile.** Tile is often used as a floor covering in bathrooms, kitchens, and laundry rooms (not to mention as countertops, back splashes, and shower and tub enclosures). Large floor tiles may also be used in high traffic areas such as hallways. You will definitely need an underlayment below the tile. Often tile is set early in the finishing process at the same time hardwood floors are laid.

**Stone.** Stone entryways are an impressive, if costly, first impression. In California, many upper-end homes have limestone entryways.

**Step 6: Cabinets and countertops.** Cabinets are usually thought of as part of the kitchen and the bathrooms. Cabinets can also be installed in your family room (a convenient hiding place for the TV), in the bedrooms, and in an office. Some buyers even request built-in cabinets in the laundry room and garage.

There are three basic types of cabinets: pre-fabricated, semi-custom and custom. Pre-fabricated cabinets such as those made by Merillat, Riviera, and Master Craft often are advertised in home magazines and on showroom floors in local lumber and home stores.

Pre-fabricated cabinets are available in a number of stock sizes. A cabinet representative measures your kitchen and bath areas to create a "schematic" of the cabinet design. If you can't fill the space up exactly, they may adjust cabinet sizes or the installer may fill in with a matching strip of wood to hide the gaps.

Some pre-fabricated cabinets are made of particle board covered with laminate and can look very cheap. Others are made of solid panels of hardwoods such as oak and are stained or painted to look quite attractive. Still other cabinets may have real wood doors with particle board and laminate "boxes." Shelves or doors may be a wood veneer over particle board. The basic rule of thumb: the price varies depending on how much real wood is used.

Semi-custom cabinets have more options for woods/styles than basic stock cabinets and as such are more expensive. They still come in stock sizes, however, and can be ordered more quickly than custom options.

Custom cabinets are noticeably more expensive because they are designed from scratch to fit your particular home. Often made in more exotic woods such as walnut and cherry, custom cabinets are usually of much higher quality construction than pre-fabricated options.

Here are four elements to look for in a good cabinet:

**1** **"Dovetailed," solid wood drawers** that are not stapled or hot-glued.

**2** **Shelves that don't bow when weight is added** (you might want to bring in a couple small barbells or other weights to test the sample cabinets). If the shelves in the showroom have a center support, ask whether this will be installed in your cabinets.

**3** **Drawers that glide easily.** The best cabinets feature drawers that don't stick and glide smoothly.

**4** **All-metal, hidden hinges**. The best cabinets have all-metal hinges that are hidden inside the door and are not visible when the door is shut. You'll note the quality of this hardware will vary widely in different price ranges.

After the kitchen flooring is installed, cabinet installation is usually done by an installer working for the cabinet manufacturer or their local representative. Occasionally, the builder or one of his workers will install your cabinets—it's probably preferable to have the cabinet manufacturer or their reps do the install, since it is their specialty. Check to make sure the cabinets are level before the countertops are installed.

**Countertops.** Countertops may come in any variety of shape, form, or style. A chart on the following page compares and contrasts different countertop surfacing options.

The most common countertop material (because it is the most cost-effective) is laminate. Laminates are popular because they come in so many colors and designs. The most famous manufacturer of laminates is Formica (others include Wilsonart, Nevamar, Pionite, and

Micarta). There are approximately 300 different colors, textures, and designs in Formica's sample kit—if you can imagine it, it's available. The cost of "color through" laminate ranges from $10 to $30 per lineal foot.

Of course, laminate countertops have some drawbacks. The disadvantages include scratching, lack of heat resistance, and seams that can be rather visible. One inexpensive way to dress up laminate countertops is to edge them in a wood that matches your cabinets. We did that in our kitchen—a "faux granite" Formica countertop was edged with maple to match the cabinets and flooring.

**Ceramic tile** is a step up in price and in elegance. The sub that installs any bath tile or floor tile will install your countertops as well. The least expensive option is the basic colored tile, either glazed or unglazed in solid colors such as black, white, mauve, etc. Some folks go hog wild with custom glazed and designed tile with scenes painted on it. Specially textured tiles are also in vogue. Prices can range from $15 to $50 a foot. Tile also has a few disadvantages: the grout between the tiles can be a burden to clean (one tip: consider a darker grout color to make cleaning easier). Tile can chip or crack if something heavy drops on it (although repairs are relatively affordable and easy). On the plus side, tile is reasonably stain resistant and hot pots and pans can be set directly on it.

**Solid surfacing materials** are made by manufacturers such as Avonite (800-4-AVONITE; www.avonite.com), Corian (800-4-CORIAN; www.corian.com) or Fountainhead (410-551-5000). Corian is a combination of acrylic and natural minerals, while the other brands include such ingredients as polyester or resin. Solid surfaces have color that goes all the way through. One advantage of solid surfacing materials: light sanding can easily repair scratches and burns. Solid surfaces can be shaped into sinks, too—the result is an ultra-modern, seamless look. New to the solid surfacing market are Zodiaq (made by Corian, www.corian.com) and Silestone (www.silestoneusa.com). Both use quartz and other polymers to give more of a stone look but with the advantages of solid surfacing material.

Unfortunately, you will pay through the nose for solid surfacing materials—about ten times the cost of laminates. In fact, the price ranges from $50 to $175 per lineal foot for the products. As a result, you tend to see Corian and its cousins in high-end luxury homes.

A couple of tips on solid surface countertops: lighter colors hide scratches better. And skip the high-gloss finish, which shows wear quicker.

**Granite** gives solid surfacing a run for its money as the preferred countertop material in high-end homes (it runs $100 to $225 per foot). In the move back to the "natural" look, many luxury buyers are choosing granite over the pre-fab solid surfacing stuff.

However, granite is very heavy, requiring more support from the cabinets. Also, it has no "give"—a glass dropped on granite will definitely break. If you can afford it, granite is an incredible option to consider. Colors are limited to nature (we've seen pinks, grays, blacks, and rusty reds), but the uniqueness of this product is fascinating.

Depending on the type of granite, a protection sealant may have to be applied periodically to keep it from staining. If your budget is tight, consider granite TILES, which are less than a solid slab of granite.

Of course, granite isn't the only stone that can be used for countertops: marble and limestone are two other options. **Marble** is very expensive, but gives a high-end look. One downside to marble: it requires regular maintenance (a sealant must be applied) to prevent staining and the absorption of oils. Instead of an entire countertop of marble, some designers just use a small slab as a pastry area. **Limestone** requires less maintenance than marble and is less costly as well. **Slate** is a pricey option (about twice granite) but provides a nice alternative for those tired of granite countertops.

Finally, there are three more countertop options that are quickly gaining popularity: concrete, butcher block and stainless steel. Yes, cutting edge kitchen designers are now using **concrete** countertops for a sleek look. A color can be added to give a unique appearance, but concrete is rather cost-

## COUNTERTOP OPTIONS COMPARED

| MATERIAL | PROS | CONS |
|---|---|---|
| LAMINATE | A ZILLION COLORS; LOW MAINTENANCE, AFFORDABLE | CAN CHIP, SCRATCH OR BURN |
| TILE | MANY DESIGN OPTIONS; HEAT RESISTANT | GROUT CAN DISCOLOR, TILES CAN CHIP OR CRACK |
| SOLID SURFACE | STAIN-RESISTANT, SLEEK, DURABLE | VERY EXPENSIVE AND HEAVY |
| GRANITE | SCRATCH/STAIN RESISTANT, DURABLE, HIGH-END LOOK | VERY EXPENSIVE; CAN RUIN KNIVES |
| MARBLE | DURABLE; LUXURIOUS LOOK | ABSORBS OILS UNLESS REGULARLY SEALED; VERY EXPENSIVE |
| CONCRETE | HIP NEW "NATURAL" LOOK | VERY EXPENSIVE; NEW TO MARKET |
| BUTCHER BLOCK | COUNTRY LOOK; EASY TO CLEAN | EASILY BURNS, SCRATCHES DENTS; NEEDS REGULAR MAINTENANCE |
| STAINLESS STEEL | SLEEK COMMERCIAL KITCHEN LOOK; VERY HEAT RESISTANT | EASILY SCRATCHES; VERY EXPENSIVE |

ly. And you have to live with cracks and other imperfections on the concrete.

**Butcher block** ($50 to $100 per square foot) is another trend. Typically made of hardwoods like maple, butcher block is easy to clean but burns, scratches and dents. Regular maintenance (mineral oil and sealant) is a must. If retro country isn't for you, consider the contemporary look of a **stainless steel** countertop. New steel fabrications limit fingerprints and give a commercial kitchen feel. While steel is heat resistant, it isn't money resistant—these countertops can be very expensive.

Most builders can install simple countertops (like laminates) themselves; if you want a exotic material, however, make sure a specialist does the install.

**Step 7: Lights.** One of the last finishing jobs will be putting in the light fixtures. Surprisingly, many people don't realize they might have to supply the **light bulbs** for each fixture—an unexpectedly expensive proposition. The light bulb tab for a simple home can top $200.

By this stage in the construction process, the electricity should be hooked up to the house. The electrician usually installs the light fixtures for you, but he needs those light bulbs to test each fixture. If ceiling fans are installed at this stage, make sure adequate supports have been installed to carry the load of the fans. Simply attaching the fan to the ceiling electrical junction box doesn't cut it—the fan could fall.

**Step 8: Appliances.** Some builders will have the appliances installed by a representative of the manufacturer, but others will do it themselves. The exception: a gas stove or dishwasher, which must be hooked up by a plumber or specially licensed contractor. Your inspector should test each appliance once it's been installed—run the dishwasher for a full cycle, grind up some food in the garbage disposal, and so on. The finishing inspection is the ultimate tire-kicking exercise.

The range of choices among appliances is incredible in this day and age, and we simply don't have enough room in this book to discuss all the best options available. As you might expect, we found **Consumer Reports** magazine to be the best authority for the latest scoop on appliances. Their August 1999 report on the "Ultimate Kitchen" is an excellent review of high-end appliances like Sub-Zero refrigerators and Viking ranges. Back issues of the magazine may be available through your local library or you can surf these articles online at www.consumerreports.com. The annual *Consumer Reports Buying Guide* book summarizes their reviews for items as well.

**Step 9: Plumbing fixtures.** Plumbing fixtures will also be installed at this stage. Your inspector will want to check that these fixtures work without leaking. Toilets should be flushed several times and faucets and shower heads should be run. Check to see whether the water from the hot water faucet gets hot—sometimes the hot and cold handles get switched. Also, make sure there are no leaks under the sinks—letting the water run for a few minutes will help determine this. Another problem: plumbers sometimes run hot water to the toilet by accident, instead of cold. While it seems nice to have a steaming hot toilet to warm the seat, it can be very destructive—the hot water can destroy the toilet seals, flooding the house.

## Eco-Friendly Alternatives

◆ **Image Carpets.** Ever wonder what you can do with used plastic soda bottles? Image Carpets are woven from yarn whose fibers are derived from melted plastic bottles. www.imageind.com

◆ **Bamboo and cork flooring** are new, environmentally friendly options for flooring. Bamboo plants grow rapidly and hence are a "sustainable" option for flooring (bamboo costs about the same has high-end hardwood). Cork is also resource-efficient, easy to clean and is easy on the feet. Read more about Bamboo at Enviornmental Building New's site (www.buildinggreen.com/products/bamboo.html), which includes a list of bamboo floor makers and their products. The same site has a similar report on cork flooring at www.buildinggreen.com/products/cork_flooring.html.

◆ **IsoUnderlay** (503) 242-7345 is an underlayment panel made of wheat straw fiber, a renewable resource. These panels are used instead of wood underlayment under carpeting and flooring. 503-242-7345 or www.isoboard.com.

◆ Pioneer Millworks (800) 951-9663 sells pine flooring recovered from buildings constructed from 1880 and 1920. www.pioneermillworks.com.

◆ **Armstrong,** (800) 233-3823, manufactures ceiling tiles and panels that are made in part from recycled newsprint. The wood fiber in the tiles is 22% recycled. The company also offers a new vinyl flooring that eliminates the need for a wood sub-floor. In addition to smoothing out lumps in the existing floor sheathing, the flooring also requires less adhesive than regular vinyl flooring.

◆ **Water-saving faucets, toilets, shower heads, and dishwashers** are available from many national manufacturers. Some communities are requiring their use in new construction. The best deal: areas that offer utility rebates for the installation of low-volume toilets and the like. Contact your local utility company to see whether they offer any incentives.

As for specifics, Delta Faucets, (317) 848-1812, offers an Embracer shower head that meets mandatory conservation codes. Speakman's Model SD 8068 Sensorflo faucet conserves up to 85% of normal water use by using touch-free controls. For a Speakman dealer near you, call (302) 764-9100. Be wary of cheap low-volume toilets. Some work so poorly they require you to flush twice.

◆ **Asko** (800) 367-2444; web: www.askousa.com makes a dishwasher and washing machine that use less water and energy.

◆ **General Electric** (800) 626-2000; web: www.ge.com has an induction cooktop that uses less energy than traditional models.

## Money Bombs with Interior Finishing

**Money Bomb #1: Substituting cheaper materials.**
*"In our specs we listed special faucets with water-control devices. However, when we visited the site and looked at the faucet boxes, we discovered that the wrong faucets were ordered. The builder thought we wouldn't notice the difference once they were installed."*

In the next chapter, we'll discuss a builder's disease called the "diminishing-profit syndrome." Basically, this drives builders to make substitutions toward the end of the project to boost their profits.

This could happen with molding, doors, windows, tubs, faucets, and carpet—basically, any aspect of the finishing work. When we were building our first home, our builder decided not to install a shower door in our master bath to save himself the expense. Later, on a subsequent remodel of another home, a contractor installed a natural gas fireplace in our home, even though our agreement said it should be a propane fireplace.

**Solution:** To protect yourself from diminishing-profit syndrome, get every detail in writing, down to the specific model number. Our problem with the shower door occurred because we assumed every master bath shower has a shower door (it wasn't on the spec list, however). The fireplace was a more complex matter: the model number of the natural gas fireplace was very close to the propane model—just one digit was different. We didn't check it closely and got stuck with the wrong unit. (Some $400 later, we were able to convert the fireplace to propane, but the experience still leaves a bitter taste in our mouths).

If you suspect your builder might try to pull a fast one with the type of product you've specified, ask to see the boxes and look carefully at each receipt. If you're supposed to get redwood molding, be sure the receipt from the lumber yard doesn't say "birch." Being on top of everything is the only way to keep the builder from substituting cheaper materials. Once again, the strategy is "trust but verify."

**Money Bomb #2: Builders in a hurry leave out important items**.
*"To finish our house on time, our builder worked around the clock. After moving in, we noticed that no one had connected the motor for the whirlpool tub. However, we couldn't connect the tub ourselves because the builder didn't cut an access panel out to get to the motor. This is insane!"*

Whenever you have a system such as a whirlpool motor, a water heater, a furnace, etc., you'll need to be certain it's hooked up and working before you close on the home. Don't assume something is hooked up because it's there. The major culprit is, of course, the rush to finish the home by a certain date. While a little deadline pressure is helpful, some builders bite off more than they can chew. The resulting work is sloppy, incomplete or worse.

**Solution:** Your inspector should be able to test each mechanical system as soon as water and/or electricity is available. If you discover such a goof, most red-faced builders will fix the problem quickly.

## Money Bomb #3: Costly last-minute changes.

*"When we first designed our home, we didn't want a whirlpool tub. However, we changed our mind midway through construction and asked the builder to get us a whirlpool. He told us there would be a substantial restocking fee for the already delivered tub as well as a change-order fee. Needless to say, we decided to stick with the original tub."*

Some builders do a lousy job of informing consumers about change-order charges and restocking fees. When you decide to change one or more of the specs you chose earlier, the builder may have already ordered the item. When the builder sends it back, he may be charged a restocking fee—this is passed on to you.

Change order fees are another bugaboo. Many builders claim this charge is necessary to cover the administrative time and expense from the change. If you want a different tub, it may only be $25 more. But the builder may spend all afternoon calling around town to get information on prices and availability. Some contractors take advantage of consumers by charging huge fees to change items at this stage.

**Solution:** Ask up front about any change-order fees. In fact, get a schedule from the builder of exactly what it costs for minor or major alterations to your project. Also, ask about deadlines after which changes incur such a fee.

## Money Bomb #4: Overzealous carpet installers freezing you out.

*"When we moved into our new home this summer, we were really excited about the place. But once winter hit, we noticed the house was rather cold. Finally, we figured out the problem—and it wasn't the furnace. It turns out the carpet installers never cut out holes for the heat vents!"*

Yes, it's hard to believe that some subs can be so incompetent, but it happens. And heating a home is a little difficult when vents are covered.

**Solution:** Make a note of where all the heat vents are on your copy of the plans before the floor coverings go in. Then when the subcontractors are finished, go back through the house and match up vents with your plans. This will help you make certain the vents are clear.

## Money Bomb #5: New-carpet fumes.

*"Right after we moved into our house, my daughter began to suffer from severe headaches and respiratory problems. We thought it might be a problem with the air conditioning, but we soon learned it was the fumes from the new carpet. What's being done about this?"*

In 1992, Congress held hearings regarding the potential health hazard of new-carpet fumes. Consumers testified that they became sick when they moved into homes with new carpet installed. A CBS News report cited a lab that found evidence that mice exposed to new-carpet fumes experienced severe health problems—like convulsions. Meanwhile, the carpet industry denies there is any problem and the EPA says they'll study the problem. If you're concerned, you may want

---

# The Best New Products for New Homes

Every year we attend builders' shows nationwide to ferret out the best new products—yes, it's all in our never-ending effort to find the best stuff for you, our readers. Sure, we have to endure endless power tool demonstrations and cocktail parties announcing the latest drywall improvements. But, hey, it's our job. Here is a round-up of what's new for new homes:

◆ **Spot-heated tile floors.** Ever walk onto a bathroom tile floor one winter morning and wish you were in Hawaii? SunTouch by Bask Technologies provides a solution: spot heated floor tiles. By installing this special electrical mat under your bathroom tile, you'll have warm and cozy feet all winter. The cost: $11 per square foot; the system includes timers to pre-warm your tile in the morning and shut it off at a pre-determined time. 888-432-8932; www.bask.net.

◆ **IBM's Home Director.** Want to add high-speed 'net access to your home, but wonder how you'll get it to both your home office and junior's bedroom? Want to check the status of your home security system from bed? Or adjust the thermostat? Home Director is a "complete home networking solution" that is both affordable ($1000 to $3000, depending on the configuration) AND easy to use. 800-426-7144, www.homedirector.net

◆ **Fisher & Paykel's "DishDrawer."** First, SubZero made large refrigerators "disappear" behind matching cabinet doors; now New Zealand's Fisher & Paykel has done the same for dishwashers. Their innovative DishDrawer comes in both single ($1000) and double ($1600) versions and as an additional benefit: it looks really cool. Plus, it uses as little as 2.4 gallons per wash. 888-936-7872; www.dishdrawer.com

to pay close attention to the debate by getting the latest information. Consumer advocates want new carpeting to carry a warning label.

A smart tip: air out a house with new carpet for several days BEFORE moving in. This should prevent any problems. Another solution: contact Planetary Solutions of Boulder, CO (303) 442-6228 (www.planetearth.com) for suppliers of "natural" flooring that don't use the chemicals which produce problems.

### Money Bomb #6: No underlayment down under.

*"I love my linoleum in the kitchen but there's a huge step up from the kitchen to the living room carpet. There are also lumps and bumps under the linoleum. What causes this?"*

◆ **Virtual bricks.** Want a brick home but can't decide amongst the ZILLION or so brick colors out there? Check out "BoralVision" by Boral Bricks (800-5-BORAL-5). Scan in your home plan, pick any color and poof! You can get a realistic picture of what the home will look like. You can change brick colors as well as paint accents for trim, roofing and even mortar color.

◆ **Tornado Guard.** With all the weird weather across U.S. lately, interest in this product should be high—The Tornado Guard shelter. This $2500 underground shelter is made of acrylic reinforced with fiberglass and is set in your foundation at the time of your home's construction. It can hold several people and features power, ventilation, and telephone links. (512) 259-6500; web: www.tornado-guard.com.

◆ **FloLogic.** This automatic water shutoff value prevents water damage if your washing machine or dishwasher springs a leak. An excellent idea for any new home, these valves should be required by insurance companies to stop water damage from frozen pipes and other water disasters. Check their web site www.flologic.com for details. The price: $495.

◆ **Zoned forced-air heat.** Ever wish you could adjust the heat in your house by the room? Until now, most forced air systems had just one thermostat—you got the same amount of heat whether upstairs or downstairs, in a sunny area or a shady spot. Honeywell has fixed this problem with their Temperature Zone Systems, basically a system of dampers that sends heat or cool air where you want it. Thermostats in each room or zone can keep one area of your home warmer or cooler. Bonus: you save energy costs by using your furnace or AC more efficiently. www.honeywell.com

You probably don't have the proper underlayment under your linoleum. Many floor-covering manufacturers won't honor their warranties if an underlayment isn't put down first. Call your installer and/or builder immediately and have this remedied—if left uncorrected, this problem causes uneven wear and damage to the floor.

**Solution:** When you draw up your spec list, be certain to include underlayment in the contract. In one case, a builder tried to get out of using underlayment because it wasn't in the contract. Once again, don't assume anything. And if you notice lumps and bumps (caused by drywall mud or sawdust) in the floor, or the floor is lower than an adjoining floor, get the builder to fix it.

## CLEAN-UP

No one wants to move into a dirty house and the clean-up of the new home requires much more effort than simple vacuuming. Stickers must be removed from windows, excess paint cleaned up, layers of dust and dirt cleaned from inside cabinets—this process can take several days. Some buyers of fancy custom homes even specify the level of cleaning they expect the contractor to do; it might be worth asking about this before you sign a contract.

## FINAL GRADING

Final grading occurs when the house is completed and the builder has cleaned up the site. Grading is absolutely necessary to make certain that water drains away from the house, thus avoiding leaky basements or standing water in the crawl space. The goal is to slope the dirt away from the house to ensure that water drains away too. Watch out: Many builders skimp on the final grading, causing you major headaches down the line.

Any landscaping will also occur during this stage. Some builders merely offer to re-seed disturbed areas with a natural grass seed. Others offer a "landscaping allowance" or package for more extensive options.

# New Home 911: When Things Go Wrong... And How to Fix It

## CHAPTER 11

**O**ne of the things that just amazes us about most "how-to" books is how darned optimistic they can be. When we read other books on building or buying a new home, we were amazed at how happy-go-lucky this process is supposed to be. Friction, arguments or even minor disagreements with the contractor are never mentioned. Everything just moves swiftly along without any hitches, glitches or semi-automatic weapons fire.

Well, as the veterans of the home building experience, we'd like to throw cold water on this notion. In interviewing other homebuyers across the country, we found a similar pattern: in the real world, building a new home is no joy ride.

Sure, some of this tension is generated between spouses who argue over where that window should be or what color the carpet is in the master bedroom. Yes, but the real fountain of frustration for new homebuyers is that darned builder.

No matter how carefully you select your builder, negotiate the contract and plan the design, there are going to be moments when you will want to shoot your builder. And not with any small handgun. We're talking a rocket launcher.

Given this natural urge on the part of all homebuyers, we'd like to give you some advice on the subject.

## Top Three Reasons Why You Shouldn't Kill Your Builder

**1** Murdering your builder is against the law in most states.

**2** It leaves a big mess on the new carpet.

**3** **You actually need this person.** Seriously, this last reason is for real. After you move into your home, you'll need the builder to come back to fix those minor problems you discover. Some of these will be on the "punch list" you draw up prior to closing—other problems may develop later, like a leaking skylight. Maintaining a relationship with your builder so you're still on speaking terms greatly increases the chances you'll get this stuff done.

This does not mean you should be walked all over like a cheap rug. You must stand up for your rights. At the same time, you still must have a working relationship, not letting any dispute degenerate into a collapse of the deal.

## Reality Check: Six Construction Crisis ... and Possible Solutions

To understand why many homeowners feel like killing their builder, it's important to understand the root causes of much of the friction. Here are the top suspects.

**1 Inept subs.** Remember, your builder is not really doing much of the work on your new home—subcontractors do most of it. Ideally, every sub would be an expert, competently accomplishing every task. In the real world, you'll get some good ones and some stinky ones. On our home, we gave the electrician an A-, while the plumber deserved a D. The reason: The plumber sent in a "second-string" crew to do our home. Without proper supervision, the crew botched the job—THREE of the six sinks in our brand new home leaked. If you're building a home in a hot market, all the good subs will probably be busy and your builder may opt for an un-tried sub to get your home finished on time. Or the good subs may quickly add crews to handle the increased the demand. The work of these second- or third-string crews often isn't up to snuff, which causes friction.

Another factor: immigrant labor and language barriers. It's the dirty little secret of the new home business: many large production builders are heavily depenedent on immigrant labor. Amazingly, many builders do NOT have supervisors who are billingual. A San Diego architecit who has studied the issue (and wrote a thesis on defective construction) recently told Builder magazine "many of (a builders') workers can't read blueprints or installation instructions. And they have absoltuety no clue about code standards."

◆ **Solution:** While the builder is not *directly* at fault for poor sub work, it is his responsibility to supervise the subs and to make sure any poor work is fixed. And fast. In nearly all cases, the builder picks the subcontractors and it's the builder's neck on the line. Let the builder play the bad guy with lousy subs—he should crack the whip to make sure the work is done right. You have to make it clear to the builder in no uncertain terms that you will not accept lousy subcontractor work and you expect him to make it right. Or else you'll find another builder who can better supervise or control his subcontractors.

**2** **Builder/architect animosity.** While both of these people should work together on the same team, the reality is friction often develops between architects and builders. Some builders just have a bad attitude about architects—perhaps they're jealous of architects' high-dollar fees and design skills. Other builders think all architects are idiots who design pretty houses but don't know one thing about the actual construction. And they resent having someone looking over their shoulder.

During the actual construction, the builder and architect may come to loggerheads at a number of flash points. The bane of many a residential architect is builders who make "field changes" to their design without permission. Or builders who try to nit-pick the smallest design mistakes, charging the buyer multiple change orders for omissions on the plans. On the other hand, builders may be frustrated by an architect who specs a material that is hard to source or install.

Builder-architect disputes can get rather nasty. Sometimes the fighting escalates to the point where the builder insists that you fire the architect. Big mistake—remember, the architect is working for you, on your side. Some builders would love to see an architect eliminated— the lack of tough oversight enables the builder to substitute cheap materials, get away with substandard work, and more. In one case, we heard of a builder who sabotaged a new home project by delaying or slowing down the work, blaming the architect for unspecified "design" mistakes. By wearing down the buyer, the builder succeeded in getting the buyer to fire the architect. What happened next wasn't pretty: Totally unsupervised, the builder's defective construction was a disaster, costing $300,000 to repair.

◆ **Solution:** Communication is the key to solving these problems. Calling a "summit meeting" of you, the architect and the builder at a neutral location (such as Iceland) might be helpful. You may have to act as a diplomatic mediator, attempting to reach a compromise to keep your home moving forward. Face-to-face meetings tend to defuse tensions, as opposed to phone conversations, where it is easier to be a "difficult" person. In the worst case, you may have to fire the builder and find another. When should you fire an architect? Only in cases of clear incompetence (you may want to get a second opinion from another design professional about this). Builders may whisper in your ear, "Fire the architect," but we urge you to think twice before you do this.

As a side note, keep a detailed record of the communication between all parties. That means copying all letters and faxes sent to the builder and architect. Keep a phone log of conversations. Take photographs/video during construction as well. Require that the builder notify you of any code violations found by building inspectors during the construction—this keeps everyone on their toes.

**3** **Cost overruns.** It seems that even a sneeze can increase the price of your home. Cost overruns tend to fall into one of two categories: those you pay for directly and those you pay for indirectly. Direct cost overruns are items that exceed allowances—if your builder runs into rock while digging your foundation (for custom or semi-custom homes), you may have to come up with hundreds of extra bucks. A mistake in the blueprints could also cost you (although you may "discuss" this with your architect, who should cough up the money). In some cases, cost overruns are all your fault—when you change or upgrade something, you must pay . . . not only for the item itself but perhaps a "change-order" fee as well.

Another category is cost overruns that you pay for *indirectly.* For example, if the cost of lumber goes through the roof, the builder is the one who pays for this (out of the home's profit). That's because most builders do homes on a fixed-price basis—if costs go up, they eat it. Or do they? A builder (and buyer) may fall into the "shrinking-profit syndrome," described next.

◆ **Solution:** If a home always costs more than anyone expects, it makes sense to plan for this in advance. First, budget an extra 5% to 10% for cost overruns. Yes, we realize that means coming up with another $30,000 on a $300,000 home (see whether you can increase your mortgage or dip into savings). Control mistakes in the plans by hiring an experienced residential architect. Beware of the low-ball allowance game, a common source of cost overruns described earlier in this book. Do your research on windows, appliances, and other products *before* construction begins—this lessens the chance of you wanting to make a change mid-course. Recognize that you can easily be "100-dollared to death" when you may be tempted to upgrade a towel rack or faucet "because it's just another $100."

**4** **Shrinking-profit syndrome.** Near the end of your home's construction, your builder may be become afflicted with a sickness we call the shrinking-profit syndrome. What's this? When the ACTUAL costs of building a house exceed the builder's own ESTIMATED costs, the builder's profit quickly shrinks . . . or disappears altogether. As you can imagine, this is a very unpleasant situation for most contractors—and it has serious implications for both your new home and your relationship with your builder.

As the profit shrinks, some unethical builders look for ways to make it back. They may cut corners on finishing items like flooring or trim, hoping you won't notice slipshod installation or the substitution of inferior products. Or they may outright renege on a contract provision, refusing to pay for an item in your contract. For our home, the shrinking-profit syndrome led to the builder denying his responsibility to put in a $200 shower door in the master bath. Another home buyer we visited was socked with a $6000 bill for utility tap fees when the builder reneged on his written agreement to pay for them—he claimed his profit on their home was too small at that point.

This scam is particularly potent since it comes at the end of the construction—when the pressure to move in or close on a mortgage is greatest. Some shady builders know you're worn down emotionally or that your mortgage-rate lock is about to expire. Since you're vulnerable, strong-arm tactics are more successful.

Playing the "blame game" (as in, who's at fault for the shrinking profit) is a moot point. Sometimes, it's no one's fault. Weather delays can push up costs. Mistakes by suppliers and subs create delays—and it all costs

## Infomercials promise "get home quick" schemes

A mong the late night infomercials for food processors and exercise equipment, there is a new product: the American dream. Fast-talking pitchmen PROMISE you can get a new home QUICKLY and for very little money. As it turned out, most consumers who fell for the pitch got burned.

One of the key players in the "get a home quick" scheme was Reno, Nevada-based National Affordable Housing Coalition. With a name that sounded like a non-profit or grass-roots group and a slew of slick infomercials, the NAHC ran infomercials that invited consumers to a $10 seminar that would reveal the secret to buying a home on the cheap. The seminar then turned into a high-pressure pitch to "join" the Coalition for $500 a head, which gave consumers access to the NAHC's alleged exclusive network of lenders and real estate agents. This network promised the American dream for those folks whom never though they could afford a home.

Nice, but it was a scam. According to the *Washington Post*, 20,000 consumers paid the NAHC their $500 fee, but only 275 were able to buy homes. Some 50,000 people attended the NAHC seminars nationwide from 1996 to 1998.

Things began to unravel for the NAHC in 1998. First, attorneys general filed numerous lawsuits against the NAHC, alleging fraud and misrepresentation. ABC's 20/20 filmed an undercover segment at one of the NAHC's seminars which exposed their high-pressure tactics and false promises.

By the end of 1998, the National Affordable Housing Coalition filed for bankruptcy and closed its doors. Founder Craig M. Meyer is no where to be found.

There are several lessons in all this for new homebuyers. While it is tempting to think there is some magic "secret" to buying a new home, don't fall for the bait. High-pressure hotel seminars are there to enrich the seminar presenters; these folks get rich selling membership, audiotape courses and other paraphernalia—not helping folks buy homes.

And remember that much of the "expert" advice on home buying can be found for little or no cost. For example, Fannie Mae's "Home Path" web site (www.homepath.com) provides FREE advice on home buying. No need to spend $500.

money. Other times it is the builder's fault. If the builder incorrectly estimates the cost of certain items, it's his neck on the line for the difference.

◆ **Solution:** Use a "bad cop" to get your way. Instead of confronting the builder directly (and destroying any remaining goodwill), have a surrogate bad cop tell the builder that the last-minute substitution/omission is not acceptable. The bad cop could be a private inspector, buyer's broker, construction manager or architect. If the builder still balks, withhold an appropriate amount of money at the closing from the builder's final profit check/disbursement. While this sounds drastic, the mere threat of such action may get results. Consult with an attorney if the situation deteriorates further—a letter from an attorney may also get the builder's attention.

**5** **Time, time, time.** Delays are inevitable when you build a home. A sudden rainstorm may prevent the gluing of the sub-floor to the foundation. Bitter cold may delay a plumber from finishing work in a damp basement. Even weather that's thousands of miles away can work against you—many home buyers find lumber in short supply (and at higher prices) after a hurricane hits the U.S, creating high demand for materials.

The most frustrating delays, however, are builder-generated. A builder's incompetence at scheduling crews can lead to long delays. Inability to find a quality framing crew or good roofing subcontractor is often due to a builder's inexperience or lack of contacts. If the labor supply is tight, a builder may shift a crew who is working on your house to another, more expensive house the builder is rushing to finish.

◆ **Solution:** Monitor the construction carefully. Try to visit the job site two to three times a week. If little progress is being made, confront the builder. Try to get specific commitments as to when certain phases are to be completed—stay on the builder when he begins to slip a deadline.

Understanding why delays are occurring is important. Your builder may blame the weather, but you might question him as to why other builders in your area are still working. Getting to the bottom of the excuses will help you decide on a course of action. If you find the builder intentionally dragging his feet, action must be taken. Have your "bad cop" discuss the situation with the builder. If nothing happens, write a "gentle" letter that you expect work on your home to get going. If more delays occur and the situation appears hopeless, consult with your attorney about firing the builder.

Above all, don't paint yourself into a corner. Putting yourself under pressure to move in or close by a certain date is a prescription for trouble. Build extra time into your own schedule (one month is smart) to account for "normal" delays.

**6** **Take-the-money-and-run builders: a vanishing breed.** A builder who's having financial problems may collapse into bankruptcy, leaving you with unpaid bills on your home. Even worse are builders who disappear altogether, fleeing the state with a trail of unhappy homebuyers behind them. Yes, this is a not an every day occurrence, but it does happen.

Telltale signs of the vanishing builder are a significant slowing in the work on your home. Failure to return phone calls or messages is a red flag. Some builders don't disappear quickly, but fade slowly. Like the witch in The Wizard of Oz, they slowly melt into a pile of goo. It's critical for you, your private inspector or construction manager to monitor the construction. While it's not important to be there every hour of every day, checking the home every few days is important.

You can also take several other precautions. First, give the builder as LITTLE of a deposit as you can get away with. Any builder who asks for your entire down payment up front in cash may be on shaky financial footing. One buyer we spoke with gave the builder a $10,000 cash deposit and lost it all when the builder went under.

Any deposit should be put into an escrow account (a buyer's broker, title company or mortgage lender can help you with this). The money is not to be released from escrow until the home is completed to your satisfaction. Never write the builder a check directly.

Control the construction loan if you can. Don't disburse money to the builder directly; instead write checks to the subcontractors or suppliers for specific invoices presented on your home. Some construction lenders don't like this process. They'd prefer to give the money to the builder and hope he'll pay the subs. Shop for a lender that will do it your (and the safe) way.

Don't close on the home until you get lien wavers from ALL the sub-contractors, suppliers and workers. Ask the builder for a list of everyone that worked on your home and call him or her to make sure they were paid. If you're paying the sub-contractors directly, stamp the back of each check with a lien waver restrictive endorsement.

Pay the builder his profit only *after* the home is finished to your satisfaction.

◆ **Solution:** What if you're careful and the builder disappears anyway? What if the builder suddenly declares bankruptcy? Immediately, you will want to contact your attorney—an experienced real estate attorney can help you navigate the choppy waters ahead. Among the potential problems are unpaid subcontractors who may file huge liens on your home.

The second step is to call an emergency meeting of your "building team": the lender, architect/designer, private inspector and others. Keeping the channels of communication open at a time of crisis is important to keep anyone from panicking (including yourself). You and/or your architect will need to begin contacting other builders to finish the home. The lender may need reassurance that the deal isn't going south. As a side note, some

# THE CAULK REFLEX

If anything goes wrong with your house, it's likely your builder's first reaction will be to grab a caulk gun. Got a leak on your roof? Water dripping on your stucco? Gutters leaking? Caulk is so often the builder's answer you'd think it was programmed into all contractors' genetic code.

That's why we call it the "caulk reflex." It's the miracle drug of builder fix-its. If builders had problems with their marriage, we'd expect them to first try squirting some caulk on their spouses.

All this reliance on caulk would be fine if it actually worked. But often it doesn't. Why? First, understand that caulk is just silicone or acrylic sealant. While caulking metal-to-metal surfaces is acceptable, many builders try to use it on wood roofs—a use that even caulk manufacturers say isn't going to work. That's because the caulk doesn't form a complete seal to wood, thereby enabling water to seep in.

In other cases it has nothing to do with caulk itself, but the way it's used. Just like glue, caulk can only stretch so far. Specifications are printed right on the tube—they say caulk won't work for joints over 1/2" wide. Some builders ignore this and squirt caulk into huge gaps. A thick strip of caulk often loses its elastic properties, causing the joint to fail when the materials it's adhered to shrink or expand. The result: it doesn't work.

One homebuyer we interviewed came face to face with the ugly reality of the caulk reflex. Water was leaking off the homeowners' garage roof and damaging the stucco facade on the front of their home. The reason? An architect called in by the buyer blamed it on faulty design—the roofline was draining right onto the stucco. Who designed the home? The builder (who had no architectural background), of course.

We have to hand it to the builder—at least he didn't abandon the homebuyer. Every week, he would come by and caulk the leak. After a while, there was probably three tons of caulk glopped up there. And guess what? It still leaked. Damage to the stucco was mounting.

An architect told the buyer the only way to solve the problem was to re-construct the roof over the garage. This would cost more than a $1000. And, frankly, the builder probably realized this, but he preferred to buy $4 tubes of caulk, squirt it up there once a week and pray it would work. After it was clear the caulk wasn't working, the builder balked at doing more than the quick fix. At last word, the buyer was hiring an attorney to try to pressure the builder into really fixing the leak.

Sadly, the caulk reflex is symptomatic of the "quick-fix" mentality of too many building professionals today. Whipping out a caulk gun is a simple way for lazy and cheap contractors to avoid addressing the real problem—faulty design or poor workmanship.

Should you be leery of builders who suggest caulking any problem? Not necessarily; in some cases, caulk may actually work. However, if the answer to each and every problem is caulk, you should begin to worry.

states have set up recovery funds to compensate homebuyers who were jilted by bankrupt builders.

Unfortunately, the problem of "take-the-money-and-run" builders is nationwide in scope. Over 4200 general contractors declare bankruptcy each year, leaving behind over $600 million in unpaid bills, according to the latest Dun & Bradstreet statistics. Even more builders never get around to filing a formal bankruptcy; most just close up shop and leave town in the middle of the night. And these business failures occur in both good and bad times—builders can go bankrupt even in a booming economy.

Even if you find a builder who's skipped town, most states have very weak laws when it comes to builder fraud. For example, in Maryland, if you steal property worth over $300, you could go to jail for up to 15 years. But, if you're a *builder* and you take $20,000 or more in deposits but never finish the home (leaving it full of defects and subject to liens from unpaid subcontractors), what's the biggest penalty you face? A massive fine of no more than $1000 and/or a year in jail. It's only a *misdemeanor* to steal the life savings of homebuyers in Maryland.

## The Legal System: Why Suing a Builder Rarely Produces Victory

Say what you want about lawyers and courts, but the U.S. legal system rarely gives any relief to victimized homeowners. In fact, many homebuyers who've tried to sue their builder say they felt victimized TWICE: first, by a shoddy contractor and second by the courts.

To understand why this occurs, consider what it takes to actually file a lawsuit against a homebuilder. First, you need to hire an attorney—not a cheap proposition at $100 to $250 per hour, plus expenses. Second, you will need experts. Thanks to the complicated nature of construction disputes, you may have to spend THOUSANDS on engineers, construction experts, and appraisers to prove something wrong was done and how much damage it has caused. The result: you have to spend $10,000 to $30,000 to bring even simple disputes to trial. Even if you win a judgement against a homebuilder, the legal fees and costs may outweigh any settlement.

And forget about criminal prosecution. Most local district attorneys and state attorney generals are busy with all sorts of other crimes to prosecute. The complex "white collar" crime of a homebuilder that rips off consumers is difficult for them to understand, much less pursue. Weak laws that classify contractor crime as a misdemeanor also play a role, as we mentioned above.

That's why we often tell consumers that home scams have few cures—the key is prevention. Avoiding trouble in the first place is the best strategy; trying to sue a builder who's committed fraud and misrepresentation is not.

# Top 6 Excuses that Builders Give for Shoddy Work and Mistakes

We'd be the first to acknowledge that builders are only mere mortals. And, yes, they do make mistakes. Some are honest goofs, while others are intentional efforts to pass off shoddy work. What particularly galls us about builder mistakes, however, is the peculiar "excuses" they concoct to explain away the situation. Here are some of our favorites:

**1** **"We're not cutting diamonds here."** This whopper is often used to explain away "minor" imperfections like poor trim work, painting or other finishing details. The implication is that you must accept little "imperfections that add to the beauty and character" of your home. Please. Many builders (big or small) spend exorbitant amounts of time and money selling you on their expert craftsmanship. Yet when problems crop up with your home, somehow the contractor morphs from Bob Vila to Barney Fife. Our advice: hold your ground here. You are paying for a PROFESSIONAL job; don't settle for less.

**2** **"I'm doing you a favor by building your home."** This often goes with the reasoning that "you're getting a steal of a deal on this home," so shut up and accept the flaws. It's quite amazing that anyone in business could demand $200,000, $300 000, or $400,000 for something and then give you an attitude that they're doing a you a favor by taking your money. The reality is that no one held a gun to the head of the builder during the negotiating process, forcing him to accept an allegedly ultra-low price. You agreed to pay X dollars and he agreed to build a certain home. There's not much to do in a case like this, but remind the builder that you are the customer. It's your money, not his. It'll be your home, not his. If he doesn't get it, perhaps he'd like to just refund all your money and both of you can part company and go your separate ways.

**3** **"But replacing it would require such a delay."** It would shock most buyers to know how often the wrong materials arrive at the construction site. Sinks that are the wrong color, a tub that's the wrong style, carpet that's not yours . . . just about anything can go wrong. Instead of sending the stuff back and getting the correct items, builders often give you a line that such a replacement would take **so long**. And it might delay the home's construction by DAYS or WEEKS. And you want to move in, don't you? Such pressure convinced one homebuyer to accept the wrong roof trusses that showed up one day— the resulting re-design nixed several windows in the living room. The home is now much darker than the buyer expected. In other cases, buyers have had to accept wrong faucets, incorrect colors and other mistakes because the builder pressured them with the delay excuse.

## Turning the Tables: When a Builder is a Buyer

Every year, 65,000 homebuilders gather for their national convention, the "Builder's Show." Contractors play with the latest power tools, attend seminars on design trends and (most importantly) party with their friends. One of the most popular activities: bash the homebuyer. There are always several seminars on "Homebuyers from Hell" and similar topics, complete with gory details of how nasty consumers tortured their poor contractors during a construction project.

Excuse us for failing to sympathize. Instead, we urge a new exercise for every builder that moans about terrible homebuyers—become a homebuyer himself. Yep, if we ruled the world, we'd decree than anyone who wants to build homes for a living must first buy one himself or herself.

That was the theme of a 1998 article in *Builder* magazine: "Turning the Tables: Sometimes it takes building a house for yourself to understand what your customers go through." The magazine interviewed several builders who did just that and their insights were very interesting.

First, many contractors-turned-buyers had trouble making up their minds about home finishes like flooring. Builders love to bitch about indecisive homebuyers, but the sheer volume of choices makes it hard for ANYONE to make decisions.

Another builder was upset by a granite subcontractor who was insulting to him (imagine that!) and a tile man who barely spoke English—and installed the wrong tile in the master bath. "In my early days as a builder, I had a tendency to feel that every homeowner was being irrational, and I believed all my subcontractors and site supervisors when they said everything was finished," admitted one builder who built a home for himself. "Since building this house, I realize that site supervisors and subcontractors have a completely different perception of what 'finished' means. I've gained a higher degree of sensitivity and follow-through."

We wish all builders would go through this before they want to lambaste consumers for their foibles.

The fact is replacing these items will incur some delay, but it should be the builder who gets on the phone and insists that the supplier fixes it ASAP. It's probably better to wait until the correct stuff arrives than to regret a compromise down the road.

**4** **"It must be the subcontractor's fault."** You see, builders never make mistakes . . . in their own minds. At least they never admit them. It's always someone else's fault—the architect drew defective plans, the subs screwed up the installation, or the supplier shipped the wrong materials. This excuse often degenerates into a ping-pong game of delay. When a skylight leaks, the roofer comes out and blames the skylight company. The skylight guys look it over and pronounce that the problem is with the flashing—the roofer's responsibility. The roofer comes back and looks at the flashing and says it is actually the seal on the skylights. Ping. Pong. Ping. You're like a ball that's bounced back and forth. The fact is, it is the builder's ultimate responsibility to make sure the skylight doesn't leak—even though he didn't personally flash the roof or install the skylight. The builder must whip the subs into shape and resolve the problem.

**5** **"That's not the way we do it here."** Building is a highly regionalized business—sometimes regional custom and traditions are adhered to like some sort of gospel. Hence, if you move to a different part of the country, you may find that builders have some strange ideas about "sound construction techniques."

Frankly, in some parts of the country building practices are deplorable. When a builder tells you, "That's not how we do it here," a translation closer to reality is, "I don't care if you're from an area where

## MOLD: THE NEXT ASBESTOS?

**$** 32 million. That's the recent jury award to an Austin homeowner who sued his home insurer when they failed to clean up the mold in his Central Texas home.

With big jury award like that, both builders and insurers are considering how to handle the next big liability issue: mold. Thanks to better and tighter insulation in houses, water infiltration (due to faulty flashing around windows or defective siding) can often mean mold. And certain types of molds (namely "black mold" or stachybotrys chartum) have been shown to cause severe health problems.

In Minneapolis, the *Star Tribune* newspaper reported on several homes that had mold problems in June 2000. One case: a $550,000 home that had mushrooms sprouting from a wall in the master suite. Cost to repair the damage from mold: $400,000.

In June 2001, 86 homeowners in Modesto, California filed a $10 million lawsuit against KB Homes (formerly Kaufman and Broad) over mold-damaged homes.

The upshot: many insurers are now excluding mold from their homeowner policies. And builders are wearily eyeing an upcoming mold crisis, which some compare to litigation over asbestos and tobacco combined.

What can you do if you suspect your home is threatened by mold? Get it tested. Companies like HomeTest.com 800-604-1995 offer kits. The EPA (epa.gov) also has info on mold on their web site.

homes are built with quality—here we do it fast and sloppy."

If you get into a dispute with a builder, get a second opinion from your private inspector or architect. These people are working for you and should have a good grounding in what's right and what's wrong. The building code may provide some help, but it's usually just a series of *minimum* standards. The dispute may be over an extra measure of quality the builder may be trying to avoid just to save a buck.

**6** **"The Building Code is not in line with current building practices."** Here's a favorite excuse builders give when home-buyers or private inspectors turn up a violation of building codes. The fact is that 99% of local and state building codes are very up-to-date—in fact, they are *too* up-to-date for many builders. The codes require builders to use sound construction techniques and often provide extra protection for consumers. In Florida, for example, hurricane clips that attach the roof to the walls are used to prevent damage from wind gusts. In California, anchor bolts that tie the walls to the foundation hopefully limit damage during earthquakes.

These strict building codes are the bane of shoddy builders, who find the requirements too much of a hassle. Some builders try to blame the code for their problems. "Current building practices" that ignore consumer protection and sound construction are certainly not in line with the building code—but it isn't the code's problem. It's the builder's.

## Tᴴᴇ Mᴏsᴛ Cᴏᴍᴍᴏɴ "Cᴀʟʟ-Bᴀᴄᴋs"

No matter how much homework you do and how carefully you pick a builder, there will probably still be a few things the builder needs to fix after you move in. In industry parlance, these are called "call-backs."

The most common callbacks are for problems with the plumbing, floors/walls/ceilings, doors/windows and the roof. Complaints about grading and landscaping are more common with big builders (especially in the South), while contractors in the Northeast see the biggest number of complaints with plumbing and heating/mechanical systems. Less common are complaints with the electrical system, appliances or driveways. (See the following box for more details).

How long is the typical wait to get a builder to come back to fix an item? While most builders respond in under a week, a survey by the National Home Builder's Association revealed as many as one-quarter of builders take one to three **weeks** to fix problems. Asking references how quickly the builder responded to warranty work is a good way to ferret out those builders who care about their customers—and those who'll drag their feet to the end of time to fix minor items.

The point of this chapter (and this entire book, for that matter) is not to make you paranoid. If you follow some of the smart consumer tactics we've outlined, you'll certainly lower your chances of falling victim to a shoddy builder.

Nonetheless, there are fights and disagreements in even the best of marriages between builder and consumer. And it **is** just like a marriage—a long-term commitment by both of you to work toward a common goal. You see or talk to the builder practically every day and that can be tiresome.

Overall, building a home is a series of highs and lows. At times, everyone will function like a well-oiled machine. Other times it seems that nothing is going right. Recognizing this reality and taking precautions against those unlikely worst case scenarios will better prepare you for your new home journey.

## Email from the Real World: 13 Hard-won lessons for a homebuyer

Dick and Julie Stenabaugh have been to hell and back. The Stenabaughs started building a new home in August 1994 just outside Kansas City—and several years later, they were still dealing with the horrific problems in their new home caused by a shoddy builder.

We don't have room to go into all the details about what went wrong with the Stenabaugh's home, but we did ask the couple to share their thoughts on the process. Their letter to us was full of excellent suggestions, warnings and observations for new homebuyers:

Dick wrote: "Here are my ideas which maybe others can use to avoid a similar fate as ours:

**1** **Plan on being there, or better still, pay someone else to be there.** I travel for business and this set up the scenario of a problem being a week old before I saw it. Led by the builder, the subs soon figured they need not listen to my wife, and would consciously avoid seeing her. Since I wasn't on the job site frequently, we had disputed items that were interpreted to be "change orders:" first it was done wrong, then correcting it to what we originally asked for became a change (and a charge!).

**2** **Trust but verify.** Don't confuse morals with workmanship. We are Christian; our builder is Christian. We thought this to be ideal, and if the builder said something was thus and so, we took him at his word. This further made the task of terminating him more emotionally charged, and actually prevented us from making the tough decision earlier. Do not expect people in the building trades to abide by the Golden Rule. In fact, if they even suspect you are of that persuasion, they love you, man. They have an effective "grapevine," and once spotted, you're dog meat.

**3** **Get to know Guido.** We have no family in this area, nor are we from here. Sleazy contractors and subs can take advantage of this, rationalizing that you won't be able to bad mouth them to potential clients.

**4** **Loose lips sink ships.** Keep your financial information between you and the bank. Any appearance of wealth can undermine you when working with a contractor and his subs. We made the mistake of telling our builder we had saved a large down payment and were going to request upgrades to his standard finishes. This is viewed as "deep pockets."

**5** **Define "quality."** We quickly determined what we call quality and what the builder calls quality are NOT the same reality. Even when seeking references we missed this point, and if quality is something you seek, we suggest you get it well defined before you move ahead.

**6** **Dip your toe before diving in.** This was our first building experience. We truly wish that we had attempted a smaller home, one we planned to sell, before attempting to build our "dream" home. We would have learned a few pitfalls, if not deciding to forget the whole ugly experience.

**7** **Surround yourself with knowledgeable people.** I know just enough about construction to get into trouble. We took solace in the fact that

## CONSTRUCTION DEFECTS: THE BIG 6

Here's an amazing statistic: a whopping one-third of California homeowners had "major defects" in their new homes, according to a 2001 survey of the California Department of Real Estate reprinted in Builder magazine. Yes, that's one out of three, folks. Here are the most common defects:

| | |
|---|---|
| Plumbing, drainage & other leaks | 21% |
| Building structure<br>Foundation, walls, siding, floors, masonry, decks, termites | 19% |
| Infrastructure<br>Landscaping, sewers, lighting, erosion, asphalt, driveways. | 17% |
| Roof leaks and defects | 12% |
| Internal systems<br>Electrical, heating, etc. | 10% |
| Other<br>Paint, stucco, everything else. | 21% |

*Our thoughts:* Like other surveys, we were not surprised to find leaks (whether from poor grading/drainage to shoddy roofs) to top the list. Note how complaints about the "building structure" (foundation, walls) are almost twice the level of "internal systems" complaints (electrical, HVAC).

we had done a lot of work restoring a 125-year-old home in Iowa. I can plumb, I can drywall, I can insulate, I can nail, I can saw, etc. NONE of this is building a custom home, and don't be fooled into thinking these kinds of experiences translate.

**8** **Never, never, believe the line, "that's the way we always do it."** In fact, it should set off an alarm that something is wrong. Many of the problems in our house were caused by subs that used that line to explain something that looked amiss.

**9** **Never pay everything in full until you are absolutely sure the work meets your agreement.** The pain of listening to their lies about how they have to have your money will be quickly overcome by the pleasure of them coming back to fix a problem if necessary. Never pay in advance. Although I will say of all the stupid times we did pay in advance, I was rewarded by the deck guy who did finish the work . . . albeit two years late.

**10** **You cannot be nice when the other party is not nice, or when they owe you.** They don't understand nice; they DO understand "in your face" and sincere threats of getting into their pocketbook. Our attorney can get nasty, and we used that to our benefit. Be bold, use nasty. I'm not suggesting stooping to their level and getting vulgar, just don't be a softy. Remember, too, time is your enemy, therefore his weapon. Try to not allow things to drag on . . . the longer it takes, the worse it gets.

**11** **Strike up a relationship with the city inspector, your builder already has.** No sense in letting the builder play the inspector without any balance. We didn't know better. We lived in this house over two years on a temporary occupancy permit good for a mere 60 days. The week we threatened to file suit against the builder, the inspector came by and provided our final—despite the fact the contractor NEVER finished any of the required work. I view that as more than mere coincidence.

**12** **Beware the sub of a sub of a sub.** First, the whole intent gets distorted in the trickle down. But then you have no recourse because you can't find out who is responsible.

**13** **A few positive suggestions.** Keep a diary every day; write it all down, especially conversations otherwise not written. Take plenty of pictures or video, and keep every scrap of paper. We have found pictures taken for no particular reason have revealed much in the aftermath. Another great investment is a quality tape recorder on your telephone; tape every conversation related to the project. Keep the tapes labeled and in a journal. (Legal note: be sure to ask your attorney if you need permission of the caller to tape phone calls—some states require this; others do not).

# Bargains for Home

W e realize that throughout this book we've been good at spending your money—recommending you use professionals such as an inspector or architect, for example.

So, to be fair, we wanted to include a chapter on home bargains—creative ways to save money on your new home. First, we'll go over discount catalogs that can save you money on everything from lighting to plumbing fixtures. Next, we'll explore the discount stores such as Home Depot and Costco. Finally, you'll learn about several mail-order discount companies that offer additional discounts.

A great source for bargains on all types of products is *Wholesale by Mail* (HarperPerennial, $21). This annual, 700-page book has discount deals on everything you could ever want to buy—it's must-reading for new homebuyers.

If you're looking for deals on furniture, check out *The Fine Furniture and Furnishings Discount Shopping Guide: Why Pay Retail* by M. K. Gladchun ($15.95, Resources, Inc.). You'll learn how to save 20% to 70% on shopping for furniture, including discount sources in North Carolina.

Along the same lines is T*he Insider's Guide to Buying Home Furnishings* by Kimberly Causey ($24.95, Home Décor Press; 800-829-1203). This 356-page book is a great resource for bargain furniture shoppers. While the book sports a 1996 copyright, much of the info is up to date (the author updates it with every printing). The same author has also published a book called the *Furniture Factory Outlet Guide"* ($24.95, 2002 edition) in with more updated material. You can surf the author's web page at: www.smartdecorating.com.

All the aforementioned books can be found in bookstores or online at Amazon.com.

## Meet the Shopping 'Bots

Before we list some of the best discount catalog for home items, we'd be remiss to not mention that hot topic among bargain shoppers right now: the 'net. Quite simply, the bargains on the net (for items small and large) are amazing. If you don't have access to the web, this might be a good excuse to get wired.

Now that you've fired up that web browser, where do you go to find the deals? A good first place to stop is a shopping robot site (or shopping 'bots for short). These sites electronically scan other web sites for the best prices and selection, pointing you to the best deals. How do they work? You select a category or enter a product brand/name and zap! They give you a list of the best places and prices on the 'net.

Shopping 'bots used to just cover a limited number of categories like books or computer equipment, but in recent months they've expanded to include "house and home items." Here is an overview of the best shopping 'bots:

◆ **My Simon** (www.mysimon.com). Simon says, BARGAINS! This easy to use site has a "Home & Garden" section which lets you search for lamps and lighting, home accents, appliances, tools, outdoor furniture, gardening items and more. MySimon's "one click" searches give you quick access to certain products.

◆ **Yahoo's** shopping page (shopping.yahoo.com) lets you compare prices and brand names with a fast search engine. Click on the "Home & Garden" section to access info/prices on appliances, furnishings, lawn and garden and more.

# Discount Catalogs

**The Container Store**
**(800) 733-3532, fax (214) 484-2560**
**www.containerstore.com**

Based in Texas, the Container Store has 25 stores in 15 markets (Atlanta, Denver, Chicago, Columbus (OH, New York, Southern California, Miami and Washington, D.C.) But the best part about the Container Store is that you don't have to visit one to shop there—several catalogs and an extensive web site let you browse their storage solutions from anywhere in the U.S. and Canada.

Among the best of their catalogs is the Container Store's "Closet Planning Guide." If you want to use your closet space efficiently, check out their "elfa" line of closet components. The catalog has storage solutions for the office, laundry room and kid's rooms. We liked the step-by-step planner in the back of the catalog and suggestions for planning walk-in, bi-fold, or hall closets—even your kitchen pantry.

We highly recommend The Container Store for their cost-effective, space-efficient closet components. While The Container Store is not a discount haven, their unique storage solutions are worthy of mention.

## Home Decorators Collection
**(800) 245-2217, (314) 993-6045, fax (314) 993-6395**
**www.homedecorators.com**

Home Decorators Collection sells a diverse number of offerings. From chairs and tables to Tiffany-style lamps, they seem to cover all the bases with products for the home.

We were most impressed by their lighting supplies. For example, we noted flush-mounted dome lights, wall scones, cast aluminum outdoor lighting as well as post lights. Beyond lighting, this catalog also features accessories, bath hardware, furniture and floor coverings.

Home Decorators Collection web site is easy to use and lets you order online—we were most impressed with the deals on "clearance items." We saw one ceiling dome light marked down from $59 to a mere $17.95 and dining room chairs for $60 to $80 (down from $129 to $169). Be sure to check out their outlet store (www.homedecoratorsoutlet.com) for the best savings.

## Renovators Supply
**www.renovatorssupply.com**
**(800) 659-2211, (603) 447-8500**

Renovators Supply is one of the most amazing home catalogs we've run across. They offer everything from sinks and toilets to copper weather vanes.

The catalog is stuffed with sinks, faucets, floor and wall tile and more. What most impressed us was The Renovators' extensive lighting fixture selection, which takes up 14 pages. This includes track lighting, recessed lighting, outdoor fixtures, and traditional chandeliers and sconces.

Renovators Supply includes quite a few other items from cabinet knobs to architectural accents, and bathroom accessories to embossed wall coverings. Even weather vanes and cupolas can be ordered, including an outstanding copper eagle weather vane for $125. All Renovators products have a one-year warranty—a definite plus.

While the catalog is superb, Renovators Supply's web site is rather primitive but does allow you to view and order a selection of their offerings.

## More discount web sites that sell furniture and accessories:

◆ **Behome.com** has an excellent series of "help" features, including live online help and articles like "All you ever wanted to know about leather" and "Easy living with slipcovers." And, oh yeah, you can also buy furniture for the bedroom, office and dining room. The company that owns Behome.com also runs has an outlet store near Kansas City; surf the web page for directions and offerings.

◆ **Reflections** (www.reflectionsfurniture.com) is a North Carolina-based furniture discounter that sells name brand leather furniture at big savings. We've ordered ourselves from this company and were impressed with their service and pricing. Their web site was still "under construction" as we went to press, but you can get their basic info online.

◆ **Warren's Interiors** (www.warrensinteriors.com) is another North Carolina furniture discounter that sells a wide variety of items, from dining room tables to rugs, lighting, upholstered furniture and more. You find what you want and then call them for a quote (800-743-9792). We've also personally ordered from this company and found their pricing and service to be excellent.

Look to our web site (www.yournewhousebook.com) for updates on these and new sites that are recommended by our readers.

# More Deals: Home Stores

You gotta love those giant home center warehouses that have sprung up nationwide in the last ten years—they can be very addictive for new homebuyers. Particularly impressive are the "design centers" where you can actually touch those lighting, plumbing and kitchen fixtures you've seen in glossy magazines. Best of all, the prices can be a bargain, especially compared to the builder's inflated prices. Here's an overview.

◆ **Home Depot** (www.homedepot.com). The King of home centers is Home Depot. With 1300 stores in the US and Canada, Home Depot emphasizes low prices and good selection. Look for Home Depot's "EXPO Design Centers" which feature complete bath, kitchen and lighting displays, plus advice from consultants. Home Depot was slow to embrace the web, but their web site now lists thousands of products you can buy online.

◆ **Lowe's** (www.lowes.com). The #2 home improvement chain boasts 600 stores in 40 states. Lowe's base is the Eastern U.S., although they've been expanding in recent years in the Midwest and West. Lowe's has been expanding their design centers in recent years (with kitchen and bath displays) and recently added appliances to their mix.

◆ **Great indoors** (www.greatindoors.com). If you are lucky enough to have a Great Indoors store near you (there are 14 locations as of this writing with another 5 scheduled to open soon), count your blessings. These mammoth design centers and home stores feature an amazing selection of stuff: appliances, plumbing fixtures, cabinetry, bath, home theater, decor, lighting and more. It's hard to believe the Great Indoors is a subsidiary of Sears (although they don't make much mention of this online or in their stores). We found the prices at the Great Indoors to be good deals, especially on plumbing fixtures (which are often discounted below retail). Appliance prices are more likely to be full retail, but the lighting store has good deals as well.

. . . . . . . . . . . . . . . . . . . . . . . . .

While not home improvement centers, the warehouse clubs **Sam's**, **Costco** and **BJ's** should not be overlooked for bargains. You can pick up lighting and plumbing fixtures for rock-bottom prices at these member-only warehouses (which require a small annual fee to join). Sam's (www.samsclub.com) is the oldest example of this category with 500 stores nationwide selling "buy it bulk" products at low prices, but competitors Costco (www.costco.com) and BJ's (www.bjswholesale. com) offer similar deals. BJ's has 90 locations in 13 states, mostly in the Northeast, and accepts several credit cards (unlike its competitors). Costco boasts 300 stores in the U.S. and Canada—Costco even offers discount mortgages for its members.

Among the best deals at wholesale clubs are their seasonal items, like lawn and garden furniture and accessories.

# Discount Lighting Sources

**Lamps Plus**
**(Retail stores)**
**(800) 360-LAMP**
**www.lampsplus.com**

This 38-store chain based in California also has stores in Washington, Arizona, Nevada, and Colorado. We were impressed by their well-stocked showroom that featured several big-name brands. Selections ranged from ultra-contemporary to traditional and even antique reproductions.

Best of all are the "factory-direct" prices—up to half off regular retail. For example, we found verdigris outdoor carriage lamps for $49.95—the same light at a regular lighting store topped $100. Periodic sales provide even better deals. Lamps Plus stores also have a small lighting lab, where you can experiment with different lighting fixtures. The service is good, although the store we visited got rather crowded on weekends.

Lamps Plus' web site includes lighting tips, a store locator and even a few online bargains. Be sure to look for an online coupon for even more savings.

**Golden Valley Lighting/Bella Decor**
**(Mail-order company)**
**(800) 735-3377 or (336) 882-7330**
**www.bellacor.com**

This North Carolina-based mail-order company (now part of Bella Decor) offers discounts of up to 50% off retail. More than 200 man-ufacturers are available, including Casablanca, Waterford, and American Lantern. Golden Valley has indoor and outdoor lighting, lamps, track lighting, ceiling fans—you name it. Styles range from "colonial" to "Oriental" and just about everything in between.

Here's how it works: you shop local lighting stores, find the fixtures you want, and get the manufacturer's name, model number, color and finish. Then call Golden Valley for a price quote. A 50% deposit is required, with the balance due prior to shipment.

You can also find deals online, including close-outs and one of a kind specials.

### AJP Coppersmith & Co.
### (Mail-order and factory showroom near Boston, MA)
### (800) 545-1776, (781) 245-1216

AJP Coppersmith specializes in period reproductions. Their 30-page color catalog is filled with colonial lanterns, chandeliers, and other Early American lighting fixtures.

Four finishes are available: antique copper, antique brass, verdigris and black. Prices are reasonable, considering the quality and craftsmanship—we liked their 28-inch Cape Cod outdoor lantern and "onion lamps" (their most popular style). The Country Brass Collection features five styles of chandeliers that were quite attractive.

If you're looking for handcrafted antique reproductions, AJP is one company to check out. They do take credit cards and offer a 15-day money-back guarantee if you're not satisfied. AJP also has a "factory showroom" open to the public just in Wakefield, MA. One bummer: AJP's web site was under construction as we went to press.

### Shades of Light
### (800) 262-6612
### www.shades-of-light.com

While we liked this catalog, their web site is even better. We loved the "Lighting Solutions" section with tips and decorating ideas. Best of all, the easy-to-navigate site is well-organized into categories such as wall sconces and bath lamps. The emphasis here is on unique and stylish options; fixtures you won't see at a Home Depot. Accordingly, the prices can be somewhat steep, but we found the closeouts page had some great deals (40% to 60% off).

### Other Discount Lighting Sources

◆ **Luigi Crystal** (215) 338-2978, specializes in crystal lighting fixtures. The company offers up to 50% savings. A $2 catalog is available.

◆**American Light Source** (800) 741-0571; web: www.americanlightsource.com. Save up to 40% with this Greensboro, NC discounter. Over 100 manufacturers are represented. A $5 catalog is available. There is a $100 minimum order.

◆ **Brass Light Gallery** (800) 243-9595; www.brasslight.com. Milwaukee, Wisconsin-based Brass Light Gallery makes their own brand of brass lights in a variety of architectural styles. Brass Light

Gallery's web site is well-designed and includes their catalogs, viewable online as PDF files.

◆ **Circle Lighting** (www.circlelighting.com) is the online outpost for a New Jersey lighting store. The site lists an impressive array of brand names, but you have to call their toll-free number for a price quote or to order.

◆ **Union Lighting** (unionlighting.com) discounts several high-end chandelier brands, as well as table lamps, wall sconces and ceiling fixtures.

# Discount Carpeting and Flooring

Buying carpet can be an exercise in frustration. Many large carpet makers "private label" their offerings—hence you can see the exact same carpet at different stores, all under different names. Another problem: outright fraud. Carpet sellers are famous for "shading the truth" on their carpet weight, features and warranty. While detailed advice on this subject is beyond the scope of the book, we do recommending checking out Consumer Reports August 1998 issue for general tips. We also liked an honest carpet discounter **Carpet Discounts** (www.carpet-discounts.com) who posted an excellent primer on 'net carpet buying on their site—it is must reading.

◆ **American Carpet Wholesalers** (706) 278-3209; web: www.carpet-wholesale.com offers savings up to 70% off retail. When we visited their web site, we saw a 48oz nylon trackless carpet for just $8 per square yard. Free samples are available on request.

◆ **American Home Showplace/Carpets of Dalton** (800) 262-3132; www.carpetsofdalton.com. "Incredible bargains" is how a reader in Arizona described this discounter in Georgia. Good discounts on carpeting and flooring, plus plenty of free samples. Discounts are 25% to 50%. The company's web site wasn't functioning when we visited at press time.

◆ **Bearden Bros. Carpet and Textiles Corporation** (800) 433-0074; www.beardenbrothers.com. Bearden Bros. specializes in carpet and padding, plus vinyl and wood flooring. Manufacturers include Armstrong, Interloom and Burlington. Savings up to 80%, and a free brochure is available. Bearden's web page is rather extensive, with pricing for many of their products online.

◆ **Beaver Flooring** (888) 595-HOME, web: www.beaverhome.com is a Canadian manufacturer of hardwood flooring that sells directly to the public in the U.S. at factory-direct prices. Their excellent web site includes detailed info on the offerings with prices, specifications and more. Beaver Flooring sells ash, cherry, maple, red oak and white oak flooring, as well as Canadian made carpet and Oriental rugs.

◆ **Paradise Mills Inc.** (800) 338-7811. Call for a brochure or free samples on this discount flooring outlet. You'll find carpet, vinyl and wood flooring at up to 60% discounts. They sell Armstrong, Horizon and many other brand names.

◆ **Warehouse Carpets, Inc.** (800) 526-2229. Warehouse Carpets sells vinyl flooring as well as carpet and padding. They carry famous brands including Mannington, Armstrong and Congoleum at up to 50% off retail.

# Discount Plumbing

◆ **Baths from the Past, Inc.** (800) 697-3871; www.faucetfactory. com. Looking for authentic Victorian bath hardware but don't want to spend a fortune? This company in Rockland, Maine sells reproductions of faucets, sinks and other accessories at 30% off comparable retail. A free 40-page brochure is available. Baths from the Past does have a rather primitive web page, but you can at least see photos (but no prices) of the items they sell.

◆ **The Faucet Outlet** (888) 381-8837; www.faucet.com. Request the $2 catalog from this Middletown, NY company and you'll find fixtures from Delta, Price Pfister, Elkay, Grohe, Kohler at a 33% discount off retail. On their web page, you can receive a free email newsletter with product specials and free online quotes. Besides faucets, this discounter also sells sinks, claw foot tubs, whirlpools and more.

◆ **Faucetsource.com** (800) 669-1707 is a sophisticated online web site with offerings from Moen and Delta among others. Check out their "monthly specials" section with discounts ranging from 30% to 50%. We liked the site's java-based shopping cart system, which calculated your total as you shop (the site was offering free shipping on our last visit).

# Miscellaneous: Discount Roofing and Auctions

◆ **New England Slate Co.** (802) 247-8809; www.neslate.com. New England Slate is unique among slate roofing companies: not only do they sell brand-new slate, but they also offer "recycled" slate recovered from old buildings on the East Coast. With savings of up to 50% and six different colors, they offer quite a deal. New England Slate's web site has an excellent FAQ for those considering a slate roof.

# What Does It All Mean?

CONCLUSION

**A**t this point, you may be wondering, "Am I crazy? Why don't I just rent an apartment somewhere and forget this home stuff?" Your head may be swimming with foreign terms such as joists and load-bearing walls.

It might be a good time to take a deep breath and look at the "wide view." What exactly is the goal here? Okay, besides spending obscene amounts of money. Yes, you're getting a new home. And it's more than just wood, bricks, glass, steel, and a few thousand nails.

Think of the new home process as a roller-coaster ride. You start off by waiting in line for what seems like an eternity. Suddenly, you're at the front and step inside a car. Then there's the long, slow climb to the top of the hill—think of this as the design process.

Next you reach the top of the hill and begin the construction. Whoosh! You plunge downhill, screaming all the way. There are going to be incredible highs and depressing lows. When the shell of the home takes shape, you'll be elated. When the builder announces yet another delay and cost overrun, you'll be crushed.

As you zoom around the corner, the end is in sight. After all the twists and turns, you suddenly find yourself in your new home. And, the best part is, it's your home. If you follow the advice in this book and hire an architect or professional designer, the home will fit you like a glove. The kitchen is a perfect dream. The layout of the rooms is just what you want. Everything in the home fits your needs, not the builder's or another homeowner's.

So, we urge you to keep your eye on the prize. The key to getting a good home is being a smart consumer. While the process of building or buying a new home may be a rollercoaster ride, the paper-scissors-rock strategy will keep you firmly strapped in.

And, of course, if you do decide to build, we have one final piece of advice: Good luck and Godspeed.

# Product Reviews: Windows, Plumbing, Plus Roofing Tips

APPENDIX A

**W**hat are the best brands of windows? Plumbing? This section includes our opinions as to the best choices in both categories. In order to come up with these ratings, we evaluated products at trade shows and interviewed both buyers, architects and homebuilders. The opinions are our own, based on this research.

First, let's look at what BUILDER'S think are the highest quality brands. Publisher Hanely-Wood surveyed 2247 builders in 2001 as to their favorite brands. Here is list of which brands they used most and which ones they thought were the highest quality (not always the same, of course).

| Category | Brand Used Most | Highest Quality |
|---|---|---|
| Disposers | In-Sink-Erator | In-Sink-Erator |
| Range Hoods | GE | Jenn-Aire |
| Ranges/Cooktops | GE | Viking |
| Refrigerators | GE | Sub-Zero |
| Water Heaters | A.O. Smith | A.O. Smith |
| Cabinetry (semi-custom) | KraftMaid | Wood-Mode |
| Cabinets (stock) | Merillat | KraftMaid |
| Patio Doors | Andersen | Andersen |
| Hardboard siding | Masonite | Georgia-Pacific |
| Housewrap | Dupont Tyvek | Dupont Tyvek |
| Insulation | Owens-Corning | Owens-Corning |
| Vinyl Siding | CertainTeed | CertainTeed |
| Bath Fixtures | Kohler | Kohler |
| Faucets | Moen | Kohler |
| Kitchen Sinks | Kohler | Kohler |
| Laminate Flooring | Pergo | WilsonArt & Armstrong (tie) |

| | | |
|---|---|---|
| Vinyl Flooring | Armstrong | Armstrong |
| Wood Flooring | Bruce | Bruce |
| Fireplaces | Heatilator | Vermont Castings |
| HVAC | Carrier | Lennox |
| Shingles: Asphalt | GAF (Timberline) | Elk |
| Clay/Concrete Roof | Monier/Lifetile | Monier/Lifetile |
| Metal roof | Alcan | N/A |
| Ceramic tile | Dal-Tile | Laufen |
| Laminate surfacing | Formica/WilsonArt (tie) | WilsonArt |
| Solid surfacing | Corian | Corian |
| Metal windows | Alencoe/Reynolds(Tie) | Reynolds |
| Skylights | Velux | Velux |
| Vinyl Windows | Milgaurd | Milgaurd |
| Wood Windows | Andersen | Andersen |
| Foundation Waterproofing | Tuff-N-Dry | Tuff-N-Dry |
| Underlayment | Georgia-Pacific | James Hardie |

*Source: Hanley Wood Brand Use Study, 2001.*

# Windows

Here are our picks as the best window makers in the U.S. and Canada:

**Andersen** These widely available windows are priced similar to Pella and other expensive brands. Several energy-efficient options are available, including argon-filled and "high-performance" sun glass windows. Andersen says the latter option is 58% more energy efficient than a regular double-pane window. As with other high-end windows, Andersen windows are double sealed. The company backs its windows with an extensive warranty: 20 years for the glass; 10 years on all other parts. Andersen often tops builder surveys of top quality windows. (800) 426-4261, (651) 439-5150. Web: www.andersenwindows.com. **Rating: A**

**Hurd** Our pick as one of the best quality windows around is Hurd. What most impressed us about this brand is their "heat mirror" technology. Instead of a mere coating on the glass, heat mirror is a thin layer of invisible metal on Mylar film that is placed between the two panes of glass. The result is super energy efficiency—Hurd formulates different versions of the heat mirror for hot and cold climates. Heat mirror also blocks 99% of furniture-damaging UV rays—compare that to 60% to 70% for other brands' top-of-the-line low-E windows. The only disadvantage: Hurd's aluminum-clad windows can be a bit pricey. For the budget-conscious, Hurd has a line of lower-price vinyl windows/ You can read more about both Hurd on the company's excellent web site, which is easy-to-navigate and explains window technology in plain English. Hurd warranties its windows for 10 years. (800) 223-4873. Web: www.hurd. com. **Rating: A**

**Kolbe & Kolbe**   This Wisconsin-based company makes quality (if not somewhat pricey) windows. Standard features include insulated low-E, argon-filled glass and double weather-stripping. Kolbe & Kolbe was founded in 1946 by brothers Herb and Ervin Kolbe; the company branched out into vinyl windows in 1998 with their new subsidiary, KVW Windows. The company's web site lets you explore both their wood, aluminum and vinyl windows, with "home tips," FAQ's and more. (715) 842-5666. Web: www.kolbe-kolbe.com. **Rating: A–**

**Marvin**   Minnesota-based Marvin touts itself as a "made-to-order" window maker. That probably explains why they are so expensive—we priced a 5x4 casement window at twice the price Hurd was charging. What do you get for that price? Marvin offers six glass options (including low-E, argon-filled glass) and nine exterior finish options. Dual-sealed, insulating glass is standard. Both wood and aluminum-clad windows are available. Marvin windows are long on razzle-dazzle—their line includes seamless corner windows and curved glass windows. Marvin's "sash pack" for replacing windows is very good. Like many other window makers, Marvin branched out into the "non-wood" window market recently. The company's "Integrity" line of windows are clad in "Ultrex," which Marvin describes as a made of glass fibers combined with a liquid polyester resin, then hardened in the shape of a window or door. Integrity has its own web site at www.integritywindows.com; Marvin's web site is excellent—we liked the case studies and custom tour of the site. (888) 537-8268, (218) 386-1430. Web: www.marvin.com. **Rating: A–**

**Peachtree**   An architect we interviewed recommend this brand, which comes with a "non-stop" warranty: all Peachtree windows are guaranteed for as long as you own them. The Ariel line features aluminum clad exteriors, with a choice of three baked-on enamel finishes. Among the best offers from Peachtree is a top-of-the-line patio door called the Citadel, which offers a maintenance-free aluminum clad exterior. Peachtree's "Aspire" line combines a aluminum exterior and vinyl clad interior. (800) PEACH99 Web: www.peachtreewindows.com. **Rating: B+**

**Pella**   The Cadillac of windows has everything you'd expect in a high-end product, including the high-end price tag. Pella windows come in three flavors: the Architect, Designer and Pro lines. The Architect series is the most expensive and features authentic reproductions of separate-pane glass. The Designer line is intriguing—Pella has designed these windows with a pleated shade between the panes of glass. Meanwhile, the Pro line is their "builder" (read: cheaper) series that has fewer options, different hardware and a slider style available. As for prices, the Designer line is about 20% more than the Pro line; and the Architect series is about 20% more than the Designer. Yes, these windows are very expensive but worth it.

Among Pella's stand-outs is their Surelock system, which adds more security to their Designer and Architect series casement windows. Also innovative is the Pella CornerView window, which won design awards for it's energy performance and clear views (with no distortion). We love their "Rolscreen" window screen that disappears when not in use.

Pella touts the energy efficiency of all its windows. Key features include double-coated, low-E glass and double seals. Pella says you'd save 28% off your heating and cooling bills with their windows, compared to single-pane wood windows. Pella windows come with a 10-year warranty. (800) 84-PELLA, (515) 628-1000. Web: www.pella.com. **Rating: A**

## What about other brands?

As you can see from the above reviews, the best known window makers all make a very good product. Depending upon your needs and budget, just about any of these companies will do a good job.

But what about other brands? We consistently get email from readers who wonder about the funky off-brand windows a production builder is using. To be honest, there are HUNDREDS of small window makers in the U.S. and Canada—and we have not researched many of the smaller, obscure brands. Call us cynics, but we've found most production builders use the CHEAPEST window they can find. If you come across a funky brand, compare how it stands up to a window from a reliable brand like those above.

## General Money–Saving Tip for Windows

Go with stock sizes. Many window makers stock certain common sizes—these are generally much less than windows that have to be custom made. Don't design a fancy opening in your new house that requires a custom-size window—you'll pay through the nose.

# PLUMBING

**American Standard** We always seem to see American Standard's basic lines at those discount home centers and have rarely been impressed. However, their full-line catalog does offer some surprises. There are upper-end options that let you mix and match spouts and handles. One plus: American Standard's excellent web site includes some helpful design tips, written in a breezy style. (800) 752-6292; (732) 980-3000. Web: www.us.amstd.com. **Rating: C+**

**Delta** Fairly basic and rarely ostentatious, Delta is the bread-and-butter brand of faucets. Most of the line is chrome or brass, although col-

ors are available as well. Prices are moderate. We liked their new "Brilliance" brass finish, which Delta promises will never lose its luster, corrode or discolor. Delta's web site won't win any tech design awards, but is functional—much of their catalog is online. For the budget conscious, check out the "Delta Select" series that offers high style at "value prices." (800) 345-DELTA, (317) 848-1812. Web: www.deltafaucet.com. **Rating: B**

**Dornbracht** Looking on the wild side for faucets? Check out the German company Dornbracht, whose faucets are quite amazing. Our favorite is the "Edition Delphini" which are faucets shaped like dolphins. Finish options include chrome, gold-plate, silver nickel and "durabrass." Ultra-contemporary "Edition Point" has conical and cylindrical forms with neon accents. Meanwhile, the Jefferson line is more classical and antique looking. Prices? Are you sitting down? A single Dornbracht bathroom faucet will set you back $500 or more. (800) 774-1181. Web: www.dornbracht.com. **Rating: B–**

**Grohe America** A very European look from Germany, Grohe includes sleek, ultra-contemporary designs. Prices are in line with Kohler; for example, bathroom faucets were $175 to $350. Penny-pinchers will want to pass up the optional 24K gold finish. Grohe's web site gives you a good overview of the line with a special section that highlights new products. (630) 582-7711. Web: www.groheamerica.com. **Rating: B**

**Kohler** Wisconsin-based Kohler is probably the best-known brandname in plumbing fixtures today. We divide Kohler's offerings into three categories: slightly expensive, very expensive, and out-of-thisworld expensive. In the slightly expensive category, the "Sterling" line is entry-level Kohler. Don't expect much design pizzazz here, as most of the fixtures have a plain vanilla look. Things start getting interesting in the regular Kohler and upper-end Kallista lines—both have stunning faucets, sinks and other accessories in just about every finish, color and style imaginable. Kohler's web site will give you a good overview of each line, complete with sharp graphics. Of course, Kohler makes more than just faucets—the company cranks out all variety of tubs, sinks and whirlpools. Among the standouts is their "BodySpa" which offers a "personal hydro-massage system" with up to ten powerful jets. The cost ranges from $3500 to $10,000, depending on the number of jets. Overall, Kohler is perhaps the most creative plumbingfixture manufacturer out there. With nearly 3 BILLION dollars in sales each year, Kolher's track record and quality is unsurpassed—the faucet's single-cartridge system makes repairs easier, for example. They've got a color and style for anyone's fancy—the only problem is that Kohler's sky-high prices make extensive use of their products beyond the means of many home buyers. (800) 4-KOHLER. (920) 457-4441. Web: www.kohlerco.com. **Rating: A**

**Moen** This middle of the road brand is priced between entry-level brands and Kohler. In recent years, the company has added some innovative products. Examples include their "Inspirations" line with mix and match faucet finishes and accents and Moen's "LifeShine" brass finish, which promises not to tarnish or corrode. Also new: Moen's "Extensa" kitchen faucet that has added height and reach to help with cleaning. Finally, Moen offers their version of a filter-in faucet, called the "PureTouch." (440) 962-2000. www.moen.com. **Rating:A–**

**Price Pfister** You've probably seen the ads for this well-known brand. Priced similarly to Delta, Price Pfister spices up their offerings with some unique styles. The all-white Flying Colors collection includes interchangeable solid brass rings. PP's basic line is quite affordable and available in many discount home centers. While PP doesn't have the "wow" factor that Kohler offers, we have been impressed with the company's innovative products. A good example is their "Pfilter Pfaucet, " which incorporates a Teledyne Water Pik filter. You can turn on or off the filter and easily pop in new replacement cartridges. (818) 896-1141. Web: www.pricepfister.com. **Rating: B**

**Swirl-Way Tubs** This Texas-based company (owned by Mansfield) makes several interesting tub styles. All Swirl-Ways are made from acrylic and the color goes all the way through (this prevents chips and scratches like those that can happen with porcelain tubs). Our personal favorite is the sculpted, two-person Andiamo tub. Just about every color is available (40 in all), as well as optional mood lights, massage jets, and more. Swirl-Way's web page does have an online catalog and advice on selecting the right tub for your needs. You just have to get past the bad design, hard-to-read text and annoying music intro. (800) 999-1459; www.swirlway.com. **Rating:A**

# Roofing

Suspect your builder is installing the roof incorrectly? Here are some sources that give tips on proper roof installation, as well as general information on various roofing options.

◆ **Asphalt Roofing Manufacturers Association** (301) 231-9050; www.asphaltroofing.org has a homeowner's guide to quality asphalt roofing. The brochure "Good application makes a good roof better" is an excellent primer on installation. We also liked their excellent web page, which includes a "Roofing 101" tutorial.

◆ **Cedar Shake and Shingle Bureau** (800) 843-3578; www.cedarbureau. org has a publication called "New Roof Construction" that includes drawings and other useful tips. The organization's web site is a bit difficult to navigate but does have some useful info.

GLOSSARY

**2x4 construction** Exterior walls are approximately four inches deep (actually $1\frac{1}{2}$" by $3\frac{1}{2}$").

**2x6 construction** Exterior walls are approximately six inches deep (actually $1\frac{1}{2}$" by $5\frac{1}{2}$").

**2-10 warranties** A third-party insured warranty purchased by the builder from such companies as Home Owners Warranty Corporation and Home Buyer's Warranty. The builder is responsible for covered repairs during the first two years. The remaining eight years are covered by the third party insurer.

**16 on center (16 O. C.)** Width between wall studs. "Sixteen On Center" means the studs are 16 inches from the center of one stud to the center of another stud.

**acreage** The amount of land area a property has, expressed in acres. One acre equals 43,560 square feet.

**adjustable rate mortgage (ARM)** a mortgage whose interest rate is adjusted periodically. The times and amount of the adjustment are defined in the terms of the loan.

**allowances** Sums of money that are "rebated" back to you to purchase various items such as light fixtures. A $500 allowance would allow you to purchase up to $500 worth of fixtures. Additional fixtures would be paid out of your own pocket.

**aluminum clad** Usually found on wood windows, the exterior is sheathed with aluminum

**anchor bolt** Required in many areas with seismic activity, the bolt is set in the concrete foundation and connects to the walls of the home. The goal is to prevent the home from moving or swaying in an earthquake.

**Annual Percentage Rate (APR)** The yearly interest rate percentage of a loan after all fees and charges are factored in.

**appraisal** An independent opinion of the value of a piece of property. One method of appraising a property is "market value" in which recently sold, comparable properties are used to determine the value of your property.

**arbitration** Third party dispute resolution method in which an arbitrator sits down with both sides, listens to their arguments and renders a decision (this decision could be binding or non-binding). It is used in some disputes to try to avoid legal action. American Arbitration Association or National Association of Conciliators are examples of organizations that offer dispute resolution.

**argon-filled glass** Specialized window with argon gas inserted between two panes of glass. Argon is used as an insulator, making such windows more energy efficient.

**back fill** Dirt used to fill in around the foundation after the foundation walls are poured or constructed.

**blueprints (design, plans)** Detailed plan that is used to construct a home.

**boilerplate contract** Contract so standard that you merely "fill in the blanks."

**builder-grade materials** Typically the least expensive, lowest quality materials available.

**building codes** Series of state and local laws that set a minimum standard for building practices.

**buyer's broker** Real estate agent who works exclusively for the buyer. Negotiates on behalf of and owes loyalty to the buyer.

**carriage lamps** Outdoor lighting that resembles lights once used on horse-drawn carriages.

**cash flow** Revenue less expenses. Does not include tax related expenses such as depreciation.

**caulk** Silicone or acrylic sealant used for filling small cracks and holes.

**change orders** Written order to change an item in the home. May incur an additional charge for administrative time.

**closing** Final exchange of money for the title to the lot or the home or for a construction loan.

**closing fees** Fees charged by the title company and lender to process the closing documents.

**collar beams** Used in a traditional rafter system for a roof. Collar beams tie together the rafters.

**columns** Vertical supports for the home made of steel, concrete blocks and brick or treated wood.

**commitment letter** Letter issued by a lender that says you have qualified for a certain mortgage amount on a specific property.

**construction documents** These documents include the blueprints, specs and materials lists and other instructions on the building of a home.

**construction loan** Short-term loan to construct a house.

**construction manager** Individual who works for the home buyer to supervise day-to-day operations at the building site.

**construction to permanent loan** Loan that finances the construction and then rolls over into a permanent mortgage loan.

**contingencies** Conditions/events that must occur before contract is binding.

**conventional loan** Mortgage that is financed and obtained from a private lender, not a government institution.

**cooperating agent** Agent who finds a buyer, but is working for and must negotiate the best price for the seller. Hence, the agent is "cooperating" with the seller.

**covenants** Specifically as found in subdivisions, covenants are restrictions and rules placed on homes and property uses.

**crawl space** Half-size basement about four feet or less in height.

**credit report** History of a loan applicant with regard to loan payments, credit worthiness and any bankruptcies.

**cul-de-sac** A street that dead-ends into a large circle.

**curb appeal** How attractive a home looks from the curb or street.

**default** Failure of a party to a contract to take some action as required.

**depreciation** Due to age or obsolescence, the decrease in a property's value over time.

**designer** Person who offers architectural services limited to drawing blueprints. Typically not licensed by states, designers cannot refer to themselves as architects.

**dimension plans** Very basic blueprints that give a rough layout of a home's rooms. Such plans are missing separate framing, electrical and plumbing/heating plans as well as specifications and materials.

**dovetail joints** Locking in a zig-zag pattern, this joint resembles the feathers of a dove. Much stronger than other joint options for cabinets.

**downspouts** Gutters that empty water off the roof to the ground.

**draws** Payments from the construction loan to satisfy subcontractors' and suppliers' bills.

**drywall (gypboard, sheetrock)** A sheet of gypsum sandwiched between two sheets of paper. Used to cover studs and create walls.

**dual agent** A real estate broker who claims to represent both the seller and the buyer in a real estate transaction. Some dual agents represent *neither* the seller nor the buyer—they simply provide general advice and help with the transaction. Also referred to as a "facilitator" or "mediator."

**elevations** Exterior view of a home design.

**Errors and omissions insurance** Special insurance for builders and architects to cover mistakes in the home design or construction.

**excavation** Removal of dirt and trees at a home site in preparation for the foundation.

**exclusive agency** This contract between builder and real estate agent gives the builder the right to sell directly to consumers without the agent receiving a commission.

**exclusive right to sell** This contract between builder and real estate agent mandates the agent receive a commission on the sale of property—even if the builder sells the home directly and the agent plays no role.

**Fannie Mae** The Federal National Mortgage Association, a private company that both buys and sells mortgages from lenders.

**FHA loan** Loan insured by the Federal Housing Administration, enabling buyers to get loans with low down payments.

**field changes** Alterations made to a home on the construction site not in accordance with the blueprints.

**fill dirt** Soil used to back fill foundations.

**fixed-rate mortgage** Mortgage whose rate is fixed for the term of the loan.

**flashing** Sheet-metal strips installed under the shingles, around the chimney, in seams where different roof lines meet, and around skylights, vents, windows, and doors. Flashing prevents water infiltration.

**floating walls** In the basement, these walls are engineered to allow movement in the basement floor without damage to the walls.

**footings** Structural element at the base of foundations, piers or columns used to support the home.

**Freddie Mac** A private company that buys and sells mortgages from lenders.

**free-market lots**  Any building site where you are free to choose any builder you wish.

**gag rule**  Contract provision that prohibits your ability to hang signs outside your home complaining about the builder. Many gag rules also prohibit picketing the builder's offices or model homes as well.

**general contractor**  Builder who is in charge of project and hires all subcontractors and materials' suppliers.

**girders**  Cross-beams that support the floor joists.

**good-faith estimate**  Lenders are required by law to provide an estimate of all closing costs and escrows within three days of your application.

**green**  A product that is environmentally friendly.

**hazard insurance**  Insurance that covers the home against damage by such hazards as fire, hail, wind and so on. The perils covered vary by policy.

**headers**  Cross- beams above windows and doors.

**heat mirror**  Thin layer of invisible metal on Mylar film placed between two panes of glass.

**Homeowners associations**  When subdivisions or communities are established, the developer may incorporate a series of "covenants, conditions and restrictions" on the lots. A homeowners association is usually set up to enforce the covenants.

**house wrap**  Energy-saving air barrier that is wrapped around a house during construction. Made from polyethylene fibers, house wrap keeps air from penetrating the walls.

**impact fees**  Taxes imposed by local communities on new homes to fund schools, parks, etc.

**implied warranty of habitability**  Established by the courts, this doctrine states that all new homes are assumed to be suitable for habitation, to be built in a workmanlike manner and to meet all building codes.

**impounds**  Amounts of money collected by a lender to pay for insurance and real estate taxes on your property.

**joists**  Small beams placed parallel on top of the sills. Supported by columns or piers, the joists in turn form the support for the sub-floor.

**limited warranty**  Any warranty that has specific exclusions and conditions.

**listing agent**  Agent who obtains the listing from the seller/ builder. This agent is working for and owes loyalty to the builder.

**load-bearing wall**  Structural element of a home that is carrying a substantial weight. Without it, the home would collapse.

**lock**  Agreement by a lender to give you a certain mortgage at a certain percentage rate providing you close within a specified number of days.

**"low-doc" loan**  Mortgage loan that requires little documentation of income and asset levels.

**low-E**  Window type that has "low emissivity," a measure of how much heat a window allows to escape or infiltrate.

**managed-competition lots**  Building site where you must choose from among a list of several approved builders.

**mechanic's lien**  Encumbrance placed against a property to satisfy any unpaid invoices to a subcontractor or supplier.

**mortgage**  Loan to purchase real property (vacant land or a house).

**mortgage brokers**  Companies that make mortgage loans but do not fund them from their own money.

**Multiple Listing Service (MLS)** Catalog of all real estate that is listed by real estate agents in a certain area.

**municipal housing inspector** Employed by a city or county, this person inspects construction sites to determine whether builders are adhering to local building codes.

**negative slope driveway** Driveway that drops in elevation from the street to the garage.

**no-competition lots** Building site that requires you to use a specified builder. The lot is usually owned by the builder.

**"no-doc" loan** Mortgage loans that require no documentation of income. Granted only in cases of large down payments.

**origination fee** A fee that covers the lender's cost of making a loan.

**percolation (perc) test** Checks the feasibility of a site for a septic system.

**permanent loan** Typically a 30-year mortgage loan.

**piers** *See* columns.

**points** Fee associated with obtaining a mortgage. One point equals one percent of the mortgage amount.

**pre-approval letter** Letter from a lender indicating that a buyer can qualify for a certain size mortgage at a specified rate.

**primer** Paint undercoat used to prepare siding for top coat.

**production home** Mass-produced homes built in a development by one builder. Buyers usually have limited ability to customize this type of home.

**punch list** List of items that require repair or correction. Prepared before closing (usually at the "walk-through").

**quit claim deed** Giving over title to a property but not admitting or ensuring that the seller has any ownership rights.

**R-value** How resistant a material is to air infiltration.

**rafters** Support beams in a roof.

**Realtor** Real estate agent who is a member of the National Association of Realtors.

**recording fees** Charges at the time of closing to record legal documents with the county.

**ridge board** Top board of roof that runs horizontally above the rafters.

**rough-in** Installation of various mechanical systems such as plumbing, electrical, heating, etc.

**schematic designs** Rough sketches of a home's floor plan and exterior.

**seller carrybacks** Financing arrangement in which the seller loans the purchaser money to purchase the property.

**selling agent** *See* listing agent.

**semi-custom home** Type of home where the buyer can make changes to the design, except for exterior and load-bearing walls.

**septic system** Waste removal process utilizing micro-organisms to break down wastes.

**setback** The minimum distance between a lot line and the location of structures or buildings.

**sills** Wood that sits atop the foundation walls.

**slab-on-grade foundation** Foundation that is built directly over dirt with no basement or crawl space.

**soils test** Test to determine subsoil conditions that impact on the foundation's design.

**spec (speculation) home** Home that is built on speculation—without a buyer at the start of construction.

**specifications (specs)** Brand names, types of materials, and installation methods to be used in a new home's construction.

**stucco** Exterior finish of a home made from wet plaster or concrete.

**studs** These are the 2x4s and 2x6s that make up the skeleton of your home.

**sub-floor** Plywood sheathing that sits atop the joists.

**sub-agent** *See* cooperating agent.

**subcontractors (subs)** Independent companies or workers who are hired by the general contractor to perform various construction tasks on the home.

**survey** Measurement to determine the exact boundary lines of a property.

**tap fees** Charges by utility companies to hook up new homes.

**title** Ownership of a piece of real property.

**title company** Company that issues title insurance and participates in the closing of property transactions.

**tract home** *See* production home.

**trusses** Prefabricated roof system.

**Two-step loan (7/23, 5/25)** Mortgage that has one rate for a beginning period (five or seven years) and then adjusts to another rate for the remaining years.

**underlayment** Layer of wood between sub-floor and floor covering.

**VA loan** A loan for veterans, insured by the Veteran's Administration.

**vinyl-clad windows** Wood windows that have a vinyl-sheathed exterior.

**walk-out basement** For houses on sloping lots, basements can sometimes be built with a door to walkout at ground level.

**water witch** Person who helps find a good location for a well. Interesting superstition many people swear by.

**zero-lot-line homes** Homes built right next to each other, with "zero clearance" between the structures. Also referred to as "cluster" or "patio" homes. Most have little or no yards.

**zoning** Laws that restrict the use of property to defined applications.

**BIBLIOGRAPHY**

**100 Questions Every First-Time Home Buyer Should Ask,** 2000, by Ilyce R. Glink, Times Books, New York, $17. An excellent guide by syndicated columnist Ilyce Glink, who combines wit and wisdom to create a primer every home buyer (not just first-timers) should read. Glink has several other real estate books available; surf her web page at www.thinkglink.com for details.

**And They Built a Crooked House**, 1991, $12.95; **Crumbling Dreams**, 1993, $8; Ruth S. Martin, Lakeside Press, 5124 Mayfield Rd., #191, Cleveland, OH, 44124. Books can be ordered by calling toll-free 1-800-247-6553. A fascinating tale of a defective house and the exhaustive legal battle the author endured. **Crumbling Dreams** rehashes the first book and adds in tales of woe from other home buyers. Although a little rambling at times, both books are recommended reading for new home buyers.

**Build it Right! What to Look For In Your New House,** 1997, Myron Ferguson, Home User's Press, $18.95. This is a good book that points out the pitfalls and mistakes one can make when building a new home. We liked the section on siting your home (the end of a cul-de-sac can mean headlights flashing in your master bedroom) as well as the helpful photos and illustrations.

**Everything You Need to Know About Building the Custom Home**, 1990, John Folds and Roy Hoopes, Taylor Publishing Co., Dallas, TX. Advice on how to be your own general contractor. While not over-ly-technical, the book's charts are somewhat ponderous.

**Kiplinger's Buying & Selling a Home**, 1999, the staff of Kiplingers Personal Finance Staff magazine, Kiplinger Books, Washington, D.C. $17.95. A good overall introduction to buying a home with solid advice from Kiplinger's. Best section: house-hunting strategies.

**The Not So Big House**, 1998, Sarah Susanka, Taunton Press, $30. The single best home design book on the market, architect Susanka's book rejects the "bigger is better" school of new home design in this fascinating look at construction today. 200 color photos show you how to design a house with smaller "personal" spaces. Highly recommended. Susanka also has authored a sequel to this book called "Creating the Not So Big Home" ($34.95) in 2000.

**The Well-Built House**, revised edition, 1992, Jim Locke, Houghton Mifflin, New York, NY. $15. Stuffed with good (if somewhat technical) information on the actual construction process, this book is a good read. The only negative is the skimpy advice on the design process and what can go wrong during construction.

◆ *These titles are out of print. Try to find them at a local library; each is a good read.*

**Getting a Good House: Tips and Tricks for Evaluating New Construction**, 1994, Bob Syvanen, Globe Pequot Press, Chester, CT. $12.95. An illustrated 135-page book that gives advice on chimneys, gutters, foundations and more. Best for very basic homes, the simplistic advice is somewhat helpful.

**The Anatomy of a House**, 1991, Fayal Greene, Doubleday, New York, NY. $9.95. Ever wonder about the difference between crown molding and a dentil? This slim book has more than 100 pages of illustrations of stonework, molding, shingles, and more. Helpful in the design process.

**Tom Philbin's Do-It-Yourself Bargain Book**, 1992, Tom Philbin, Warner Books, New York, NY. $10. An incredible guide that gives money-saving advice on everything from power tools to building materials. Specific brands/prices are quoted. Highly recommended.

**The Walls Around Us**, 1993, David Owen, Villard Books, New York, NY. $12. A funny and ingenious look at what makes a house tick. Author Owen uses his own Connecticut home as a blackboard, dispensing good advice on the "fear of lumber" and "the best paint in the world." Highly recommended.

◆ *Other books of interest:* **The National Association of Home Builders** publishing arm (Home Builders Press; www.builderbooks.com) produces several interesting books. Yes, these titles are meant for builders—however, consumers might be interested to see what tips and tricks contractors are learning. You can call them at 800-223-2665 for a catalog; or better yet their offerings on the web at www.builderbooks.com. Yes, some of the titles can be pricey ($30 or so), but where else can you find construction cost guides, the dirt on contracts and more?

# About the Authors

**D**enise and Alan Fields are consumer advocates who have made a career out of chronicling life's milestones.

The Fields first national book, *Bridal Bargains*, was inspired by their wedding in 1989. After Oprah recommended the book to her viewers in 1991, the book became a best-seller with over 400,000 copies in print. *Bridal Bargains'* expose of rip-offs and consumer abuse of engaged couples was hailed by the *Wall Street Journal*, which said the book was "stirring up a commotion in the bridal industry."

The Fields' next book, *Your New House*, grew out of the couple's own experience building a new home in Monument, Colorado. "This book is, by far, the best book available on how to buy or build a new home," raved *Chicago Tribune* syndicated columnist Robert Bruss. The *San Francisco Examiner* picked the book as one of the Top 10 Best Real Estate Books for 1993 and again in 1996. *Your New House* guides home buyers through the new home construction process, with detailed tips on hiring a builder, what to get in writing and which scams to watch out for.

*Baby Bargains* continued this tradition, a consumer guide inspired by the birth of their sons, Ben in 1993 and Jack in 1996. The Fields scoured the country for the best deals on cribs, bedding, maternity clothes and more. *Baby Bargains* has been featured on the *Today Show*, *Oprah*, and *DATELINE NBC*.

The Fields' latest books include the *Bridal Gown Guide*, a price guide for wedding dresses and *CyberBride: The Complete Online Guide to Planning a Wedding*.

The Fields have been writing together since 1987, after meeting in college in Colorado. Their first book was a local how-to guide for engaged couples in Austin, Texas called *Austin Weddings*.

A native of Dallas, Texas, Alan Fields has a bachelor's degree in business from the University of Colorado and a masters in business administration from the University of Texas at Austin. His hobby (and fascination) with the weather inspired him to write *Partly Sunny: The Weather Junkie's Guide to Outsmarting the Weather* in 1994. Denise Fields holds a bachelor of arts degree from the University of Colorado. A native of Colorado, Denise grew up in Loveland.

The Fields live in Boulder, Colorado with their sons, Ben & Jack.

# Phone/Web Directory

**W**onder where these contact names appear in the book? Check the index for a page number. Remember that some of the contacts for building supplies do not sell to the public directly; the phone numbers are so you can find a dealer/store near you. Refer to the chapter in which they are mentioned to see which companies offer a consumer catalog, sell to the public, etc. Note: we've omitted the "www." prefix before the web address for space reasons.

| Contact Name | Toll-Free | Phone | Web Site |
|---|---|---|---|
| Authors, Denise & Alan Fields | | (303) 442-8792 | YourNewHouseBook.com |

### Chapter 2: Mortgages

| | | | |
|---|---|---|---|
| Eloan | | | eloan.com |
| HSH | | | hsh.com |
| Microsoft's Home Advisor | | | homeadvisor.msn.com |
| Bankrate.com | | | Bankrate.com |
| Countrywide.com | | | Countrywide.com |
| Getsmart.com | | | Getsmart.com |
| iOwn.com | | | iOwn.com |
| IndyMac.om | | | IndyMac.com |
| LendingTree.com | | | LendingTree.com |
| Mortgagebot.com | | | mortgagebot.com |
| Mortgagelocator.com | | | Mortgagelocator.com |
| Quickenmortgage.com | | | Quickenmortgage.com. |
| Realestate.com | | | Realestate.com |

### Chapter 3: Building Team

| | | | |
|---|---|---|---|
| American Institute of Architects | (800) 365-ARCH | (202) 626-7351 | aiaonline.com |
| American Society of Home Inspectors | (800) 743-2744 | | ashi.com |
| National Association of Home Inspectors | (800) 448-3942 | (612) 928-4641 | www.nahi.org |

### Consumer Groups

| | | | |
|---|---|---|---|
| Homeowners Organization for Mediation and Education | | (817) 924-3737 | flash.net/~carlton2/home.htm |

| Homeowners Against Deficient Dwellings | (816) 781-1590 | www.hadd.com |
| Improvenet.com | | Improvenet.com |
| Nolo.com | | Nolo.com |
| FreeAdvice.com | | FreeAdvice.com |
| Findlaw.com | | Findlaw.com |
| Law.com | | Law.com |

## Chapter 4: If Dirt Were Dollars
| | | |
| --- | --- | --- |
| Sourcebook of Zip Code Demographics | | demographics.caci.com |
| USA City Link | | usacitylink.com |
| SmartHomeBuy | | smarthomebuy.com |
| 2001 Beyond | | 2001beyond.com |
| Near My Home | (800) 733-7606 | nearmyhome.com |
| Environmental Assessment Assoc | (320) 763-4320 | iami.org |

## Chapter 5: Real Estate Agents
| | | |
| --- | --- | --- |
| National Association of Realtors | | realtor.com |
| National Association of Home Builders | | homebuilder.com |
| Microsoft's Home Advisor | | homeadvisor.msn.com |
| HomeSeekers | | homeseekers.com |
| Buyer's Resource | (800) 359-4092 | www.buyersresource.com |
| National Assoc. of Exclusive Buyer Agents (NAEBA) | (800) 986-2322 | www.naeba.com |
| Hoover's Online | | hoovers.com |
| KnowX.com | | knowx.com |

## Chapter 6: Design
| | | | |
| --- | --- | --- | --- |
| Home Planners | | | homeplanners.com |
| Home Plan Network | | | homeplan-network.com |
| Homestyles | | | homestyles.com |
| Residential Technologies | | | residential.com |
| United Designs | | | designconcepts.com |
| Home-Plan Finder | (800) 345-HOME | | abbisoft.com |
| BuildingScience | | | buildingscience.com |
| American Association of Retired People | | | www.aarp.org |
| Davis Instruments | (800) 678-3669 | | davisnet.com |
| U.S. Tec | (800) 836-2312 | (716) 924-1740 | ustechnet.com |
| Environmental Building News | (802) 257-7300 | | ebuild.com |
| Manufactured Home Institute | | | mfghome.org |
| Log Homes Council | (800) 368-5242 | | loghomes.org |
| Building Systems Council | | | buildingsystems.org |

### Manufactured Home Builders
| | |
| --- | --- |
| Champion Enterprises | (248) 340-9090 |
| Fleetwood Enterprises | (909) 351-3500 |
| Oakwood Homes | (336) 664-2400 |
| Horton Homes | (706) 485-8506 |
| Skyline Corp. | (219) 294-6521 |
| Palm Harbor Homes | (972) 991-2422 |
| Cavalier Homes | (256) 747-9800 |
| Southern Energy Homes | (256) 747-8589 |
| Four Seasons Housing | (219) 825-9999 |
| Cavco Industries | (602) 256-6263 |

| | | |
|---|---|---|
| Modular Connection | | modularconnection.com |
| Dome Homes | | www.dnaco.net/~michael/domes/domes.html |
| Timberpeg | (603) 542-7762 | timberpeg.com |
| Cheng Design | (510) 549-2805 | chengdesign.com |
| GE | (800) 626-2000 | ge.com |

*Chapter 7: Builder*

| | |
|---|---|
| Homebuilder.com | homebuilder.com |
| New Home Network | newhomenetwork.com |
| American Builders Network | americanbuilders.com |
| BuildFind.com | buildfind.com |
| Lonergan Homes | www.lonerganhomes.com |

*Top 10 Builders*

| | |
|---|---|
| Pulte* | pulte.com |
| Centex | centex.com |
| K B Home | kbhome.com |
| Lennar/US Home | lennar.com |
| D.R. Horton | drhorton.com |
| Ryland Group | ryland.com |
| NVR | nvrinc.com |
| Del Webb* | delwebb.com |
| Beazer Homes | beazer.com |
| MDC/Richmond | richmondamerican.com |

| | | |
|---|---|---|
| Hoovers's | | hoovers.com |
| Anti-Ryland site | | orbitworld.net/johncoby |
| Homeowners Against Defective Dwellings (HADD) | (816) 781-1590 | hadd.com |
| Homeowners Organization for Mediation and Education (HOME) | (817) 924-3737 | flash.net/~carlton2/home.htm |
| Homeowners for Better Building | (210) 402-6800 | orbitworld.net/johncoby/hobb.htm |
| Home Buyer Beware | | charlotte.com/observer/special/house/ |
| Advocates for Quality Home Construction | (408) 803-HOME | jps.net/hollister1/ |
| National Fenestration Rating Council | (301) 589-6372 | nfrc.org |
| KnowX.com | | knowx.com |
| Bigfoot.com | | bigfoot.com |

*Chapter 8: Contracts*

| | | |
|---|---|---|
| Home Builder Press | (800) 368-5242 | builderbooks.com |
| Reprofile | | www.reprofile.com |
| AIA | (800) 365-ARCH | www.aiaonline.com |

*Chapter 9: Building Part I: Framing*

| | | | |
|---|---|---|---|
| National Ground Water Association | (800) 551-7379 | (614) 898-7791 | ngwa.org |
| Arxx Wallsystems | (800) 293-3210 | | arxxbuild.com |
| SmartBlock | (800) CONFORM | | smartblock.com |
| Insulating Concrete Form Association | | | forms.org |

| Oak Ridge National Laboratory's | | | |
|---|---|---|---|
| "Building Technology Center" | | | ornl.gov/roofs+walls/ |
| Tyvek | (800) 44-TYVEK | | |
| Trus Joist Corp. | (800) 628-3997 | | tjm.com |

| American Iron and Steel Institute's | | | |
|---|---|---|---|
| Steel Home Hotline | (800) 79-STEEL | (202) 452-7100 | steel.org. |
| Stormguard nails by Maze Nails | | (815) 223-8290 | mazenails.com |
| LO/MIT-1 by Solar Energy Corp. | | (609) 883-7700 | |
| Defective Siding web page | | | orbitworld.net/johncoby/siding.htm |

| Radiant Panel Information | | | |
|---|---|---|---|
| Association | (800) 660-7187 | (970) 613-0100 | rpa-info.com |
| Owens Corning | (800) 447-3759 | | owenscorning.com |

| Nature Guard Insulation | | (503) 221-0800 | lpcorp.com |
|---|---|---|---|
| Cellulose Insulation Manufacturer's | | | |
| Association (CIMA) | | (937) 222-1024 | |
| Copper Development Association | | | www.copper.org |
| Eco Products | | | ecoproducts.com |

*Chapter 10 Building Part II: Finishing*

| Cedar Shake and Shingle Bureau | | (800) 843-3578 | cedarbureau.org |
|---|---|---|---|
| Vinyl Siding Institute | | (888) FOR-VSI-1 | vinylsiding.org |
| Cultured Stone Corp | | (800)-255-1727 | culturedstone.com |
| TREX | (800) BUY-TREX | | trex.com |
| Eco-Shakes | (800) 420-7576 | (918) 485-5803 | oikos.com/esb/49/renew.html |

| Northern Virginia Stucco Homeowners Association | | novashoc.org. |
|---|---|---|
| EFIS Industry Members Association | | eifsfacts.com |

| Avonite | (800) 4-AVONITE | avonite.com |
|---|---|---|
| Corian | (800) 4-CORIAN | corian.com |
| Fountainhead | (410) 551-5000 | |

| Image Carpets | | (706) 857-6481 | |
|---|---|---|---|
| FibreBond wallboard | | (503) 221-0800 | |
| Armstrong | (800) 233-3823 | | |
| Premium windows | | (419) 248-8000 | owenscorning.com |
| Delta Faucets | | (317) 848-1812 | |
| Speakman | | (302) 764-9100 | |
| Asko | (800) 367-2444 | | askousa.com |
| Frigidaire | (800) 451-7007 | | frigidaire.com |
| General Electric | (800) 626-2000 | | ge.com |
| Sage Advance water heaters | | (541) 485-1947 | |
| Planetary Solutions | | (303) 442-6228 | |

*Best New Products*

| SunTouch by Bask Technologies | | (888) 432-8932 | bask.net |
|---|---|---|---|
| IBM Home Director | (800) 426-7144 | | ibm.com/homedirector |
| Fisher & Paykel's "DishDrawer" | | (888)936-7872 | dishdrawer.com |
| BoralVision | (800) 5-BORAL-5 | | |
| Advantage 2000 | | (206) 448-0354 | cmiworldwide.com |
| Tornado Guard shelter | | (512) 259-6500 | |
| Zoned forced-air heat | | | honeywell.com |

**Chapter 11: New Home 911**
Fannie Mae's "Home Path"                                   www.homepath.com

**Chapter 12: Bargains**
Insider's Guide to Buying Home Furnishings                 smartdecorating.com

*Discount sources for furnishings*

| | | | |
|---|---|---|---|
| The Container Store | (800) 733-3532 | | containerstore.com |
| Home Decorators Collection | (800) 245-2217 | (314) 993-6045 | homedecorators.com |
| The Renovators | (800) 659-2211 | (603) 447-8500 | |
| Behome.com | | | Behome.com |
| Reflections | | | reflectionsfurniture.com |
| Warren's Interiors | | | warrensinteriors.com |

*Home Centers*

| | |
|---|---|
| Home Depot | homedepot.com |
| Lowe's | lowes.com |
| Great Indoors | greatindoors.com |
| Sam's Club | samsclub.com |
| Costco | costco.com |
| BJ's | bjswholesale.com |

*Discount Lighting*

| | | | |
|---|---|---|---|
| Lamps Plus | (800) 360-LAMP | | lampsplus.com |
| Golden Valley Lighting | (800) 735-3377 | (332) 882-7330 | gvlight.com |
| AJP Coppersmith | (800) 545-1776 | (781) 932-3700 | ajpcoppersmith.com |
| Shades of Light | (800) 262-6612 | | shades-of-light.com |
| Luigi Crystal | | (215) 338-2978 | |
| Main Lamp/ Lamp Warehouse | (800) 52-LITES | (718) 436-8500 | nationwidelighting.com |
| American Light | (800) 741-0571 | | |
| Brass Light Gallery | (800) 243-9595 | | brasslight.com |
| Circle Lighting | | | circlelighting.com |
| Union Lighting | | | unionlighting.com |

*Discount Carpeting and Flooring*

| | | | |
|---|---|---|---|
| Carpet Discounts | | | carpet-discounts.com |
| American Home Showplace | (800) 262-3132 | | carpetsofdalton.com |
| Bearden Bros. Carpet and Textiles | (800) 433-0074 | | beardenbrothers.com |
| Beaver Flooring | (888) 595-HOME | | Beaverfloor.com |
| Martin's Flooring | | (706) 278-3209 | carpet-wholesale.com |
| Paradise Mills Inc. | (800) 338-7811 | | |
| S&S Mills | (800) 363-3758 | | ssmils.com |
| Warehouse Carpets | (800) 526-2229 | | |

*Discount Plumbing*

| | | |
|---|---|---|
| Baths from Past | (800) 697-3871 | faucetfactory.com |
| The Faucet Outlet | (800) 444-5783 | faucet.com |
| Faucetsource.com | (800) 669-1707 | |

*Discount Roofing*
New England Slate Co.          (802) 247-8809                    neslate.com

*Auction sites*
Buildscape.com

*Product Reviews*
*Windows*
Andersen          (800) 426-4261  (651) 439-5150        andersenwindows.com
Hurd              (800) 223-4873                                    hurd.com
Kolbe & Kolbe                     (715) 842-5666           kolbe-kolbe.com
Marvin            (888) 537-8268  (218) 386-1430                 marvin.com
Peachtree         (800) PEACH99                             peachtree99.com
Pella             (800) 84-PELLA  (515) 628-1000                  pella.com

*Plumbing*
American Standard  (800) 752-6292  (732) 980-3000              us.amstd.com
Delta              (800) 345-DELTA(317) 848-1812            deltafaucet.com
Dornbracht         (800) 774-1181                           dornbracht.com
Grohe America                      (630) 582-7711          groheamerica.com
Kohler             (800) 4-KOHLER (920) 457-4441              kohlerco.com
Moen                               (440) 962-2000                 moen.com
Price Pfister                      (818) 896-1141          pricepfister.com
Swirl-Way Tubs     (800) 999-1459                             swirlway.com

*Roofing*
Asphalt Roofing
Manufacturers Association          (301) 231-9050        asphaltroofing.org
Cedar Shake and Shingle Bureau     (800) 843-3578
cedarbureau.org

National Assoc. of Home
Builders Press      (800) 223-2665                         builderbooks.com

# Index

# Is this book a library loaner?

Have you checked this book
out from a library?

Do you find this book indispensable—
but the return date is approaching fast?

Now, you can get
your very own, personal copy of

## Your New House

Just

# $15.95
(Plus $3 shipping)

Call toll-free

# 1-800-888-0385
or order online at www.windsorpeak.com

# BRIDAL BARGAINS

## The Fields' first best-seller, over 400,000 copies sold!

*"If you're getting married, you need this book!"*
—Oprah Winfrey

**W**OW! Finally, a book on weddings you can actually use! With average U.S. wedding costs soaring near $20,000, you need creative and innovative solutions to planning a wonderful wedding on a realistic budget. *BRIDAL BARGAINS* in the answer! Inside you'll discover:

- ◆ HOW TO SAVE up to 40% on brand new, nationally advertised wedding dresses.
- ◆ THE BEST WEB SITES to save on everything from flowers to gowns, invitations to, well, you name it.
- ◆ Fourteen creative ways to CUT THE CATERING BILL at your reception.
- ◆ How to order FLOWERS AT WHOLESALE over the internet.
- ◆ ELEVEN QUESTIONS YOU SHOULD ASK ANY PHOTOGRAPHER— and seven money saving tips to lower that photo expense.
- ◆ How to do your INVITATIONS ON A COMPUTER, saving 70%.
- ◆ A CLEVER TRICK to save big bucks on your wedding cake.
- ◆ Plus many MONEY-SAVING TIPS ON WEDDING VIDEOS, RINGS, ENTERTAINMENT and more!

MONEY BACK GUARANTEE: If *BRIDAL BARGAINS* doesn't save you at least $500 on your wedding, then we will give you a complete refund. No kidding.

*Just*
# $14.95
*(Plus $3 shipping)*

*Call toll-free to order!*
*1-800-888-0385*
*or order online at www.windsorpeak.com*

*Mastercard, VISA, American Express and Discover Accepted!*